SAUDI ARABIA

T0295821

BUSINESS LAW HANDBOOK
VOLUME 1
STRATEGIC INFORMATION AND BASIC LAWS

International Business Publications, USA
Washington DC, USA- Saudi Arabia

SAUDI ARABIA
BUSINESS LAW HANDBOOK
VOLUME 1 STRATEGIC INFORMATION AND BASIC LAWS

UPDATED ANNUALLY

We express our sincere gratitude to all government agencies and international organizations which provided information and other materials for this handbook

Cover Design: International Business Publications, USA

International Business Publications, USA. *has used its best efforts in collecting, analyzing and preparing data, information and materials for this unique handbook. Due to the dynamic nature and fast development of the economy and business environment, we cannot warrant that all information herein is complete and accurate. IBP does not assume and hereby disclaim any liability to any person for any loss or damage caused by possible errors or omissions in the handbook.*
This handbook is for individual use only. Use this handbook for any other purpose, included but not limited to reproducing and storing in a retrieval system by any means, electronic, photocopying or using the addresses or other information contained in this handbook for any commercial purposes requires a special written permission from the publisher.

2016 Edition Updated Reprint International Business Publications, USA
ISBN 1-5145-0181-3

For additional analytical, business and investment opportunities information,
please contact Global Investment & Business Center, USA
at (703) 370-8082. Fax: (703) 370-8083. E-mail: ibpusa3@gmail.com
Global Business and Investment Info Databank - www.ibpus.com

Printed in the USA

For additional analytical, business and investment opportunities information,
please contact Global Investment & Business Center, USA
at (202) 546-2103. Fax: (202) 546-3275. E-mail: ibpusa3@gmail.com
Global Business and Legal Information Databank: www.ibpus.com

SAUDI ARABIA

BUSINESS LAW HANDBOOK
VOLUME 1
STRATEGIC INFORMATION AND BASIC LAWS

TABLE OF CONTENTS

For additional analytical, business and investment opportunities information,
please contact Global Investment & Business Center, USA
at (202) 546-2103. Fax: (202) 546-3275. E-mail: ibpusa3@gmail.com
Global Business and Legal Information Databank: www.ibpus.com

**For additional analytical, business and investment opportunities information,
please contact Global Investment & Business Center, USA
at (202) 546-2103. Fax: (202) 546-3275. E-mail: ibpusa3@gmail.com
Global Business and Legal Information Databank: www.ibpus.com**

**For additional analytical, business and investment opportunities information,
please contact Global Investment & Business Center, USA
at (202) 546-2103. Fax: (202) 546-3275. E-mail: ibpusa3@gmail.com
Global Business and Legal Information Databank: www.ibpus.com**

**For additional analytical, business and investment opportunities information,
please contact Global Investment & Business Center, USA
at (202) 546-2103. Fax: (202) 546-3275. E-mail: ibpusa3@gmail.com
Global Business and Legal Information Databank: www.ibpus.com**

**For additional analytical, business and investment opportunities information,
please contact Global Investment & Business Center, USA
at (202) 546-2103. Fax: (202) 546-3275. E-mail: ibpusa3@gmail.com
Global Business and Legal Information Databank: www.ibpus.com**

/

For additional analytical, business and investment opportunities information,
please contact Global Investment & Business Center, USA
at (202) 546-2103. Fax: (202) 546-3275. E-mail: ibpusa3@gmail.com
Global Business and Legal Information Databank: www.ibpus.com

STRATEGIC AND DEVELOPMENT PROFILES

Capital and largest city	Riyadh 24°39′N 46°46′E24.650°N 46.767°E
Official languages	Arabic
Ethnic groups	90% Arab 10% Afro-Arab
Religion	Sunni Islam (official)
Demonym	• Saudi Arabian • Saudi (informal)
Government	Unitary Islamic absolute monarchy
• King	Salman bin Abdulaziz
• Crown Prince	Mohammad bin Nayef
• Deputy Crown Prince	Mohammad bin Salman
Legislature	None (Legislation passed by the Council of Ministers)
	Establishment
• Kingdom founded	23 September 1932
	Area
• Total	2,149,690 km² (13th) 830,000 sq mi
• Water (%)	0.7
	Population
• Estimate	30,770,375 (41st)
• Density	12.3/km² (216th) 31/sq mi
GDP (PPP)	2015 estimate
• Total	$1.668 trillion (14th)
• Per capita	$53,149 (12th)
GDP (nominal)	2015 estimate
• Total	$648.971 billion (20th)
• Per capita	$20,677 (38th)
HDI	▲ 0.837 very high · 39th
Currency	Saudi riyal (SR) (SAR)
Time zone	AST (UTC+3)
Drives on the	right
Calling code	+966
ISO 3166 code	SA
Internet TLD	• .sa • السـعودية.

a. Legislation is by king's decree. The Consultative Assembly exists to advise the king.

Saudi Arabia officially known as the **Kingdom of Saudi Arabia (KSA)**, is an Arab state in Western Asia constituting the bulk of the Arabian Peninsula. With a land area of approximately 2,150,000 km² (830,000 sq mi), Saudi Arabia is geographically the fifth-largest state in Asia and second-largest state in the Arab world (after Algeria). Saudi Arabia is bordered by Jordan and Iraq to the north, Kuwait to the northeast, Qatar, Bahrain, and the United Arab Emirates to the east, Oman to the southeast, and Yemen to the south. It is the only nation with both a Red Sea coast and a Persian Gulf coast, and most of its terrain consists of arid inhospitable desert or barren landforms.

The area of modern-day Saudi Arabia formerly consisted of four distinct regions: Hejaz, Najd, and parts of Eastern Arabia (Al-Ahsa) and Southern Arabia ('Asir). The Kingdom of Saudi Arabia was founded in 1932 by Ibn Saud. He united the four regions into a single state through a series of conquests beginning in 1902 with the capture of Riyadh, the ancestral home of his family, the House of Saud. The country has since been an absolute monarchy, effectively a hereditary dictatorship governed along Islamic lines. The ultra-conservative Wahhabism religious movement within Sunni Islam has been called "the predominant feature of Saudi culture", with its global spreading largely financed by the oil and gas trade. Saudi Arabia is sometimes called "the Land of the Two Holy Mosques" in reference to Al-Masjid al-Haram (in Mecca), and Al-Masjid an-Nabawi (in Medina), the two holiest places in Islam. The Kingdom has a total population of 28.7 million, of which 20 million are Saudi nationals and 8 million are foreigners.

Petroleum was discovered in 1938 and followed up by several other finds in the Shia-majority Eastern Province. Saudi Arabia has since become the world's largest oil producer and exporter, controlling the world's second largest oil reserves, and the sixth largest gas reserves. The kingdom is categorized as a World Bank high-income economy with a high Human Development Index, and is the only Arab country to be part of the G-20 major economies. However, the economy of Saudi Arabia is the least diversified in the Gulf Cooperation Council, lacking any significant service or production sector (apart from the extraction of resources). It is a monarchical autocracy and is ranked as "Not Free" by Freedom House. Saudi Arabia has the fourth highest military expenditure in the world, and in 2010–14, SIPRI found that Saudi Arabia was the world's second largest arms importer. Saudi Arabia is considered a regional and middle power. In addition to the GCC, it is an active member of the Organisation of Islamic Cooperation and OPEC.

Limitations on women's rights in Saudi Arabia make it the only country where women are not permitted to drive. The country is also criticised for its capital punishment, which is condemned internationally because of the wide range of crimes which can result in the death penalty. It is usually carried out by public beheading and sometimes crucifixion. It applies even to individuals who were under the age of 18 at the time of their alleged crimes, which is a violation of international law

STRATEGIC PROFILE

GEOGRAPHY

Location: Middle East, bordering the Persian Gulf and the Red Sea, north of Yemen
Geographic coordinates: 25 00 N, 45 00 E
Map references: Middle East

Area:
total: 1,960,582 sq km
land: 1,960,582 sq km
water: 0 sq km

Area—comparative: slightly more than one-fifth the size of the US

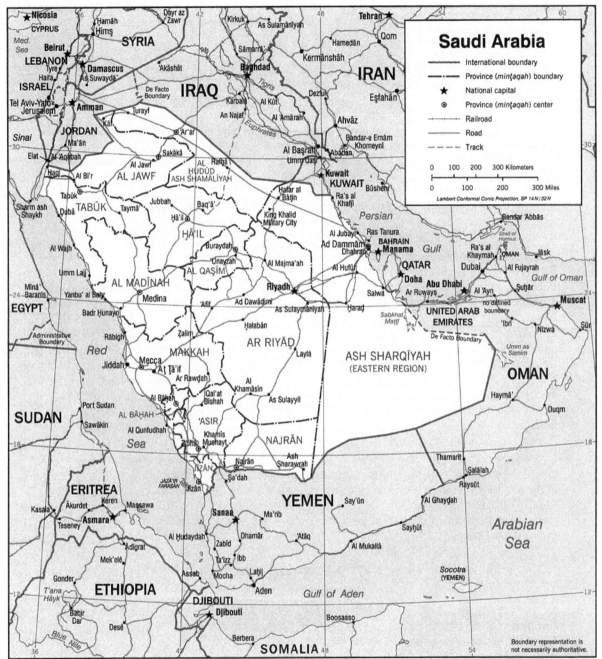

Land boundaries:
total: 4,415 km
border countries: Iraq 814 km, Jordan 728 km, Kuwait 222 km, Oman 676 km, Qatar 60 km, UAE 457 km, Yemen 1,458 km

Coastline: 2,640 km
Maritime claims:
contiguous zone: 18 nm

For additional analytical, business and investment opportunities information,
please contact Global Investment & Business Center, USA
at (202) 546-2103. Fax: (202) 546-3275. E-mail: ibpusa3@gmail.com
Global Business and Legal Information Databank: www.ibpus.com

continental shelf: not specified
territorial sea: 12 nm
Climate: harsh, dry desert with great extremes of temperature
Terrain: mostly uninhabited, sandy desert
Elevation extremes:
lowest point: Persian Gulf 0 m
highest point: Jabal Sawda' 3,133 m
Natural resources: petroleum, natural gas, iron ore, gold, copper

Land use:

arable land: 2%
permanent crops: 0%
permanent pastures: 56%
forests and woodland: 1%
other: 41%

Irrigated land: 4,350 sq km
Natural hazards: frequent sand and dust storms

Environment—current issues: desertification; depletion of underground water resources; the lack of perennial rivers or permanent water bodies has prompted the development of extensive seawater desalination facilities; coastal pollution from oil spills

Environment—international agreements:
party to: Climate Change, Desertification, Endangered Species, Hazardous Wastes, Law of the Sea, Ozone Layer Protection
signed, but not ratified: none of the selected agreements

Geography—note: extensive coastlines on Persian Gulf and Red Sea provide great leverage on shipping (especially crude oil) through Persian Gulf and Suez Canal.

PEOPLE

Nationality:
noun: Saudi(s)
adjective: Saudi or Saudi Arabian

Ethnic groups:
Arab 90%, Afro-Asian 10%

Languages:
Arabic (official)

Religions:
Muslim (official; citizens are 85-90% Sunni and 10-15% Shia), other (includes Eastern Orthodox, Protestant, Roman Catholic, Jewish, Hindu, Buddhist, and Sikh) (2012 est.)
note: despite having a large expatriate community of various faiths (more than 30% of the population), most forms of public religious expression inconsistent with the government-sanctioned interpretation of Sunni Islam are restricted; non-Muslims are not allowed to have Saudi citizenship and non-Muslim places of worship are not permitted (2013)

Population:
27,752,316 (July 2015 est.)
note: immigrants make up more than 30% of the total population, according to UN data (2015)
country comparison to the world: 47

Age structure:
0-14 years: 27.07% (male 3,850,992/female 3,661,194)
15-24 years: 19.11% (male 2,839,161/female 2,463,216)
25-54 years: 45.9% (male 7,244,386/female 5,495,284)
55-64 years: 4.68% (male 710,827/female 587,281)
65 years and over: 3.24% (male 460,209/female 439,766) (2015 est.)

Dependency ratios:
total dependency ratio: 45.9%
youth dependency ratio: 41.7%
elderly dependency ratio: 4.2%
potential support ratio: 24% (2015 est.)

Median age:
total: 26.8 years
male: 27.6 years
female: 25.8 years (2015 est.)

Population growth rate:
1.46% (2015 est.)
country comparison to the world: 81

Birth rate:
18.51 births/1,000 population (2015 est.)
country comparison to the world: 94
Death rate:
3.33 deaths/1,000 population (2015 est.)
country comparison to the world: 219

Net migration rate:
-0.55 migrant(s)/1,000 population (2015 est.)
country comparison to the world: 137

Urbanization:
urban population: 83.1% of total population (2015)
rate of urbanization: 2.1% annual rate of change (2010-15 est.)
Major urban areas - population:
RIYADH (capital) 6.195 million; Jeddah 4.076 million; Mecca 1.771 million; Medina 1.28 million; Ad Dammam 1.064 million (2015)

Sex ratio:
at birth: 1.05 male(s)/female
0-14 years: 1.05 male(s)/female
15-24 years: 1.15 male(s)/female
25-54 years: 1.32 male(s)/female
55-64 years: 1.21 male(s)/female
65 years and over: 1.05 male(s)/female

For additional analytical, business and investment opportunities information,
please contact Global Investment & Business Center, USA
at (202) 546-2103. Fax: (202) 546-3275. E-mail: ibpusa3@gmail.com
Global Business and Legal Information Databank: www.ibpus.com

total population: 1.19 male(s)/female (2015 est.)

Maternal mortality rate:
12 deaths/100,000 live births (2015 est.)
country comparison to the world: 133

Infant mortality rate:
total: 14.09 deaths/1,000 live births
male: 16.16 deaths/1,000 live births
female: 11.9 deaths/1,000 live births (2015 est.)
country comparison to the world: 108

Life expectancy at birth:
total population: 75.05 years
male: 73 years
female: 77.2 years (2015 est.)
country comparison to the world: 108

Total fertility rate:
2.12 children born/woman (2015 est.)
country comparison to the world: 105

Contraceptive prevalence rate: 23.8%

Health expenditures:
3.2% of GDP (2013)
country comparison to the world: 178

Physicians density:
2.49 physicians/1,000 population

Hospital bed density:
2.1 beds/1,000 population

Drinking water source:
improved:
urban: 97% of population
rural: 97% of population
total: 97% of population
unimproved: urban: 3% of population
rural: 3% of population
total: 3% of population (2015 est.)

Sanitation facility access:
improved:
urban: 100% of population
rural: 100% of population
total: 100% of population

unimproved:
urban: 0% of population
rural: 0% of population
total: 0% of population (2015 est.)

For additional analytical, business and investment opportunities information,
please contact Global Investment & Business Center, USA
at (202) 546-2103. Fax: (202) 546-3275. E-mail: ibpusa3@gmail.com
Global Business and Legal Information Databank: www.ibpus.com

Obesity - adult prevalence rate:
33.7%
country comparison to the world: 19

Children under the age of 5 years underweight:
5.3%
country comparison to the world: 88

Education expenditures:
5.1% of GDP
country comparison to the world: 68

Literacy:
definition: age 15 and over can read and write
total population: 94.7%
male: 97%
female: 91.1% (2015 est.)

School life expectancy (primary to tertiary education):
total: 16 years
male: 16 years
female: 17 years

Unemployment, youth ages 15-24:
total: 29.5%
male: 21.1%
female: 55.3% (2013 est.)
country comparison to the world: 29

GOVERNMENT

Country name:

conventional long form: Kingdom of Saudi Arabia
conventional short form: Saudi Arabia
local long form: Al Mamlakah al Arabiyah as Suudiyah
local short form: Al Arabiyah as Suudiyah

Government type:

monarchy

Capital:

name: Riyadh
geographic coordinates: 24 39 N, 46 42 E
time difference: UTC+3 (8 hours ahead of Washington, DC, during Standard Time)

Administrative divisions:

13 provinces (mintaqat, singular - mintaqah); Al Bahah, Al Hudud ash Shamaliyah (Northern Border), Al Jawf, Al Madinah (Medina), Al Qasim, Ar Riyad (Riyadh), Ash Sharqiyah (Eastern), 'Asir, Ha'il, Jazan, Makkah (Mecca), Najran, Tabuk

For additional analytical, business and investment opportunities information,
please contact Global Investment & Business Center, USA
at (202) 546-2103. Fax: (202) 546-3275. E-mail: ibpusa3@gmail.com
Global Business and Legal Information Databank: www.ibpus.com

Independence:

23 September 1932 (unification of the kingdom)

National holiday:

Unification of the Kingdom, 23 September (1932)

Constitution:

1 March 1992 - Basic Law of Government, issued by royal decree, serves as the constitutional framework and is based on the Qur'an and the life and tradition of the Prophet Muhammad

Legal system:

Islamic (sharia) legal system with some elements of Egyptian, French, and customary law; note - several secular codes have been introduced; commercial disputes handled by special committees

International law organization participation:

has not submitted an ICJ jurisdiction declaration; non-party state to the ICCt

Suffrage:

21 years of age; male

Executive branch:

chief of state: King and Prime Minister SALMAN bin Abd al-Aziz Al Saud (since 23 January 2015); Crown Prince and Deputy Prime Minister MUHAMMAD BIN NAYIF bin Abd al-Aziz Al Saud (born 30 August 1959); Crown Prince and Second Deputy Prime Minister MUHAMMAD BIN SALMAN bin Abd al-Aziz Al Saud (born 31 August 1985); note - the monarch is both chief of state and head of government
head of government: King and Prime Minister SALMAN bin Abd al-Aziz Al Saud (since 23 January 2015); Crown Prince and Deputy Prime Minister MUHAMMAD BIN NAYIF bin Abd al-Aziz Al Saud (born 30 August 1959); Crown Prince and Second Deputy Prime Minister MUHAMMAD BIN SALMAN bin Abd al-Aziz Al Saud (born 31 August 1985)
cabinet: Council of Ministers appointed by the monarch every 4 years and includes many royal family members
elections/appointments: none; the monarchy is hereditary; note - an Allegiance Commission created by royal decree in October 2006 established a committee of Saudi princes to a role in selecting future Saudi kings

Legislative branch:

description: unicameral Consultative Council or Majlis al-Shura (150 seats; members appointed by the monarch to serve 4-year terms); note - in early 2013, the monarch granted women 30 seats on the Council

Judicial branch:

highest court(s): High Court (consists of the court chief and organized into circuits with 3-judge panels except the criminal circuit which has a 5-judge panel for cases involving major punishments)
judge selection and term of office: the High Court chief and chiefs of the High Court

For additional analytical, business and investment opportunities information, please contact Global Investment & Business Center, USA at (202) 546-2103. Fax: (202) 546-3275. E-mail: ibpusa3@gmail.com Global Business and Legal Information Databank: www.ibpus.com

Circuits appointed by royal decree following the recommendation of the Supreme Judiciary Council, a 10-member body of high level judges and other judicial heads; new judges and assistant judges serve 1- and 2- year probations, respectively, before permanent assignment
subordinate courts: Court of Appeals; first-degree courts composed of general, criminal, personal status, and commercial courts, and the Labor Court; hierarchy of administrative courts
note: in 2005, former King Abdullah issued decrees approving an overhaul of the judicial system and which were incorporated in the Judiciary Law of 2007; changes include the establishment of a High Court and special commercial, labor, and administrative courts

Political parties and leaders:

Political pressure groups and leaders:

gas companies; religious groups

International organization participation:

ABEDA, AfDB (nonregional member), AFESD, AMF, BIS, CAEU, CP, FAO, G-20, G-77, GCC, IAEA, IBRD, ICAO, ICC (national committees), ICRM, IDA, IDB, IFAD, IFC, IFRCS, IHO, ILO, IMF, IMO, IMSO, Interpol, IOC, IOM (observer), IPU, ISO, ITSO, ITU, LAS, MIGA, NAM, OAPEC, OAS (observer), OIC, OPCW, OPEC, PCA, UN, UNCTAD, UNESCO, UNIDO, UNRWA, UNWTO, UPU, WCO, WFTU (NGOs), WHO, WIPO, WMO, WTO

Diplomatic representation in the US:

chief of mission: Ambassador FAISAL TURKI Al Saud (since 28 January 2016)
chancery: 601 New Hampshire Avenue NW, Washington, DC 20037
telephone: [1] (202) 342-3800
FAX: [1] (202) 944-3113
consulate(s) general: Houston, Los Angeles, New York

Diplomatic representation from the US:
chief of mission: Ambassador Joseph William WESTPHAL (since 26 March 2014)
embassy: Collector Road M, Diplomatic Quarter, Riyadh
mailing address: American Embassy, Unit 61307, APO AE 09803-1307; International Mail: P. O. Box 94309, Riyadh 11693
telephone: [966] (1) 488-3800
FAX: [966] (1) 488-7360
consulate(s) general: Dhahran, Jiddah (Jeddah)

Flag description:

green, a traditional color in Islamic flags, with the Shahada or Muslim creed in large white Arabic script (translated as "There is no god but God; Muhammad is the Messenger of God") above a white horizontal saber (the tip points to the hoist side); design dates to the early twentieth century and is closely associated with the Al Saud family which established the kingdom in 1932; the flag is manufactured with differing obverse and reverse sides so that the Shahada reads - and the sword points - correctly from right to left on both sides *note:* one of only three national flags that differ on their obverse and reverse sides - the others are Moldova and Paraguay

National symbol(s):

palm tree surmounting two crossed swords

National anthem:

name: "Aash Al Maleek" (Long Live Our Beloved King)

ECONOMY

Saudi Arabia has an oil-based economy with strong government controls over major economic activities. It possesses about 16% of the world's proven petroleum reserves, ranks as the largest exporter of petroleum, and plays a leading role in OPEC. The petroleum sector accounts for roughly 80% of budget revenues, 45% of GDP, and 90% of export earnings.

Saudi Arabia is encouraging the growth of the private sector in order to diversify its economy and to employ more Saudi nationals. Diversification efforts are focusing on power generation, telecommunications, natural gas exploration, and petrochemical sectors. Over 6 million foreign workers play an important role in the Saudi economy, particularly in the oil and service sectors, while Riyadh is struggling to reduce unemployment among its own nationals. Saudi officials are particularly focused on employing its large youth population, which generally lacks the education and technical skills the private sector needs.

In 2015 the Kingdom incurred a budget deficit estimated at 20% of GDP, and it faces deficits for the foreseeable future because it requires an oil price greater than $100 per barrel to balance its budget. Although the Kingdom can finance high deficits for several years by drawing down its considerable foreign assets or by borrowing, it has announced plans to cut capital spending in 2016.

GDP (purchasing power parity):
$1.681 trillion (2015 est.)
$1.625 trillion (2014 est.)
$1.571 trillion (2013 est.)

note: data are in 2015 US dollars
country comparison to the world: 15

GDP (official exchange rate):
$665.5 billion (2015 est.)

GDP - real growth rate:
3.4% (2015 est.)
3.5% (2014 est.)
2.7% (2013 est.)

country comparison to the world: 85

GDP - per capita (PPP):
$54,600 (2015 est.)
$52,800 (2014 est.)
$51,100 (2013 est.)
note: data are in 2015 US dollars
country comparison to the world: 21

Gross national saving:
26.1% of GDP (2015 est.)
38.1% of GDP (2014 est.)
44.4% of GDP (2013 est.)
country comparison to the world: 43

GDP - composition, by end use:
household consumption: 38.3%
government consumption: 31%
investment in fixed capital: 29.3%
investment in inventories: 4%
exports of goods and services: 35%
imports of goods and services: -37.6%
(2015 est.)

GDP - composition, by sector of origin:
agriculture: 2.3%
industry: 46.9%
services: 50.8% (2015 est.)

Agriculture - products:
wheat, barley, tomatoes, melons, dates, citrus; mutton, chickens, eggs, milk

Industries:
crude oil production, petroleum refining, basic petrochemicals, ammonia, industrial gases, sodium hydroxide (caustic soda), cement, fertilizer, plastics, metals, commercial ship repair, commercial aircraft repair, construction

Industrial production growth rate:
2.8% (2015 est.)
country comparison to the world: 91

Labor force:
11.67 million
note: about 80% of the labor force is non-national (2015 est.)
country comparison to the world: 49

Labor force - by occupation:
agriculture: 6.7%
industry: 21.4%
services: 71.9%

Unemployment rate:
11.4% (2015 est.)

11.6% (2014 est.)
note: data are for Saudi males only (local bank estimates; some estimates are as high as 25%)
country comparison to the world: 129

Budget:
revenues: $193 billion
expenditures: $318 billion (2015 est.)

Taxes and other revenues:
29% of GDP (2015 est.)
country comparison to the world: 90

Budget surplus (+) or deficit (-):
-18.8% of GDP (2015 est.)
country comparison to the world: 216

Public debt:
7.8% of GDP (2015 est.)
9.3% of GDP (2014 est.)
country comparison to the world: 170

Fiscal year:
calendar year

Inflation rate (consumer prices):
2.3% (2015 est.)
2.7% (2014 est.)
country comparison to the world: 122

Central bank discount rate:
2.5%
country comparison to the world: 109

Commercial bank prime lending rate:
6.7% (31 December 2015 est.)
6.8% (31 December 2014 est.)
country comparison to the world: 124

Stock of narrow money:
$341.3 billion (31 December 2015 est.)
$304.8 billion (31 December 2014 est.)
country comparison to the world: 16

Stock of broad money:
$513.3 billion (31 December 2015 est.)
$461.2 billion (31 December 2014 est.)
country comparison to the world: 23

Stock of domestic credit:
$24 billion (31 December 2015 est.)
$-38.16 billion (31 December 2014 est.)
country comparison to the world: 82

For additional analytical, business and investment opportunities information, please contact Global Investment & Business Center, USA at (202) 546-2103. Fax: (202) 546-3275. E-mail: ibpusa3@gmail.com
Global Business and Legal Information Databank: www.ibpus.com

Market value of publicly traded shares:
$373.4 billion (31 December 2012 est.)
$338.9 billion (31 December 2011)
$353.4 billion (31 December 2010 est.)
country comparison to the world: 26

Current account balance:
-$22.38 billion (2015 est.)
$76.92 billion (2014 est.)
country comparison to the world: 188

Exports: 🔢
$222.6 billion (2015 est.)
$342.3 billion (2014 est.)
country comparison to the world: 22

Exports - commodities:
petroleum and petroleum products 90%

Exports - partners:
China 13.3%, Japan 13%, US 12.9%, South Korea 10%, India 8.9%, Singapore 4%
(2014)

Imports:
$160 billion (2015 est.)
$158.5 billion (2014 est.)
country comparison to the world: 28

Imports - commodities:
machinery and equipment, foodstuffs, chemicals, motor vehicles, textiles
Imports - partners: 🔢
China 13.3%, US 12.1%, India 8.3%, Germany 6.5%, South Korea 5.4%, Japan 4.9%
(2014)

Reserves of foreign exchange and gold:
$660.1 billion (31 December 2015 est.)
$732.4 billion (31 December 2014 est.)
country comparison to the world: 4

Debt - external:
$166.1 billion (31 December 2014 est.)
$155.7 billion (31 December 2013 est.)
country comparison to the world: 39

Stock of direct foreign investment - at home:
$250.3 billion (31 December 2015 est.)
$242.6 billion (31 December 2014 est.)
country comparison to the world: 26

Stock of direct foreign investment - abroad:
$37.32 billion (31 December 2015 est.)
$32.46 billion (31 December 2014 est.)

For additional analytical, business and investment opportunities information,
please contact Global Investment & Business Center, USA
at (202) 546-2103. Fax: (202) 546-3275. E-mail: ibpusa3@gmail.com
Global Business and Legal Information Databank: www.ibpus.com

country comparison to the world: 49

Exchange rates:
Saudi riyals (SAR) per US dollar -
3.75 (2015 est.)
3.75 (2014 est.)
3.75 (2013 est.)
3.75 (2012 est.)
3.75 (2011 est.)

ENERGY

Electricity - production:

255.2 billion kWh
country comparison to the world: 19

Electricity - consumption:

231.6 billion kWh
country comparison to the world: 20

Electricity - exports:

0 kWh
country comparison to the world: 188

Electricity - imports:

0 kWh
country comparison to the world: 192

Electricity - installed generating capacity:

53.2 million kW
country comparison to the world: 20

Electricity - from fossil fuels:

99.9% of total installed capacity
country comparison to the world: 30

Electricity - from hydroelectric plants:

0% of total installed capacity
country comparison to the world: 193

Electricity - from other renewable sources:

0.1 % of total installed capacity
country comparison to the world: 118

Crude oil - production:

9.735 million bbl/day
country comparison to the world: 1

country comparison to the world: 2

For additional analytical, business and investment opportunities information,
please contact Global Investment & Business Center, USA
at (202) 546-2103. Fax: (202) 546-3275. E-mail: ibpusa3@gmail.com
Global Business and Legal Information Databank: www.ibpus.com

Crude oil - exports:
7.658 million bbl/day (
country comparison to the world: 1

Crude oil - imports:
0 bbl/day
country comparison to the world: 119

Crude oil - proved reserves:
268.3 billion bbl (1 January 2015 est.)
country comparison to the world: 2

Refined petroleum products - production:
1.971 million bbl/day (2012 est.)
country comparison to the world: 10

Refined petroleum products - consumption:
2.961 million bbl/day (2013 est.)
country comparison to the world: 7

Refined petroleum products - exports:
1.524 million bbl/day (2012 est.)
country comparison to the world: 6

Refined petroleum products - imports:
338,800 bbl/day (2012 est.)
country comparison to the world: 20

Natural gas - production:
102.4 billion cu m (2014 est.)
country comparison to the world: 9

Natural gas - consumption:
102.4 billion cu m (2014 est.)
country comparison to the world: 8

Natural gas - exports:
0 cu m (2014 est.)
country comparison to the world: 172
Natural gas - imports:
0 cu m (2014 est.)
country comparison to the world: 127

Natural gas - proved reserves:
8.235 trillion cu m (1 January 2014 est.)
country comparison to the world: 5

Carbon dioxide emissions from consumption of energy:
582.7 million Mt (2012 est.)
country comparison to the world: 10

For additional analytical, business and investment opportunities information,
please contact Global Investment & Business Center, USA
at (202) 546-2103. Fax: (202) 546-3275. E-mail: ibpusa3@gmail.com
Global Business and Legal Information Databank: www.ibpus.com

COMMUNICATIONS

Telephones - main lines in use:

4.8 million
country comparison to the world: 31

Telephones - mobile cellular:

53 million
country comparison to the world: 26

Telephone system:

general assessment: modern system including a combination of extensive microwave radio relays, coaxial cables, and fiber-optic cables
domestic: mobile-cellular subscribership has been increasing rapidly
international: country code - 966; landing point for the international submarine cable Fiber-Optic Link Around the Globe (FLAG) and for both the SEA-ME-WE-3 and SEA-ME-WE-4 submarine cable networks providing connectivity to Asia, Middle East, Europe, and US; microwave radio relay to Bahrain, Jordan, Kuwait, Qatar, UAE, Yemen, and Sudan; coaxial cable to Kuwait and Jordan; satellite earth stations - 5 Intelsat (3 Atlantic Ocean and 2 Indian Ocean), 1 Arabsat, and 1 Inmarsat (Indian Ocean region)

Broadcast media:

broadcast media are state-controlled; state-run TV operates 4 networks; Saudi Arabia is a major market for pan-Arab satellite TV broadcasters; state-run radio operates several networks; multiple international broadcasters are available (2007)

Internet country code:

.sa

Internet hosts:

145,941
country comparison to the world: 79

Internet users:

9.774 million (2009)
country comparison to the world: 30

TRANSPORTATION

Airports:

214
country comparison to the world: 26

total: 82
over 3,047 m: 33
2,438 to 3,047 m: 16
1,524 to 2,437 m: 27
914 to 1,523 m: 2
under 914 m: 4

For additional analytical, business and investment opportunities information,
please contact Global Investment & Business Center, USA
at (202) 546-2103. Fax: (202) 546-3275. E-mail: ibpusa3@gmail.com
Global Business and Legal Information Databank: www.ibpus.com

Airports - with unpaved runways:

total: 132
2,438 to 3,047 m: 7
1,524 to 2,437 m: 72
914 to 1,523 m: 37
under 914 m:
16

Heliports:

10

Pipelines:

condensate 209 km; gas 2,940 km; liquid petroleum gas 1,183 km; oil 5,117 km; refined products 1,151 km

Railways:

total: 1,378 km
country comparison to the world: 81
standard gauge: 1,378 km 1.435-m gauge (with branch lines and sidings) (2008)

Roadways:

total: 221,372 km
country comparison to the world: 22
paved: 47,529 km (includes 3,891 km of expressways)
unpaved: 173,843 km (2006)

Merchant marine:

total: 72
country comparison to the world: 61
by type: cargo 1, chemical tanker 25, container 4, liquefied gas 2, passenger/cargo 10, petroleum tanker 20, refrigerated cargo 3, roll on/roll off 7
foreign-owned: 15 (Egypt 1, Greece 4, Kuwait 4, UAE 6)
registered in other countries: 55 (Bahamas 16, Dominica 2, Liberia 20, Malta 2, Norway 3, Panama 11, Tanzania 1)

Ports and terminals:

major seaport(s): Ad Dammam, Al Jubayl, Jeddah, Yanbu al Bahr
container port(s) (TEUs): Ad Dammam (1,492,315), Jeddah (4,010,448)

MILITARY

Military branches:

Ministry of Defense and Aviation Forces: Royal Saudi Land Forces, Royal Saudi Naval Forces (includes Marine Forces and Special Forces), Royal Saudi Air Force (Al-Quwwat al-Jawwiya al-Malakiya as-Sa'udiya), Royal Saudi Air Defense Forces, Royal Saudi Strategic Rocket Forces, Saudi Arabian National Guard (SANG)

Military service age and obligation:

For additional analytical, business and investment opportunities information,
please contact Global Investment & Business Center, USA
at (202) 546-2103. Fax: (202) 546-3275. E-mail: ibpusa3@gmail.com
Global Business and Legal Information Databank: www.ibpus.com

17 is the legal minimum age for voluntary military service; no conscription

Manpower available for military service:

males age 16-49: 8,644,522
females age 16-49: 6,601,985

Manpower fit for military service:

males age 16-49: 7,365,624
females age 16-49: 5,677,819

Manpower reaching militarily significant age annually:

male: 261,105
female: 244,763

Military expenditures:

7.98% of GDP
country comparison to the world: 3
7.25% of GDP 7.98% of GDP

TRANSNATIONAL ISSUES

Disputes - international:

Saudi Arabia has reinforced its concrete-filled security barrier along sections of the now fully demarcated border with Yemen to stem illegal cross-border activities; Kuwait and Saudi Arabia continue discussions on a maritime boundary with Iran; Saudi Arabia claims Egyptian-administered islands of Tiran and Sanafir

Refugees and internally displaced persons:

stateless persons: 70,000 ; note - thousands of biduns (stateless Arabs) are descendants of nomadic tribes who were not officially registered when national borders were established, while others migrated to Saudi Arabia in search of jobs; some have temporary identification cards that must be renewed every five years, but their rights remain restricted; most Palestinians have only legal resident status; some naturalized Yemenis were made stateless after being stripped of their passports when Yemen backed Iraq in its invasion of Kuwait in 1990; Saudi women cannot pass their citizenship on to their children, so if they marry a non-national, their children risk statelessness

Trafficking in persons:

current situation: Saudi Arabia is a destination country for men and women subjected to forced labor and, to a lesser extent, forced prostitution; men and women from Bangladesh, India, Sri Lanka, Nepal, Pakistan, the Philippines, Indonesia, Sudan, Ethiopia, Kenya, and many other countries voluntarily travel to Saudi Arabia as domestic servants or other low-skilled laborers, but some subsequently face conditions indicative of involuntary servitude (many are forced to work months or years beyond their contract term because employers withhold passports and required exit visas); women, primarily from Asian and African countries, are believed to be forced into prostitution in Saudi Arabia; others were reportedly kidnapped and forced into prostitution after running away from abusive employers; Yemeni, Nigerian, Pakistani, Afghan, Chadian, and Sudanese children were subjected to forced

For additional analytical, business and investment opportunities information,
please contact Global Investment & Business Center, USA
at (202) 546-2103. Fax: (202) 546-3275. E-mail: ibpusa3@gmail.com
Global Business and Legal Information Databank: www.ibpus.com

labor as beggars and street vendors in Saudi Arabia, facilitated by criminal gangs

tier rating: Tier 3 - Saudi Arabia does not fully comply with the minimum standards for the elimination of trafficking and is not making significant efforts to do so; fewer victims were identified and referred to protection services than in the previous reporting period; the sponsorship system, including the exit visa requirement, continues to restrict the freedom of movement of migrant workers and hamper the ability of victims to pursue legal cases against their employers; however, the government has implemented regulations mandating the formation of unified recruitment companies to replace the sponsorship model; no specialized shelter was available to victims of sex trafficking or male victims of trafficking

Illicit drugs:

death penalty for traffickers; improving anti-money-laundering legislation and enforcement

IMPORTANT INFORMATION FOR UNDERSTANDING THE KINGDOM OF SAUDI ARABIA
Official Name: Kingdom of Saudi Arabia

PROFILE

Geography
Area: 1,960,582 million sq. km. (784,233 sq. mi.), slightly more than one-fifth the size of the continental United States.
Cities (est.): *Capital*--Riyadh (pop. 4.3 million). *Other cities*--Jeddah (3.4 million), Makkah, (1.6 million), Dammam/Khobar/Dhahran, (1.6 million).
Terrain: Primarily desert with rugged mountains in the southwest.
Climate: Arid, with great extremes of temperature in the interior; humidity and temperature are both high along the coast.

People
Nationality: *Noun*--Saudi(s). *Adjective*--Saudi Arabian or Saudi.
Population (est.): 31.54 million). 90% Arab and 10% Afro-Asian
Annual population growth rate: (est.): 1.8%.
Ethnic groups: Arab (90% of native pop.), Afro-Asian (10% of native pop.).
Religion: Islam.
Language: Arabic (official).
Education: *Literacy*--total 78.8% (male 84.7%, female 70.8%).
Health: *Infant mortality rate* (est.)--11.57 deaths/1,000 live births. *Life expectancy*--male 74 years, female 78 years.
Work force: 6.49 million, about 35% foreign workers (est.); *industry*--25%; *services* (including government)--63%; *agriculture*--12%.

Government
Type: Monarchy with Council of Ministers and Consultative Council.
Unification: September 23, 1932.
Constitution: The Holy Qur'an (governed according to Islamic Law), Shari'a, and the Basic Law.
Branches: *Executive*--King (chief of state and head of government; rules under the title Custodian of the Two Holy Mosques). *Legislative*--a Consultative Council with advisory powers was formed September 1993. *Judicial*--Supreme Court, Supreme Judicial Council, Islamic Courts of First Instance and Appeals.

For additional analytical, business and investment opportunities information, please contact Global Investment & Business Center, USA at (202) 546-2103. Fax: (202) 546-3275. E-mail: ibpusa3@gmail.com Global Business and Legal Information Databank: www.ibpus.com

Administrative divisions: 13 provinces.
Political parties: None; formal political parties are not recognized by the government and have no legal status.

PEOPLE

The population of Saudi Arabia as of July 2013 is estimated to be 26.9 million, including between 5.5 million and 10 million non-nationalized immigrants, though the Saudi population has long proved difficult to accurately estimate due to Saudi leaders' historical tendency to artificially inflate census results. Saudi population has grown rapidly since 1950 when it was estimated to be 3 million, and for many years had one of the highest birthrates in the world at around 3% a year.

The ethnic composition of Saudi citizens is 90% Arab and 10% Afro-Asian. Most Saudis live in Hejaz (35%), Najd (28%), and the Eastern Province (15%).Hejaz is the most populated region in Saudi Arabia.

As late as 1970, most Saudis lived a subsistence life in the rural provinces, but in the last half of the 20th century the kingdom has urbanized rapidly. As of 2012 about 80% of Saudis live in urban metropolitan areas—specifically Riyadh, Jeddah, or Dammam.

Its population is also quite young with over half the population under 25 years old. A large fraction are foreign nationals. (The CIA Factbook estimated that foreign nationals living in Saudi Arabia made up about 21% of the population. Other estimates are 30% or 33%

Saudi Arabia is known as the birthplace of Islam, which in the century following the Prophet Muhammad's death in 632 A.D. spread west to Spain and east to India. Islam obliges all Muslims to make the Hajj, or pilgrimage to Makkah, at least once during their lifetime if they are able to do so. The cultural environment in Saudi Arabia is highly conservative; the country officially adheres to the strict Wahhabi interpretation of Islamic religious law (Shari'a). Cultural presentations must conform to narrowly defined standards of ethics. Men and women often are not permitted to attend public events together and are segregated in the work place.

Most Saudis are ethnically Arab. Some are of mixed ethnic origin and are descended from Turks, Iranians, Indonesians, Indians, Africans, and others, most of whom immigrated as pilgrims and reside in the Hijaz region along the Red Sea coast. Many Arabs from nearby countries are employed in the kingdom. There also are significant numbers of Asian expatriates mostly from India, Pakistan, Bangladesh, Indonesia, and the Philippines. Westerners in Saudi Arabia number under 100,000.

HISTORY

Except for a few major cities and oases, the harsh climate historically prevented much settlement of the Arabian Peninsula. People of various cultures have lived in the peninsula over a span of more than 5,000 years. The Dilmun culture, along the Gulf coast, was contemporaneous with the Sumerians and ancient Egyptians, and most of the empires of the ancient world traded with the states that existed on the peninsula, which lay along important trade routes.

The Saudi state began in central Arabia in about 1750. A local ruler, Muhammad bin Saud, joined forces with an Islamic reformer, Muhammad Abd Al-Wahhab, to create a new political entity. Over the next 150 years, the fortunes of the Saud family rose and fell several times as Saudi rulers contended with Egypt, the Ottoman Empire, and other Arabian families for control on the

**For additional analytical, business and investment opportunities information,
please contact Global Investment & Business Center, USA
at (202) 546-2103. Fax: (202) 546-3275. E-mail: ibpusa3@gmail.com
Global Business and Legal Information Databank: www.ibpus.com**

peninsula. The modern Saudi kingdom was founded by the late King Abdul Aziz Al Saud (known internationally as Ibn Saud, or "Son of Saud"). In 1902, Abdul Aziz recaptured Riyadh, the Al Saud dynasty's ancestral capital, from the rival Al-Rashid family. Continuing his conquests, Abdul Aziz subdued Al-Hasa in the east, the rest of the central Nejd region, and the Hijaz along the Red Sea coast between 1913 and 1926. In 1932, Abdul Aziz declared these regions unified as the Kingdom of Saudi Arabia.

Boundaries with Jordan, Iraq, and Kuwait were established by a series of treaties negotiated in the 1920s, with two "neutral zones"--one with Iraq and the other with Kuwait--created. The Saudi-Kuwaiti neutral zone was administratively partitioned in 1971, with each state continuing to share the petroleum resources of the former zone equally. Tentative agreement on the partition of the Saudi-Iraqi neutral zone was reached in 1981, and partition was finalized by 1983. The country's southern boundary with Yemen was partially defined by the 1934 Treaty of Taif, which ended a brief border war between the two states. A June 2000 treaty further delineated portions of the boundary with Yemen. The location and status of Saudi Arabia's boundary with the United Arab Emirates is not final; a de facto boundary reflects a 1974 agreement. The border between Saudi Arabia and Qatar was resolved in March 2001.

King Abdul Aziz died in 1953 and was succeeded by his eldest son, Saud, who reigned for 11 years. In 1964, Saud abdicated in favor of his half-brother, Crown Prince Faisal, who had served as both prime minister and foreign minister. Because of fiscal difficulties, King Saud had been persuaded in 1958 to delegate direct conduct of Saudi Government affairs to Faisal as prime minister; Saud briefly regained control of the government in 1960-62. In October 1962, Faisal outlined a broad reform program, stressing economic development. Proclaimed King in 1964 by senior royal family members and religious leaders, Faisal also continued to serve as prime minister. This practice has been followed by subsequent kings.

The mid-1960s saw external pressures generated by Saudi-Egyptian differences over Yemen. When civil war broke out in 1962 between Yemeni royalists and republicans, Egyptian forces entered Yemen to support the new republican government, while Saudi Arabia backed the royalists. Tensions subsided only after 1967, when Egypt withdrew its troops from Yemen.

Saudi forces did not participate in the Six-Day (Arab-Israeli) War of June 1967, but the government later provided annual subsidies to Egypt, Jordan, and Syria to support their economies. During the 1973 Arab-Israeli war, Saudi Arabia participated in the Arab oil boycott of the United States and the Netherlands. A founding member of the Organization of Petroleum Exporting Countries (OPEC), Saudi Arabia had joined other member countries in moderate oil price increases beginning in 1971. After the 1973 war, the price of oil rose substantially, dramatically increasing Saudi Arabia's wealth and political influence.

In 1975, King Faisal was assassinated by a nephew, who was executed after an extensive investigation concluded that he acted alone. Faisal was succeeded by his half-brother Khalid as King and Prime Minister; their half-brother Prince Fahd was named Crown Prince and First Deputy Prime Minister. King Khalid empowered Crown Prince Fahd to oversee many aspects of the government's international and domestic affairs. Economic development continued rapidly under King Khalid, and the kingdom assumed a more influential role in regional politics and international economic and financial matters.

In June 1982, King Khalid died, and Fahd became King and Prime Minister in a smooth transition. Another half-brother, Prince Abdallah, Commander of the Saudi National Guard, was named Crown Prince and First Deputy Prime Minister. King Fahd's full brother, Prince Sultan, the Minister of Defense and Aviation, became Second Deputy Prime Minister. Under King Fahd, the Saudi economy adjusted to sharply lower oil revenues resulting from declining global oil prices.

For additional analytical, business and investment opportunities information, please contact Global Investment & Business Center, USA at (202) 546-2103. Fax: (202) 546-3275. E-mail: ibpusa3@gmail.com Global Business and Legal Information Databank: www.ibpus.com

Saudi Arabia supported neutral shipping in the Gulf during periods of the Iran-Iraq war and aided Iraq's war-strained economy. King Fahd played a major part in bringing about the August 1988 cease-fire between Iraq and Iran and in organizing and strengthening the Gulf Cooperation Council (GCC), a group of six Arabian Gulf states dedicated to fostering regional economic cooperation and peaceful development.

In 1990-91, King Fahd played a key role before and during the Gulf war, helping consolidate the coalition of forces against Iraq and define the tone of the operation as a multilateral effort to reestablish the sovereignty and territorial integrity of Kuwait. Acting as a rallying point and personal spokesman for the coalition, King Fahd helped bring together his nation's GCC, Western, and Arab allies, as well as nonaligned nations from Africa and the emerging democracies of Eastern Europe. He used his influence as Custodian of the Two Holy Mosques to persuade other Arab and Islamic nations to join the coalition.

King Fahd suffered a stroke in November 1995. From 1997, Crown Prince Abdallah took on much of the day-to-day responsibilities of running the government. Upon King Fahd's death on August 1, 2005, Abdallah assumed the throne as King. Prince Sultan, Minister of Defense and Aviation, became Crown Prince and First Deputy Prime Minister. Since ascending to the throne, King Abdallah has continued to pursue an incremental program of social, economic, and political reforms. In September 2009, he inaugurated the King Abdallah University of Science and Technology (KAUST), a graduate-level research institution and Saudi Arabia's first co-educational university.

In 2005, King Fahd died and his half-brother, Abdullah ascended to the throne. Despite growing calls for change, the king has continued the policy of moderate reform.

The country's continued reliance on oil revenue is of particular concern. King Abdullah has pursued a policy of limited deregulation, privatization and seeking foreign investment. In November 2005, following 12 years of talks, the World Trade Organization gave the green light to Saudi Arabia's membership.

In December 2006, Saudi Arabia pressured Britain into halting a fraud investigation into the £43bn Al-Yamamah arms deal with Saudi Arabia. Then, in September 2007, Saudi Arabia agreed a deal to buy 72 Eurofighter Typhoon combat jets from Britain. A British High Court later ruled that the British government had acted unlawfully in dropping the corruption inquiry, but this was overturned by the British House of Lords in July 2008 because Saudi Arabia had threatened to withdraw cooperation with Britain on security matters.

Terrorist attacks continued to be a major problem. In September 2005, five gunmen and three police officers were killed in clashes in the eastern city of Dammam. The government claimed it had foiled a planned suicide bomb attack on a major oil-processing plant at Abqaiq in February 2006. Six men allegedly linked to al-Qaeda were killed in a shootout with police in Riyadh in June 2006. Four French nationals were killed in a suspected terror attack near the popular tourist destination of Madain Saleh in February 2007.

Saudi justice came under criticism over the Qatif rape case in which a 19-year-old rape victim was sentenced to 6 months in prison and 90 lashes. The king eventually issued a pardon. A ban had to be placed on the Mutaween (religious police) from detaining suspects as they had come under increasing criticism over the number of deaths in custody. A royal decree ordered an overhaul of the judicial system in October 2007. In December 2007, authorities announced the arrest of a group of men suspected of planning attacks on holy sites during the Hajj pilgrimage. In February 2009, Interpol issued security alerts for 85 men suspected of plotting attacks in Saudi

For additional analytical, business and investment opportunities information, please contact Global Investment & Business Center, USA at (202) 546-2103. Fax: (202) 546-3275. E-mail: ibpusa3@gmail.com Global Business and Legal Information Databank: www.ibpus.com

Arabia, in its largest group alert. All but two were Saudis. In February 2009, King Abdullah sacked the head of religious police, his most senior judge and the head of the central bank in a rare government reshuffle. He also appointed the country's first woman minister.

In July 2009, US President Barack Obama arrived in Saudi Arabia and held talks with King Abdullah at the start of a Middle East tour aimed at increasing US engagement with the Islamic world. In October 2010, US officials confirmed a plan to sell $60 billion worth of arms to Saudi Arabia - the most lucrative single arms deal in US history. Relations were hurt over the United States diplomatic cables leak by the whistle-blowing website Wikileaks in December 2010. They suggested that the USA was concerned that Saudi Arabia was the *most significant* source of funding for Sunni terrorist groups worldwide. Nevertheless, a major sale of US fighter jets to Saudi Arabia was confirmed in December 2011.

Security measures included a policy of mass arrests.

In April 2007, Saudi police claimed they had arrested 172 terror suspects, some of whom were allegedly trained as pilots for suicide missions. In April 2009, police said they had arrested 11 al-Qaeda militants who were allegedly planning attacks on police installations, armed robberies and kidnappings. A court issued verdicts in the first explicit terrorism trial for al-Qaeda militants in the country. Officials said 330 people had been put on trial, but did not specify how many had been found guilty. In August 2009, Saudi Arabia said it had arrested 44 more suspected militants with alleged links to al-Qaeda. A year later, officials announced the arrest of 149 militants over an eight months period, most of them allegedly belonging to al-Qaeda. In April 2012, fifty men suspected of having links to al-Qaeda went on trial. Charges included the 2003 bombing of an expatriates' compound.

As the Arab Spring unrest and protests began to spread across Arab world in early 2011, King Abdullah announced an increase in welfare spending amounting to $10.7 billion. This included funding to offset high inflation, aid for young unemployed people and Saudi citizens studying abroad, as well as writing off some loans. State employees saw their incomes increase by 15 per cent, and additional cash was made available for housing loans. No political reforms were announced as part of the package, though some prisoners indicted for financial crimes were pardoned. After a number of small demonstrations in the mainly Shia areas of the east, public protests were banned in March 2011, and King Abdullah warned that threats to the nation's security and stability would not be tolerated.

At the same time Saudi troops were sent to participate in the crackdown on unrest in Bahrain. King Abdullah gave asylum to deposed President Zine El Abidine Ben Ali of Tunisia and telephoned President Hosni Mubarak of Egypt (prior to his deposition) to offer his support. In July 2012, security forces detained several people in Qatif, Eastern Province, after witnessing police open fire on Shia protesters demanding the release of Shia cleric Sheikh Nimr al-Nimr and others. Two people were killed at a rally against his arrest earlier in the month. Human-rights activists Mohammad al-Qahtani and Abdullah al-Hamid were put on trial in September 2012; the former was charged with setting up an unlicensed organisation.

In June 2011 Saudi women mounted a symbolic protest drive in defiance of the ban on female car drivers. A few months later, King Abdullah did announce more rights for women, including the right to vote, stand in municipal elections and to be appointed to the consultative Shura Council - the most influential political body. In September 2011, the king overturned a sentence of 10 lashes on a woman who was found guilty of driving - the first time that a legal punishment had been handed down for violation of the ban on women drivers. Saudi Arabia agreed to allow its women athletes to compete in the 2012 Olympics for the first time, amidst speculation that the entire Saudi team might have been disqualified on grounds of gender discrimination.

In August 2013, Saudi Arabia emerged as a supporter of the Egyptian military leaders that were cracking down on Islamists. They openly supported the leaders with their wealth received from oil mining and used their diplomatic presence to aid Egypt in resisting pro-Western influence. Just a month later, word spread that President Obama intended to keep up his presence in the Middle East, and continue trying to work towards preventing the development of nuclear weapons in Iran. Saudi Arabia, like many other gulf states, saw Iran to be a large threat to the area with its growing nuclear program.

Citizens have also taken initiative to address discrimination that women face in the region and on October 26, have called for a day where the women in Saudi Arabia break the norm. On that day, over 60 women in the region drove their cars in defiance to their limitation. Since then, an online petition regarding the event and its cause, has gathered thousands of signatures, however, they still await government recognition. Authorities followed up after the event by stating that it will deal with such violations forcefully.

Around the end of the month of April in 2014, President Obama announced that he would travel to Saudi Arabia in March in an effort to mend the relationship between the two countries. Saudi Arabia and the gulf states have been frustrated with policies that the United States has been placing on Syria and Iran. Iran especially, has been expressing desire to be relieved of the Iran Sanctions Act. Obama's visit to Saudi Arabia proved to be successful as Obama reassured King Abdullah of Saudi Arabia that America still intended to strengthen Saudi Arabia's standing in the Syrian war. There were no concrete details of the meeting, but speculation from the aides has presented information on the meeting. President Obama's visit to the Middle East ended on the 30th of March with a private ceremony, and he returned home. Still there was little word about what really transpired at the convening.

During the month of April in 2014, there has been a severe outbreak of Middle Eastern Respiratory Syndrome, or MERS. MERS has been present in Saudi Arabia since 2012, and has affected over 200 people since then. There have been nearly 100 deaths as a result of MERS, and due to the new cases that have reemerged, King Abdullah has replaced Arabia's health minister. From April 21, 2014 to the 25th, there have been almost 100 new cases reported and six deaths from MERS.

In May 2014, on the 6th it was reported that 62 military men were arrested because of alleged accusations for having ties linked to terrorist groups in Yemen and Syria. Saudi Arabia believes that they were planning an attack on Saudi Arabia in the form of assassinations of Arabian officials. Maj. Gen. Mansour al-Turki, the spokesman of the interior ministry program states that the men had communicated with members of the Al Qaeda terrorist group, and they were in the process of planning on to make trades and smuggling weapons for an attack on the Saudi Arabia's clerics and government officials.

On 2 January 2015, Abdullah was hospitalized for pneumonia and died on 22 January, to be succeeded by his brother Salman

GOVERNMENT AND POLITICAL CONDITIONS

The central institution of Saudi Arabian Government is the monarchy. The Basic Law adopted in 1992 declared that Saudi Arabia is a monarchy ruled by the sons and grandsons of King Abdul

Aziz Al Saud, and that the Holy Qur'an is the constitution of the country, which is governed on the basis of Islamic law (Shari'a). There are no officially recognized political parties. Following the first municipal elections in 2005, elections to select half of all municipal councilors have been scheduled for September 2011. The king has broad powers with limitations coming from a need to observe Shari'a and other Saudi traditions. He also must maintain consensus among the Saudi royal family, religious leaders (ulema), and other important elements in Saudi society. In the past the leading members of the royal family chose the king from among themselves with the subsequent approval of the ulema. In November 2006, King Abdallah established an Allegiance Commission that will select future kings and crown princes, a step designed to help formalize the selection process.

Saudi kings gradually have developed a central government. Since 1953, the Council of Ministers, appointed by and responsible to the king, has advised on the formulation of general policy and directed the activities of the growing bureaucracy. This council consists of the king (as prime minister), the first and second deputy prime ministers, 20 ministers, two ministers of state, and a small number of advisers and heads of major autonomous organizations.

Legislation is by resolution of the Council of Ministers and the Consultative Council, ratified by royal decree, and must be compatible with Shari'a. Justice is administered according to Shari'a by a system of religious courts. A 2007 law created a new Supreme Court to replace the Supreme Judicial Council (SJC) as Saudi Arabia's highest court authority. The same law transfers powers that the Ministry of Justice formerly exercised to the SJC, such as the authority to ability to establish and abolish courts, and name judges to the Courts of Appeal and First Instance. The independence of the judiciary is protected by law. The king has the authority to hear appeals and has the power to pardon in cases where the punishment is not ordained in the Qur'an. Access to high officials (usually at a public audience, or majlis) and the right to petition them directly are well-established traditions.

The kingdom is divided into 13 provinces governed by princes or close relatives of the royal family. All governors are appointed by the king.

In March 1992, King Fahd issued several decrees outlining the basic statutes of government and codifying for the first time procedures concerning the royal succession. Fahd's political reform program also provided for the establishment of a national Consultative Council, with appointed members having advisory powers to review and give advice on issues of public interest. It also outlined a framework for councils at the provincial level.

In September 1993, King Fahd issued additional reform decrees, appointing the members of the national Consultative Council and spelling out procedures for the new council's operations. He announced reforms regarding the Council of Ministers, including term limitations of 4 years and regulations to prohibit conflict of interest for ministers and other high-level officials. The members of 13 provincial councils and the councils' operating regulations also were announced in September 1993. In February, March, and April 2005, Saudis voted in the country's first municipal elections in more than 40 years. Only male, nonmilitary citizens at least 21 years old were permitted to vote.

In July 1997, the membership of the Consultative Council was expanded from 60 to 90 male members, and again in May 2001 from 90 to 120 members. In 2005, membership was expanded to 150 members. The Council also includes female non-voting advisors; in 2010, their numbers were increased from 10 to 13. Membership has changed significantly during expansions of the council as many members have not been reappointed. The role of the royally appointed Council is gradually expanding as it gains experience.

In November 2006, King Abdallah announced the formation of an Allegiance Commission which, in the future, will select a king and crown prince upon the death or incapacitation of either. A December 2007 royal decree named the initial members of the Commission, all of whom are sons, grandsons, or great-grandsons representing each branch of the descendants of the kingdoms' founder, King Abdul Aziz. Only direct male descendants of Abdul Aziz are eligible to become crown prince or king.

Principal Government Officials

Saudi Council of Ministers

Portfolio	Minister	Since
Prime Minister	King Salman bin Abdulaziz Al Saud	2015
First Deputy Prime Minister and Minister of Interior	Mohammad bin Nayef bin Abdulaziz Al Saud	2015
Second Deputy Prime Minister and Minister of Defense	Mohammad bin Salman bin Abdulaziz Al Saud	2015
Minister of the National Guard	Mutaib bin Abdullah bin Abdulaziz Al Saud	2013
Minister of Foreign Affairs	Adel bin Ahmed Al Jubeir	2015
Minister of Islamic Affairs, Endowments, Call and Guidance	Saleh bin Abdulaziz Al Ash-Shaikh	2015
Minister of Education	Ahmed bin Mohammed Al-Issa	2015
Minister of Justice	Waleed bin Mohammad Al Samaani	2015
Minister of Petroleum and Mineral Resources	Ali bin Ibrahim Al Naimi	1995
Minister of Transport	Abdullah bin Abdulrahman Al Muqbel	2014
Minister of Commerce and Industry	Tawfiq bin Fawzan Al Rabiah	2012
Minister of Social Affairs	Majid bin Abdullah Al Qasabi	2015
Minister of Economy and Planning	Adel bin Mohammad Fakeih	2015
Minister of Health	Khalid bin Abdulaziz Al Faleh	2015
Minister of Culture and Information	Adel bin Zaid Al Toraifi	2015
Minister of Labor	Mufarrej bin Saad Al-Haqbani	2015
Minister of Civil Service	Khalid bin Abdullah Al Araj	2015
Minister of Finance	Ibrahim bin Abdulaziz Al Assaf	1996
Minister of Water and Electricity	Abdullah bin Abdul Rahman Al Hussein	2004
Minister of Agriculture	Abdulrahman bin Abdulmuhsen Al Fadhly	2015
Minister of Hajj	Bandar bin Mohammad Al Hajjar	2011
Minister of Housing	Majed bin Abdullah Al Hogail	2015
Minister of Communication and Information Technology	Mohamed bin Ibrahim Al Suwaiyel	2015
Minister of Municipal and Rural Affairs	Abdullatif bin Abdulmalik Al AsShaikh	2015
Minister of State	Abdulaziz bin Abdullah Al Saud	2015
Minister of State for Foreign Affairs	Nizar bin Obaid Madani	1997
Minister of State	Muttlab bin Abdullah Al Nafissa	1995
Minister of State for Shura Affairs	Mohammad bin Faisal Abu Saq	2014
Minister of State	Essam bin Saad bin Saeed	2015

For additional analytical, business and investment opportunities information, please contact Global Investment & Business Center, USA at (202) 546-2103. Fax: (202) 546-3275. E-mail: ibpusa3@gmail.com Global Business and Legal Information Databank: www.ibpus.com

Minister of State	Saad bin Khalid Al Jabry	2015
Minister of State	Mohammad bin Abdulmalik Al AsShaikh	2015
Minister of State	Khalid bin Abdulrahman Al Eissa	2015
Minister of State	Musaad bin Mohammed Al Aiban	1995

The **Embassy** of the Kingdom of Saudi Arabia is located at 601 New Hampshire Avenue NW, Washington, DC 20037; tel. 202-342-3800.

ECONOMY

Currency	Saudi Riyal (harr, SR)
Fiscal year	Calendar year
Trade organisations	WTO, OPEC, G-20 major economies, BIS, ICS, IOS, WCO, GCC, World Bank IMF
Statistics	
GDP	$906.8 billion (PPP; 19th) $745.273 billion (nominal; 19th)
GDP growth	5.13%
GDP per capita	$53,780 (PPP; 8th)
GDP by sector	agriculture: 3.2%; industry: 60.4%; services: 36.4%
Inflation (CPI)	2.90%
Labour force	7.63 million (2009 est.) note: about 80% of the labor force is non-national
Labour force by occupation	agriculture: 6.7%; industry: 21.4%; services: 71.9%
Unemployment	5.7%
Main industries	crude oil production, petroleum refining, basic petrochemicals, ammonia, industrial gases, sodium hydroxide (caustic soda), cement, fertilizer, plastics, metals, commercial ship repair, commercial aircraft repair, construction
Ease-of-doing-business rank	22nd
External	
Exports	$381.5 billion
Export goods	petroleum and petroleum products 90%
Main export partners	United States 14.3% China 13.7% Japan 13.7% South Korea 9.9% India 8.2% Singapore 4.3%
Imports	$136.8 billion
Import goods	machinery and equipment, foodstuffs, chemicals, motor vehicles, textiles
Main import partners	China 13.5% United States 13.2% South Korea 6.7% Germany 6.5% India 6.3%

	Japan 6.0%
Gross external debt	$127.4 billion
	Public finances
Public debt	9.4% of GDP
Revenues	$293.1 billion
Expenses	$210.6 billion
Economic aid	(Donor) $100 million in 1993 to Lebanon; since 2000, Saudi Arabia has committed $307 million to Palestinians; pledged $240 million to Afghanistan; pledged $1 billion in export guarantees and soft loans to Iraq.
Credit rating	Standard & Poor's: AA- (Domestic) AA- (Foreign) AA+ (T&C Assessment) Outlook: Stable Moody's: Aa3 Outlook: Stable Fitch: AA- Outlook: Stable

Saudi Arabia has an oil-based **economy** with strong government control over major economic activities. Saudi Arabia possesses 18% of the world's proven petroleum reserves, ranks as the largest exporter of petroleum, and played a leading role in OPEC for many years. The petroleum sector accounts for almost all of Saudi government revenues, and export earnings. Most workers, particularly in the private sector, are foreigners.

Oil was discovered in Saudi Arabia by U.S. geologists in the 1930s, although large-scale production did not begin until after World War II. Oil wealth has made possible rapid economic development, which began in earnest in the 1960s and accelerated spectacularly in the 1970s, transforming the kingdom.

Saudi oil reserves are the largest in the world, and Saudi Arabia is the world's leading oil producer and exporter. Oil accounts for more than 90% of the country's exports and nearly 75% of government revenues. Proven reserves are estimated to be 263 billion barrels, about one-quarter of world oil reserves.

More than 95% of all Saudi oil is produced on behalf of the Saudi Government by the parastatal giant Saudi ARAMCO. In June 1993, Saudi ARAMCO absorbed the state marketing and refining company (SAMAREC), becoming the world's largest fully integrated oil company. Most Saudi oil exports move by tanker from Gulf terminals at Ras Tanura and Ju'aymah. The remaining oil exports are transported via the east-west pipeline across the kingdom to the Red Sea port of Yanbu.

Due to a sharp rise in petroleum revenues in 1974 following the 1973 Arab-Israeli war, Saudi Arabia became one of the fastest-growing economies in the world. It enjoyed a substantial surplus in its overall trade with other countries; imports increased rapidly; and ample government revenues were available for development, defense, and aid to other Arab and Islamic countries.

But higher oil prices led to development of more oil fields around the world and reduced global consumption. The result, beginning in the mid-1980s, was a worldwide oil glut, which introduced an element of planning uncertainty for the first time in a decade. Saudi oil production, which had increased to almost 10 million barrels per day (b/d) during 1980-81, dropped to about 2 million b/d in 1985. Budgetary deficits developed, and the government drew down its foreign assets. Responding to financial pressures, Saudi Arabia gave up its role as the "swing producer" within OPEC in the summer of 1985 and accepted a production quota. Since then, Saudi oil policy has been guided by a desire to maintain market and quota shares and to support stability in the international oil market.

Saudi Arabia was a key player in coordinating the successful 1999 campaign of OPEC and other oil-producing countries to raise the price of oil to its highest level since the Gulf War by managing production and supply of petroleum. That same year saw establishment of the Supreme Economic Council to formulate and better coordinate Saudi economic development policies in order to accelerate institutional and industrial reform.

In response to increasing international demand for oil, Saudi ARAMCO engaged in an expansion of its oil production capacity and raised its capacity from 11 million barrels/day (mb/d) to 12 mb/d in 2009. Saudi ARAMCO is also increasing production of associated and non-associated natural gas to feed the expanding petrochemical sector. Notably, Saudi Arabia has awarded contracts to foreign companies to conduct gas exploration in selected regions of the country--the first such foreign participation in the petroleum sector upstream since the nationalization of ARAMCO began in the 1970s.

Saudi Arabia continues to pursue rapid industrial expansion, led by the petrochemical sector. The Saudi Basic Industries Corporation (SABIC), a parastatal petrochemical company, is now one of the world's leading petrochemical producers, and the government promotes private sector involvement in petrochemicals. The government also plans new investments in the mining sector and in refining,

After Saudi Arabia announced its intention to join the World Trade Organization (WTO), negotiations focused on increasing market access to foreign goods and services and the timeframe for becoming fully compliant with WTO obligations. In April 2000, the government established the Saudi Arabian General Investment Authority to encourage foreign direct investment in the country. Saudi Arabia signed a Trade Investment Framework Agreement with the U.S. in July 2003, and joined the WTO in December 2005.

Through 5-year development plans, the government has sought to allocate its petroleum income to transform its relatively undeveloped, oil-based economy into that of a modern industrial state while maintaining the kingdom's traditional Islamic values and customs. Although economic planners have not achieved all their goals, the economy has progressed rapidly. Oil wealth has increased the standard of living of most Saudis. However, significant population growth has strained the government's ability to finance further improvements in the country's standard of living. Heavy dependence on petroleum revenue continues, but industry and agriculture now account for a larger share of economic activity. The mismatch between the job skills of Saudi graduates and the needs of the private job market at all levels remains the principal obstacle to economic diversification and development; about 4.6 million non-Saudis are employed in the economy.

Saudi Arabia's first two development plans, covering the 1970s, emphasized infrastructure. The results were impressive--the total length of paved highways tripled, power generation increased by a multiple of 28, and the capacity of the seaports grew tenfold. For the third plan (1980-85), the emphasis changed. Spending on infrastructure declined, but it rose markedly on education, health, and social services. The share for diversifying and expanding productive sectors of the economy (primarily industry) did not rise as planned, but the two industrial cities of Jubail and Yanbu--built around the use of the country's oil and gas to produce steel, petrochemicals, fertilizer, and refined oil products--were largely completed.

In the fourth plan (1985-90), the country's basic infrastructure was viewed as largely complete, but education and training remained areas of concern. Private enterprise was encouraged, and foreign investment in the form of joint ventures with Saudi public and private companies was welcomed. The private sector became more important, rising to 70% of non-oil GDP by 1987. While still concentrated in trade and commerce, private investment increased in industry, agriculture, banking, and construction companies. These private investments were supported by generous government financing and incentive programs. The objective was for the private sector to have 70% to 80% ownership in most joint venture enterprises.

The fifth plan (1990-95) emphasized consolidation of the country's defenses; improved and more efficient government social services; regional development; and, most importantly, creating greater private-sector employment opportunities for Saudis by reducing the number of foreign workers.

The sixth plan (1996-2000) focused on lowering the cost of government services without cutting them and sought to expand educational training programs. The plan called for reducing the kingdom's dependence on the petroleum sector by diversifying economic activity, particularly in the private sector, with special emphasis on industry and agriculture. It also continued the effort to "Saudiize" the labor force.

The seventh plan (2000-2004) focused more on economic diversification and a greater role of the private sector in the Saudi economy. For the period 2000-04, the Saudi Government aimed at an average GDP growth rate of 3.16% each year, with projected growths of 5.04% for the private sector and 4.01% for the non-oil sector. The government also set a target of creating 817,300 new jobs for Saudi nationals.

The eighth plan (2005-2010) again focused on economic diversification in addition to education and inclusion of women in society. The plan called for establishing new universities and new colleges with technical specializations. Privatization as well as emphases on a knowledge-based economy and tourism would help in the goal of economic diversification.

The ninth plan (2010-2014) aspires to eliminate poverty and increase development in infrastructure, medical services, educational capacity, and residential housing. The plan also aims to increase real GDP by 15% over 5 years and calls for substantial government investment in human resource development, in order to decrease Saudi unemployment from 9.6% to 5.5%.

FOREIGN RELATIONS

Saudi foreign policy objectives are to maintain its security and its paramount position on the Arabian Peninsula, defend general Arab and Islamic interests, promote solidarity among Islamic governments, and maintain cooperative relations with other oil-producing and major oil-consuming countries.

Saudi Arabia signed the UN Charter in 1945. The country plays a prominent and constructive role in the International Monetary Fund, the World Bank, and Arab and Islamic financial and development assistance institutions. One of the largest aid donors in the world, it still gives some aid to a number of Arab, African, and Asian countries. Jeddah is the headquarters of the Secretariat of the Organization of the Islamic Conference and its subsidiary organization, the

Islamic Development Bank, founded in 1969.

Membership in the 11-member OPEC and in the technically and economically oriented Arab producer group--the Organization of Arab Petroleum Exporting Countries--facilitates coordination of Saudi oil policies with other oil-exporting governments. As the world's leading exporter of petroleum, Saudi Arabia has a special interest in preserving a stable and long-term market for its vast oil resources by allying itself with healthy Western economies which can protect the value of Saudi financial assets. It generally has acted to stabilize the world oil market and tried to moderate sharp price movements.

The Saudi Government frequently helps mediate regional crises and supports the Middle East peace process. A charter member of the Arab League, Saudi Arabia supports the position that Israel must withdraw from the territories which it occupied in June 1967, as called for in United Nations Security Council Resolution 242. Saudi Arabia supports a peaceful resolution of the Arab-Israeli conflict but rejected the Camp David accords, claiming that they would be unable to achieve a comprehensive political solution that would ensure Palestinian rights and adequately address the status of Jerusalem. Although Saudi Arabia broke diplomatic relations with and suspended aid to Egypt in the wake of Camp David, the two countries renewed formal ties in 1987. In March 2002, then-Crown Prince Abdallah offered a Middle East peace plan, now known as the Arab Peace Initiative, at the annual summit of the Arab League in which Arab governments would offer "normal relations and the security of Israel in exchange for a full Israeli withdrawal from all occupied Arab lands, recognition of an independent Palestinian state with Jerusalem as its capital, and the return of Palestinian refugees." In March 2007 the Arab League reiterated its support for the Arab Peace Initiative by emphasizing that it could be the foundation for a broad Arab-Israeli peace. In November 2007, Saudi Foreign Minister Prince Saud al-Faisal attended the Annapolis Conference, along with more than 50 representatives of concerned countries and international organizations. The conference was convened to express the broad support of the international community for the Israeli and Palestinian leaders' courageous efforts and was a launching point for negotiations designed to lead to the establishment of a Palestinian state and the realization of Israeli-Palestinian peace.

Saudi Arabia supports the establishment of a unified, independent, and sovereign Iraq. The kingdom is a charter member of the International Compact with Iraq and participates in the Expanded Iraq Neighbors process. In January 2008, Foreign Minister Prince Saud al-Faisal reiterated Saudi Arabia's intention to open a diplomatic mission in Baghdad and appoint an ambassador.

In 1990-91, Saudi Arabia played an important role in the Gulf War, developing new allies and improving existing relationships between Saudi Arabia and some other countries, but also suffering diplomatic and financial costs. Relations between Saudi Arabia and Tunisia, Algeria, and Libya deteriorated. Each country had remained silent following Iraq's invasion of Kuwait but called for an end to violence once the deployment of coalition troops began. Relations between these countries and Saudi Arabia later returned to their pre-war status. Saudi Arabia's relations with those countries which expressed support for Saddam Hussein's invasion of Kuwait--Yemen, Jordan, and Sudan--were severely strained during and immediately after the war. For example, several hundred thousand Yemenis were expelled from Saudi Arabia after the Government of Yemen announced its position, thus exacerbating an existing border dispute. Saudi Arabia's relations with the Yemeni Government have improved, but the current instability in Yemen remains a significant concern to the Saudi Government. The Palestine Liberation Organization's support for Iraq cost it financial aid as well as good relations with Saudi Arabia and other Gulf states. Saudi Arabia's relations with Jordan and the Palestinian Authority later improved, with the Saudi Government providing assistance for the Palestinian Authority.

For additional analytical, business and investment opportunities information, please contact Global Investment & Business Center, USA at (202) 546-2103. Fax: (202) 546-3275. E-mail: ibpusa3@gmail.com Global Business and Legal Information Databank: www.ibpus.com

During and after the Gulf War, the Government of Saudi Arabia provided water, food, shelter, and fuel for coalition forces in the region, and also made monetary payments to some coalition partners. Saudi Arabia's combined costs in payments, foregone revenues, and donated supplies were $55 billion. More than $15 billion went toward reimbursing the United States alone.

Since ascending to the throne, King Abdallah has followed a more activist foreign policy, offering Saudi assistance and support in efforts to resolve regional crises in Lebanon, Sudan, and Somalia; fostering Israeli-Palestinian peace efforts; and increasing Saudi diplomatic engagement around the world. In particular, he has pursued an Interfaith Dialogue Initiative to encourage religious tolerance on a global level, which was endorsed in a session of the UN General Assembly in November 2008.

U.S.-SAUDI ARABIAN RELATIONS

Saudi Arabia's unique role in the Arab and Islamic worlds, its possession of the world's largest reserves of oil, and its strategic location make its friendship important to the United States. Diplomatic relations were established in 1933; the U.S. embassy opened in Jeddah in 1944 and moved to Riyadh in 1984. The Jeddah embassy became a U.S. consulate general. The U.S. consulate general in Dhahran opened in 1944 in response to the growing oil-related U.S. presence in eastern Saudi Arabia.

The United States and Saudi Arabia share common concerns about regional security, oil exports and imports, and sustainable development. Close consultations between the U.S. and Saudi Arabia have developed on international, economic, and development issues such as the Middle East peace process and shared interests in the Gulf. The continued availability of reliable sources of oil, particularly from Saudi Arabia, remains important to the prosperity of the United States as well as to Europe and Japan. Saudi Arabia is one of the leading sources of imported oil for the United States, providing more than one million barrels/day of oil to the U.S. market. The U.S. is Saudi Arabia's largest trading partner, and Saudi Arabia is the largest U.S. export market in the Middle East.

In addition to economic ties, a longstanding security relationship continues to be important in U.S.-Saudi relations. The U.S. Army Corps of Engineers has a role in military and civilian construction activities in the kingdom reaching back to the 1950s. A U.S. military training mission established at Dhahran in 1953 provides training and support in the use of weapons and other security-related services to the Saudi armed forces. In 1973, another security assistance organization (SAO) was established to assist in the modernization of the Saudi Arabian National Guard. More recently a SAO was authorized to train and equip a Facility Security Force, part of the Ministry of Interior. All three of these SAOs are funded through the U.S. Foreign Military Sales (FMS) program. The United States has sold Saudi Arabia military aircraft (F-15s, AWACS, and UH-60 Blackhawks), air defense weaponry (Patriot and Hawk missiles), armored vehicles (M1A2 Abrams tanks and M-2 Bradley infantry fighting vehicles), and other equipment. In September 2010 the U.S. announced a major new FMS program to sell fighter aircraft and helicopters to the Saudi military services in support of defense modernization plans.

Although Saudi Arabia's relations with the United States were strained after September 11, 2001, Saudi Arabia is now one of the United States' strongest partners against terrorism. Fifteen of the suicide bombers in the attacks of September 11 were Saudi citizens. In May 2003, a terrorist organization directly affiliated with al-Qaeda launched a violent campaign of terror in Saudi Arabia. On May 12, suicide bombers killed 35 people, including nine Americans, in attacks at three housing compounds for Westerners in Riyadh. On November 8, 2003, terrorists attacked another compound housing foreign workers from mainly Arab countries. At least 18 people, including five children, died in this attack, and more than 100 were injured. On May 1, 2004,

For additional analytical, business and investment opportunities information, please contact Global Investment & Business Center, USA at (202) 546-2103. Fax: (202) 546-3275. E-mail: ibpusa3@gmail.com Global Business and Legal Information Databank: www.ibpus.com

terrorists killed two Americans in the Yanbu oil facility in the western part of the country. On May 29, 2004, terrorists killed one American and wounded several others in attacks on an official building and housing compound in al-Khobar in the Eastern Province. On June 6, terrorists shot and killed a BBC journalist. On June 9 and June 12, 2004, terrorists killed Americans Robert Jacobs and Kenneth Scroggs. On June 18, 2004, terrorists kidnapped and beheaded American Paul Johnson. On December 6, 2004, terrorists attacked the U.S. Consulate in Jeddah, killing five consulate employees. Terrorists also targeted and killed other foreign nationalities during this time. As a result, in 2005, the Saudi Arabian Government enacted new laws to increase punishment for terrorist-related crimes.

Saudi security services have waged an active counterterrorism campaign that has largely neutralized this terrorist organization, though sporadic instances of terrorism still occur. In May 2006, terrorists attempted to attack the major ARAMCO oil-processing facility at Abqaiq. In February 2007, four French nationals were killed in western Saudi Arabia in a suspected terrorist attack. In August 2009, an al-Qaeda in the Arabian Peninsula (AQAP) suicide bomber attempted to assassinate a Saudi royal and senior Ministry of Interior official.

Saudi Arabia is a strong partner in the campaign against terrorism, providing military, diplomatic, and financial cooperation. Counterterrorism cooperation between Saudi Arabia and the United States increased significantly after the May 12, 2003, bombings in Riyadh and continues today. In February 2005, the Saudi Government sponsored the first-ever Counterterrorism International Conference in Riyadh. The Saudis were instrumental in thwarting the planned October 2010 "printer bomb" attack against the United States. They also provided crucial information on the planned May 2010 Times Square terrorist attack. In addition, they work closely with U.S. law enforcement to ensure the security of both countries' national security interests.

Human Rights
Despite generally good relations, the United States remains concerned about human rights conditions in Saudi Arabia. Principal human rights issues include abuse of prisoners and incommunicado detention; prohibitions or severe restrictions on freedom of speech, press, peaceful assembly and association, and religion; denial of the right of citizens to change their government; systematic discrimination against women and ethnic and religious minorities; and suppression of workers' rights.

Principal U.S. Officials
Ambassador-- Joseph W. Westphal

Joseph W. Westphal was sworn in as the U.S. Ambassador to the Kingdom of Saudi Arabia on March 26, 2014.

Deputy Chief of Mission--Susan L. Ziadeh
Counselor for Consular Affairs--Glen Keiser
Counselor for Economic Affairs--Angus Simmons
Counselor for Management Affairs--Alison Barkley
Counselor for Political Affairs--Lisa Carle
Counselor for Political-Military Affairs--Scott McGehee
Counselor for Public Affairs--Bonnie Gutman
Consul General, Dhahran--Timothy Pounds
Consul General, Jeddah--Tom Duffy

The **U.S. Embassy** in Saudi Arabia is located in the Diplomatic Quarter of Riyadh (tel. 966-1-488-3800). The Consulate General in Jeddah is located on Palestine Road, Ruwais, Jeddah (tel. 966-2-667-0080); and the Consulate General in Dhahran is located between ARAMCO Headquarters and the King Abdul Aziz Airbase (tel. 966-3-330-3200). The embassy and consulates are open for business Saturday through Wednesday, in accordance with the official workweek of Saudi Arabia.

TRAVEL AND BUSINESS INFORMATION

Travel Alerts, Travel Warnings, Trip Registration
The U.S. Department of State's Consular Information Program advises Americans traveling and residing abroad through Country Specific Information, Travel Alerts, and Travel Warnings. **Country Specific Information** exists for all countries and includes information on entry and exit requirements, currency regulations, health conditions, safety and security, crime, political disturbances, and the addresses of the U.S. embassies and consulates abroad. **Travel Alerts** are issued to disseminate information quickly about terrorist threats and other relatively short-term conditions overseas that pose significant risks to the security of American travelers. **Travel Warnings** are issued when the State Department recommends that Americans avoid travel to a certain country because the situation is dangerous or unstable.

For the latest security information, Americans living and traveling abroad should regularly monitor the Department's Bureau of Consular Affairs Internet web site at http://travel.state.gov, where current Worldwide Caution, Travel Alerts, and Travel Warnings can be found. The travel.state.gov website also includes information about passports, tips for planning a safe trip abroad and more. More travel-related information also is available at http://www.usa.gov/Citizen/Topics/Travel/International.shtml.

The Department's Smart Traveler app for U.S. travelers going abroad provides easy access to the frequently updated official country information, travel alerts, travel warnings, maps, U.S. embassy locations, and more that appear on the travel.state.gov site. Travelers can also set up e-tineraries to keep track of arrival and departure dates and make notes about upcoming trips. The app is compatible with iPhone, iPod touch, and iPad (requires iOS 4.0 or later).

The Department of State encourages all U.S. citizens traveling or residing abroad to register via the State Department's travel registration website or at the nearest U.S. embassy or consulate abroad (a link to the registration page is also available through the Smart Traveler app). Registration will make your presence and whereabouts known in case it is necessary to contact you in an emergency and will enable you to receive up-to-date information on security conditions.

Emergency information concerning Americans traveling abroad may be obtained by calling 1-888-407-4747 toll free in the U.S. and Canada or the regular toll line 1-202-501-4444 for callers outside the U.S. and Canada.

Passports
The National Passport Information Center (NPIC) is the U.S. Department of State's single, centralized public contact center for U.S. passport information. Telephone: 1-877-4-USA-PPT (1-877-487-2778); TDD/TTY: 1-888-874-7793. Passport information is available 24 hours, 7 days a week. You may speak with a representative Monday-Friday, 8 a.m. to 10 p.m., Eastern Time, excluding federal holidays.

RELIGIOUS FREEDOM AND GOVERNMENT POLICY IN THE COUNTRY[1]

The laws and policies restrict religious freedom, and in practice, the government generally enforced these restrictions. Freedom of religion is neither recognized nor protected under the law and is severely restricted in practice. The country is an Islamic state governed by a monarchy; the king is head of both state and government. According to the basic law, Sunni Islam is the official religion and the country's constitution is the Qur'an and the Sunna (traditions and sayings of the Prophet Muhammad). The legal system is based on the government's application of the Hanbali School of Sunni Islamic jurisprudence. The public practice of any religion other than Islam is prohibited, and there is no separation between state and religion.

The government did not respect religious freedom in law, but generally permitted Shia religious gatherings and non-Muslim private religious practices. Some Muslims who did not adhere to the government's interpretation of Islam faced significant political, economic, legal, social, and religious discrimination, including limited employment and educational opportunities, underrepresentation in official institutions, restrictions on religious practice, and restrictions on places of worship and community centers.

There was no change in the status of respect for religious freedom by the government during the reporting period. The Commission for the Promotion of Virtue and Prevention of Vice (CPVPV) and security forces of the Ministry of Interior (MOI) conducted some raids on private non-Muslim religious gatherings, and sometimes confiscated the personal religious materials of non-Muslims. However, there were fewer reported charges of harassment and abuse at the hands of the CPVPV compared with the previous reporting period. Although many intolerant statements had been removed, some school textbooks continued to contain overtly intolerant statements against Jews and Christians and intolerant references by allusion against Shia and Sufi Muslims and other religious groups. For example they stated that apostates from Islam should be killed if they do not repent within three days of being warned and that treachery is a permanent characteristic of non-Muslims, especially Jews.

There were reports of societal abuses and discrimination based on religious affiliation, belief, or practice. Conservative vigilantes sometimes harassed and assaulted citizens and foreigners.

Senior U.S. officials discussed a number of key policies concerning religious practice and tolerance with the government, as well as specific cases involving

infringement on the right to religious freedom. On January 16, 2009, the Secretary of State redesignated the country as a Country of Particular Concern (CPC). In connection with this redesignation, the Secretary issued a waiver of sanctions on the same date "to further the purposes of the act."

RELIGIOUS DEMOGRAPHY

The country has an area of 830,000 square miles and a population of 27.1 million persons, of whom approximately 18.6 million are citizens, according to the government. There is no accurate figure for the number of foreign residents. The government estimated there were 8.5 million foreign workers in the country in 2010. Figures from foreign embassies indicated the foreign population in the country, including many undocumented migrants, may be even higher,

---

[1] US State Departmetn Materials

For additional analytical, business and investment opportunities information, please contact Global Investment & Business Center, USA at (202) 546-2103. Fax: (202) 546-3275. E-mail: ibpusa3@gmail.com Global Business and Legal Information Databank: www.ibpus.com

exceeding 12 million. Estimates provided by foreign embassies include two million Indians, two million Bangladeshis, 1.5 million Filipinos, 1.5 million Pakistanis, 1.5 million Indonesians, one million Egyptians, one million Yemenis, 400,000 Syrians, 500,000 Sri Lankans, 350,000 Nepalese, 250,000 Palestinians, 150,000 Lebanese, and 100,000 Eritreans.

Approximately 85 to 90 percent of citizens are Sunni Muslims, who predominantly adhere to the Hanbali School of Islamic jurisprudence. A number of Sunni citizens also adhere to the other Sunni schools of jurisprudence (the Hanafi, Maliki, and Shafi schools).

Shiites constitute 10 to 15 percent of the population. Approximately 80 percent of Shia are "Twelvers" (followers of Muhammad ibn Hasan al-Mahdi, whom they recognize as the Twelfth Imam) and are primarily located in the Eastern Province. Twelver Shia adhere to the Jafari school of jurisprudence. Most of the remaining Shiite population are Sulaimaniya Isma'ilis, also known as "Seveners" (those who branched off from the Twelvers to follow Isma'il ibn Jafar as the Seventh Imam).Seveners reside primarily in Najran Province, around the residence of their sect's spiritual leader in Al Mansourah. In the western Hejaz region, there are approximately 100,000 Ashraf (descendants of the Prophet Muhammad) and 150,000 Nakhawala, or "Medina Shia." Additionally, statistics put the number of Zaydis (followers of Zayd ibn Ali , whom they recognize as the fifth Imam) at approximately 500,000. The Zaydis reside primarily in the cities of Jizan and Najran along the border with Yemen.

Comprehensive statistics for the religious denominations of foreigners are not available, but they include Muslims from the various branches and schools of

Islam, Christians (including Eastern Orthodox, Protestants, and more than one million Roman Catholics), Jews, over 250,000 Hindus, over 70,000 Buddhists, approximately 45,000 Sikhs, and others. In addition to European and North American Christians, there are Christians from East African, Lebanon, Syria, Egypt, the Palestinian territories, India, Pakistan, and other South Asian countries. The Filipino community is 90 percent Christian.

In 2010 the country hosted approximately three million Muslim pilgrims during the annual three-day Hajj pilgrimage and four million Umra pilgrims throughout the year from throughout the world.

LEGAL/POLICY FRAMEWORK

Current laws and policies restrict freedom of religion. According to the basic law, Islam is the official religion, and the country's constitution is the Qur'an and the Sunna. There is no legal recognition or protection of religious freedom, and the government allowed only private practice of non-Muslim religions.

The basic law establishes the country as a sovereign Arab Islamic state and establishes the Qur'an and the Sunna as the constitution. Neither the government nor society in general accepts the concept of separation of state and religion.

The government considers its legitimacy to rest in part on its custodianship of the two Holy Mosques in Mecca and Medina and its promotion of Islam. The official interpretation of Islam is derived from the writings and teachings of 18th-century Sunni religious scholar Muhammad ibn 'Abd Al-Wahhab, who advocated a return to what he considered the practices of the first three generations of the Muslim era and urged Muslims to be stricter in their obedience to Islam. The country's religious teaching opposes attempts by the Muslim reform movements of the 19th, 20th, and 21st centuries to reinterpret aspects of Islamic law in light of economic and social developments, particularly in areas such as gender relations, personal autonomy, family law, and participatory democracy. Outside the country this branch of Islam is often referred to as " Wahhabi ," a term the Saudis do not use.

The Islamic judicial system is based on laws derived from the Qur'an and the Sunna and on legal opinions and fatwas (rulings) of the Council of Senior [Religious] Scholars. Established in 1971, the council is an advisory body of 20 persons that reports to the king. The council, supported by the Board of Research and Religious Rulings, is recognized as the supreme authority on religious rulings by the basic law. It is headed by the grand mufti and is composed of Sunni religious scholars and jurists, as well as the minister of justice. Government universities provide training on all the Sunni schools of jurisprudence but focus on the Hanbali school; consequently, most Sharia judges follow its system of interpretation. Three members of the council belong to non-Hanbali schools, representing the Maliki, Hanafi, and Shaf'i schools; however, there are no Shiite members. Scholars are chosen at the king's discretion and serve renewable four-year terms, with most members serving for life. Sharia is not based on precedent and rulings can diverge widely. In theory rulings can be appealed to the appellate and supreme courts, but these higher courts must agree to hear the case. In 2009 for the first time ever, a member of the council was dismissed after he criticized the king's establishment of a mixed-gender university.

The government permits Shiite judges presiding over courts in the Eastern Province to use the Jafari school of Islamic jurisprudence to adjudicate cases in family law, inheritance, and endowment management. There were six Shiite judges, all located in the Eastern Province cities of Qatif and al-Ahsa, where the majority of Shia lived. Shia living in other parts of the Eastern Province, Najran Province, and the western Hejaz region had no access to local, regional, or national Shiite courts.

The Majlis al-Shoura (the Consultative Council) is responsible for drafting resolutions for approval by the Council of Ministers and the king. The king appoints the Consultative Council's 150 full-time male members and 13 part-time, female, non-voting advisors. Advisors can attend sessions and may offer their opinion, but have no voting power. There are five Shiite members. According to the council charter, the members should be "scholars and men of learning." There are no term limits for the Consultative Council's members; however, every four years the king must replace 50 percent of the council.

The two mosques in Mecca and Medina do not come under Ministry of Islamic Affairs, Endowment, Call, and Guidance (MOIA) jurisdiction. They are the responsibility of the General Presidency for the Affairs of the Two Holy Shrines, which reports directly to the king; its head holds a rank equivalent to a government minister. Thousands of other mosques existed in private homes, at rest stops along

highways, and elsewhere throughout the country. There were no public non-Muslim houses of worship, but private Christian religious gatherings took place throughout the country.

The CPVPV is a semiautonomous agency authorized to monitor social behavior and enforce morality consistent with the government's interpretation of Islam. The law defines the CPVPV's mission as "guiding and advising people to observe the religious duties prescribed by Islamic Sharia, and to prevent committing [acts] proscribed and prohibited [by Sharia], or adopting bad habits and traditions or taboo [sic] heresies." The purview of the CPVPV includes public gender mixing and illegal private contact between men and women; practicing or displaying non-Muslim faiths or disrespecting Islam; displaying or selling media contrary to Islam, including pornography; producing, distributing, or consuming alcohol; venerating places or celebrating events inconsistent with approved Islamic practices; practicing sorcery or magic for profit; and

For additional analytical, business and investment opportunities information, please contact Global Investment & Business Center, USA at (202) 546-2103. Fax: (202) 546-3275. E-mail: ibpusa3@gmail.com Global Business and Legal Information Databank: www.ibpus.com

committing or facilitating lewdness, including adultery, homosexuality, and gambling. Full-time CPVPV field officers are known as mutawwa'een; they do not wear uniforms, but are required to wear identification badges and can only legally act in their official capacity when accompanied by a regular policeman. In practice CPVPV officers often act as public morality enforcers. According to the latest public statistics, the CPVPV has more than 5,000 staff members, including 3,583 CPVPV field offices throughout all 13 provinces. Additionally there are over 1,600 administrative support personnel. The CPVPV reports to the king through the Council of Ministers, and the minister of interior oversees its operations on the king's behalf. Religious vigilantes and/or volunteers unaffiliated with the CPVPV also exist but often act alone, sometimes even harassing and assaulting citizens and foreigners.

The 24-member Human Rights Commission (HRC) was established in 2005 by the Council of Ministers to address human rights abuses and promote human rights within the country. The board does not include women, but each regional branch includes a women's branch operated and staffed by women. The board previously did not have Shia members, but now includes at least one. The HRC regularly follows up on citizen complaints, including complaints of favoritism or unfair court decisions, but has not specifically addressed issues of religious freedom and tolerance and does not issue a report on its actions.

No law specifically requires all citizens to be Muslims, but non-Muslim foreigners and many foreign and Saudi national Muslims whose beliefs are deemed not to conform with the government's interpretation of Islam must practice their religion in private and are vulnerable to discrimination, harassment, detention, and

deportation for noncitizens. Legally children born to Muslim fathers are deemed Muslim, and conversion from Islam to another religion is considered apostasy and punishable by death. Blasphemy against Sunni Islam is also punishable by death, but the more common penalty is a long prison sentence. There have been no confirmed reports of executions for either apostasy or blasphemy in recent years.

The law discriminates against adherents of religions deemed polytheistic and to a lesser extent against Christians and Jews, who are mentioned in the Qur'an as "People of the Book." The government officially does not permit non-Muslim clergy to enter the country to conduct religious services, although some do so under other auspices and are able to hold services. These entry restrictions make it difficult for non-Muslims to maintain regular contact with clergy. This is particularly problematic for Roman Catholics and Orthodox Christians, whose faiths require that they receive sacraments from a priest on a regular basis. However, many non-Muslims continue to gather for private worship, and the government generally allows the discreet performance of religious functions of all faiths.

Shia face systematic and pervasive official and legal discrimination, including in education, employment, the military, housing, political representation, the judiciary, religious practice, and media. Primary reasons include the widely-held view that Shia are polytheists and that they commit apostasy by practicing some of their worship activities, historical Sunni-Shia animosity, and suspicion of Iranian influence on their actions.

The MOIA determines the qualifications of Sunni clerics and is responsible for investigating complaints against them, particularly clerics who issue intolerant fatwas or promote intolerance, violence, or hatred. In 2003 the MOIA created a program to monitor all government-paid clerics. Provincial committees of senior religious scholars supervise full-time MOIA employees who monitor all mosques and clerics, through scheduled and unscheduled visits and receipt of public complaints. Based on their reports, the committees summon clerics accused of preaching extremist ideologies. If the provincial committees are not able to dissuade these clerics from their thinking, the clerics are referred to a central committee or dismissed. Under this program, the MOIA has removed 3,500 imams from duty since 2003, but none were removed during the reporting period. On August 12, in a move to curb extremist and absurd fatwas, King Abdullah bin Abdul Aziz decreed that only members of the Council of Senior [Religious] Scholars, and those whom the king permits, may issue public fatwas. The MOIA also monitors and posts counter-arguments on extremist online forums and Web sites.

The government requires noncitizen legal residents to carry an identity card containing a religious designation for "Muslim" or "non-Muslim." Older residency cards bear religious denominations such as "Christian."

The Naturalization Law requires that applicants attest to their religious affiliation and requires applicants to get a certificate endorsed by their local cleric.

Freedom of religious assembly is severely limited, because the government does not allow individuals to publicly assemble based on religious affiliation. This freedom is also limited in other ways, including the government's hindering of the establishment and maintenance of non-Sunni places of worship. All new mosques require the permission of the MOIA, the local municipality, and the provincial government, which is functionally part of the MOI. The MOIA supervises and finances the construction and maintenance of most Sunni mosques, including the hiring of clerical workers, while the other approximately 30 percent of Sunni mosques are at private residences or were built and endowed by private persons. Individuals responsible for the supervision of a mosque are selected from the local community. The imams received monthly MOIA salaries ranging from 2,500 to 5,000 riyals ($667 to $1,333), depending on the seniority and educational level of the individual. The MOIA estimated that in 2010 it was financially and administratively responsible for 75,000 Sunni mosques, 15,000 of which are Friday mosques (larger mosques that host Friday prayers and include a sermon). According to data provided by the MOIA in October, it employs approximately 75,000 Sunni imams and 15,000 Sunni Friday khateebs (sermon leaders) to staff these mosques.

Unlike for Sunni mosques, the government does not finance construction or maintenance of Shiite mosques, and the process for obtaining a government-required license for a Shiite mosque is reportedly unclear and arbitrary. However, Shia have the right to manage their own mosques and to be supervised by Shiite scholars.

Discussion of sensitive religious issues such as sectarian differences was rare, and criticism of Islam is forbidden. Officially the government allows religious materials for personal use in the country; customs officials and the CPVPV do not have the authority to confiscate personal religious materials. Furthermore, the government's stated policy for its diplomatic and consular missions abroad is to

inform foreign workers applying for visas that they have the right to worship privately and possess personal religious materials and to provide the name of the appropriate offices where grievances can be filed.

The government prohibits the public propagation of Islamic teachings that differ from the official interpretation of Islam and restricts the public religious training of non-Sunni groups and clergy.

Regardless of a student's personal religious traditions, public school students at all levels receive mandatory religious instruction based on the government's interpretation of Islam. Students in private international schools are not required to study Islam. Muslim students of other nationalities must obtain a waiver from the Ministry of Education (MOE) to attend private international schools, but obtaining the waiver was rarely a problem. Private religious schools not based on the official interpretation of Islam are not permitted.

The government observes the following religious holidays as national holidays: Eid al-Fitr and Eid al-Adha.

Shiite courts' powers are limited by the fact that any litigant who disagrees with a ruling can seek a new decision from a Sunni court. Sunni court rulings can void Shiite court rulings, and government departments can choose not to implement judgments rendered by Shiite judges. Jurisdictionally these courts are only allowed to rule on cases in the Qatif and al-Ahsa areas; Shia from other regions cannot use such courts.

Discrimination is manifested in the calculation of accidental death or injury compensation. In the event a court renders a judgment in favor of a plaintiff who is a Jewish or Christian male, the plaintiff is only entitled to receive 50 percent of the compensation a Muslim male would receive; all other non-Muslims are only entitled to receive one-sixteenth of the amount a male Muslim would receive. Furthermore, judges may discount the testimony of non-practicing Muslims or individuals who do not adhere to the official interpretation of Islam and disregard the testimony of a non-Muslim in favor of the testimony of a Muslim. Moreover, courts adhere to the Qur'anic stipulation that in cases of capital punishment the value of a woman's testimony is only one-half that of a man's.

RESTRICTIONS ON RELIGIOUS FREEDOM

The government generally enforced legal and policy restrictions on religious freedom vigorously. There was no change in the status of respect for religious freedom by the government during the reporting period.

Sunni clerics, who received government stipends, occasionally used anti-Semitic, anti-Christian, and anti-Shiite language in their sermons. It was common for preachers in mosques, including the mosques of Mecca and Medina, to end Friday sermons with a prayer for the well-being of Muslims and for the humiliation of polytheism and polytheists.

Most Shia expressed general concerns about discrimination in religious practice, education, employment, political representation, the judiciary, and the media.

The government generally limited public religious practice to activities that conform to the official interpretation of Islam. Practices that diverged from the official interpretation, such as celebrating Maulid Al-Nabi (the birthday of the Prophet Muhammad) and visits to the tombs of renowned Muslims, were forbidden. Enforcement was more relaxed in some communities than in others. For example, authorities allowed Shia in the Eastern Province city of Qatif greater freedom in their religious practices, including the public commemoration of Ashura (the "day of grief"). This event was held with minimal government interference. In other areas with large Shiite populations, such as al-Ahsa and Dammam, authorities restricted Shiite religious activities, including public observances of Ashura, public marches, loudspeaker broadcasts of clerics' lectures from Shiite community centers, and, in some instances, gatherings within those centers.

Shia described restrictions on their visits to Mecca and Medina as interference by Riyadh-based authorities in private Muslim worship. In addition government religious authorities continued the practice of destroying ancient Islamic historical sites.

Shiite mosques in mixed religious neighborhoods reportedly were required to recite the Sunni call to prayer, which is distinct from the Shiite call, at prayer times. Moreover, although Shia combine two of the five daily Sunni prayers, Shiite businessmen were often forced to close their shops during all five prayer times, in accordance with the country's official Sunni practices.

The government's stated policy is to permit private worship for all, including non-Muslims, and address violations of this policy by government officials; however,

the CPVPV sometimes did not respect this policy. Individuals whose ability to worship privately had been infringed could address their grievances through the MOI, the government's official Human Rights Commission (HRC), the National Society for Human Rights (NSHR, a quasi-autonomous NGO), and when appropriate, the Ministry of Foreign Affairs. The HRC and the NSHR reported that they did not receive any complaints against the CPVPV in the past year and that they have never received complaints regarding violations of religious freedom.

The government restricted the ability of religious leaders and activists to express views critical of the religious establishment. Consequently some Shia faced obstacles in constructing their mosques. For example, provincial officials in Al-Ahsa have blocked construction of some new Shiite mosques and community lecture halls, as well as withdrawn some permits for existing mosques and lecture halls. Shia in other parts of Saudi Arabia were not allowed to build Shia-specific mosques. However, the government did approve construction of some new Shiite mosques in Qatif and Al-Ahsa -- sometimes after lengthy delays due to the numerous approvals required -- but did not approve construction of Shiite mosques in Dammam, home to many Shia.

The government did not officially recognize several centers of Shiite religious instruction located in the Eastern Province, provide financial support for them, recognize certificates of educational attainment for their graduates, or provide employment for their graduates, all of which it does for Sunni religious training institutions. In contrast to previous reporting periods, none of these centers were subject to forced closures.

The government refused to approve construction or registration of Shiite community centers, so Shia were forced to build such facilities in private homes. These community centers sometimes did not meet safety codes, and the lack of legal recognition made their long-term financing and continuity considerably more difficult.

During the reporting period, there was significant public discussion, including in the media, questioning the official version of religious traditions and criticizing their enforcement. However, discussion of sensitive religious issues such as sectarian differences remained limited, and criticism of Islam was forbidden. Individuals who publicly criticized the official interpretation of Islam risked harassment, intimidation, and detention, and foreigners who did so risked deportation. Journalists and activists who wrote critically about the religious

leadership or who questioned theological dogma risked detention, travel bans, and government shutdowns of their publications.

Moreover, the government continued to exclude Shiite perspectives from the state's extensive religious media and broadcast programming. The government sporadically imposed bans on the importation and sale of Shiite books and audiovisual products. The government also blocked access to some Web sites with religious content it considered offensive or sensitive, including the Al-Rasid Web site, in line with a broader official policy of censoring objectionable content, including political discourse and illicit materials. In addition, terms like "rejectionists," which are insulting to Shia, were commonly found in public discourse and could be found on the MOIA official Web site.

In higher education the government discriminated against Shia in the selection process for students, professors, and administrators at public universities. For example, Shia constituted an estimated 2 percent of professors at a leading university in al-Ahsa, an area with a population that is at least 50 percent Shiite.

At the primary and secondary levels of education in al-Ahsa, there continued to be severe underrepresentation of Shia among school principals, with approximately 1 percent of area principals Shiite, and none in al-Ahsa schools for females.

In Qatif, where Shia constitute approximately 90 percent of the population, many male principals and even some male religious teachers in primary schools were Shiite; however, there were no Shiite principals or religious teachers in Qatif's public female primary schools. There are a small number of private schools for girls in Qatif.

A new curriculum was implemented throughout the country in 2010 for first, fourth, and seventh grades. Math, science, and English textbooks for these grades were improved by the removal of all religious references. The new religious sciences and Arabic textbooks for those grades, however, continue to contain intolerant language. Approximately 100 schools piloted a new curriculum for second, fifth, and eighth grades in 2010 that reportedly contains a reduction in intolerant language, which is scheduled to be implemented in all schools next year. Reform programs for the other grades are being developed, but most schoolchildren used textbooks that retained language intolerant of other religious traditions, especially Jewish, Christian, and Shiite beliefs, and included commands to hate infidels for their kufr (unbelief) and kill apostates. Unrevised school textbooks continued to contain intolerant statements alluding to Shia and Sufi

Muslims, and other religious groups, some inciting to violence. For example, the monotheism textbook for twelfth grade boys states that those who worship tombs -- a likely allusion to include Shia and Sufi Muslims' practice of visiting tombs of venerated Imams -- thereby commit apostasy by action. The text goes on to state that once a finding of apostasy has been confirmed, legal consequences apply, including that if the apostate refuses to repent, he must be killed.

Shia faced significant employment discrimination in the public and private sectors. A very small number of Shia occupied high-level positions in government-owned companies and government agencies. Many Shia believed that openly identifying themselves as Shia would negatively affect career advancement. Shia were significantly underrepresented in national security-related positions, including the Ministry of Defense and Aviation, the National Guard, and the MOI. Shia were better represented in the ranks of traffic police, municipalities, and public schools in predominantly Shiite areas. There was no formal policy concerning the hiring and promotion of Shia in the private sector, but anecdotal evidence suggested that in some companies, including the oil and petrochemical industries, a "glass ceiling" existed and well-qualified Shia were passed over for less qualified Sunni colleagues.

Qatif community leaders described allegedly prejudicial zoning laws that prevent construction of buildings over a certain height in various Shiite neighborhoods. The leaders claimed the laws prevented investment and development in these areas and aimed to limit the density of the Shiite population in any given area.

In contrast to previous reporting periods, there were no reports that MOI officials and/or CPVPV members pressured sponsors and employers not to renew the residency cards of non-Muslims they had sponsored for employment if it was discovered or suspected that those individuals had led, sponsored, or participated in private non-Muslim worship services. Similarly there were no reports that CPVPV members pressured employers and sponsors to reach verbal agreements with non-Muslim employees that they would not participate in private non-Muslim worship services.

Members of the Shiite minority were also subjected to political discrimination. For example, although Shia constitute approximately 10 to 15 percent of the citizen population and approximately one-third to one-half of the Eastern Province population, they were underrepresented in senior government positions. There were no Shiite ministers, deputy ministers, governors, deputy governors, or ministry branch directors in the Eastern Province, and only three of the 59

government-appointed municipal council members were Shiite. However, the Shia were proportionally represented among the elected members of the municipal councils, as they held 10 of 11 seats on the Qatif and al-Ahsa councils. An elected Shia headed the Qatif municipal council. However, the Majlis al-Shura (Consultative Council) -- the 150 strong, all-male, all-appointed body that advises the king and in some cases can initiate legislation -- only has five Shiite members.

Judicial discrimination against Shia was evident during the reporting period. Shiite leaders argue that the one court of appeals on which Shiite judges sit has no real authority and only verifies documents.

In addition to these discriminatory practices, Nakhawala leaders claimed the Shia in their community faced even more problems, particularly in comparison to the Twelvers in the Eastern Province. They claimed to hear anti-Shiite sermons and statements regularly in their neighborhoods. Unlike the case with Shia from the Eastern Province, there were no prominent Nakhawala Shia in government bodies such as the Consultative Council or the HRC. The Nakhawala also averred that their surname ("al-Nakhly," which roughly translates as "farmers" and identifies their minority status and sect) facilitated systematic discrimination against them in employment and education.

The Sulaimaniya Isma'ili community also continued to face additional obstacles in Najran Province. Community leaders asserted that the government discriminated against them by prohibiting their religious books; allowing Sunni religious leaders to declare them unbelievers; denying them government employment; and relocating them from the southwest to other parts of the country, or encouraging them to emigrate.

IMPROVEMENTS AND POSITIVE DEVELOPMENTS IN RESPECT FOR RELIGIOUS FREEDOM

During the reporting period, the government implemented policies that sought to address issues of religious freedom in the country. Moreover, the king and other government and religious leaders showed efforts that aimed to expand interfaith and national dialogues to promote tolerance and moderation through broadly targeted seminars and media campaigns.

For additional analytical, business and investment opportunities information,
please contact Global Investment & Business Center, USA
at (202) 546-2103. Fax: (202) 546-3275. E-mail: ibpusa3@gmail.com
Global Business and Legal Information Databank: www.ibpus.com

- 53 -

Improvements included the implementation of a completely new curriculum in three grades and continued teacher training, better protection of the right to possess and use personal religious materials, augmented efforts to curb and investigate harassment by the CPVPV (particularly through specialized training to improve the performance of the CPVPV), increased media coverage and criticism of the CPVPV, greater authority and capacity for official human rights entities to operate, and measures to combat extremist ideology.

The king continued a national dialogue campaign to increase tolerance and encourage moderation and understanding. During the reporting period, the King Abdulaziz Center for National Dialogue (KACND) had 2,000 certified trainers. Over the past five years, the KACND has trained over 500,000 men and women in over 17,000 training programs in 42 cities on "the culture and importance of open dialogue and communication skills." Beginning in June 2010, the KACND launched an eight-month awareness campaign using television advertisements and print media. The government-owned Saudi Channel One donated free airtime to the KACND for this campaign. All of the advertisements focused on spreading tolerance and dialogue, with some specifically focused on interaction with different cultures. During the reporting period, a mix of high-level government and religious officials openly supported this campaign. They advocated against religious extremism and intolerant language, especially in mosques and schools. The center continued to conclude memoranda of understanding with government ministries and institutions, including the Ministry of Islamic Affairs, the CPVPV, universities, and charities. Training sessions with CPVPV members were ongoing. In October 2010 the KACND trained over 100 CPVPV members in communication skills to promote dialogue and help prevent conflicts.

The government continued to combat extremist ideology by scrutinizing religious clerics and teachers closely and dismissing those found to be promoting intolerant and extreme views. The MOIA supervised clerics through regular inspections, surprise inspections, receiving complaints from worshipers, and investigating accusations in the press. In July 2010 for example, 2,000 teachers reportedly were either fired or transferred to administrative positions due to fear that they were indoctrinating their young students with dangerous content. According to Mansour al-Turki, spokesman for the MOI, his ministry assesses teachers' beliefs and viewpoints prior to hiring them to identify extremist ideologies.

Additionally some leading government and religious officials, including the king and crown prince, made strong public statements against extremism and instead advocated tolerance and moderation. For example, on September 26, during the symposium on "The Saudi Moderate Approach," Minister of Interior Prince Nayef said, "Terrorism has harmed our country and because of it we lost many of our sons, we have approached it in a moderate way such as giving advice to those who have extremist thoughts to bring them back to their senses." Additionally according to press reports, on November 11, three days before the Hajj, the king called on citizens "to look at the common points of different religions, creeds, and cultures and to stress the shared principles in order that we sidestep our differences, narrow

the distance between us, and build a world dominated by peace and understanding, enjoying progress and prosperity."

On August 12 King Abdullah bin Abdul Aziz decreed that only members of the Council of Senior [Religious] Scholars, and those whom he permits, may issue public fatwas. The decree was in direct response to a spate of controversial and sometimes contradictory fatwas issued by scholars and imams outside the council. The decree exempted religious opinions given in private at the request of an individual. Individuals may continue to seek religious opinions on the day-to-day aspects of life or specific situations that may arise and are not otherwise addressed in the official public fatwas. Following the decree, the Saudi Communications and Information

Technology Center blocked three Web sites and the sites' text messaging services. Several similar sites voluntarily stopped issuing fatwas.

There were fewer reports that government officials confiscated religious materials, and no reports that customs officials confiscated religious materials from travelers, whether Muslims or non-Muslims. Individuals reportedly were able to bring personal Bibles, crosses, DVDs of sermons, and other religious materials into the country without difficulty.

The MOIA confirmed that it continues to monitor educational materials used at religious summer camps to prevent the teaching of extremist ideologies to children.

ENJOYMENT OF RELIGIOUS FREEDOM

There were reports of societal abuses and discrimination based on religious affiliation, belief, or practice. In addition to the religious basis on which the government claims its authority, and the significant role the country's religious leadership plays in the country, the culture also exerts intense pressure on the population to conform to socio-religious norms. As a result a majority of citizens supported a state based on Islamic law, although there were differing views as to how this should be realized in practice.

Discrimination based on religion was a factor in mistreatment of foreign workers by citizen employers and coworkers.

Religious vigilantes and/or volunteers, unaffiliated with the CPVPV and acting on their own, sometimes harassed and assaulted citizens and foreigners.

Media criticism of government educational materials continued during the reporting period.

Editorial cartoons occasionally exhibited anti-Semitism characterized by stereotypical images of Jews along with Jewish symbols and comparisons of Israeli government actions to those of Nazis, particularly at times of heightened political tensions with Israel. For example, on September 15 the daily newspaper *Al-Madina* showed a caricatured Jew whipping an Arab toward "concessions" in a new round of peace talks. Anti-Semitic editorial comments appeared in government and private print and electronic media in response to regional political events.

U.S. GOVERNMENT POLICY

U.S. policy is to press the government to respect religious freedom and honor its public commitment to permit private religious worship by non-Muslims, eliminate discrimination against minorities, promote respect for non-Muslim religious belief, and combat violent extremism. Senior U.S. government officials raised these issues at the highest levels within the MOIA, MOI, HRC, MOE, and Ministry of Culture and Information during the reporting period. U.S. government officials also continued to meet with minority religious groups to discuss religious freedom concerns, including Shia groups and non-Muslim expatriates.

Additionally, Saudi government officials regularly participate in U.S. government visitor programs to promote tolerance and interfaith dialogue. Previous participants in these programs continued to commend the openness and tolerance they witnessed on their trips to the United States in lectures and television and radio programs that reached a broad audience.

REGIONS OF THE KINGDOM

LARGEST CITIES OR TOWNS IN SAUDI ARABIA

Rank	Name	Regions	Pop.	Rank	Name	Regions	Pop.
1	Riyadh	Riyadh	5,328,228	11	Tabuk	Tabuk	569,797
2	Jeddah	Makkah	3,456,259	12	Ha'il	Ha'il	412,758
3	Mecca	Makkah	1,675,368	13	Hafar Al-Batin	Eastern	389,993
4	Medina	Al Madinah	1,180,770	14	Jubail	Eastern	378,949
5	Hofuf	Eastern	1,063,112	15	Al-Kharj	Riyadh	376,325
6	Ta'if	Makkah	987,914	16	Qatif	Eastern	371,182
7	Dammam	Eastern	903,597	17	Abha	'Asir	366,551
8	Khamis Mushait	'Asir	630,000	18	Najran	Najran	329,112
9	Buraidah	Al-Qassim	614,093	19	Yanbu	Al Madinah	298,675
10	Khobar	Eastern	578,500	20	Al Qunfudhah	Makkah	272,424

GEOGRAPHIC REGIONS OF THE KINGDOM

Geographically, Saudi Arabia is divided into four (and if the Rub al-Khali is included, five) major regions. The first is the Central Region, a high country in the heart of the Kingdom; secondly, there is the Western Region, which lies along the Red Sea coast. The Southern Region, in the southern Red Sea-Yemen border area, constitutes the third region. Fourthly, there is the Eastern Region, the sandy and stormy eastern part of Saudi Arabia, the richest of all the regions in petroleum. It is important to note that, for administrative purposes, the Kingdom is divided into fourteen Administrative Regions.

RUB AL-KHALI

In the south of the Kingdom is the famous Rub al-Khali (the Empty Quarter), a massive, trackless expanse of shifting sand dunes - one of the largest sand deserts in the world - which covers an area of more than 250,000 square miles (650,000 square kilometers) and extends to 1,200 by 500 kilometers. The Rub al-Khali is one of the driest places on earth, receiving almost no rain at all. Nevertheless, many parts of this dry desert support some hardy plants (in particular, the scarlet-fruited abal and the hadth saltbush).

CENTRAL REGION

The Central Region, considered the heartland of Saudi Arabia both physically and culturally, is a vast eroded plateau, consisting of areas of uplands, broad valleys and dry rivers. The area also contains a number of marshes. These are thought to be the remnants of inland seas which existed in ancient geological times. Most of the Central Region is arid, with some oases in the north around Qasim. At the center of the Central Region is the royal capital of Riyadh.

The area around Kharj which lies south of Riyadh has now become a major source of wheat, part of the Kingdom's burgeoning agricultural industry; while 300 miles to the north of Riyadh lies the Qasim region, an even larger farming area which has contributed on a massive scale to the Kingdom's self-sufficiency in wheat and poultry. The climate of the region is hot and dry in summer and cold in winter. Summer temperatures sometimes exceed 45 degrees centigrade, while in winter the temperature falls to 5 degrees centigrade or lower.

WESTERN REGION

The Western Region (the Hijaz) includes the west coast of the Kingdom, north of Asir. It contains a mountain chain (with peaks rising to 3,000 meters), running south to north, decreasing gradually in elevation as it moves northward, and the coastal plain bordering the Red Sea.

In this region is the busy seaport of Jeddah, known as the Islamic Port of Jeddah, a thriving commercial center. Of greatest note is that the Western Region contains the holiest cities of Islam - Makkah and Madinah - which are visited by some two million Muslims annually.

The coastal area of the Western Region is renowned for its humidity, with summer temperatures rising to above 40 degrees centigrade

SOUTHERN REGION

The Southern Region (Asir) is the relatively fertile area of coastal mountains in the extreme southwest (near Yemen). Mountain peaks rise to 3,000 meters and there is ample rainfall to support natural vegetation and cultivation.

Asir, with some juniper trees, wild olive trees and even some larger trees is the only part of the Kingdom of Saudi Arabia to support forest.

The Southern Region has always been relatively densely populated. With the implementation of government irrigation schemes, the agricultural potential of the region is being increasingly exploited.

EASTERN REGION

The Eastern Region contains the Kingdom's massive petroleum resources. The headquarters of Saudi oil industry is located in this region in Dhahran, a few miles from the administrative capital and port of Dammam. Ras Tanura, the world's largest petroleum port, is located to the north of Dhahran.

Up the coast is the site of the Kingdom's new industrial complex at Jubail. The fertile oasis-cities of Qatif and Hofuf are also located here.

A special weather phenomenon affecting chiefly the Eastern Region is the north-westerly winds called the Shamals. These are prevalent during late spring and early summer, reaching their greatest frequency in June.

DHAHRAN

Dhahran is located 6 miles (10 km) west of Khobar.

Dhahran, with Dammam and Al Khobar, forms the Dammam Area.

Dhahran was the site of the headquarters of what was Aramco (the Arabian American Oil Company). For obvious reasons, it is also the site of the King Fahd Petroleum and Minerals University.

Dhahran is served by one of the Kingdom's three international airports, a construction of outstanding architectural beauty which combines traditional Islamic design with the most modern building technology.

DAMMAM

In the early 1980s Dammam, the capital of the Eastern Region, was a separate city but so close to Al Khobar and Dhahran that the traveler could pass from one to the other in a few minutes. With the continuing expansion of all parts of the Kingdom, the three towns inevitably merged into one, creating a single municipality known as Dammam Area. Each of the three towns which compose the Dammam Area retain their own character and some local administrative functions but, in terms of its place in the Kingdom, the Dammam Area forms a single administrative entity.

AL KHOBAR

Al Khobar lies in the Dammam Area in the Eastern region of the Kingdom, close to Dammam and Dhahran. The municipality of Al Khobar was founded in 1942, prompted by the discovery of oil and the ensuing development of commercial activity.

RIYADH

Riyadh, which lies in the Central Region, is the capital city of the Kingdom of Saudi Arabia and now rivals any modern city in the world in the splendor of its architecture. Broad highways sweep through the city, passing over or under each other in an impressive and still growing road network. Trees now bedeck the broad streets and avenues, giving pleasure to passers-by and shade to those who linger beneath them. Today the city extends for some 600 square miles (1600 square kilometers) and has a population of more than 3 million. The name Riyadh is derived from the Arabic word meaning a place of gardens and trees ("rawdah"). With many wadis (a former water course, now dry) in the vicinity, Riyadh has been since antiquity a fertile area set in the heartland of the Arabian peninsula.

Of all the Kingdom's developmental achievements, Riyadh is perhaps the most obvious and accessible to the foreign visitor. From the moment he lands at the King Khalid International Airport, itself a marvel of design wedding the traditional Arab style with the best of modern architecture in a happy marriage of spacious practicality, the traveler is aware that he has reached a city that must be counted one of the wonders of modern times.

RIYADH: BACKGROUND

The history of Riyadh and its growth from a relatively small settlement into a great modern city is inextricably involved with the rise of the Saudi state. With Riyadh as the capital of the Saudi Arabian Kingdom which Abdul Aziz bin Abdul Rahman Al Saud (Ibn Saud) founded, it was inevitable that the city would grow. By 1955 (1375 AH), all ministries and government offices had been moved to or established in Riyadh. In the same year, a Royal Decree was issued raising the status of the municipality of Riyadh to that of mayoralty. Its scope of responsibility was greatly enlarged and its resources increased to enable it to cope with its growing size and population.

In the midst of the city's extraordinary growth, the history of the city has not been forgotten. Preservation orders now ensure the survival of the Musmak fort which Abdul Aziz (Ibn Saud) scaled in 1902 (1319/20 AH), a fitting reminder of a turning point in the history of the city and, indeed, the Arabian Peninsula.

For additional analytical, business and investment opportunities information, please contact Global Investment & Business Center, USA at (202) 546-2103. Fax: (202) 546-3275. E-mail: ibpusa3@gmail.com Global Business and Legal Information Databank: www.ibpus.com

DIPLOMATIC QUARTER

Apart from its importance as a seat of government and as a thriving commercial center, Riyadh is also a center of Arab diplomacy. Located five miles (8 km) from the center of the city of Riyadh, on high ground overlooking the Wadi Hanifa and the vast expanse of desert behind, lies the Diplomatic Quarter. This unique complex of diplomatic buildings and facilities, housing the embassies and consulates of many countries, occupies an area of 8.4 million square yards (7 million square meters) and is the venue for many international Arab meetings.

FOREIGN MINISTRY COMPLEX

The Foreign Ministry Complex in Riyadh is one of the most outstanding examples of modern architecture in the entire Kingdom of Saudi Arabia. Its combination of elements of traditional Arabic design with the most modern construction techniques furnishes a magnificent example of the harmony that can be achieved when tradition and modernity are blended together with care and sensitivity.

KING FAHD INTERNATIONAL STADIUM

The King Fahd International Stadium, which can accommodate 80,000 spectators, was established by the General Presidency of Youth Welfare in 1988. Its remarkable tent-like design, constructed from hard-wearing, fireproof material, is the venue for many major events in the Kingdom.

KING KHALID INTERNATIONAL AIRPORT

The King Khalid International Airport was opened in 1983 (1403/04 AH). Located 35 kilometers north of Riyadh, with a land area of 225 square kilometers, the King Khalid International Airport is a masterpiece of modern architecture, blending traditional Arab design with the requirements of efficiency, and incorporating into the whole the essential Islamic character of the Kingdom. It is decorated with the works of many Saudi artists. It has four terminals and, from its inauguration, had the capacity to handle 7.5 million passengers a year. By the year 2000 (1420/21 AH), its capacity will have been doubled.

QASR-AL-HUKM AREA DEVELOPMENT PROJECT

The Qasr-al-Hukm Area Development Project lies in the center of the city of Riyadh where the office of the Governor of the Riyadh region is located. The Project was designed to develop the area around the Governor's palace, while preserving the sites of historical interest which lie within the area - most notably, the Al-Masmak Palace from which Abdul Aziz (Ibn Saud) set out to unify the Kingdom early in the 20th century.

The site includes both cultural and commercial centers, together with all the other facilities of a modern city center.

In the heart of the development is Qasr-al-Hukm, the office of the Governor of Riyadh, containing the administrative offices of the Governorate and the Grand Reception Hall where, in the Kingdom's tradition of consultation, the Governor receives citizens, listens to their problems and ensures that he is kept fully informed of all aspects of the region's life.

SAUDI ARABIA LEGAL SYSTEM BASICS

SAUDI ARABIA LAWS AND PRACTICES UNDER SHARIA - MAJOR LEGAL AREAS

The **legal system of Saudi Arabia** is based on Sharia, Islamic law derived from the Qu'ran and the Sunnah (the traditions) of the Islamic prophet Muhammad. The sources of Sharia also include Islamic scholarly consensus developed after Muhammad's death. Its interpretation by judges in Saudi Arabia is influenced by the medieval texts of the literalist Hanbali school of Islamic jurisprudence. Uniquely in the Muslim world, Sharia has been adopted by Saudi Arabia in an uncodified form. This, and the lack of judicial precedent, has resulted in considerable uncertainty in the scope and content of the country's laws.

 The government therefore announced its intention to codify Sharia in 2010, but this is yet to be implemented. Sharia has also been supplemented by *regulations* issued by royal decree covering modern issues such as intellectual property and corporate law. Nevertheless, Sharia remains the primary source of law, especially in areas such as criminal, family, commercial and contract law, and the Qu'ran and the Sunnah are declared to be the country's constitution. In the areas of land and energy law the extensive proprietorial rights of the Saudi state (in effect, the Saudi royal family) constitute a significant feature.

The current Saudi court system was created by King Abdul Aziz, who founded the Kingdom of Saudi Arabia in 1932, and was introduced to the country in stages between 1927 and 1960. It comprises general and summary Sharia courts, with some administrative tribunals to deal with disputes on specific modern regulations. Trials in Saudi Arabia are bench trials. Courts in Saudi Arabia observe few formalities and the country's first criminal procedure code, issued in 2001, has been largely ignored. King Abdullah, in 2007, introduced a number of significant judicial reforms, although they are yet to be fully implemented.

Criminal law punishments in Saudi Arabia include public beheading, stoning, amputation and lashing. Serious criminal offences include not only internationally recognized crimes such as murder, rape, theft and robbery, but also apostasy, adultery, witchcraft and sorcery. In addition to the regular police force, Saudi Arabia has a secret police, the *Mabahith*, and "religious police", the *Mutawa*. The latter enforces Islamic social and moral norms. Western-based human rights organizations, such as Amnesty International and Human Rights Watch, have criticized the activities of both the Mabahith and the Mutawa, as well as a number of other aspects of human rights in Saudi Arabia. These include the number of executions, the range of offences which are subject to the death penalty, the lack of safeguards for the accused in the criminal justice system, the treatment of homosexuals, the use of torture, the lack of religious freedom, and the highly disadvantaged position of women. The Albert Shanker Institute and Freedom House have also reported that "Saudi Arabia's practices diverge from the concept of the rule of law

CONSTITUTIONAL LAW

Saudi Arabia is an absolute monarchy, and has no legally binding written constitution. However, in 1992, the Basic Law of Saudi Arabia was adopted by royal decree. The Basic Law outlines the responsibilities and processes of the governing institutions but is insufficiently specific to be considered a constitution. It declares that the king must comply with Sharia (that is, Islamic law) and that the Quran and the Sunna (the traditions of Muhammad) are the country's constitution.

Interpretation of the Quran and the Sunna remains necessary, and this is carried out by the ulema, the Saudi religious establishment.

The Basic Law further states:

> Monarchy is the system of rule in the Kingdom of Saudi Arabia. Rulers of the country shall be from amongst the sons of the founder King Abdulaziz bin Abdulrahman Al-Faisal Al-Saud, and their descendants. The most upright among them shall receive allegiance according to Almighty God's Book and His Messenger's Sunna (Traditions)...Government in the Kingdom of Saudi Arabia derives its authority from the Book of God and the Sunna of the Prophet (PBUH), which are the ultimate sources of reference for this Law and the other laws of the State...Governance in the Kingdom of Saudi Arabia is based on justice, shura (consultation) and equality according to Islamic Sharia.

CRIMINAL LAW

Saudi Arabia uses the bench trial system. Its courts observe few formalities. The country's first criminal procedure code was introduced in 2001 and contains provisions borrowed from Egyptian and French law. Human Rights Watch, in a 2008 report, noted that judges were either ignorant of the criminal procedure code or were aware of it but routinely ignored the code.

Criminal law is governed by Sharia and comprises three categories: hudud (fixed Quranic punishments for specific crimes), Qisas (*eye-for-an-eye* retaliatory punishments), and Tazir, a general category. Hudud crimes are the most serious and include theft, robbery, blasphemy, apostasy, adultery, sodomy and fornication. Qisas crimes include murder or any crime involving bodily harm. Tazir represents most cases, many of which are defined by national regulations such as bribery, trafficking, and drug abuse. The most common punishment for a Tazir offence is lashing.

A conviction requires proof in one of three ways. The first is an uncoerced confession. Alternatively, the testimony of two male witnesses can convict (four in the case of adultery), unless it is a hudud crime, in which case a confession is also required. Women's evidence normally carries half the weight of men in Sharia courts, however in criminal trials women's testimony is not allowed at all. Testimony from non-Muslims or Muslims whose doctrines are considered unacceptable (for example, Shia) may be discounted. Lastly, an affirmation or denial by oath can be required. Giving an oath is taken particularly seriously in a religious society such as Saudi Arabia's, and a refusal to take an oath will be taken as an admission of guilt resulting in conviction.

The Saudi courts impose a number of severe physical punishments. The death penalty can be imposed for a wide range of offences including murder, rape, armed robbery, repeated drug use, apostasy, adultery, witchcraft and sorcery and can be carried out by beheading with a sword, stoning or firing squad, followed by crucifixion. The 345 reported executions between 2007 and 2010 were all carried out by public beheading. Two executions for "witchcraft and sorcery" were carried out in 2011. There were no reports of stoning between 2007 and 2010. Stoning has, however, occurred relatively recently and, for example, between 1981 and 1992 there were four cases of execution by stoning reported. Of the 90, 51 of those executed were Saudi citizens. Pakistanis – 13 of whom were convicted on heroin smuggling charges – formed the largest group among the 39 foreigners executed.

Although repeated theft can be punishable by amputation of the right hand and aggravated theft by the cross-amputation of a hand and a foot, only one instance of judicial amputation was reported between 2007 and 2010. Homosexual acts are punishable by flogging, imprisonment or death. Lashings are a common form of punishment and are often imposed for offences against religion and public morality such as drinking alcohol and neglect of prayer and fasting obligations.

Retaliatory punishments, or Qisas, are practised: for instance, an eye can be surgically removed at the insistence of a victim who lost his own eye. This occurred in a case reported in 2000 Families of someone unlawfully killed can choose between demanding the death penalty or granting clemency in return for a payment of diyya, or blood money, by the perpetrator. There has been a growing trend of exorbitant blood-money demands, for example a sum of $11 million was reported as being recently demanded. Saudi officials and religious figures have criticized this trend and said that the practise of diyya has become corrupted.

FAMILY LAW

Laws relating to marriage, divorce, children and inheritance are not codified and fall within the general jurisdiction of the Sharia courts.

Polygamy is permitted for men but is limited to four wives at any one time. There is evidence that its practice has increased, particularly among the educated Hejazi elite, as a result of oil wealth. The government has promoted polygamy as part of a return to "Islamic values" program. In 2001, the Grand Mufti (the highest religious authority) issued a fatwa, or opinion, calling upon Saudi women to accept polygamy as part of the *Islamic package* and declaring that polygamy was necessary "to fight against...the growing epidemic of spinsterhood".There is no minimum age for marriage in Saudi Arabia and the Grand Mufti reportedly said in 2009 that girls of the age of 10 or 12 were marriageable.

Men have a unilateral right to divorce their wives (talaq) without needing any legal justification. The divorce is effective immediately. The husband's obligation is then to provide financial support for the divorced wife for a period of four months and ten days. A woman can only obtain a divorce with the consent of her husband or judicially if her husband has harmed her. In practice, it is very difficult for a Saudi woman to obtain a judicial divorce. The divorce rate is high, with 50% of marriages being dissolved.

In the event of divorce, fathers have automatic custody of sons from the age of 7 and daughters from the age of 9. The right for men to marry up to four wives, combined with their ability to divorce a wife at anytime without cause, can translate to unlimited polygamy. King Abdul Aziz, the founder of the country, reportedly admitted to marrying over two hundred women. However, his polygamy was considered extraordinary even by Saudi Arabian standards.

With regard to the law of inheritance, the Quran specifies that fixed portions of the deceased's estate must be left to the so-called *Quranic heirs*. Generally, female heirs receive half the portion of male heirs. A Sunni Muslim can bequeath a maximum of a third of his property to non-Quranic heirs. The residue is divided between agnatic heirs.

COMMERCIAL AND CONTRACT LAW

Business and commerce are governed by Sharia, commercial jurisdiction rests with the Board of Grievances composed of Sharia-trained judges, but "Special Tribunals" tasked with "finding ways to circumnavigate the more restrictive aspects of Shariah Law" have been established.

For foreign investors, uncertainties around the content of commercial law, because of the Sharia aspect, constitutes a disincentive to invest in Saudi Arabia. As it is governed by Sharia, contract law is not codified. Within the general limitations of Sharia, it allows considerable freedom for the parties to agree contract terms. However, contracts involving speculation or the payment of interest are prohibited and are not enforceable. If a contract is breached, Saudi courts will only award compensation for proven direct damage. Claims for loss of profit or opportunity will not be allowed as these would constitute speculation, which is not permitted under Sharia.

The non-sharia "Special Tribunals" or "Special Committees" hear "most commercial law cases" ranging from "breach of contract suits to trade mark infringement and labour disputes." The Tribunals enforce *nizam* (decrees) issued by the King. Specific modern aspects of commercial law, for example, commercial paper and securities, intellectual property, and corporate law are governed by modern regulations, and specialist government tribunals deal with related disputes. The government recently revised its intellectual property laws to meet World Trade Organization standards, as part of its admission to the WTO in 2004. Because of a lack of resources, when the new patent law went into effect in 2004, the Saudi Patent office had only registered 90 patents since 1989, with a back-log of 9,000 applications. It is believed the back-log has now been reduced.

The Saudi government is also putting greater resources into combating unauthorized distribution of software, printed material, recordings and videos. However, illegally copied material is still widely available. Enforcement efforts have been supported by a fatwa, or religious ruling, that copyright infringement of software is forbidden under Islam. Saudi Arabia had been on the Special 301 Watchlist, the U.S.'s running log of countries considered to inadequately regulate or enforce intellectual property rights, but was removed in 2010.

Saudi law recognizes only corporate or partnership entities established under Sharia or the Saudi Company Law of 1982. A contract with any other type of company will be void and the persons who made the contract in the company's name will be personally liable for it. Under Sharia, corporations can take a number of forms, but the most common in Saudi Arabia is *Sharikat Modarabah* where some partners contribute assets and others contribute expertise. In addition, the Company Law (which is based on Egyptian company law) identifies eight permissible forms of corporate entity including joint ventures, and limited liability partnerships.

LABOR LAW

Employers have a number of obligations, including at least 21 days paid holiday after a year's employment and will be 30 days after five years of continuous service. Terminated employees must receive an "end-of-service" payment of a half a months' salary for each year employed going up to one month if employed for more than 5 years.

LAND LAW

Most land in Saudi Arabia is owned by the government and only cultivated land and urban property are subject to individual ownership. All land titles must be registered, but there is no accurate information as to the extent of registration. Real estate could only be owned by Saudi citizens until 2000, when the property laws were amended to allow foreigners to own property in Saudi Arabia. Property investments by non-Saudis of more than 30 million Saudi riyals require approval of the Council of Ministers and foreigners remain prohibited from owning property in Medina and Mecca.

Saudi Arabia has three categories of land: developed land (*amir*), undeveloped land (*mawat*), and "protective zones" (*harim*). Developed land comprises the built environment of towns and villages and agriculturally developed land, and can be bought, sold and inherited by individuals. The undeveloped land comprises rough grazing, pasture and wilderness. Rough grazing and pasture is owned in common and everyone has equal rights to its use. The wilderness is owned by the state and may be open to everyone unless specific restrictions are imposed. *Harim* land is a protective buffer between the owned land and the undeveloped land, and is defined, in the case of a town, as the area that can be reached and returned from in a day for the purposes of collecting fuel and pasturing livestock.

Saudi law utilizes the *Waqf*, which is a form of land ownership whereby a Muslim can transfer property to a foundation for long-term religious or charitable purposes. The property cannot then be alienated or transferred.

ENERGY LAW

Saudi Arabia's vast oil reserves are owned by the Saudi government, in effect the Saudi royal family. Article 14 of the Basic Law states:

> *All natural resources that God has deposited underground, above ground, in territorial waters or within the land and sea domains under the authority of the State, together with revenues of these resources, shall be the property of the State, as provided by the Law. The Law shall specify means for exploitation, protection and development of these resources in the best interest of the State, and its security and economy.*

The Ministry of Petroleum and Mineral Resources is responsible for general strategy in the oil and gas sectors and for monitoring the state-owned oil company, Saudi Aramco. The oil, gas and refining industries in Saudi Arabia are controlled by law by Saudi Aramco, which has a near monopoly in these areas. It is the world's biggest oil producer, the Middle East's biggest company and is generally considered to be the most important energy company in the world. However, in 2003, the law was changed to allow foreign companies to look for Saudi Arabia's vast reserves of natural gas, believed to represent 4% of the world's reserves. This was the first time since the 1970s that foreign companies have been permitted to search for oil or gas.

Currently, the electricity industry is in the hands of the 75% state-owned Saudi Electric Company, but plans have been announced to privatize the industry.

HUMAN RIGHTS LAWS

Human rights issues and failings in the rule of law in Saudi Arabia have attracted strong criticism. These include criminal law punishments that are considered as cruel, as well as the position of women, religious discrimination, the lack of religious freedom and the activities of the Saudi Mutaween.

Between 1996 and 2000, Saudi Arabia acceded to four UN human rights conventions and, in 2004, the government approved the establishment of the National Society for Human Rights (NSHR), staffed by government employees, to monitor their implementation. To date, the activities of the NSHR have been limited and doubts remain over its neutrality and independence. Saudi Arabia was one of only eight countries that did not accept the UN's Universal Declaration of Human Rights when it was launched in

RULE OF LAW

Because Sharia, as applied by Saudi courts, is uncodified and because judges are not bound by judicial precedent, the scope and content of the law is uncertain. A study published by the Albert Shanker Institute and Freedom House has criticized a number of aspects of the administration of justice in Saudi Arabia and concluded that the country's "practices diverge from the concept of the rule of law." The study goes on to assert that qadis (judges) reach decisions without following due process and "only the bravest of lawyers ... challenge decisions of the qadis; usually appeals to the king are based on mercy, not on justice or innocence." It also claimed that members of the Saudi royal family are not forced to appear before Saudi courts.

As in many countries, those with influence may receive favorable treatment before the law. According to a former managing editor at *Arab News*, the ruling House of Saud is so unwilling "to let one of their own face the consequences of his criminal activity" that on the rare occasions that they are arrested for a crime, the perpetrating prince is pardoned (Prince Fahd bin Naif, who was 19, gunned down Mundir al-Qadi in 2002) or released, and further media mention of the incident forbidden by the Ministry of Culture and Information (four princes that participated in the disruption of a 2002 Eid al-Fitr gathering on the corniche of Jeddah)

On the other hand blue collar foreign workers have sometimes been unable to collect salaries due even when the Saudi Labor Office has ruled in their favor, since employers can stall payment until the worker' work permits have expired.

WOMEN'S RIGHTS

The U.S. State department considers that "discrimination against women is a significant problem" in Saudi Arabia and that women have few political or social rights. After her 2008 visit, the UN special rapporteur on violence against women noted the lack of women's autonomy and the absence of a law criminalizing violence against women. The World Economic Forum 2012 Global Gender Gap Report ranked Saudi Arabia 131st out of 135 countries for gender parity, ahead of Syria, Chad, Pakistan and Yemen.

Every adult woman has to have a close male relative as her "guardian".

As a result, Human Rights Watch has described the position of Saudi women as no different from being a minor, with little authority over their own lives. The guardian is entitled to make a number of critical decisions on a woman's behalf. These include giving approval for the woman to travel, to hold some types of business licenses, to study at a university or college and to work if the type of business is not "deemed appropriate for a woman." Even where a guardian's approval is not legally required, some officials will still ask for it. Women also face discrimination in the courts, where the testimony of one man equals that of two women, and in family and inheritance law

The religious police *mutawa* impose restrictions on women when in public. These restrictions include requiring women to sit in separate specially designated family sections in restaurants, to wear an abaya (a loose-fitting, full-length black cloak covering the entire body) and to conceal their hair. Women also risk arrest for riding in a vehicle driven by a male who is not an employee or a close male relative. Although there is no written ban on women driving cars, a Saudi driving license is required by law and these are not issued to women. Thus, it is effectively illegal for women to drive, and the ban is enforced by the *mutawa*. In 2013, Saudi Arabia registered its first female trainee lawyer, Arwa al-Hujaili.

POLITICAL FREEDOM AND FREEDOM OF SPEECH

No political parties or national elections are permitted in Saudi Arabia and according to *The Economist's* 2010 Democracy Index, the Saudi government is the seventh most authoritarian regime from among the 167 countries rated. There is no legal protection of freedom of speech and Saudis are prohibited from publicly criticizing the government, Islam, or the royal family. The Saudi press is strictly censored and articles on Saudi dissidents are banned. Saudi censorship is considered among the most restrictive in the world and the country blocks broad swathes of the Internet. After protests occurred in early 2011, the government banned all public demonstrations and marches.

CRIMINAL TRIALS AND PUNISHMENT

Western-based organisations such as Amnesty International and Human Rights Watch have condemned both the Saudi criminal justice system and its severe punishments. However, most Saudis reportedly support the system and say that it maintains a low crime rate.

Human Rights Watch, in their 2008 report on Saudi Arabian criminal justice system, noted that the criminal procedure code introduced in 2002 lacked some basic protections but, as mentioned above, had been ignored by judges in any case. Those arrested are often not informed of the crime of which they are accused or given access to a lawyer and are subject to abusive treatment and torture if they do not confess. At trial, there is a presumption of guilt and the accused is often unable to examine witnesses and evidence or present a legal defense. Most trials are held in secret, that is, without the public or press. The physical punishments imposed by Saudi courts, such as beheading, stoning, amputation and lashing, and the number of executions have also been strongly criticized.

RELIGIOUS FREEDOM

In 2010, the U.S. State Department stated that in Saudi Arabia "freedom of religion is neither recognized nor protected under the law and is severely restricted in practice" and that "government policies continued to place severe restrictions on religious freedom". No faith other than Islam is permitted to be practised, although there are nearly a million Christians, nearly all foreign workers, in Saudi Arabia. There are no churches or other non-Muslim houses of worship permitted in the country. Even private prayer services are forbidden in practice and the Saudi religious police reportedly regularly search the homes of Christians. Foreign workers must observe Ramadan and are not allowed to celebrate Christmas or Easter. Conversion by Muslims to another religion (apostasy) carries the death penalty, although there have been no confirmed reports of executions for apostasy in recent years. Proselytizing by non-Muslims is illegal, and the last Christian priest was expelled from Saudi Arabia in 1985. Compensation in court cases discriminates against non-Muslims: once fault is determined, a Muslim receives all of the amount of compensation determined, a Jew or Christian half, and all others a sixteenth.

According to Human Rights Watch, the Shia minority face systematic discrimination from the Saudi government in education, the justice system and especially religious freedom. Restrictions are imposed on the public celebration of Shia festivals such as Ashura and on the Shia taking part in communal public worship.

In March 2014, the Saudi interior ministry issued a royal decree branding all atheists as terrorists, which defines terrorism as "calling for atheist thought in any form, or calling into question the fundamentals of the Islamic religion on which this country is based".

**For additional analytical, business and investment opportunities information,
please contact Global Investment & Business Center, USA
at (202) 546-2103. Fax: (202) 546-3275. E-mail: ibpusa3@gmail.com
Global Business and Legal Information Databank: www.ibpus.com**

LGBT RIGHTS

Saudi Arabia is one of the few countries in the world where homosexual acts are not only illegal but punishable by execution. However, there have been no executions for homosexuality reported in Saudi Arabia since 2002 when three men from Abha were beheaded. There have, however, reportedly been raids on "gay parties" and men have been arrested for "behaving like women".The usual penalties inflicted have been limited to flogging and imprisonment

ISLAMIC ECONOMICS FUNDUMENTALS

Islamic economics economics in accordance with Islamic law. Islamic economics can refer to the application of Islamic law to economic activity either where Islamic rule is in force or where it is not; i.e. it can refer to the creation of an Islamic economic system, or to simply following Islamic law in regards to spending, saving, investing, giving, etc. where the state does not follow Islamic law.

The former paradigm, particularly as developed by modern Shia scholars such as Mahmoud Taleghani, and Mohammad Baqir al-Sadr, seeks not only to enforce Islamic regulations on issues such as Zakat, Jizya, Nisab, Khums, Riba, insurance and inheritance, but to implement broader economic goals and policies of an Islamic society. It seeks an economic system based on uplifting the deprived masses, a major role for the state in matters such as circulation and equitable distribution of wealth and ensuring participants in the marketplace are rewarded for being exposed to risk and/or liability. Islamists movements and authors will generally describe this system as being neither Socialist nor Capitalist, but a third way with none of the drawbacks of the other two systems.

The latter paradigm is of necessity more limited, revolving around a few main tenets of Islam: the payment of zakat charity by believers, borrowing and lending without payment of fixed interest (riba), and socially responsible investing. The key difference from a financial perspective is the no-interest rule since most other religions favor charitable giving and socially responsible investing. The belief that the prohibition of investment with interest charges is essential for an Islamic society is widespread, though liberal movements within Islam may deny the need for this prohibition, since they see Islam as generally compatible with modern secular institutions and law.

ISLAMIC ECONOMICS IN THE WORLD

Islamic economics in practice, or economic policies supported by self-identified Islamic groups, has varied throughout its long history.

Traditional Islamic concepts having to do with economics included

- *zakat* - the "taxing of certain goods, such as harvest, with an eye to allocating these taxes to expenditures that are also explicitly defined, such as aid to the needy."
- *Gharar* - "the interdiction of chance ... that is, of the presence of any element of uncertainty, in a contract (which excludes not only insurance but also the lending of money without participation in the risks)"
- *Riba* - "referred to as usury"

For additional analytical, business and investment opportunities information,
please contact Global Investment & Business Center, USA
at (202) 546-2103. Fax: (202) 546-3275. E-mail: ibpusa3@gmail.com
Global Business and Legal Information Databank: www.ibpus.com

These concepts, like others in Islamic law and jurisprudence, came from the "prescriptions, anecdotes, examples, and words of the Prophet, all gathered together and systematized by commentators according to an inductive, casuistic method." Sometimes other sources such as al-urf, (the custom), al-aql (reason) or al-ijma (consensus of the jurists) were employed. In addition, Islamic law has developed areas of law that correspond to secular laws of contracts and torts.

EARLY REFORMS UNDER ISLAM

Main article: Early reforms under Islam
Some argue early Islamic theory and practice formed a "coherent" economic system with "a blueprint for a new order in society, in which all participants would be treated more fairly". Michael Bonner, for example, has written that an "economy of poverty" prevailed in Islam until the 13th and 14th centuries. Under this system God's guidance made sure the flow of money and goods was "purified" by being channeled from those who had much of it to those who had little by encouraging zakat (charity) and discouraging riba (usury/interest) on loans. Bonner maintains the prophet also helped poor traders by allowing only tents, not permanent buildings in the market of Medina, and not charging fees and rents there.

CORPORATE SOCIAL RESPONSIBILITY IN COMMERCE

Social responsibility and corporate social responsibility in commerce was stressed in Islamic sociology. The development of Islamic banks and Islamic economics was a side effect of this sociology: usury was rather severely restrained, no interest rate was allowed, and investors were not permitted to escape the consequences of any failed venture -- all financing was equity financing (*Musharaka*). In not letting borrowers bear all the risk/cost of a failure, an extreme disparity of outcomes between "partners" is thus avoided. Ultimately this serves a social harmony purpose. Muslims also could not and cannot (in shariah) finance any dealings in forbidden goods or activities, such as wine, pork, gambling, etc. Thus ethical investing is the only acceptable investing, and moral purchasing is encouraged.

LEGAL INSTITUTIONS

HAWALA AGENCY

The *Hawala*, an early informal value transfer system, has its origins in classical Islamic law, and is mentioned in texts of Islamic jurisprudence as early as the 8th century. *Hawala* itself later influenced the development of the agency in common law and in civil laws such as the *aval* in French law and the *avallo* in Italian law. The words *aval* and *avallo* were themselves derived from *Hawala*. The transfer of debt, which was "not permissible under Roman law but became widely practiced in medieval Europe, especially in commercial transactions", was due to the large extent of the "trade conducted by the Italian cities with the Muslim world in the Middle Ages." The agency was also "an institution unknown to Roman law" as no "individual could conclude a binding contract on behalf of another as his agent." In Roman law, the "contractor himself was considered the party to the contract and it took a second contract between the person who acted on behalf of a principal and the latter in order to transfer the rights and the obligations deriving from the contract to him." On the other hand, Islamic law and the later common law "had no difficulty in accepting agency as one of its institutions in the field of contracts and of obligations in general."

WAQF TRUST

The *waqf* in Islamic law, which developed in the medieval Islamic world from the 7th to 9th centuries, bears a notable resemblance to the English trust law. Every *waqf* was required to have

For additional analytical, business and investment opportunities information,
please contact Global Investment & Business Center, USA
at (202) 546-2103. Fax: (202) 546-3275. E-mail: ibpusa3@gmail.com
Global Business and Legal Information Databank: www.ibpus.com

a *waqif* (founder), *mutawillis* (trustee), *qadi* (judge) and beneficiaries. Under both a *waqf* and a trust, "property is reserved, and its usufruct appropriated, for the benefit of specific individuals, or for a general charitable purpose; the corpus becomes inalienable; estates for life in favor of successive beneficiaries can be created" and "without regard to the law of inheritance or the rights of the heirs; and continuity is secured by the successive appointment of trustees or *mutawillis*."

The only significant distinction between the Islamic *waqf* and English trust was "the express or implied reversion of the *waqf* to charitable purposes when its specific object has ceased to exist", though this difference only applied to the *waqf ahli* (Islamic family trust) rather than the *waqf khairi* (devoted to a charitable purpose from its inception). Another difference was the English vesting of "legal estate" over the trust property in the trustee, though the "trustee was still bound to administer that property for the benefit of the beneficiaries." In this sense, the "role of the English trustee therefore does not differ significantly from that of the *mutawalli*."

The trust law developed in England at the time of the Crusades, during the 12th and 13th centuries, was introduced by Crusaders who may have been influenced by the *waqf* institutions they came across in the Middle East. After the Islamic waqf law and madrassah foundations were firmly established by the 10th century, the number of Bimaristan hospitals multiplied throughout throughout Islamic lands. In the 11th century, every Islamic city had at least several hospitals. The waqf trust institutions funded the hospitals for various expenses, including the wages of doctors, ophthalmologists, surgeons, chemists, pharmacists, domestics and all other staff, the purchase of foods and remedies; hospital equipment such as beds, mattresses, bowls and perfumes; and repairs to buildings. The waqf trusts also funded medical schools, and their revenues covered various expenses such as their maintenance and the payment of teachers and students.

CLASSICAL MUSLIM COMMERCE

During the Islamic Golden Age, guilds were formed though officially unrecognized by the medieval Islamic city. However, trades were recognized and supervised by officials of the city. Each trade developed its own identity, whose members would attend the same mosque, and serve together in the militia.

Technology and industry in Islamic civilization were highly developed. Distillation techniques supported a flourishing perfume industry, while chemical ceramic glazes were developed constantly to compete with ceramics imported from China. A scientific approach to metallurgy made it easier to adopt and improve steel technologies from India and China. Primary exports included manufactured luxuries, such as wood carving, metal and glass, textiles, and ceramics. The systems of contract relied upon by merchants was very effective. Merchants would buy and sell on commission, with money loaned to them by wealthy investors, or a joint investment of several merchants, who were often Muslim, Christian and Jewish. Recently, a collection of documents was found in an Egyptian synagogue shedding a very detailed and human light on the life of medieval Middle Eastern merchants. Business partnerships would be made for many commercial ventures, and bonds of kinship enabled trade networks to form over huge distances. Networks developed during this time enabled a world in which money could be promised by a bank in Baghdad and cashed in Spain, creating the cheque system of today. Each time items passed through one of the cities along this extraordinary network, the city imposed a tax, resulting in high prices once the items reached their final destinations. These innovations made by Muslims and Jews laid the foundations for the modern economic system.
Transport was simple, yet highly effective. Each city had an area outside its gates where pack animals were assembled; found in the cities' markets were large secure warehouses; while

accommodations were provided for merchants in cities and along trade routes by a sort of medieval motel.

The concepts of welfare and pension were introduced in early Islamic law as forms of *Zakat* (charity), one of the Five Pillars of Islam, since the time of the Abbasid caliph Al-Mansur in the 8th century. The taxes (including *Zakat* and *Jizya*) collected in the treasury of an Islamic government was used to provide income for the needy, including the poor, elderly, orphans, widows, and the disabled. According to the Islamic jurist Al-Ghazali (Algazel, 1058-1111), the government was also expected to store up food supplies in every region in case a disaster or famine occurs. The Caliphate was thus one of the earliest welfare states, particularly the Abbasid Caliphate.

AGE OF DISCOVERY

The Islamic Empire significantly contributed to globalization during the Islamic Golden Age, when the knowledge, trade and economies from many previously isolated regions and civilizations began integrating due to contacts with Muslim explorers, sailors, scholars, traders, and travelers. Some have called this period the "Pax Islamica" or "Afro-Asiatic age of discovery", in reference to the Muslim South-west Asian and North African traders and explorers who travelled most of the Old World, and established an early global economy across most of Asia and Africa and much of Europe, with their trade networks extending from the Atlantic Ocean and Mediterranean Sea in the west to the Indian Ocean and China Sea in the east. This helped establish the Islamic Empire (including the Rashidun, Umayyad, Abbasid and Fatimid caliphates) as the world's leading extensive economic power throughout the 7th-13th centuries. Several contemporary medieval Arabic reports also suggest that Muslim explorers from al-Andalus and the Maghreb may have travelled in expeditions across the Atlantic Ocean between the 9th and 14th centuries.

Arabic silver *dirham* coins were being circulated throughout the Afro-Eurasian landmass, as far as sub-Saharan Africa in the south and northern Europe in the north, often in exchange for goods and slaves. In England, for example, the Anglo-Saxon king Offa of Mercia (r. 757-796) had coins minted with the Shahadah in Arabic. These factors helped establish the Arab Empire (including the Rashidun, Umayyad, Abbasid and Fatimid caliphates) as the world's leading extensive economic power throughout the 7th–13th centuries.

AGRICULTURAL REVOLUTION

During the Muslim Agricultural Revolution, the Caliphate understood that real incentives were needed to increase productivity and wealth, thus enhancing tax revenues, hence they introduced a social transformation through the changed ownership of land, where any individual of any gender or any ethnic or religious background had the right to buy, sell, mortgage and inherit land for farming or any other purposes. They also introduced the signing of a contract for every major financial transaction concerning agriculture, industry, commerce, and employment. Copies of the contract were usually kept by both parties involved.

The two types of economic systems that prompted agricultural development in the Islamic world were either politically-driven, by the conscious decisions of the central authority to develop under-exploited lands; or market-driven, involving the spread of advice, education, and free seeds, and the introduction of high value crops or animals to areas where they were previously unknown. These led to increased subsistence, a high level of economic security that ensured wealth for all citizens, and a higher quality of life due to the introduction of artichokes, spinach, aubergines, carrots, sugar cane, and various exotic plants; vegetables being available all year round without the need to dry them for winter; citrus and olive plantations becoming a common sight, market gardens and orchards springing up in every Muslim city; intense cropping and the technique of intensive irrigation agriculture with land fertility replacement; a major increase in animal husbandry; higher quality of wool and other clothing materials; and the introduction of selective breeding of animals from different parts of the Old World resulting in improved horse stocks and the best load-carrying camels.

The Islamic Empire experienced a growth in literacy, having the highest literacy rate of the Middle Ages, comparable to Athens' literacy in Classical Antiquity but on a larger scale. The average life expectancy in the lands under Islamic rule also experienced an increase, due to the Agricultural Revolution as well as improved medical care. In contrast to the average lifespan in the ancient Greco-Roman world (22-28 years), the average lifespan in the early Islamic Caliphate was more than 35 years. The average lifespans of the Islamic scholarly class in particular was much higher: 84.3 years in 10th-11th century Iraq and Persia, 72.8 years in the 11th century Middle East, 69-75 years in 11th century Islamic Spain, 75 years in 12th century Persia, and 59-72 years in 13th century Persia.

JUDICIAL SYSTEM REFORMS

On April 2, 2005, a Royal Order was issued which approved principle amendments to the organization of the judicial system, including the establishment of specialized courts in Saudi Arabia for the first time. According to the 2005 Royal Order, specialized courts in labor, commercial, domestic, and criminal cases will have complete jurisdiction over their areas of specialization. The jurisdiction of the new specialized courts and the General Courts will be defined so as to avoid conflict over jurisdiction.

On October 1, 2007, King Abdullah bin Abdul-Aziz issued a Royal Decree approving a new body of laws regulating the judiciary and the Board of Grievances. The new laws replaced regulations in force for more than 30 years in the case of the judiciary, and about 25 years for the Board of Grievances. The Kingdom allocated a budget of seven billion riyals ($1.8 billion), ".for the King Abdullah bin Abdul-Aziz project to revamp the judicial sector, which aims at upgrading the judiciary and developing it in a comprehensive and integrated manner." These funds will be used to upgrade and build new courts while also training judges. The Saudi Judicial System will pass through a transition period lasting two to three years in which the new judicial system will be implemented.

The intention of the new law is to shape the Saudi Judicial system so that it can meet a higher judicial standard set by ongoing reforms started by the passage of the Law of Criminal Procedures and Procedures before Shari'ah Courts Law in 2001 to 2002. The new law came as a response to the social and economic needs of Saudi society. It represents a major step toward meeting the requirements of a modern and thriving economy, while also improving the business environment. The new law affirms the Saudi justice system's independence and impartiality; it will also ensure the highest possible fair trial standards.

THE NEW ROLE OF THE SUPREME JUDICIAL COUNCIL

Under the new Judiciary Law of 2007, the Supreme Judiciary Council will no longer serve as the Kingdom's highest court. However, it will continue to oversee administrative aspects of the judiciary. The Supreme Judicial Council will be composed of a president and ten members: the Chief of the High Court, four full-time members of the rank of Chief of the Appellate Court appointed by the King, the Deputy Minister of Justice, the Chief of the Bureau of Investigation and Prosecution, and three members who will possess the qualifications required by the Appellate Judge, appointed by the King. All Supreme Judicial Council members will serve for a period of four years, which will be renewable for other periods.

For additional analytical, business and investment opportunities information,
please contact Global Investment & Business Center, USA
at (202) 546-2103. Fax: (202) 546-3275. E-mail: ibpusa3@gmail.com
Global Business and Legal Information Databank: www.ibpus.com

Under the new law, the Supreme Judicial Council performs several administrative roles. In its administrative capacity, the Council, as stated in Article 6 of the new law, will have a supervisory role over Shari'ah Courts and Judges in accordance with the Law of the Judiciary, adopted in 2007. The Council will primarily supervise the courts, administering the employment-related affairs of all members of the judiciary within those limits laid down by the law. Such affairs include promotions, transfers, assignments, secondments, and training. The Council will also monitor the proper discharge of their duties in accordance with established rules and procedures, in order to ensure the independence of judges. The Council will have the authority to:

- Issue regulations on matters related to judges duties, subject to the King's approval;
- Issue judicial inspection regulations; establish, merge, or abolish courts;
- Specify the areas of their jurisdiction, and the formation of their circuits;
- Name the Appellate Courts' chiefs and their deputies, and First-Degree Courts chiefs and their deputies;
- Issue rules governing the functions and powers of the Courts' chiefs and their deputies;
- Issue rules governing the method of selecting judges;
- Regulate assistant judges' duties;
- Set counterpart judicial work required to fill judicial levels; and
- Propose what it deems necessary and relevant to its competency.

At the end of each year, the Council will prepare a comprehensive report containing all achievements, constraints and proposals, which will then be submitted to the King.

In addition, the Supreme Judicial Council will have a Jurisdictional Conflict Committee that has jurisdiction to solve jurisdictional conflicts and conflicts arising out of two final judgments entered by the Judiciary Courts and the Board of Grievances Courts. Meetings of the Council's Permanent Panel are governed according to regulations that administer attendance and voting.

Moreover, the Council will encompass several committees, including a Judicial Disciplinary Committee and a Department for Judicial Inspection.

THE NEW COURTS SYSTEM

The new Law of the Judiciary organizes the Courts System in the following hierarchical structure in descending order:

- High Court;
- Courts of Appeals; and,
- First-Degree Courts, which are composed of:
  o General Courts;
  o Criminal Courts;
  o Personal Status Courts;
  o Commercial Courts; and,
  o Labor Court (see Chart 3).

HIGH COURT

The High Court will assume the previous Supreme Judicial Council's main function as the highest authority in the judicial system. The High Court will be seated in Riyadh and will be composed of a president-who possesses the qualifications required of the Chief Appellate Judge and will be appointed by a Royal Order, along with a sufficient number of judges holding the rank of Chief of the Appellate Court- appointed by a Royal Order on the recommendation of the Supreme Judiciary Council. The High Court will exercise its jurisdictions through specialized circuits (as needed), which will be comprised of three-judge panels-except for the Criminal Circuit, which will review judgments involving certain major punishments, such as the death sentence. These will be composed of a five judge panel. Chief Judges of the High Court Circuits will be appointed by decisions of the Supreme Judicial Council on the recommendation of the Chief of the High Court.

The High Court will perform several legislative, consultative, and judicial roles. In addition to the function set forth by the Law of Procedure, before Shari'ah Courts and the Law of Criminal Procedure, the Court will supervise the implementation of Islamic law (Shari'ah) and regulations enacted by the King which are consistent with the issues that fall within the general jurisdiction of the judiciary. The High Court will review rulings issued or upheld by the Courts of Appeals, including those which relate to cases punishable by death, and other certain major crimes. In addition, the High Court will review judgments and decisions issued or supported by the Courts of Appeals on matters not previously mentioned. These include questions of law or questions of procedure-not questions of fact-if the objection to judgments are based on:

- A violation of the of Islamic Shari'ah provisions and regulations issued by the King that does not contradict with Shari'ah rules;

- Entry of judgment from a Court not properly constituted as provided for by the Law of the Judiciary and other regulations;

- Entry of judgment from an incompetent Court or Circuit Court; and

- Fault in the framing of an incident, or impropriety in its description of said case.

The High Court will have a General Council presided over by the Chief of the High Court.

The General Council will play a very crucial role in establishing general principles and precedents that have to be followed by lower courts, and considering other issues set forth by the Law of the Judiciary or other laws. Decisions of the General Council will be rendered by a vote of the majority of members in attendance. In the event of a tie, the Chief Judge will cast the deciding vote. All decisions adopted by the High Court's General Council will be final. Lastly, if one of the High Court Circuits, while reviewing a case, deems it necessary to depart from an interpretation adopted by either that same Circuit Court or by a different Circuit of the same Court in previous judgments, the case will be referred to the Chief of the High Court, who will refer it to the High Court General Council for a decision.

COURTS OF APPEALS

The new reforms announced by King Abdullah are aimed at introducing safeguards-such as Courts of Appeal-which can overturn decisions by lower courts. The new law will establish one or more Courts of Appeals in each of the Kingdom's provinces. Each court will function through specialized circuits comprised of three three-judge panels, except for the Criminal Circuit, which reviews judgments involving certain major crimes, including those which bear the death sentence. It will be composed of five judge panels.

Courts of Appeals will consist of the following circuits: Labor Circuits, Commercial Circuits, Criminal Circuits, Personal Status Circuits, and Civil Circuits. It will also be possible to establish

For additional analytical, business and investment opportunities information,
please contact Global Investment & Business Center, USA
at (202) 546-2103. Fax: (202) 546-3275. E-mail: ibpusa3@gmail.com
Global Business and Legal Information Databank: www.ibpus.com

specialized Appeals Circuits in the counties of each province where a Court of Appeals is established. Each circuit will be composed of a president appointed by the Chief of the Appellate Court and judges holding the rank of Appellate Judge. The Courts of Appeals will hear appealable decisions from lower courts. They will render their judgment after hearing the litigants' arguments in accordance with the Law of Procedure before Shari'ah Courts and the Law of Criminal Procedure.

FIRST-DEGREE COURTS

The First-Degree Courts will be established in the Kingdom's provinces, counties and districts in accordance to the needs of the system. First-Degree Courts will consist of General Courts, Criminal Courts, Commercial Courts, Labor Courts, and Personal Status Courts. General Courts will be established in provinces and will consist of specialized circuits including Implementation and Approval Circuits and Traffic Cases Circuits. General Courts will be composed of one or three-judge panels as specified by the Supreme Judicial Council. The Criminal Court will consist of the following specialized circuits: Qisas (Retaliatory Punishment) Cases Circuits, Hudud Cases Circuits (Prescribed Punishment), Ta'zir (Discretionary Punishment) Cases Circuits, and Juvenile Cases Circuits. The Criminal Court will be composed of a three-judge panel. Other cases (offences) specified by the Supreme Judicial Council will be heard by one judge. It is worth noting that all existing Summary Courts will be transmitted to Criminal Courts.

Other Personal Status, Commercial, and Labor Courts will consist of specialized circuits as needed, and will be composed of one or more judges as specified by the Supreme Judicial Council. It is worth mentioning that Commercial and Labor Courts will oversee disputes that had previously been handled by "special committees" at the Ministry of Commerce and Industry, and the Ministry of Labor. These committees were previously criticized because their decisions were not always enforceable and they were challenged in the courts. There were also questions regarding the impartiality and independence of these committees. Existing Commercial Circuits of the Board of Grievances First-Instance Circuits and Appeal Circuits will be transferred (with all of their judges, cases, etc.) to the new judicial system's First-Degree Commercial Courts and Appellate Courts.

In addition, disputes related to divorce and other family and personal matters would be settled by their own courts. The two existing Courts of Guarantee and Marriages located in Riyadh and Makkah will be transformed into Personal Status Courts.

General Courts in counties and districts will consist of one or more specialized circuits, according to the needs of the system, and will be composed of one or more judges as specified by the Supreme Judicial Council. Specialized Criminal, Personal Status, Commercial, and Labor Circuits may be established in General Courts in Counties and Districts where no Specialized Court has been established. Moreover, where necessary, the Supreme Judicial Council may assign one or more circuits to hear pilgrims' cases.

BOARD OF GRIEVANCES REFORMS

Specialized circuits in Counties and Districts General Courts will have the same jurisdiction as the specialized courts and will be composed of one or more judges. In addition, the Supreme Judicial Council will specify the jurisdiction of the General Courts, which are comprised of one judge. However, in general and without prejudice to the Law of the Board of Grievances, courts will have jurisdiction to render decisions with respect to all disputes and crimes in accordance with the rules for the jurisdiction of courts as set forth in the Law of Procedure before Shari'ah Courts and Law of Criminal Procedure.

Finally, the new judicial system will assume jurisdiction over most of the civil, commercial and criminal disputes previously decided by Administrative Committees. A committee from the Bureau of Expert in the Council of Ministers will convene, within a year of the Law of the Judiciary's effective date, to review all laws and regulations affected by such transition and suggest their amendments accordingly.

The newly established Supreme Judicial Council will be required to study the condition of the Administrative Committees exempted from this transition (the Banking Disputes Settlement Committee, Financial Market, and Customs Committees) and will submit its finding within a year to complete the regulatory procedures. In cases other than those requiring a visit to the site of a dispute, courts may not hold their hearings in places other than their respective seats. However, by a decision of the Supreme Judicial Council, courts may, when necessary, hold their hearings elsewhere-even if the new location falls outside of their areas of jurisdiction.

King Abdullah's Royal Decree also approved an overhaul of Saudi Arabia's Board of Grievances. The pyramidal structure of the new Board Administrative Courts stands parallel to the structure of the Judicial Courts. The new law affirms that the Board of Grievances-which will be based in the city of Riyadh-is an independent administrative judicial commission responsible directly to the King.

The Board of Grievances will consist of a President of the rank of minister, at least one Vice-President, a number of Assistant Vice-Presidents, and several judges. Vice Presidents will be appointed by Royal Order from among those who possess the qualifications required to become a Chief of the Appellate Court.

Alongside the Supreme Judicial Council, the new Board of Grievances Law establishes an Administrative Judicial Council composed of the President of the Board, the Chief of the High Administrative Court, the senior Vice President of the Board, and four judges of the rank of Chief of the Appellate Court, all appointed by Royal Orders.

The Council will perform several administrative tasks similar to those of the Supreme Judicial Council. The Administrative Judicial Council will meet every two months; its meetings will be valid if attended by at least five of the members, and decisions of the Council will be made by majority vote. Finally, the Administrative Judicial Council will encompass several committees, including the Jurisdictional Conflict Committee, the Judicial Disciplinary Committee, and the Department for Judicial Inspection.

The Board of Grievances Law organizes the Board according to the following hierarchical structure:

- High Administrative Court;
- Administrative Courts of Appeals; and,
- Administrative Courts (see Chart 4).

HIGH ADMINISTRATIVE COURT

The new law also establishes a Higher Administrative Court, which will be comprised of a President holding the rank of minister-appointed by Royal Order, and a sufficient number of

For additional analytical, business and investment opportunities information,
please contact Global Investment & Business Center, USA
at (202) 546-2103. Fax: (202) 546-3275. E-mail: ibpusa3@gmail.com
Global Business and Legal Information Databank: www.ibpus.com

judges bearing the rank of Chief of the Appellate Court-appointed by Royal Order on the recommendation of the Administrative Judicial Council.

The High Court will exercise its jurisdictions through specialized circuits (as needed), which will be composed of three-judge panels. The Higher Administrative Court will have a General Council, which will be presided over by the Chief of the High Administrative Court and the membership of all of its judges. Its meetings will be valid if attended by at least two thirds of its members. The Council's decisions will be issued by majority vote. If, while reviewing a complaint, one of the High Administrative Court Circuits deems it necessary to depart from an interpretation adopted by either the same or a different circuit of the same court, the case will be referred to the Chief of the High Administrative Court, who will refer it to the High Administrative Court General Council for a decision.

The Board of Grievances High Administrative Court will have jurisdiction to review rulings issued or upheld by the Administrative Courts of Appeals if the objection to the judgment is based on:

· A violation of the Islamic Shari'ah provisions or regulations which do not contradict Shari'ah rules, as well as faults in its implementation or interpretation-including violations of judicial principles established by the High Administrative Court;

· Entry of judgment from an incompetent court;

· Entry of judgment from a court not properly constituted as provided by the Board of Grievances Law;

· Fault in framing the incident or impropriety in its description;

· Entry of a judgment contrary to another previous decision issued between the parties to the proceedings; or,

· Jurisdictional conflict among the board's courts.

ADMINISTRATIVE COURTS OF APPEALS

The new law establishes at least one Administrative Court of Appeals. Each court will function through Specialized Circuits composed of three-judge panels. The Administrative Courts of Appeals will hear appealable decisions from the lower Administrative Courts. They will render their judgment after hearing the litigants' arguments in accordance with the Law of Procedure before Shari'ah Courts and the Law of Criminal Procedure.

ADMINISTRATIVE COURTS

(A) Cases related to the rights provided for in the Civil and Military Service and Pension Laws for government employees and hired hands, and independent public entities and their heirs and claimants;

(B) Cases of objection filed by parties concerned by administrative decisions, where the reason for such an objection is lack of jurisdiction, a deficiency in form, a violation or erroneous application or interpretation of laws and regulations, or abuse of authority. The rejection or refusal of an administrative authority to take a decision that it should have taken pursuant to laws and regulations is considered to be an administrative decision;

(C) Cases of compensation filed by parties concerned against the government and independent public corporate entities resulting from their actions;

(D) Cases filed by parties regarding contract-related disputes where the government or an independent public corporate entity is a party;

(E) Disciplinary cases filed by the Bureau of Control and Investigation;

(F) Other Administrative Disputes; and,

(G) Requests for implementation of foreign judgments.

The new law establishes one or more Administrative Courts. Each court will function through specialized circuits such as Administrative Circuits, Employment, and Disciplinary Circuits, and Subsidiary Circuits, and will be composed of either a one or a three-judge panel. The Administrative Courts will have jurisdiction to decide the following:

Simple Structure of the New Board of Grievances

HIGH ADMINISTRATIVE COURT

ADMINISTRATIVE COURTS OF APPEAL

DICIPLINARY CIRCUITS	ADMINISTRATIVE CIRCUITS	SUBSIDIARY CIRCUITS	OTHER CIRCUITS

ADMINISTRATIVE COURTS

DICIPLINARY CIRCUITS	ADMINISTRATIVE CIRCUITS	SUBSIDIARY CIRCUITS	OTHER CIRCUITS

Thus, it is clear that the Board of Grievances will continue to handle administrative disputes involving government departments. It is important to note that the previous Law of Board of Grievances, adopted in 1982, empowered the Board to hear and punish offences involving bribery, forgery, exploitation of official influence or abuse of authority in criminal prosecution proceedings, or violations of human rights. However, the new law relinquished to the new Judicial Court System the jurisdiction over criminal offenses that had been granted by the Law of 1982. In addition, the Board of Grievances may not hear requests related to sovereign actions, objections filed by individuals against judgments, decisions issued by courts or legal panels which fall within their jurisdiction, or any decision issued by the Supreme Judicial Council or the Administrative Judicial Council.

Moreover, it is noteworthy that all of the existing Criminal Circuits of the Board of Grievances' First-Instance Circuits and Appeal Circuits will be transferred to the new judicial system's First-Degree Criminal Courts and Appellate Courts. Finally, the Board of Grievances will have jurisdiction over most of the Administrative Committees' administrative disputes. A committee from the Bureau of Experts in the Council of Ministers will be convened, within a year of the Law of the Judiciary becoming effective, to review all laws and regulations affected by the transition and to suggest amendments

JUDGES' QUALIFICATIONS, JOB PERFORMANCE, AND TRAINING

As Islamic Shari'ah is the main authority for Saudi Courts, a judge is required to have a higher standard of education, knowledge, and understanding of socio-cultural issues, and must be equipped with the tools of ijtihad, as well as specific professional skills that will lead to reasonable, just, and impartial judgments. The Law of the Judiciary requires each judicial candidate to hold a degree from one of the Shari'ah colleges in the Kingdom of Saudi Arabia. According to Saudi "ulama", education in Saudi universities has the purpose of producing "ulama" capable of relative degrees of "ijtihad".A candidate may hold an equivalent certificate, although he is required to pass a special examination prepared by the Supreme Judicial Council. To enable judges to attain the highest levels of education, the Kingdom has established a Judicial Academy and an Institute of Public Administration to train judges, enhance their expertise, develop their skills, and provide them with the information that they need to work effectively. In addition, to cope with the transition from the current to the new judiciary system, the new Law of the Judiciary requires all Criminal, Labor and Commercial Courts judges-and all Criminal, Labor and Commercial Courts of Appeal Circuits judges in all Provinces, Counties and Districts of the Kingdoms-to undergo at least two months of training in the Commercial, Labor and Criminal Procedure laws and other relevant regulations.

In general, there are different requirements and qualifications that a person must possess in order to be a member of the Judiciary. To be appointed as a judge, a candidate must:

- Be a Saudi national;
- Be of good character and conduct;
- Be qualified to hold the position of judge in accordance with the Shari'ah's provisions;
- Fulfill certain educational requirements;
- Be at least forty years old if he is to be appointed as an appellate judge, or be at least twenty two years old if he is to be appointed to any other rank; and,
- Not have been sentenced for a crime affecting his religion or honor or dismissed from a public office as a disciplinary action, unless he has been rehabilitated.

Assistant judgesare initially appointed on probation for a period of two years, and newly appointed judges are assigned to serve with court judges on probation for at least one year in order to become familiar with the court's procedures. During the period of probation, newly appointed assistant judgesbenefit from the experience of senior judges and work on simple cases and settlements. Their work is always reviewed by higher-ranking judges, and their judgments are reviewed or approved to ensure that they conform to the rules and procedures of the courts before they are handed down. In addition, during the period of probation, an assistant judgemay be dismissed for lack of competence by a decision of the Supreme Judicial Council. Other newly appointed judges may be dismissed during their period of probation for lack of competence by Royal Order on the recommendation of the Supreme Judicial Council.

A judge who begins his career at the bottom of the judicial hierarchy will usually be required to satisfy additional requirements in order to be promoted to a higher tier of the judiciary. These requirements include:

- A graduate degree from the High Judiciary Institute or one of the Shari'ah colleges in the Kingdom;
- A diploma in System Studies from the Institute of Public Administration in the Kingdom;
- Experience teaching Islamic law (fiqh) or Islamic jurisprudence (Usul al-Fiqh) in one of the Shari'ah colleges; or,
- Experience fulfilling comparable judicial duties for a defined period of time.

These and other requirements are strongly enforced to ensure the presence of qualified judges in each tier of the judiciary. The new ranks of the judiciary are organized according to the following hierarchical structure:

- Chairman of the High Court;
- Chief of Appellate Court;
- Appellate Judge;
- Chief of Court (A);
- Chief of Court (B);
- Deputy Chief of Court (A);
- Deputy Chief of Court (B);
- Judge (A);
- Judge (B);
- Judge (C); and,
- Assistant Judge.

The new ranking system of members of the judiciary placed the position of Chairman of the High Court at the top of the judicial ranking hierarchy, replacing the Chairman of the Supreme Judicial Council These ranks are filled in accordance with the provisions of the new Law of the Judiciary.

Chart 5: The New Ranks of the Judiciary in the Saudi Arabian Judicial System

In general, Royal Orders based on decisions of the Supreme Judicial Council affect the appointment and promotion of judges. The Supreme Council's decision must state the statutory conditions that have been fulfilled in each case. In the case of promotion, the Council usually follows the order of absolute seniority (in the service). Where two or more judges have served for equal periods of time, the selected candidate is given priority based on his proficiency reports. Where the proficiency reports are equal or there are no proficiency reports to examine, priority is based on age and seniority.

Similarly, occupation of any of the ranks of the Board of Grievances requires the qualifications specified for each rank in the Law of the Judiciary, with slight modification. The current ranks in the Board of Grievances are organized according to the following hierarchical structure:

- Assistant Head of the rank of Chief of Appellate Court;
- Assistant Head of the rank of Appellate Judge;

- Counselor (A) of the rank of Chief of Court (A);
- Counselor (B) of the rank of Chief of Court (B);
- Counselor (C) of the rank of Deputy Chief of Court (A);
- Counselor (D) of the rank of Deputy Chief of Court (B);
- Assistant Counselor (A) of the rank of Judge (A);
- Assistant Counselor (B) of the rank of Judge (B);
- Assistant Counselor (C) of the rank of Judge (C); and,
- Trainee of the rank of Assistant Judge (see Chart 6).

Appointments and promotions of Board members are carried out in accordance with procedures defined in the judicial cadre. The current Board has, "an Administrative Affairs Committee," composed of the President of the Board or his deputies and six members selected by the President from counselors whose ranks are not lower than (B). The Committee has powers similar to those of the current Supreme Judicial Council with regard to Board members. The Committee's decisions are issued by a majority vote of its members.

Ranks in the new Board of Grievances are similar to the judiciary ranks. These ranks are filled in accordance with the provisions of the new Board of Grievances Law.

The new ranking system addressing members of the Board places the position of Chairman of the High Administrative Court at the top of the Board of Grievances' hierarchy-similar to the chairman of the High Court position established by the new Law of the Judiciary (see Chart 5). The new Board of Grievances Law establishes an Administrative Judicial Council. The Council will perform several administrative roles similar to those of the new Supreme Judicial Council.

Moreover, the 1982 Law of the Judiciary formed a Department for Judicial Inspection at the Ministry of Justice. It consists of a president and a sufficient number of members selected from among the Judges of the Appellate Court or the General Courts by decision of the Supreme Judicial Council for one year-a term which is renewable for other periods. Under the new Law of the Judiciary, the Supreme Judicial Council will encompass the Judicial Disciplinary Committee, which will inspect the work of judges of Appellate and First-Degree Courts for the purpose of collecting information about their level of efficiency and their ability to perform the duties of their offices. All inspections are made by members with ranks higher than those of the judges whose work is being inspected. Inspection of the members of the judiciary is made at least once and not more than twice a year. Evaluation of the proficiency of a judge is based on the following ratings:

- Competent;
- Above average;
- Average; and,
- Below average.

If a judge receives a below average rating in three consecutive proficiency reports, he is placed on retirement by a Royal Order on the basis of a decision by the Supreme Judicial Council.

Judges are allowed to contest the findings of these reports through defined mechanisms and regulations. No member of the judiciary may be promoted unless his work has been subjected to inspection at least twice while he was in the rank from which he is to be promoted, and unless the last two reports preceding the promotion rated his proficiency as (at least) average. The current Board of Grievances has a Supervisory Committee, which assumes a supervisory role over the Board's members. The committee has provisions similar to those of the Judicial Inspection

Department. The Administrative Judicial Council of the new Board of Grievances Law will encompass a Department for Judicial Inspection.

Moreover, to provide judges with the most up-to-date working knowledge and to avoid any discrepancy in their judgments, the current and the new Law of the Judiciary establish a research department under the Ministry of Justice composed of a number of specialized members (who hold at least a Bachelors degree) to abstract, classify, and index the principles established by the Higher Courts, prepare selected collections of judgments, general rules and precedents for publication, execute research projects, and answer enquiries of judges.

The Implementation Mechanism of the Judiciary Law of 2007 also establishes a Research and Study Department in the High Court; the Department is composed of researchers who prepare studies requested by the High Court specialized Circuits. The new Law of the Board of Grievances establishes similar departments, which are comprised of a chairman, several judges, professionals and researchers. These departments provide opinions, prepare research projects,classify the Board judgments, general rules and precedents, and prepare them for publication. The Implementation Mechanism of the Law of the Board of Grievances also establishes a Research and Study Department in the High Administrative Court comprised of researchers whose role is to prepare studies requested by the High Administrative Court's specialized circuits.

In sum, the application of Islamic law in the Saudi Arabian Shari'ah Courts requires justices with specialized qualifications in complex jurisprudence. A judge's knowledge, qualifications, experience gained while in office, and successful completion of inspection all confer respect onto the judicial office and provide confidence in judicial rulings.

JUDICIAL INDEPENDENCE

The Kingdom realized that an independent judiciary is a cornerstone of the protection of rights and freedoms. Such protection cannot be accomplished without providing a fair trial under an independent and impartial Court System. The independence of the judiciary is enshrined in Article 46 of the Basic Law of Governance, which states that, "the judiciary shall be an independent authority and, in their administration of justice, judges shall be subject to no authority other than that of the Islamic Shari'ah." The same principle is embodied in many provisions of the Law of the Judiciary, which provide several safeguards. For example, Article 1 of the Law of the Judiciary explains that, "judges are independent and, in the administration of justice, they shall be subject to no authority other than the provisions of Shari'ah and laws in force." The same Article provides that, no one may interfere with the Judiciary." Article 5 of the Ordinance concerning the Prosecution of Ministers prohibits any interference with Courts affairs, and makes personal interference with the affairs of the judiciary a crime punishable by imprisonment for a term ranging from three to five years.

Moreover, the Law of the Board of Grievances recognizes the Board as an independent administrative judiciary, and the Board and its judges enjoy the same safeguards as provided in the Law of the Judiciary. Furthermore, one of the important characteristics of judicial independence is the protection of judges from removal from office or transfer. Such protection is guaranteed by the Law of the Judiciary to protect judges from any act that might compromise their independence. Article 2 states that, "[j]udges are not subject to removal from office except in the cases set forth herein." Article 3 stipulates that, "judges may be transferred to other positions only with their consent or by reason of promotion" in accordance with the provisions of the law. The Law of the Judiciary further asserts that judges are not subject to removal from office (save in cases specified by the law, such as retirement).

The accountability of judges is ensured by special procedures which provide the safeguards needed to ensure the protection and independence of judges. Article 4 of the Law of the Judiciary stipulates that, "a judge may not be sued except in accordance with the conditions and rules pertaining to the disciplining of judges."

Section 5 of the Law of the Judiciary is devoted to disciplinary sanctions against judges. To ensure that the executive authority will not interfere with the judicial system, the Law of the Judiciary stipulates that the Supreme Judicial Council is the only authority empowered to discipline a judge. The current Board of Grievances has a Disciplinary Committee which deals with the members of the Board's misconduct. The Administrative Judicial Council of the new Board of Grievances Law will encompass a Department for Judicial Inspection.

It is important to note that the new Law of the Judiciary clearly acknowledges the doctrine of separation of powers. The new law stressed the authority of judges in making decisions independent of outside influence, especially the influence of the "Executive Branch." The most prominent feature of the new law is its practical application of the judicial independence principle, as evidenced by the limiting of the Ministry of Justice's administrative control over the judiciary. Under the new law, the right to supervise all courts and judges was transferred from the Minister of Justice to the Supreme Judicial Council. The Supreme Judicial Council makes all decisions regarding judges' promotion, transfer, assignment, replacement, and training, and monitors the proper discharge of their duties and other issues that were subject to the supervision of the Ministry of Justice.

In addition, under the previous law, the Minister of Justice once enjoyed an approval authority over the decisions of the courts' high councils, such as the Courts of Appeals General Council. However, the new Law of the Judiciary removed the Minister of Justice from the decision-making process of similar bodies such as the High Court General Council which, according to the new law, renders its decisions by majority vote. All of its decisions will be final without any interference from any member of the Executive Branch. Moreover, the new law removed a provision from the Law of the Judiciary of 1975 that gave the Minister of Justice the authority to select a person to fill an absent member's seat at a Supreme Judicial Council meeting.

Furthermore, the Supreme Judicial Council is now the sole authority in determining the composition of the First-Degree Courts and designating their seats and jurisdictions, which were previously effected by decisions made by the Minister of Justice on the recommendation of the Supreme Judicial Council.

The Council also became the sole authority in naming the Appellate Courts' Chiefs and their Deputies, and First-Degree Courts' Chiefs and their Deputies. The Council also became the sole authority in deciding when the First-Degree Courts could hold their hearings outside of their areas of jurisdiction. Special examinations for candidate judges who hold "Shari'ah Degrees" from one of Saudi Arabia's Shari'ah Colleges will now be prepared by the Supreme Judicial Council instead of the Ministry of Justice. The Supreme Judicial Council now has the authority to specify what is meant by judicial duties which are mentioned as a requirement in the appointment and promotion process for judges. Such determinations had been made by the Council of Ministers on the recommendation of the Minister of Justice.

The principles of judicial independence from the Executive Branch were further preserved when the new law transferred the Department for Judicial Inspection from a committee under the Ministry of Justice authority to the Supreme Judicial Council authority.

For additional analytical, business and investment opportunities information, please contact Global Investment & Business Center, USA at (202) 546-2103. Fax: (202) 546-3275. E-mail: ibpusa3@gmail.com Global Business and Legal Information Databank: www.ibpus.com

The new law also moved the authority to issue regulations and procedures of judicial inspection, the authority to institute a disciplinary action, and the authority to implement judges' reprimands from the authority of the Minister of Justice to the Supreme Judicial Council authority. Finally, it should be noted that under the new law, the interaction between the Ministry and the Courts is limited to matters of:

- Administrating and financially supervising the courts and other judicial panels;
- Assuaging the effective functioning of the judiciary;
- Modernizing the judiciary; and,
- Improving its efficiency.

However, it has been argued that the decisions pertaining to the appointment of judges are made, to a great extent, by administrative authorities. For instance, the Supreme Judicial Council members, and the Chief of the High Court, are appointed by the King.

To understand why higher-ranking Judges are appointed by the King, it is important to realize that under Islamic Shari'ah, a Muslim ruler is mainly responsible for the administration of justice and the maintenance of the independence and dignity of the judiciary. It is his duty to look for those who are highly qualified and well-versed in Islamic law and to nominate them to the Highest Courts and Councils in the Kingdom. This process is part of the King's constitutional role-asserted in Article 55 of the Basic Law of Governance-in carrying out, ".the policy of the nation, a legitimate policy in accordance with the provisions of Islam; the King oversees the implementation of the Islamic Shari'ah, the system of government, the state's general policies; and the protection and defense of the country."

Thus, it is the type of responsibilities and authorities that the ruler enjoys as prescribed by Islamic Jurists for the Head of the Islamic State, which has been exercised by Muslim rulers throughout the history of Islamic States. It is also worth mentioning that although the King appoints judges so that they may put Islamic Shari'ah into effect, the applied law (Islamic Shari'ah) remained independent from the King and outside the state's domain. In other words, while a Muslim ruler appoints judges, a ruler may not interfere in the judicial process by altering decisions or redirecting cases. Thus the principle of separation of powers exists between the King and the Judiciary.

In addition, it is true that the right to an independent and impartial court is a basic and absolute right, ".that may suffer no exception." Due to the fundamental nature of the right to a fair trial, it, ".requires compliance in appearance as well as fact." The requirement of independence has been interpreted to mean that the, ".courts must be independent of both the executive and the parties." This independence must be institutional and functional. For instance, the European Court on Human Rights clarified that for impartiality to exist, two conditions must be satisfied, "(i) the tribunal must be subjectively free of personal prejudice or bias; and (ii) the tribunal must be impartial from an objective point of view" (that is, it must offer sufficient guarantees to exclude any legitimate doubt of partiality).

The overall effect of the administrative power should be weighed against other aspects of judicial statues that provide guarantees of independence and impartiality. "The international instruments and guidelines require that the courts operate in a manner strictly consistent with fair trial requirements." The limited administrative involvement in the judiciary could be tolerated only as long as sufficient safeguards are in place to guarantee the court and judges' independence and impartiality. The law in Saudi Arabia recognizes the principle of the independence of the judiciary and judges. The administrative involvement in the judicial nomination process is restricted and

For additional analytical, business and investment opportunities information,
please contact Global Investment & Business Center, USA
at (202) 546-2103. Fax: (202) 546-3275. E-mail: ibpusa3@gmail.com
Global Business and Legal Information Databank: www.ibpus.com

based on other administratively stipulated standards, such as seniority among judges of advanced seniority in the judicial corps.

The new Judicial System clearly asserted the independence of judges and their adherence to Islamic rules while providing them with adequate safeguards to protect them from arbitrary transfer, dismissal, or legal action. Therefore, there is no legitimate reason to fear that a particular judge lacks independence or impartiality due to the limited level of administrative involvement in the Saudi judicial system.

SOURCES OF LAW

All official legal materials in Saudi Arabia are written in Arabic, the official language of Saudi Arabia. Legal materials take many forms but can be classified under three main sources: Islamic Law, Statutory Law, and Royal Orders.

The legal system in Saudi Arabia relies on the two main sources of Islamic Shari'ah: Qur'an and Sunnah. The first source is: the Islamic law which is availed from the Holy Book of Islam, "the Qur'an", and the second is the teachings and precedents of the Prophet Muhammad, which is called "the Sunnah". In addition, there is a consensus of opinion and Islamic rulings regarding the medieval Islamic institutions of learning that specialize in interpreting the divine law (fiqh). These rulings, based on the interpretation of the Qur'an and Sunnah, are considered to be one of the sources of Islamic law which take on different forms known as 'the striving of a legitimate scholar to reach a religious verdict' (ijtihad), Islamic rulings dealing with issues not present at the time of the Prophet (fatwa), consensus of the earliest generations of Muslims (ijma), rulings based on analogy (qiyas), other sources of fiqh such as unrestricted public interest (al-Maslahah al-Mursalah), and custom (urf), which are called Usul al-Fiqh rules. Broadly speaking, the body of Islamic Law is divided into three main categories:

- Worship and rituals matters (ibadat);
- Civil and other legal obligations which cover, in a contemporary sense, commercial, constitutional, administrative, labor, employment, family, and civil laws (mua'malat); and,
- Punishments (uqubat).

To learn the law of Saudi Arabia, one turns first to the "fiqh", or Islamic Law. In other words, one turns not to state legislation or court precedents but to the opinions, the "ijtihad," of religious-legal scholars from both the past and the present who, by their piety and learning, have become qualified to interpret the scriptural sources and to derive laws. Most of the Islamic Law applied today, according to the recognized Islamic schools of law, can be found in books of "fiqh" that were written by Muslim Scholars (ulama) over a period of nearly fourteen centuries. Judges in Saudi Arabia consult these books (especially those books considered the primary sources in each Islamic school of thought) to make their rulings. Professor Frank Vogel, who studied the Saudi Legal System, states:

> Except for the Qur'an, all of the . sources of Saudi law, even the collection of the Prophet conducts, were compiled or written by scholars, the 'ulama.' The authority of 'ulama' to produce these texts rests on their status as scholars, and not on any official or formal positions they may hold such as judge or instructor in a scholarly institution.From these sources, then, other 'ulama', such as the Mufti and judges of Saudi Arabia, produce fiqh to guide others or to decide disputes. Ordinarily, it does take a scholar to evaluate these sources and create a ruling. A non-scholar is under conscientious obligation to seek the advice of a person

more skilled than he or she in interpretation, either obtaining his fatwa or consulting a book where he has recorded his opinions.

The application of Islamic law in Saudi Arabian Courts is mainly based on the rules of Islamic Shari'ah in accordance with the interpretation of the Hanbali School-the fourth orthodox school of law within Sunni Islam. The existence of one school of Islamic law in the Kingdom, however, did not remove differences in rulings and procedures, leading to further difficulties in obtaining an authoritative legal opinion. The diversity of interpretations continued due to variations in opinions and philosophies amongst the scholars of the Hanabli School of Islamic law.

In order to try to rectify the inconsistencies, the Judicial Board of Saudi Arabia issued a resolution in June 1928, affirmed by the King, proclaiming that rulings are to be in accordance with the established decisions found in the school of Islamic law of Imam Ahmed ibn Hanbal because of the ease and clarity of its references and books, the consensus of those scholars who follow this school, and the presentation of evidence addressing whichever problems happen to be under consideration

The Judicial Board declared particular publications within the Hanabali School as the official and main sources for Shari'ah Courts in its jurisdiction. Paragraph (C) of the resolution asserted that judges were to rely on the two late Hanbali authoritative works authored, by the famous Hanbali jurist Mansur ibn Yunus al-Bahuti al-Hanbali (1052H/1642):

(1) Sharh Muntaha al-Iradat (Explanation of Muntaha al-Iradat Manual); and,

(2) Sharh al-Iqna (Explanation of al-Iqna Manual).

In seeking out a resolution to a given problem, Judges ought to follow the answer that either both books agreed upon or which was provided by one of them and not the other. However, in the event of a discrepancy, Sharh al-Muntaha prevails; when neither of the two books is available, nor do they provide an answer to a given problem, judges revert to abridgment or summarization:

(1) Zad al-Mustaqni fi Ikhtisar al-Muqni (A Summary of al-Muqni, and al-Iqna) by Sharf al-Din Abu al-Naja al-Hajjawi (968H/1560); and,

(2) Dalil al-Talib li Nayl al-matalib, (A Summary of Muntaha al-Iradat) by Mar'i ibn Yusuf al-Karmi (961H/1554).

If an answer still cannot be obtained, then other Hanbali law books may be consulted and decisions issued according to the prevailing opinion they contain.

In conformity with this resolution, a Royal Decree, issued in 1349H (1930), stated that, "it will be sufficient to rule by what is found in the authentic law books of the school of Imam Ahmed ibn Hanbal, which can be applied without the meeting of court members, while judgment with no basis in these text will require an obligatory meeting."

In addition, there are cases where the teaching of other Sunni schools ought to or may be-depending on the circumstances-followed by the judge entertaining such cases. The previous resolution quickly included an important exception in paragraph (b), where the courts would apply the opinion of other schools of Islamic law if they determined that it was better to apply it so as to reach a more appropriate ruling which would best serve the public welfare.

To date, there is no formal code, legislation, or act passed by the two Councils (the Council of Ministry, and the Shura Council), as well as the King, which codifies criminal law, family law, heritage or inheritance, and many aspects of the Islamic law of contracts. It is worth mentioning that there is a controversy over "codification of Islamic Law", which has been opposed strongly by traditionalists who support the application of Islamic Law as stated in the Qur'an and the Sunnah, and understood by the Prophet's noble companions, and with the help of explanations provided in traditional jurisprudential sources. Although that is not the subject of this research, from the scholars' point of view, limiting the number of scientific sources from the divine law (fiqh), which were leading to confusion and varying opinions when they were applied in court rulings, was an initial step toward codification as well as an important step toward uniting the Justice System in Saudi Arabia.

In addition to Islamic Law, the development of the Saudi Council of Ministers in 1958 into a formal decision-making body-with legislative, executive and administrative functions-lead to a massive introduction of modern laws and regulations into the Saudi legal system covering various areas in the fields of both public and private law. Many of these legal codes have been influenced by other legal systems, especially the Egyptian and the French legal systems. A major example of the influence of French law in the area of private law is the Saudi Corporation Law enacted in (1385H/1965), which was transmitted to the Saudi legal system through "the Egyptian code which was directly patterned after the French company law before the amendments of 24 July 1966." The Saudi Law of Criminal Procedure contains several provisions that have been borrowed from Egyptian and French law. In the area of public law, several codes were enacted governing public finance, customs, ports, mines, etc.

In general, the adoptions of modern statutory provisions are lawful and enforceable as long as they do not contravene divine law. As mentioned previously, modern statutory laws and regulations can only be introduced and adopted through the doctrine of public interest (al-Maslahah al-Mursalah) as a basis for rule making. The right is exercised only were there is no clear text present in Islamic law to regulate a given issue.

Article 67 of the Basic System states that, the regulatory authority lays down regulations and motions to meet the interests of the state or remove what is bad in its affairs, in accordance with the Islamic Shari'ah." Because under Islamic Shari'ah God is sovereign and has the ultimate right to legislate, Saudi Arabia use the Arabic term "Nizam" which means "Regulations" in reference to statutory laws that are autonomous, but not fully independent of Islamic Shari'ah rules and courts. "The Arabic word [Qanun] which means 'law' is not used in Saudi Arabia.because [it] represents secular or temporal law 'and is therefore prohibited by the [Shari'ah]."

The Saudi legal materials are composed of Royal Decrees, regulations, executive regulations, lists, codes, rules, procedures, international treaties and agreements, ministerial resolutions, ministerial decisions, circular memoranda, explanatory memoranda, documents, ministerial decisions, and resolutions which have been designated by the government as the official sources of Saudi Arabian law. As mentioned previously, no Statutory Laws or regulations, treaties, international agreements or concessions may be enacted or amended unless they are approved by Royal Decrees after having been studied by both the Council of Ministers and the Shura Council.

The King also can enact rules or regulations independently by issuing Royal Orders. The King possesses this essential regulatory role in support of Shari'ah rule. In spite of the divine origin of Islamic Shari'ah, the head of the Islamic state, according to the Islamic jurists, has the authority to enact laws, either directly or by way of interpretation, so as to meet growing social needs, address developmental concerns, and protect the public interest. The King used his legislative authority to issue the Constitutional Documents that were enacted between 1992 and 1994, which include:

The Basic System;
The Shura Council Law;
The Council of Ministers Law (Amended in 1993); and,
The Regional Law.

All Saudi statutory laws and regulations are published in the Official Gazette (Umm Al-Qura). Private publishers have also published all the primary sources of the Sunni-Schools of thoughts, and most of the Saudi statutory laws and regulations in multiple volumes.

A researcher's first choice should be the printed resources. However, it is worth mentioning that the heritage books of Islamic Law and jurisprudence are now available in digital format, which makes accessible, through digital technology, a significant body of primary sources related to Islamic Law and its related sciences-including all primary sources of the Hanbali School of jurisprudence. Many independent online services provide lawyers, judges, scholars, and researchers with the full texts of all primary sources relating to the Sunni schools of thought (see research links below). As a result of modern search engine technology, the electronic versions of these primary sources provide an easy tool by which to search for one subject among hundreds of books. This enables interested parties to examine a variety of opinions in one or more Islamic schools of thought.

In addition, the Saudi National Center for Documents and Archivescollects, organizes, preserves, and provides access to all statutory laws, and regulations of the Kingdom of Saudi Arabia. The Center website provides expansive coverage of the full text of the Arabic versions of the Saudi statutory laws and regulations, along with mutual, regional and international conventions and treaties.

Moreover, the Bureau of Experts-which is affiliated with the Council of Ministers-has been translating several major Saudi statutory laws. The Bureau of Experts English online database is one of the officially authorized government sites that offers a reliable English translation of Saudi Arabia statutory laws and regulations. All translated Saudi Statutory Laws are categorized into the following categories; links for the full text versions of laws and regulations are provided under each category:

1- Basic Laws
2- Media, Culture and Publishing Laws
3- National Security, Civil Status and Criminal Laws
4- Commerce, Economy and Investment Laws
5- Protocol and Ceremonies Laws
6- Education and Science Laws
7- Hajj and Islamic Affairs Laws
8- Municipal Services, Lay Out, and Urban Development Laws
9- Civil Service Laws
10- Military Service and Affairs Laws
11- Judicial Authority and human rights Laws.
12- Tourism and Archaeological Sites Law
13- Youth and Sports Laws
14- Health Laws
15- Energy, Industry and Mining Laws

16- Labor and Civil Care Laws
17- General Financial Laws
18- Transportation and Communication Laws
19- Water, Agriculture and Biota Resources Laws
20- Other Laws

Furthermore, all official Saudi Arabian ministry and agency websites provide an expansive coverage of the full texts of most of the statutory laws and regulations related to the affairs of each body (see Ministries and Agencies links below).

Other available law sources include unofficial websites whose objective it is to publish accurate, reliable information and knowledge on both Saudi and Islamic laws in Arabic and English. One of the major online resources and legal research tools addressing Saudi Laws is the Arab Lawyers Network. This legal Internet service provides lawyers, judges, experts, and researchers with an up-to-date Encyclopedia of Saudi laws, regulations, related resolutions, instructions and decisions in both Arabicand English, in addition to journalistic folders concerned with daily follow-ups to the legal news and issues raised in the Kingdom. Other online services provide extensive coverage of Saudi Arabian publications and legal information, as well as useful resources for acquiring research materials in both Arabic and English (see research links below). However, it is worth noting that in Saudi Courts the official language is Arabic. Languages other than Arabic may be used, but the Arabic text will always prevail in court.

For additional analytical, business and investment opportunities information,
please contact Global Investment & Business Center, USA
at (202) 546-2103. Fax: (202) 546-3275. E-mail: ibpusa3@gmail.com
Global Business and Legal Information Databank: www.ibpus.com

STRATEGIC AND LEGAL INFORMATION FOR CONDUCTING BUSINESS

GOVERNMENT STRUCTURE

Saudi Arabia is an Arab and Islamic sovereign monarchy. The Custodian of the Two Holy Mosques, King Fahd Bin Abdul Aziz acts as the Prime Minister overseeing the ministries and the different departments of state. Crown Prince Abdullah Bin Abdul Aziz is the Deputy Prime Minister of Saudi Arabia and Commander of its National Guard. Prince Sultan Bin Abdul Aziz is the Second Deputy Prime Minister, Minister of Defense and Aviation, and Inspector General. Other ministers are appointed by the King and are responsible for implementing governmental policies which relate to their particular ministry. The Council of Ministers, headed by the King, is responsible for drafting and overseeing implementation of the internal, external, economic, financial, social, educational, defense, and other general matters of the state.

COUNCIL OF MINISTERS

Members - Saudi Council of Ministers

Portfolio	Minister	Since
Prime Minister	King Salman bin Abdulaziz Al Saud	2015
First Deputy Prime Minister and Minister of Interior	Mohammad bin Nayef bin Abdulaziz Al Saud	2015
Second Deputy Prime Minister and Minister of Defense	Mohammad bin Salman bin Abdulaziz Al Saud	2015
Minister of the National Guard	Mutaib bin Abdullah bin Abdulaziz Al Saud	2013
Minister of Foreign Affairs	Adel bin Ahmed Al Jubeir	2015
Minister of Islamic Affairs, Endowments, Call and Guidance	Saleh bin Abdulaziz Al Ash-Shaikh	2015
Minister of Education	Ahmed bin Mohammed Al-Issa	2015
Minister of Justice	Waleed bin Mohammad Al Samaani	2015
Minister of Petroleum and Mineral Resources	Ali bin Ibrahim Al Naimi	1995
Minister of Transport	Abdullah bin Abdulrahman Al Muqbel	2014
Minister of Commerce and Industry	Tawfiq bin Fawzan Al Rabiah	2012
Minister of Social Affairs	Majid bin Abdullah Al Qasabi	2015
Minister of Economy and Planning	Adel bin Mohammad Fakeih	2015
Minister of Health	Khalid bin Abdulaziz Al Faleh	2015
Minister of Culture and Information	Adel bin Zaid Al Toraifi	2015
Minister of Labor	Mufarrej bin Saad Al-Haqbani	2015
Minister of Civil Service	Khalid bin Abdullah Al Araj	2015
Minister of Finance	Ibrahim bin Abdulaziz Al Assaf	1996
Minister of Water and Electricity	Abdullah bin Abdul Rahman Al Hussein	2004
Minister of Agriculture	Abdulrahman bin Abdulmuhsen Al Fadhly	2015
Minister of Hajj	Bandar bin Mohammad Al Hajjar	2011
Minister of Housing	Majed bin Abdullah Al Hogail	2015
Minister of Communication and Information	Mohamed bin Ibrahim Al Suwaiyel	2015

For additional analytical, business and investment opportunities information, please contact Global Investment & Business Center, USA at (202) 546-2103. Fax: (202) 546-3275. E-mail: ibpusa3@gmail.com Global Business and Legal Information Databank: www.ibpus.com

Technology		
Minister of Municipal and Rural Affairs	Abdullatif bin Abdulmalik Al AsShaikh	2015
Minister of State	Abdulaziz bin Abdullah Al Saud	2015
Minister of State for Foreign Affairs	Nizar bin Obaid Madani	1997
Minister of State	Muttlab bin Abdullah Al Nafissa	1995
Minister of State for Shura Affairs	Mohammad bin Faisal Abu Saq	2014
Minister of State	Essam bin Saad bin Saeed	2015
Minister of State	Saad bin Khalid Al Jabry	2015
Minister of State	Mohammad bin Abdulmalik Al AsShaikh	2015
Minister of State	Khalid bin Abdulrahman Al Eissa	2015
Minister of State	Musaad bin Mohammed Al Aiban	1995

OIL IN SAUDI ARABIA

HISTORICAL BACKGROUND AND ARAMCO

The history of oil in the Middle East and the Arab world goes back many centuries during which seepages of oil and tar were used for a multitude of purposes. A mission of German experts in 1871 (1288 AH) visited Iraq and reported plentiful supplies of oil. In 1907 (1324/25 AH), another mission said Iraq was a veritable 'lake of petroleum'. In Iran, oil was found in quantity in 1908 (1325/26 AH). The major Iraqi field was discovered at Kirkuk in 1927 (1345/46 AH) and began producing oil in commercial quantities; oil flowed abroad in 1934 (1352/53 AH). In 1932 (1350/51 AH), petroleum was discovered in Bahrain.

In 1923 (1341/42 AH), a New Zealander, Major Frank Holmes, acting on behalf of a British syndicate, the "Eastern and General", obtained the first Saudi Arabian oil concession from King Abdul Aziz (Ibn Saud), an exclusive concession to explore for oil and other minerals in an area of more than 30,000 square miles in the Eastern Region.

The concession, at a bargain price of 2,000 pounds sterling per annum to be paid in gold, came to nothing. The Eastern and General Syndicate were unable to persuade any oil company to invest sufficient funds for exploration and, after paying the 2,000 pounds sterling for two years, they ceased to fulfill their part of the agreement.

The King waited for three years and then, in 1928 (1346/47 AH), revoked the concession. From the viewpoint of Major Frank Holmes and his London-based syndicate, this episode must represent one of the world's greatest lost opportunities.

In 1930 (1348/49 AH), King Abdul Aziz (Ibn Saud) was faced with a substantial fall in revenues, resulting from a drop in the number of pilgrims caused by the world-wide recession.

The King invited a wealthy American businessman and philanthropist, Charles R. Crane, to visit the Kingdom. Crane had already shown an eagerness to meet the King. In the course of Crane's visit, it was agreed that he should send a mining engineer to conduct a survey of Saudi Arabia to assess the Kingdom's water, mineral and oil resources.

In 1931 (1349/50 AH), the engineer, Karl Twitchell, arrived in Jeddah. Twitchell was a civil and mining engineer, with Middle East experience, having worked for Crane in the Yemen. After an extensive survey of many months, Twitchell submitted his report to the King. A key finding was

For additional analytical, business and investment opportunities information,
please contact Global Investment & Business Center, USA
at (202) 546-2103. Fax: (202) 546-3275. E-mail: ibpusa3@gmail.com
Global Business and Legal Information Databank: www.ibpus.com

that the geological formations in eastern region around Dhahran strongly indicated the presence of oil.

While Twitchell's survey was proceeding, Socal, the Standard Oil Company of California, which had sent two geologists to Bahrain, was becoming increasingly interested in the oil potential of the mainland of Saudi Arabia.

In 1933 (1351/52 AH), Twitchell arrived in Jeddah with a Socal representative, Lloyd Hamilton. Despite some impressive competition from the Iraq Petroleum Company, Hamilton succeeded in negotiating a concession for exclusive rights to oil in the eastern region.

The agreement which had a 60-year life (later to be extended for a further six years), received royal assent in July, 1933 (1352 AH). Thus, the Kingdom broke what had been virtually a British monopoly of oil concessions in that part of the world.

Initial exploration produced disappointing results but in 1935 (1353/54 AH) a well drilled in Dhahran found indications of oil in commercial quantities. The following year, Socal, now operating through its subsidiary the Californian Arabian Standard Oil Company (Casoc), put into effect Article 32 of the 1933 (1351/52 AH) agreement and sold one-half of its concession interest to the Texas Oil Company. Oil production began in 1938 (1356/57 AH), by which time the vast extent of the oil reserves was becoming apparent.

With this confirmation of the commercial viability of the oil reserves, another supplementary agreement was signed on 31st May, 1938 (1357 AH), adding six years to the 60-year life of the original agreement. This second instrument, known as the Supplemental Agreement, enlarged Socal's concession area by almost 80,000 square miles. It also included rights in the Saudi government's half interest in the two neutral zones shared with Iraq and Kuwait.

In 1944 (1363/64 AH), the Californian Arabian Standard Oil Company was re-named the Arabian American Oil Company - Aramco.

In 1948 (1367/68 AH), Aramco invoked an Article of the Supplemental Agreement of 1939 (1357/58 AH) by selling a 30% interest to Standard Oil of New Jersey and a 10% interest to Socony Vacuum.

The redistributed ownership of Aramco was then Standard Oil of California (now known as California Standard) - 30%; Texas Oil Company (now known as Texaco) - 30%; Standard Oil of New Jersey (later known as Exxon) - 30%; and Socony Vacuum (later known as Mobil Oil) - the last 10%.

(In 1998, Exxon and Mobil signed a definitive agreement to merge and form a new company called Exxon Mobil Corporation.)

It was inconceivable in the political and economic context of the second half of the twentieth century that so important a national resource as oil, representing as it did most of the country's national income, should remain under the ownership of foreign companies.

In 1973 (1392/93 AH), the Saudi Arabian government took a 25% stake in Aramco. In 1974 (1393/94 AH), this share was increased to 60% and in 1980 (1400/01 AH) it was amicably agreed that Aramco should become 100% Saudi-owned, with the date of ownership back-dated to 1976 (1396/97 AH).

For additional analytical, business and investment opportunities information, please contact Global Investment & Business Center, USA at (202) 546-2103. Fax: (202) 546-3275. E-mail: ibpusa3@gmail.com Global Business and Legal Information Databank: www.ibpus.com

On 6th April, 1989, The New York Times reported:

"At a quiet dinner a few days ago, the last American to preside over the world's largest oil company handed over power to its first Saudi boss. The Saudi, a man who started working there more than 40 years ago as an office boy, earned engineering and management degrees as he climbed up the ladder.

"The transfer of the Arabian American Oil Company from the American John J. Kelberer, to the Saudi Ali Naimi, took place at Hamilton House, named after an American lawyer who negotiated the first agreement that opened the Kingdom to American oil companies 56 years ago and led to the formation of Aramco, as the company is known to the world.

"While the formal transfer of power was low-key, in the Aramco tradition, the event was one of great moment both in Saudi and international terms."

Thus the oil of the Kingdom which had lain for so long beneath Saudi Arabia's deserts and which then, for decades, had been exploited by foreign interests became at last a national resource controlled and managed by those under whose soil it lay.

SAUDI ARABIA: OIL INDUSTRY PROFILE

Saudi Arabia has 16% of the world's proved oil reserves, is the largest exporter of total petroleum liquids in the world, and maintains the world's largest crude oil production capacity.[1]

Saudi Arabia is the world's largest holder of crude oil proved reserves and was the largest exporter of total petroleum liquids in 2013. In 2013, Saudi Arabia was the world's second-largest petroleum liquids producer behind the United States and was the world's second-largest crude oil producer behind Russia. Saudi Arabia's economy remains heavily dependent on petroleum. Petroleum exports accounted for 85% of total Saudi export revenues in 2013, according to the Organization of the Petroleum Exporting Countries (OPEC)'s *Annual Statistical Bulletin 2014*.

With the largest oil projects nearing completion, Saudi Arabia is expanding its natural gas, refining, petrochemicals, and electric power industries. Saudi Arabia's oil and natural gas operations are dominated by Saudi Aramco, the national oil and gas company and the world's largest oil company in terms of production. Saudi Arabia's Ministry of Petroleum and Mineral Resources and the Supreme Council for Petroleum and Minerals have oversight of the oil and natural gas sector and Saudi Aramco.

ENERGY CONSUMPTION

Saudi Arabia is the largest consumer of petroleum in the Middle East, particularly in the area of transportation fuels and direct crude oil burn for power generation. Domestic consumption growth has been spurred by the economic boom as a result of historically high oil prices and large fuel subsidies. According to the BP Statistical Review of World Energy 2014, Saudi Arabia was the world's 12th largest consumer of total primary energy in 2013 at 9 quadrillion British thermal units (Btu), of which about 60% was petroleum-based, with natural gas accounting for the rest. The King Abdullah City for Atomic and Renewable Energy (K.A. CARE) program seeks to ensure that half[2] of the electricity generated in Saudi Arabia comes from renewable sources by 2032, when forecasted electricity demand growth will necessitate power generation capacity to increase to 120 gigawatts (GW). The increased use of renewable sources allows for more oil and natural gas originally allocated for domestic power needs to be freed up for export. In the interim, Saudi Arabia is participating in the Gulf Cooperation Council's efforts to link the power grids of member countries to reduce shortages during peak power periods.

PETROLEUM AND OTHER LIQUID FUELS

More than half of Saudi Arabia's oil reserves are contained in eight fields. The giant Ghawar field, the world's largest oil field with estimated remaining reserves of 75 billion barrels, has more proved oil reserves than all but seven other countries.

RESERVES

According to the *Oil & Gas Journal* (OGJ), Saudi Arabia had approximately 266 billion barrels of proved oil reserves[3] (in addition to 2.5 billion barrels in the Saudi-Kuwaiti shared Neutral Zone, half of the total reserves in the Neutral Zone) as of January 1, 2014, amounting to 16% of proved world oil reserves. Although Saudi Arabia has about 100 major oil and gas fields, more than half of its oil reserves are contained in eight fields in the northeast portion of the country.[4] The giant Ghawar field is the world's largest oil field in terms of production and total remaining reserves. The Ghawar field has estimated remaining proved oil reserves of 75 billion barrels,[5] more than all but seven other countries.

CONSUMPTION

Saudi Arabia is the largest oil-consuming nation in the Middle East. Saudi Arabia consumed 2.9 million barrels per day (bbl/d) of oil in 2013, almost double the consumption in 2000, because of strong industrial growth and subsidized prices. Contributing to this growth is rising direct burn of crude oil for power generation, which has reached an average of 0.7 million bbl/d from 2009 to 2013 during the months of June to September, according to the Joint Oil Data Initiative (JODI), and the use of natural gas liquids (NGL) for petrochemical production. The current president and Chief Executive Officer of Saudi Aramco, Khalid al-Falih, said that domestic liquids demand was on pace to reach more than 8 million bbl/d of oil equivalent by 2030 if there were no improvements in energy efficiency.

PRODUCTION

Saudi Arabia produced on average 11.6 million bbl/d of total petroleum liquids in 2013, of which 9.6 million bbl/d[6] was crude oil production and 2 million bbl/d was non-crude liquids production. Total petroleum liquids production declined 0.13 million bbl/d from 2012, the first decline since 2009. Saudi Arabia decreased its crude oil production in 2013 to accommodate non-OPEC production growth, mainly from the United States and, to a lesser extent, Canada.

Saudi Arabia maintains the world's largest crude oil production capacity, estimated to reach about 12 million bbl/d at the end of 2014, and the country is subject to OPEC production quotas. Of this capacity, about 300,000 bbl/d is Saudi Arabia's share of the production in the Neutral Zone. Non-crude liquids, which are not subject to OPEC quotas or production targets, are produced at full capacity. There are currently no plans to increase oil production capacity. Saudi Arabia's long-term goal is to further develop its lighter crude oil potential and maintain current levels of production by offsetting declines in mature fields with newer fields.

Saudi crude streams

For additional analytical, business and investment opportunities information, please contact Global Investment & Business Center, USA at (202) 546-2103. Fax: (202) 546-3275. E-mail: ibpusa3@gmail.com Global Business and Legal Information Databank: www.ibpus.com

Saudi Arabia produces a range of crude oils, from heavy to super light. Of Saudi Arabia's total crude oil production capacity, more than 70% is considered light gravity, with the remaining crude oil considered medium or heavy gravity.[7] The country is moving to reduce the share of the latter two grades. Lighter grades generally are produced onshore, while medium and heavy grades come mainly from offshore fields. Most Saudi oil production, except for the Extra Light and Super Light crude oil types, is considered sour, containing relatively high levels of sulfur. Saudi Aramco said that its fields do not require the use of enhanced oil recovery techniques, although fields in the Neutral Zone could require steam flooding. The Ministry of Petroleum and Mineral Resources estimates that oil fields in Saudi Arabia have decline rates no higher than 2% per year.[8] Saudi Aramco has stated that it will conduct additional drilling at existing fields to help compensate for the natural declines from the mature fields.

Major oil fields in Saudi Arabia		
Field	Location	Capacity
Ghawar	onshore	5.8 million bbl/d of Arab Light crude
Safaniya	offshore	1.2 million bbl/d of Arab Heavy crude
Khurais	onshore	1.2 million bbl/d of Arab Light crude. Plans to expand capacity by 0.30 million bbl/d by 2017.
Manifa	offshore	0.90 million bbl/d of Arab Heavy crude oil after completion at end of 2014. Production will be used to offset declines in mature fields.
Shaybah	onshore	0.75 million bbl/d of Arab Extra Light. Plans to expand capacity by 0.25 million bbl/d by 2017.
Qatif	onshore	0.50 bbl/d of Arab Light crude
Khursaniyah	onshore	0.50 bbl/d Arab Light crude
Zuluf	offshore	0.50 bbl/d of Arab Medium crude
Abqaiq	onshore	0.40 bbl/d Arab Extra Light crude
Source: Saudi Aramco, Arab Oil and Gas Journal		

SAUDI-KUWAIT NEUTRAL ZONE

The Saudi-Kuwait Neutral Zone (also called the Divided Zone) is an area of 2,230 square miles between the borders of Saudi Arabia and Kuwait. The Neutral Zone contains an estimated 5 billion barrels of total proved oil reserves that are divided equally between the two countries.

According to the *Arab Oil and Gas Journal*, total crude oil production in the Neutral Zone is about 520,000 bbl/d.[9] Total crude oil production capacity in the Neutral Zone is estimated to be 600,000 bbl/d. Within the Neutral Zone, Japan's Arabian Oil Co. (AOC) traditionally operated the two offshore fields of Khafji and Hout, but in February 2000, AOC lost the concession, and Aramco took over operation of the former AOC fields. Currently the Khafji field produces about 300,000 bbl/d[10] of crude oil, while the Hout field has not been operational since 2005. Saudi Arabian Chevron and Kuwait Gulf Oil Company (KGOC) operate the Wafra, Humma, South Fuwaris, and South Umm Gudair fields in the Neutral Zone. The first phase of a steam injection project currently in discussion to boost crude oil production in Wafra by 80,000 bbl/d will cost $5 billion. The project is expected to increase crude oil production by a total of 500,000 bbl/d when it is completed, according to the Middle East Economic Survey.

For additional analytical, business and investment opportunities information, please contact Global Investment & Business Center, USA at (202) 546-2103. Fax: (202) 546-3275. E-mail: ibpusa3@gmail.com Global Business and Legal Information Databank: www.ibpus.com

PROCESSING

Saudi Aramco operates the world's largest oil processing facility and crude stabilization plant in the world at Abqaiq, in eastern Saudi Arabia, with a crude processing capacity of more than 7 million bbl/d. The plant processes the majority of Arab Extra Light and Arab Light crude oils, as well as NGL. The facility's infrastructure includes pumping stations, gas-oil separation plants (GOSPs), hydro-desulphurization units, and an extensive network of pipelines that connects the plant to the ports of Ras al-Ju'aymah, Ras Tanura, and Yanbu (for NGL). According to the *Arab Oil and Gas Journal*, more than 70% of Saudi crude is processed[12] at Abqaiq before export or delivery to refineries. The facility was the target of a terrorist attack in 2006 (see Security Issues Section).

REFINING/PETROCHEMICALS

According to OGJ, Saudi Arabia has eight domestic refineries, with a combined crude throughput capacity of about 2.5 million bbl/d[13] (of which Aramco's share is approximately 1.8 million bbl/d).[14] Saudi Arabia continues to integrate its refinery projects with large petrochemicals complexes, in what has been described as the creation of petrochemical cities.

Planned domestic refineries or refineries under development include:

- Yanbu Aramco Sinopec Refining Company (YASREF) Limited, a joint venture with Chinese Petrochemical Corporation (Sinopec), will be able to process up to 400,000 bbl/d of Arab Heavy crude oil from the planned Manifa oil development by the third quarter of 2014.
- Saudi Aramco is developing its 400,000 bbl/d Jazan refinery project in southwest Saudi Arabia. It will be able to process Arab Heavy and Arab Medium crude oil by late 2016.
- Saudi Aramco is studying an expansion of its integrated Petro Rabigh Refinery and petrochemical joint venture, which currently has a capacity of 400,000 bbl/d.

Saudi Arabia has also initiated a number of clean fuels projects to provide more ultra-low sulfur diesel fuel. The Yanbu refinery, jointly owned by Saudi Aramco and Mobil Yanbu Refining Company (a subsidiary of ExxonMobil), was upgraded to produce cleaner fuels. Similar upgrades were completed on the Jubail refinery jointly owned by Saudi Aramco and Shell Saudi Arabia Refining.

OVERSEAS REFINING INVESTMENTS

Saudi Arabia has 2.4 million bbl/d of refining capacity overseas through joint and equity ventures in facilities in the United States, China (in Fujian Province with ExxonMobil and Sinopec), South Korea (with S-Oil), and Japan (with Showa Shell). Saudi Aramco's share of overseas ventures is 0.9 million bbl/d. In the United States, Saudi Aramco and partner Royal Dutch Shell own three Motiva joint-venture refineries in Louisiana and Texas. The three facilities currently have a total capacity of about 1 million bbl/d. Saudi Aramco owns 50% of Motiva through a subsidiary, Saudi Refining. According to the Middle East Economic Survey, Saudi Aramco is expected to invest $100 billion domestically and overseas to expand its refining capacity to 8-10 million bbl/d.

Existing refineries in Saudi Arabia

Name	Company	Crude distillation capacity (thousand bbl/d)
Ras Tanura	Saudi Aramco	550
Yanbu	Saudi Aramco	250
Riyadh	Saudi Aramco	122
Jeddah	Saudi Aramco	85
SATORP Jubail	Saudi Aramco, Total S.A.	400
Petro Rabigh	Saudi Aramco, Sumitomo Chemical	400
SAMREF Yanbu	Saudi Aramco, Mobil Yanbu Refining Company Inc. (ExxonMobil)	400
SASREF Jubail	Saudi Aramco, Shell Saudi Arabia Refining, Ltd.	305

Source: Saudi Aramco, Oil and Gas Journal

SECURITY ISSUES

The Saudi petroleum pipeline and export network (and energy sector in general) has been a terrorist target in the past. In February 2006, Saudi security prevented an attempted suicide bomb attack at the Abqaiq petroleum processing facility, after Al-Qaeda leadership called for renewed attacks against the country's economic backbone. Following the 2006 incident, the government increased the National Guard and military security force to approximately 20,000 guards, in addition to the 5,000 guards employed directly by Saudi Aramco. In addition to direct security, Saudi Arabia is known to ensure export security by maintaining redundancy (i.e., multiple options for transportation and export) in its oil system, in part as a form of indirect security against any one facility being disabled.

OIL EXPORTS AND SHIPPING

Saudi Arabia is the second-largest petroleum exporter to the United States, after Canada.

EXPORTS

According to the Global Trade Information Services (GTIS), Saudi Arabia exported an estimated 7.7 million bbl/d of crude oil in 2013. Asia received an estimated 68% of Saudi Arabia's crude oil exports as well as most of its refined petroleum products.

Saudi Arabia exported an average of 1.5 million bbl/d of total petroleum liquids to the United States in the first quarter of 2014, an increase of 0.4 million bbl/d from the first quarter of 2013. Since 2012, Saudi Arabia has been the second-largest petroleum exporter annually, after Canada, to the United States. In 2013, after the United States, the next four top importers of Saudi crude and petroleum products according to GTIS were Japan (1.2 million bbl/d), China (1.1 million bbl/d), South Korea (0.9 million bbl/d), and India (0.8 million bbl/d).

MAJOR PORTS

Saudi Arabia has three primary oil export terminals:

- The port of Ras Tanura on the Persian Gulf has an average handling capacity of 3.4 million bbl/d,[16] and it handles most of Saudi Arabia's exports.
- The Ras al-Ju'aymah facility on the Persian Gulf has an average handling capacity of about 3 million bbl/d,[17] and because of the availability of various Single Point Mooring buoys, the largest oil tankers can be accommodated for crude loadings.
- The Yanbu terminal on the Red Sea, from which most of the remaining volumes are exported, has an average handling capacity of 1.3 million bbl/d.[18]

In addition to these primary export terminals, Saudi Arabia has other smaller ports including Ras al-Khafji, Jubail, and Jeddah.

MAJOR DOMESTIC PETROLEUM PIPELINES

Saudi Aramco operates more than 12,000 miles of crude and petroleum product pipelines throughout the country, including two major pipelines:

- Saudi Arabia has the 746-mile-long East-West Pipeline, also known as Petroline, which runs across Saudi Arabia from its Abqaiq complex to the Red Sea. The Petroline system consists of two pipelines with a total nameplate capacity of about 4.8 million bbl/d. The 56-inch pipeline has a nameplate capacity of 3 million bbl/d, and its current throughput is about 2 million bbl/d. In recent years, the 48-inch pipeline had been operating as a natural gas pipeline, but Saudi Arabia moved to convert it back to an oil pipeline. The switch could increase Saudi Arabia's spare oil pipeline capacity to bypass the Strait of Hormuz from 1 million bbl/d to 2.8 million bbl/d, which is only attainable if the system is able to operate at its full nameplate capacity.
- Running parallel to the Petroline is the 290,000-bbl/d Abqaiq-Yanbu NGL pipeline, which serves petrochemical plants in Yanbu.[20]

A 236-mile multi-products line between Dhahran in the Eastern Province and Riyadh and a smaller 220-mile multi-products line between Riyadh and Qassim to the north were also built in the 1980s.

INTERNATIONAL PETROLEUM PIPELINES

Saudi Aramco does not operate any major functioning international pipelines.

- The Trans-Arabian Pipeline (Tapline), built in 1947 to transport crude oil from Qaisumah through Jordon to Sidon, Lebanon, has been closed, in part, since 1984. The portion of the pipeline that runs to Jordan was closed in 1990.
- The Iraqi Pipeline in Saudi Arabia (IPSA) has a capacity of 1.65 million bbl/d and runs from Iraq, through Saudi Arabia parallel to the East-West Pipeline, and ends at the port of Mu'ajjiz, south of Yanbu. The pipeline was built in 1989 but was closed in 1990 during the Persian Gulf War. Saudi Arabia then seized IPSA in 2001. The portion of the pipeline that runs parallel to the East-West Pipeline was converted to transport natural gas to power plants, while the portion of the pipeline that goes north into Iraq remains a closed, inactive oil pipeline.

Saudi Arabia's only functioning international crude pipeline system is a 60-year old complex of four small underwater pipelines carrying Arabian Light crude from Saudi Arabia's Abu Safah field to Bahrain.[20] This aging pipeline system is expected to be decommissioned after the construction of a new pipeline with a capacity of 350,000 running between Abqaiq and Bahrain's refinery at Sitra. The new pipeline is expected to be completed in the third quarter of 2016.

SHIPPING

Saudi Aramco's shipping subsidiary, Vela International Marine Ltd., operates 15 Very Large Crude Carriers (VLCCs) that transport crude between the Middle East, Europe, and the U.S. Gulf Coast. Vela also operates five product tankers conducting coastal trade in the Red Sea and the Persian Gulf. Vela has a large number of VLCCs and product tankers employed on time or as spot charters. In addition to tankers, Saudi Aramco owns or leases oil storage facilities around the world, including Rotterdam (3.9 million barrels),[23] Sidi Kerir (the Sumed pipeline terminal on Egypt's Mediterranean coast), and Japan (6.3 million barrels),[24] according to the Middle East Economic Survey.

The National Shipping Company of Saudi Arabia (also known as Bahri) is a public company that owns and operates a modern fleet of 17 VLCCs, 24 chemical tankers, and other cargo ships. The Public Investment Fund (PIF) of the Saudi Arabian government holds 28% of the company's shares, while the remaining 72% are publicly traded shares held by the people of Saudi Arabia.

The Bahri and Vela companies announced in June 2012 that they signed a non-binding memorandum of understanding (MOU) to pursue the merger of their fleets and operations. Management responsibility for Saudi Aramco's VLCC transportation system would be implemented within the corporate structure of Bahri. The merger is expected to begin in 2014.[25]

CRUDE OIL PRICING

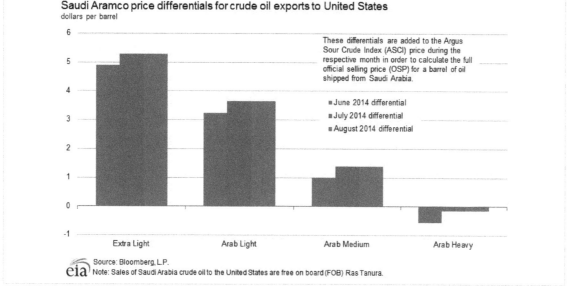

Saudi Aramco determines the official selling price (OSP) of its crude oil based on the location of the consumer and the quality of crude that is shipped. The OSP is calculated by adding a differential to a specific crude oil benchmark price. For crude oil exported to Asia, the OSP is based on the average of Dubai and Oman crude prices published by the pricing agency Platts. Crude oil exported to Europe and the Mediterranean has an OSP based on the Brent Weighted Average (BWAVE) published by Intercontinental Exchange. Crude oil exported to North America has an OSP based on the Argus Sour Crude Index (ASCI), which provides an average daily assessment on the price per barrel of a basket of medium sour crudes from the U.S. Gulf Coast including the Mars, Southern Green Canyon, and Poseidon crude streams. Saudi Arabia used West Texas Intermediate (WTI) crude oil price as the benchmark prior to 2010, but the country switched to the ASCI in part because the ASCI is viewed as being more representative of the U.S. Gulf Coast sour crude market.

NATURAL GAS

Saudi Arabia has the world's fifth-largest natural gas reserves, but natural gas production remains limited.

RESERVES

Saudi Arabia (including the Neutral Zone) had proved natural gas reserves of 291 trillion cubic feet (Tcf)[26] as of January 1, 2014, fifth largest in the world behind Russia, Iran, Qatar, and the United States, according to OGJ. The majority of natural gas fields in Saudi Arabia are associated with petroleum deposits, or are found in the same wells as the crude oil, and production increases of this type of gas remain linked to an increase in oil production.

PRODUCTION AND CONSUMPTION

Saudi Arabia does not import or export natural gas, so all consumption must be met by domestic production. Saudi Arabia's dry natural gas production and consumption was 3.6 Tcf in 2013. As of 2011, more than 70% of natural gas production consisted of associated gas from Ghawar, Safaniya, and Zuluf fields. Associated gas produced at Ghawar oil field alone accounts for more than 60% of total production.[27]

Rapid reserve development is necessary for Saudi Arabia's plans to fuel the growth of the petrochemical sector, as well as for power generation and for water desalination. All current and future gas supplies (except NGLs) reportedly remain earmarked for domestic use, in part to minimize the use of crude oil for power generation. However, natural gas production remains limited, as soaring costs of production, exploration, processing, and distribution of natural gas have squeezed supply. The National Oceanic and Atmospheric Administration (NOAA) and the World Bank Global Gas Flaring Reduction partnership estimate that in 2011, Saudi Arabia lost 131 Bcf of gas production to flaring.

PRICING

In addition to facing domestic supply shortages, Saudi Arabia has also come under pressure internationally for its subsidized natural gas prices, which are among the lowest in the Persian Gulf region. These low prices were set when most of Saudi Arabia's gas production came from inexpensive associated gas, but they are inconsistent with the much more expensive high-sulfur gas production coming from offshore fields. As of 2013, domestic natural gas prices in Saudi Arabia are set and sold to domestic consumers at a constant $0.75/million Btu (MMBtu), compared with an average of $3.73/MMBtu spot price at Henry Hub in the United States, $10.51/MMBtu in the United Kingdom,[28] and $15.96/MMBtu in Japan.[29]

For additional analytical, business and investment opportunities information,
please contact Global Investment & Business Center, USA
at (202) 546-2103. Fax: (202) 546-3275. E-mail: ibpusa3@gmail.com
Global Business and Legal Information Databank: www.ibpus.com

UPSTREAM DEVELOPMENTS AND STRATEGY

Although most of its natural gas reserves are from associated gas, Saudi Arabia is unlikely to boost its gas production from associated gas reserves in the near future because the country has completed its recent major oil development phase, and it has shifted its attention to natural gas and downstream petroleum activities.

Saudi Aramco has focused heavily on major offshore gas developments in the Persian Gulf. Exploration and development will also commence in non-producing areas such as the Red Sea, northern and western Saudi Arabia, and the Nafud basin, north of Riyadh. Saudi Aramco divides its exploration activities into three regions: the northwest portion of the country, the South Ghawar region, and the Rub al-Khali desert in the southern portion of the country.[30]Saudi Aramco also launched its Upstream Unconventional Gas program in 2011 to access Saudi Arabia's unconventional gas resources. In its 2013 Annual Review, Saudi Aramco discussed the development of a 1,000 megawatt (MW) power plant that will use shale gas for power generation.

UPSTREAM DEVELOPMENTS BY SAUDI ARAMCO

Saudi Aramco has focused on offshore fields in the Persian Gulf in its current five-year plan to expand its natural gas production. Three non-associated gas fields have been targeted:

- The Karan gas field, discovered in 2006, is Saudi Arabia's first offshore non-associated gas development. According to the *Arab Oil and Gas Journal*, the Karan field came online in 2012, producing 1.8 billion cubic feet per day (Bcf/d)[31] of sour gas that is delivered via a 68-mile subsea pipeline to the Khursaniyah gas plant.[32]
- The Arabiyah offshore gas field will have a production capacity of 1.2 Bcf/d.[33]
- The Hasbah offshore gas field will have a production capacity of 1.3 Bcf/d.[34]

According to OGJ, Saudi Arabia has a total gas processing capacity of 11.8 Bcf/d as of January 1, 2014. The Wasit Gas Program is an initiative to develop two offshore natural gas fields, the Arabiyah and Hasbah fields, and to construct the Wasit Gas Plant capable of processing 2.5 Bcf/d of natural gas from these fields. It will be one of the largest gas plants Saudi Aramco has ever built and is scheduled to be completed in 2014. However, there have been reports of delays that may push the completion date back to 2016.[35]

UPSTREAM ACTIVITIES IN CONTESTED REGIONS

Plans to develop the offshore Dorra field (located in the Saudi-Kuwait Neutral Zone) jointly with Kuwait have met opposition because a small portion of that field is also claimed by Iran, who refers to it as the Arash field. In addition, some of the maritime borders with Kuwait and Iran remain not demarcated. The Dorra field is estimated to hold 60 Tcf. In 2013, it was reported that Saudi Arabia and Kuwait put development on hold because of issues about how to transport each country's equal share of gas onto onshore facilities.[36]

UPSTREAM ACTIVITIES IN RUB AL-KHALI (KNOWN AS THE EMPTY QUARTER)

The Saudi domestic natural gas market, traditionally the sole domain of Saudi Aramco, is slowly being opened to private investment both in exploration and distribution, and to increasing competition in the market. The key component of the non-associated gas exploration strategy relies on foreign consortiums exploring for onshore gas and condensate in the Rub al-Khali, referred to as the Empty Quarter in English, which encompasses most of the southern third of Saudi Arabia.

Saudi Arabia has had four upstream joint ventures in the Empty Quarter:

- South Rub al-Khali Company, or SRAK (a venture of Saudi Aramco and Royal Dutch Shell). In 2014, Shell ended its exploration of the Empty Quarter.
- Luksar Energy Limited (a venture of Saudi Aramco and the Russian oil company, Lukoil). In 2010, Luksar gave up 90% of its exploration area to focus on a smaller area with possible gas discoveries.[37]
- Sino Saudi Gas Limited (a venture of Saudi Aramco and Sinopec).
- EniRepSa Gas Limited (a consortium of Saudi Aramco, the Italian oil company, Eni, and the Spanish oil company, Repsol). In 2012, both Eni and Repsol pulled out of the joint venture.[38]

As of July 2014, these ventures did not make significant commercial discoveries, in part because development costs would be far higher than Saudi Arabia's official domestic natural gas price.

DOMESTIC NATURAL GAS PIPELINES

Domestic demand for natural gas, particularly the delivery feedstock to petrochemical plants, has driven continued expansion of the Master Gas System (MGS), the domestic gas distribution network in Saudi Arabia first built in 1975. Prior to the MGS, all of Saudi Arabia's natural gas output was flared. The MGS feeds gas to the industrial cities including Yanbu on the Red Sea and Jubail.

To supply natural gas to the expanded gas processing facilities, several additions to the MGS are in the planning or construction phases. The largest pipeline to be built is the 132-mile conduit to the Rabigh complex and to the Yanbu NGL processing facility. Installation of four other pipelines will connect Manifa to the Khursaniyah gas plant and to Ras al-Zour for gas processing and raw power production.[39]

ELECTRICITY

Saudi Arabia plans to increase electricity generating capacity to 120 gigawatts (GW) by 2032 to meet the country's rapidly growing demand for electricity.

According to the BP Statistical Review of World Energy 2014, Saudi Arabia generated 292.2 billion kilowatthours (kWh) of electricity in 2013, 7% more than in 2012 and more than double the electricity generated in 2000. Like many developing countries in the Middle East and North Africa, Saudi Arabia faces a sharply rising demand for power. Demand is driven by population growth, a rapidly expanding industrial sector led by the development of petrochemical cities, high demand for air conditioning during the summer months, and heavily subsidized electricity rates. According to the Middle East Economic Survey, Saudi Arabia has the largest expansion plan in the Middle East for generation, with plans to increase generating capacity to 120 GW by 2032.[40] All existing generating capacity is powered by oil or natural gas, but Saudi Arabia plans to diversify fuels used for generation, in part to free up oil for export. The Saudi Electricity Company (SEC) has plans to reduce direct crude burn for electricity generation by more than 500,000 bbl/d by switching to natural gas.[41] By 2032, Saudi Arabia plans to add 41 GW of solar power, 18 GW of nuclear power, and 4 GW from other renewable sources to expand electricity supply.[42]

For additional analytical, business and investment opportunities information, please contact Global Investment & Business Center, USA at (202) 546-2103. Fax: (202) 546-3275. E-mail: ibpusa3@gmail.com Global Business and Legal Information Databank: www.ibpus.com

SECTOR ORGANIZATION

SEC is the largest provider of electricity in the Saudi Arabia, with total available generating capacity of 58 GW.[43] The state-owned Saline Water Conversion Corporation (SWCC), which provides most of the Saudi Arabia's desalinated water, is the second-largest generator of electricity. SWCC plans to rapidly increase its desalination capacity, with an equivalent increase in generation capacity. Privately-owned independent water and power plants also provide electricity to the grid. Saudi Aramco continues to build cogeneration plants to generate power for its own needs at various oil facilities.

Saudi Arabia is moving to create a more competitive power market through a series of physical and regulatory changes. In 2013, the Electricity and Cogeneration Regulatory Authority (ECRA) allowed Saudi Aramco to sell any excess electricity it produced through the intermediary of SEC, according to the *Arab Oil and Gas Journal*.[44] According to ECRA, Saudi Arabia has to invest about $140 billion through 2020 to increase SEC generating capacity to 71 GW and to satisfy increasing electricity demand.[45] In 2014, ECRA hired HSBC Holdings to explore splitting SEC into four separate power generation companies, in an attempt to privatize the electricity market.

Physical improvements will also be needed to allow more companies to sell power to the grid. SEC has ongoing and planned projects that will link power plants in the eastern, western, and southern portions of the country together. In order to meet peak demand requirements, Saudi Arabia is participating in the Gulf Cooperation Council's efforts to link the power grids of member countries. The Gulf Cooperation Council is composed of six countries. Saudi Arabia has also discussed a 3 GW cable link with Egypt, whose peak electricity demand hours vary from those of Saudi Arabia. The power link is estimated to cost $1.6 billion and bidding for the project is expected to begin in 2015.[46] Expansions to the power grid will allow Saudi Arabia to improve access to back up power generation from renewable sources.

OIL AND GAS INDUSTRIES

Organization: The Supreme Petroleum Council governs the nationalized oil industry, including Saudi Arabian Oil Co. (Saudi Aramco) crude production, refining and marketing; Saudi Basic Industries Corp. (SABIC) petrochemicals.
Major Foreign Oil Company Involvement: AOC, Mobil, Shell, Texaco
Major Ports: Jeddah, Jubail, Ras al-Khafji, Ras Tanura, Juaymah, Rabigh, Yanbu, Zuluf
Major Oil Fields: Ghawar, Safaniya, Najd, Abqaiq, Berri, Manifa, Zuluf, Shaybah, Abu Saafa, Khurusaniya
Major Pipelines (capacity - million bbl/d): Petroline (4.8), IPSA 1 (0.5), IPSA 2 (1.7), Abqaiq-Yanbu NGL line (0.4), (note: IPSA I shut since 1990)
Major Refineries (capacity, 1/1/00): Aramco - Ras Tanura 325,000 bbl/d, Rabigh 325,000 bbl/d, Yanbu 190,000 bbl/d, Riyadh 140,000 bbl/d, Jeddah 42,000 bbl/d; Aramco/Mobil - Yanbu 366,000 bbl/d; Petromin/Shell - al-Jubail 292,000 bbl/d; Arabian Oil Company - Ras al-Khafji 30,000 bbl/d

Sources for this report include: Agence France Presse; Alexander's Gas and Oil Connections; BBC Summary of World Broadcasts; Cambridge Energy Research Associates; CIA World Factbook 1999; Deutsche Presse-Agentur; Dow Jones News Wire service; Economist Intelligence Unit ViewsWire; Hart's Middle East Oil and Gas; Middle East Economic Digest; Middle East Newsfile; Oil Daily; Oil and Gas Journal; Petroleum Economist; Petroleum Finance Company; Petroleum Intelligence Weekly; International Market Insight Reports; U.S. Energy Information Administration; WEFA Middle East Economic Outlook; World Gas Intelligence.

INDUSTRIAL DEVELOPMENT AND REGULATION

A key element in the Saudi Arabian government's economic strategy is industrial diversification, a process which has as its primary objective the reduction of the Kingdom's dependence on oil revenues. To this end, the government has encouraged the development of a wide range of manufacturing industries.

The government has provided a range of incentives to encourage the private sector to participate in the Kingdom's industrial effort. Eight industrial estates provide private Saudi manufacturing companies with the necessary infrastructure and services at a very low cost. Credit facilities on generous terms are readily available for such enterprises.

The Kingdom has adopted a free market economic model. The financial, industrial and trade sectors of the economy have made rapid progress, enabling the private sector to play an increasingly important role in the development and diversification of the economy, especially in the fields of construction and farming.

Saudi Arabian Basic Industries Corporation (SABIC)
PO Box 5101
Riyadh 11422
Tel: 401 2033 / 401 2361
Fax: 401 2045 / 401 3831

Function: Joint ventures in heavy industries, primarily at Jubail and Yanbu.

The Saudi Arabian Basic Industries Corporation (SABIC) is an example, par excellence, of the practical results of the Kingdom's blend of long-range planning, long-term major investment and the judicious use of public and private sources of finance.

SABIC was established by Royal Decree in 1976 (1396/97 AH) - its task being to set up and operate hydrocarbon and mineral-based industries in the Kingdom of Saudi Arabia. The Public Investment Fund provides long-term loans to SABIC on highly concessional terms. The balance of SABIC's capital requirements come from SABIC's joint venture partners. In addition, SABIC can make use of normal commercial loans. With these sources of finance, SABIC is able to undertake industrial projects considerably in excess of its own authorized capital of 10,000 million Saudi Riyals.

Saudi Consulting House

The Saudi Consulting House, established in 1967, was a Government consulting corporation which provided a range of research and consultancy services for industry in the Kingdom. The Saudi Consulting House operated under four main departments;

- Industrial Development
- Industrial Engineering
- Industrial Information
- Finance and Administration

The Saudi Consulting House offered the following types of service;

- identification of new opportunities for industrial development

For additional analytical, business and investment opportunities information,
please contact Global Investment & Business Center, USA
at (202) 546-2103. Fax: (202) 546-3275. E-mail: ibpusa3@gmail.com
Global Business and Legal Information Databank: www.ibpus.com

- identification of opportunities for the expansion of existing industrial projects
- provision of technical advice for industry at all stages of project implementation
- provision of professional advice to government agencies, on request provision of consultancy services in such areas as marketing, cost control and quality control On 10th April, 2000, the Saudi Consulting House was dissolved. All its duties and rights were transferred all its duties and rights to the newly-established GCI

GENERAL COMMISSION FOR INVESTMENT (GCI)

On 10th April, 2000, it was announced that the Cabinet had approved the formation of the General Commission for Investment (GCI). At the same time, the Cabinet dissolved the Saudi Consulting House and transferred all its duties and rights to the newly-established GCI.

LEADING COMPANIES IN THE KINGDOM OF SAUDI ARABIA

SABIC (Market Capitalization
Saudi American Bank
Al-Rajhi Banking & Investment Corporation
Riyadh Bank
SCECO* - Central
SCECO* - Western
Saudi British Bank
Arab National Bank
Al-Bank Al-Saudi Al-Fransi
Saudi Arabian Fertilizer Company

* SCECO = Saudi Consolidated Electricity Companies

JUBAIL AND YANBU: THE INDUSTRIAL CITIES

The industrial cities at Jubail and Yanbu have played a key part in the Kingdom's determination to develop hydrocarbon-based and energy-intensive industries. The Royal Commission for Jubail and Yanbu, established in 1395 AH (1975), has created the basic infrastructure for these two cities, often described as the jewels in the Kingdom's industrial crown.

By the end of the Third Development Plan (1405 AH: 1985), fifteen primary industrial projects (ten at Jubail and five at Yanbu) were operational.

Royal Commission for Jubail & Yanbu
PO Box 5864
Riyadh 11432
Tel: 479 4444
Fax: 477 5404

Function: Construction and administration of the industrial complexes and infrastructure at Jubail and Yanbu.

For additional analytical, business and investment opportunities information, please contact Global Investment & Business Center, USA at (202) 546-2103. Fax: (202) 546-3275. E-mail: ibpusa3@gmail.com Global Business and Legal Information Databank: www.ibpus.com

AID TO OTHER COUNTRIES

The Kingdom's oil wealth and its own ambitious development programs have received wide international publicity. Perhaps less widely recognized is its commitment to helping those materially less fortunate in the developing world.

Throughout its own development, the Kingdom of Saudi Arabia has been mindful of its responsibilities in the community of nations, especially in the Arab world and amongst the less developed countries. Blessed with its vast reserves of oil and minerals, Saudi Arabia has willingly accepted the Muslim obligation to share its wealth with those less favored. Although a relatively young country, Saudi Arabia has quickly understood the reality of interdependence which exists between one nation and another. The Kingdom is, of course, particularly involved with the industrialized nations of the West, supplying much of these countries' energy requirements and importing much of the West's technology. But there is also an interdependence, both moral and economic, between rich nations and poor.

SAUDI AID TO THE DEVELOPING WORLD

Since the mid-1970s (1390s AH), Saudi Arabia has been a leading donor in terms of ODA (Overseas Development Aid) volume and ODA/GNP ratio:

Disbursements from 1975 to 1987 amounted to US$48 billion, second only to the United States of America. The ODA/GNP ratio averaged 4.2% over this period, well above the highest among DAC countries (the DAC average is 0.35%).

Under pressure of sharply falling oil revenues, uncertainties regarding the future of the oil market and the regional security situation, Saudi Arabian ODA volume declined from a peak of US $5.5 billion in 1981 to US $2.6 billion in 1985, but recovered to US $3.5 billion in 1986. In 1987, it was about US $2.9 billion. As a proportion of the Kingdom's oil revenues, ODA has risen from 10% in 1983-1985 to 15% in 1986-1987, and Saudi Arabia's ratio of ODA to GNP has remained by far the highest among all donors. Saudi aid is untied, quick-disbursing, and highly concessional, with a grant element of 96% (1986).

DEVELOPMENTAL CO-OPERATION WITH ISLAMIC COUNTRIES

The Kingdom of Saudi Arabia has played an increasingly important role in the past several years in the area of supporting economic and social development plans and programs in Third World countries in general and in Islamic developing countries in particular. The Kingdom allocates a major part of its annual national product to assisting developing countries implement their respective development programs. In some years of the past decade, this assistance has amounted to 6% of GNP, whereas the industrial countries as a group fell short of achieving the modest rate of assistance flowing from developed to developing countries as called for by the United Nations, namely 0.7% of gross national product.

The total non-reimbursable development assistance and concessional loans provided by the Kingdom during the past 15 years to the developing countries that are members of the Islamic Conference Organization amounted to about 77,000 million Saudi Riyals. These funds have contributed toward the implementation of economic and social development programs and projects in 35 sister Islamic nations.

For additional analytical, business and investment opportunities information, please contact Global Investment & Business Center, USA at (202) 546-2103. Fax: (202) 546-3275. E-mail: ibpusa3@gmail.com Global Business and Legal Information Databank: www.ibpus.com

SAUDI FUND FOR DEVELOPMENT

The Saudi Fund for Development was established by Royal Decree in the month of Sha'ban 1394 AH (1974) and began its operations in the month of Safar 1395 AH (1975). At the time of its inception, the Fund's capital amounted to 10,000 million Saudi Riyals; however, due to the developing countries' increasing need for assistance in order to implement development projects, the Fund's capital has been augmented twice, and now totals 25,000 million Saudi Riyals. Despite the fact that the Fund has been operating for a relatively short time, it has made great strides in the area of international development co-operation. The Fund now contributes to the financing of 276 projects in 61 countries.

The terms under which the Saudi Fund for Development provides loans formulated to provide recipients with the greatest possible help;

- the loans are without conditions
- funds are made available quickly and easily
- repayment terms are generous (up to 50 years with a 10-year grace period)
- the outright grant component of such loans can amount to 60% of the total
- the cost of loans is generally 1%

SAUDI AID TO RELIEVE THE PROBLEM OF DROUGHT

The onset of the drought problem in the Sahel prompted the government and the people of Saudi Arabia to come to the rescue of the African countries of the Sahel afflicted. Donations and grants were extended through bilateral channels for support of reform programs and of economic and social plans so as to ensure immediate and beneficial relief for the African peoples.

During the third Islamic Summit held in the Holy City of Makkah in 1984 (1404/05 AH), the Kingdom of Saudi Arabia announced the allocation of 382 million Saudi Riyals for the implementation of an emergency program to assist the following countries of the Sahel affected by the drought in Africa: Cape Verde, Guinea, Guinea Bissau, Gambia, Mali, Mauritania, Niger, Senegal, Burkina Faso, and Chad. 15% of this amount was allocated for the provision of large quantities of foodstuffs and their immediate distribution to the afflicted victims. The balance, amounting to 318,750,000 Saudi Riyals was allocated to a special program for digging wells and rural development in the ten countries of the Sahel.

SAUDI AID FOR REFUGEES IN AFRICA

The Kingdom of Saudi Arabia has been greatly concerned with the problem of African refugees in Sudan and Somalia, and of the victims of conflicts in Chad. The assistance in money, foodstuffs, medical supplies, and shelter provided to refugees in these areas amounted to more than 170,000 million Saudi Riyals. In addition, the Kingdom donated 122,500,000 Saudi Riyals for the UN's first and second conferences for assistance to refugees in Africa.

Some countries of the African continent have been hit by natural disasters such as the earthquakes in the Algerian city of Al-Shleif, the hurricanes in the Comoro Islands and Madagascar, and the ravaging floods in some African countries. The Kingdom has promptly come to the rescue of the victims of such disasters by providing assistance in money and in kind and by contributing in the reconstruction programs. The Kingdom provided a total of 618 million Saudi Riyals to seven countries: Algeria, Tunisia, Somalia, Comoro Islands, Madagascar and Nigeria.

SAUDI AID AT THE NATIONAL LEVEL

Due to the persistence of the drought problem in a number of the African countries for several years, growing worse and spreading its ill effects, the Custodian of the Two Holy Mosques called upon the citizens of the Kingdom to extend aid to their brothers in Africa. Official and national committees were formed in each Saudi city under the auspices of a high ministerial committee to receive contributions in money and in kind from citizens and to ensure that they are promptly delivered to the afflicted African countries. The response of the Muslim people of Saudi Arabia was prompt and generous. Through 1988 (1408 AH), assistance in money and in kind amounted to more than 325 million Saudi Riyals, including more than 152,120 tons of grains and various foodstuffs, clothing, tents, blankets, ambulances, water trucks, and fuel. It benefited more than 3.5 million victims in Sudan, Somalia, Mauritania, Mali, Niger, Djibouti, Comoro Islands and Morocco.

SAUDI AID AT THE INTERNATIONAL LEVEL

In addition to the Kingdom's intensive efforts to assist the victims of drought and other natural disasters and to support the means of sheltering refugees through bilateral channels, the Kingdom has not overlooked the support of international efforts in this area and has responded to the call addressed by the third and fourth Islamic Summits held respectively in Makkah and Casablanca under the auspices of the Organization of the Islamic Conference to provide assistance to the African countries of the Sahel afflicted by the drought. The Kingdom implemented the aforementioned special program for digging wells and rural development in African countries and contributed to several international programs in this field such as the World Food Program, the World Program for Combating River Blindness, the Arab Gulf Program for United Nations Development Organization, and the WB-IMF Programs for support of the structural adjustment of the African sub-Saharan countries as previously mentioned.

SAUDI AID: THE WORLD FOOD PROGRAM

This program is concerned with providing food to the needy all over the world, food being a vital element to human survival. Due to this program's importance, the Kingdom has recently extended to this program donations in money and in kind totaling more than 1,245 million Saudi Riyals up to 1988 (1408/09 AH), at a rate of more than 100 million Saudi Riyals per year.

Official statistics show that about 50% of this program's resources has been allocated in previous years to the African Continent because of the persistent drought in many of its countries.

SAUDI AID: THE ARAB GULF PROGRAM FOR U.N. DEVELOPMENT ORGANIZATIONS

At the beginning of 1981 (1402/03 AH), the Kingdom and the sister Arab Gulf nations established the Arab Gulf Program for the purpose of supporting the UN humanitarian and development organizations. To this program, the Kingdom has contributed about 78% of the program's resources. The program provides assistance to the poorest countries of the world, in particular African countries, through the UN humanitarian and development programs, and has allocated about 40% of its resources to UNICEF. The World Health Organization, the World Food and Agriculture Organization, the World Labor Organization, the World Food Program, the Environment Program, UNESCO, the Program for Handicapped, the UN Development Program, the High Commission for Refugee Affairs, the World Fund for Agricultural Development, and the Fund for Population Affairs have also benefited from the program.

WORLD PROGRAM FOR COMBATING RIVER BLINDNESS DISEASE

This program is concerned with the attempt to eradicate river blindness disease and to prevent it from spreading to an area of about one million and one hundred thousand square kilometers. This program was initiated by the IBRD and the World Health Organization, with the collaboration of the West African governments, namely: Ghana, Ivory Coast, Mali, Niger, Togo, Burkina Faso. Realizing the importance of such a program, the Kingdom has participated in the international meetings on the mobilization of financial and technical resources for the implementation of this program's three stages during the period 1974-1989 (1394-1410 AH). The Kingdom's contribution to such stages amounted to 92 million Saudi Riyals, representing 8.36% of the total donations of contributing countries.

U.N. HIGH COMMISSION FOR REFUGEE AFFAIRS

The Commission was established for the purpose of sponsoring refugees' affairs all over the world. It assists refugees by developing programs aimed at reaching permanent solutions, such as voluntary return of refugees to their home countries, if possible, or their long-term settlement in the local community of the first refugee country, or repatriation to any other country.

The Commission receives annual contributions from the countries of the world in support of its regular budget, as well as donations in support of emergency and special programs. In appreciation of the Commission's humanitarian role, the Kingdom of Saudi Arabia makes an annual contribution to its budget, dating back several years. The Kingdom also donated 105 million Saudi Riyals at the first conference organized by the Commission in 1981 (1401/02 AH) for the purpose of collecting donations to assist refugees in Africa. At the second conference held in 1984 (1404/05 AH), the Kingdom donated 17.5 million Saudi Riyals, and in 1988 (1408/09 AH), it donated through the Commission large quantities of flour to the refugees in Somalia, amounting to 20,000 tons valued at about 30 million Saudi Riyals.

SAUDI AID: RELIEF EFFORTS IN ASIA

The Asian continent has several areas where tension and armed conflicts prevail; some of its countries have been so greatly affected that their resources have been drained and efforts at development impeded. The unjust Israeli occupation of Palestine and some Arab territories was one of the worst events, as well as the Soviet invasion of the Muslim country of Afghanistan, the Lebanese war, and the war between Iraq and Iran. These distressing events have brought about a number of problems paramount among which are the problems of Palestinian and Afghani refugees, and the victims of war. The persistence of these problems for many years has led to an increase in the number of refugees and to the worsening of their living conditions.

The Kingdom has consistently endeavored to support security and stability in the Middle East region and in the Islamic World by various means, while seeking to provide prompt relief to the victims of such events. The Kingdom provides assistance in cash and in kind, in addition to medical assistance to the afflicted and the needy everywhere

SAUDI AID: UNRWA

This agency was established by the United Nations following the Israeli occupation of Palestine, and the expulsion of hundreds of thousands of Palestinians, for the purpose of sponsoring Palestinian refugees' affairs and providing them with humanitarian and social services, as well as for training and creating job opportunities for those who are capable of working.

For additional analytical, business and investment opportunities information, please contact Global Investment & Business Center, USA at (202) 546-2103. Fax: (202) 546-3275. E-mail: ibpusa3@gmail.com Global Business and Legal Information Databank: www.ibpus.com

In appreciation of the role played by this agency and the humanitarian activities that it provided for more than 2 million refugees, the Kingdom has contributed to the agency's annual budget the amount of 4.5 million Saudi Riyals in addition to exceptional donations on various occasions amounting to about 225 million Saudi Riyals dedicated for several purposes, including funding the budget shortfalls, implementation of the programs for construction of refugee camps in Lebanon, and providing educational services as well as relief, food and medical supplies.

SAUDI AID: INTERNATIONAL COMMITTEE OF THE RED CROSS

The International Committee of the Red Cross is an independent humanitarian foundation that works as a neutral mediator in cases of conflicts and disturbances to protect and assist the victims of world and civil wars, thus contributing to the settlement of peace in the world. The foundation provides assistance to prisoners, refugees and homeless families, as well as to Palestinian and Afghan refugees and victims of the Lebanese and the Iraq-Iran war, etc.

In appreciation of the humanitarian role played by this foundation the Kingdom has contributed 750,000 Saudi Riyals per year since 1976 (1396 AH) in addition to exceptional donations in cases of emergency totaling about 79 million Saudi Riyals to support the Foundation's budget and to enable it to implement some of the projects and programs for Palestinian refugees in Lebanon and the victims of the armed conflict in Lebanon and the Iraq-Iran war.

LEGAL, INVESTMENT AND BUSINESS CLIMATE

Saudi Arabia offers an attractive and relatively stable market for investment, particularly for investors that are able to overcome initial barriers imposed on foreigners. Despite political upheaval across the Middle East and North Africa and the transition to a new king, Saudi Arabia's economy continues to expand at a healthy pace, achieving real GDP growth of 3.8% for CY2014. Improvement of the investment climate continues to be an important part of the new Saudi Arabian government's (SAG) broader program to liberalize the country's trade and investment regime, diversify an economy overly dependent on oil, and promote employment for a young population. The government encourages investment across nearly all economic sectors, prioritizing investments in industry, transportation, education, health, communications technology, life sciences, and energy; as well as in four "Economic Cities" that are at various stages of development.

The Saudi Arabian General Investment Authority (SAGIA) provides information and assistance to foreign investors and works to foster investment opportunities across the economy, particularly in energy, transportation, health, life sciences, and knowledge-based industries (see www.sagia.gov.sa). SAGIA also maintains and periodically reviews the list of activities excluded from foreign investment. The Saudi Industrial Development Fund (SIDF), an independent entity within the Ministry of Commerce and Industry, is one important source of financing for investors.

Saudi Arabia's foreign-direct-investment law permits foreigners to invest in all sectors of the economy, except for specific activities contained in a "negative list" that currently exclude two industrial sectors and 13 service sectors, among them real estate investment in Mecca and Medina, some subsectors in printing and publishing, audiovisual services, land-transportation services excluding inter-city transport by trains, and upstream petroleum. The complete "negative list" can be found at www.sagia.gov.sa.

Investors are not required to purchase from local sources or export a certain percentage of output, and their access to foreign exchange is unlimited. There is no requirement in place for shares of foreign equity to be reduced over time. Investors are not required to disclose proprietary information to the SAG as part of the regulatory approval process, except where issues of health and safety are concerned. Other than hiring quotas for Saudi citizens, the government does not currently impose conditions on investment, such as locating in a specific geographic area, committing to specific percentages of local content or local equity, substitution for imports, export requirements or targets, or financing only by local sources.

The SIDF will grant additional incentives and better loan terms to foreign investors who set up their manufacturing facilities in the underdeveloped provinces of Jizan, Hail, and Tabuk. American and other foreign firms are able to participate in SAG-financed and/or -subsidized research-and-development programs.

Overall, Saudi Arabia offers attractive investment opportunities for American investors, and the climate has not significantly changed from the previous year.

OPENNESS TO, AND RESTRICTIONS UPON, FOREIGN INVESTMENT

Attitude toward Foreign Direct Investment

Improving the investment climate continues to be an important part of the SAG's broader program to liberalize the country's trade and investment regime, diversify an economy overly dependent on oil, and promotes employment for a young population. The government encourages investment in nearly all economic sectors, with priority given to transportation, education, health, information and communications technology, life sciences, and energy, as well as in four new "Economic Cities" that are at various stages of development. The Economic Cities are comprehensive large-scale developments in different regions focusing on particular industries, e.g., information technology. Prospective investors will find Saudi Arabia attractive for its economic stability, large market (with a population of over 30 million), sound infrastructure, and well-regulated banking system.

In the "2015 Doing Business" report, the World Bank ranked Saudi Arabia 49th out of 189 economies in terms of ease of doing business, a significant drop from 2012 where they ranked 22nd. In its "Corruption Perceptions Index 2014" report, Transparency International ranked Saudi Arabia as the 55th-cleanest out of 175 countries in terms of perceived levels of public-sector corruption, down from 57th in 2011 but still better than in 2008, when it ranked 80th. In its 2015 "Economic Freedom Index," the Heritage Foundation gave the Kingdom a score of 62.1 out of 100, a drop of 0.1 from 2014, placing it 77th out of the 178 rated countries.

There are also disincentives to investment, including a government effort to force all employers to hire larger proportions of Saudis at higher costs, an increasingly restrictive visa policy for foreign workers, extremely slow payment under some government contracts, a very conservative cultural environment, and enforced segregation of the sexes in nearly all business and social settings. Further, although the SAG is making progress towards establishing a commercial court system, there is no transparent, comprehensive legal framework for resolving commercial disputes in accordance with international standards. The indicator that most negatively affects its World Bank "Doing Business" ranking is resolving insolvency, where it ranks 163rd out of 189.

Saudi Arabia has made progress on its World Trade Organization (WTO) commitments since joining the organization in 2005. However, the SAG has yet to initiate accession procedures to join the Government Procurement Agreement, as agreed during the Kingdom's accession process to the WTO.

For additional analytical, business and investment opportunities information, please contact Global Investment & Business Center, USA at (202) 546-2103. Fax: (202) 546-3275. E-mail: ibpusa3@gmail.com Global Business and Legal Information Databank: www.ibpus.com

Other Investment Policy Reviews

Saudi Arabia underwent its first WTO Trade Policy Review in January 2012, which included investment policy, and is expected to complete its second WTO review in late 2015.

Laws/Regulations of Foreign Direct Investment

In April 2000, the Council of Ministers established the Saudi Arabian General Investment Authority (SAGIA) to provide information and assistance to foreign investors and to foster investment opportunities (see www.sagia.gov.sa). SAGIA is headed by Governor Abdullatif al-Othman, and its duties include formulating government policies regarding investment activities, proposing plans and regulations to enhance the investment climate in the country, and evaluating and licensing investment proposals.

SAGIA periodically reviews the list of activities excluded from foreign investment and submits its reviews to higher authorities for approval. Although these sectors are off-limits to 100 percent foreign investment, foreign minority ownership in joint ventures with Saudi partners may be allowed in some sectors. Foreign investors are no longer required to take local partners in many sectors and may own real estate for company activities. They are allowed to transfer money from their enterprises outside of the country and can sponsor foreign employees. Minimum capital requirements to establish business entities range from zero to 30 million Saudi riyals ($8 million) depending on the sector and the type of investment.

SAGIA's Investor Service Center (ISC) offers detailed information on the investment process, provides licenses and support services to foreign investors, and coordinates with government ministries to facilitate investment. According to SAGIA's regulations, the ISC must grant or refuse a license within 30 days of receiving an application and supporting documentation from the prospective investor. SAGIA established and posted new licensing guidelines in 2012, but many companies looking to invest in Saudi Arabia continue to work with local representation to facilitate the slow and often bureaucratic licensing process. Licenses in services and agriculture must be renewed after one year and in industry after every two years. An important SAGIA objective is to ensure that investors do not just acquire and hold licenses without investing. However, the periodic license reviews, with the possibility of cancellation, adds uncertainty for investors and can provide a disincentive to longer-term investment commitments.

SAGIA has agreements with various SAG agencies and ministries to facilitate and streamline foreign investment. These agreements permit SAGIA to facilitate the granting of visas, establish SAGIA branch offices at Saudi embassies in different countries, prolong tariff exemptions on imported raw materials to three years and on production and manufacturing equipment to two years, and establish commercial courts. SAGIA opened a Women's Investment Center in spring 2003. To make it easier for businesspeople to visit the Kingdom, SAGIA can sponsor visa requests without involving a local company. Saudi Arabia is also implementing a decree stating that sponsorship is no longer required for certain business visas. While SAGIA has set up the infrastructure to support foreign investment, many companies report that the process remains cumbersome and time-consuming.

Pursuant to commitments it made when acceding to the WTO, Saudi Arabia has opened additional service markets to foreign investment, including financial and banking services; maintenance and repair of aircraft and computer reservation systems; wholesale, retail, and franchise distribution services; both basic and value-added telecom services; and investment in the computer and related services sectors.

Industrial Promotion

Government bodies such as the Royal Commission for Jubail & Yanbu and the Al-Riyadh Development Authority have actively promoted opportunities in Saudi Arabia's industrial cities and other regions. In addition to the majority-government-owned Saudi Arabian Basic Industries Corporation (SABIC), private investment companies, such as the National Industrialization Company, the Saudi Venture Capital Group, and the Saudi Industrial Development Company, have also become increasingly active in project development and in seeking out foreign joint-venture partners.

The Saudi Industrial Development Fund (SIDF), an independent entity within the Ministry of Commerce and Industry, is an important source of financing for investors. The main objective of the SIDF is to support the development of the private industrial sector by extending medium- to long-term loans for the establishment of new factories and the expansion, upgrading, and modernization of existing ones. Foreign investors are eligible to receive low-cost financing for up to 50%, 60%, or 75% of project costs (i.e., fixed assets, pre-operating expenses, and start-up working capital) depending on the level of development of the region. Loans are provided for a maximum term of 15 to 20 years, again depending on the region, with repayment schedules designed to match projected cash flows for the project in question.

Limits on Foreign Control

There is no prohibition on foreign investment in refining and petrochemical development, and there is significant foreign investment in the downstream Saudi energy sector. ExxonMobil and Shell are both 50% partners in refineries with Saudi Aramco. ExxonMobil, Chevron Texaco, and Shell, as well as several other international investors, have formed joint ventures with SABIC to build large-scale petrochemical plants that utilize natural-gas feedstock from Saudi Aramco's existing operations at Ras Tanura. Aramco selected the Dow Chemical Company as its partner in a $20-billion joint venture to construct, own, and operate a chemicals and plastics production complex in Saudi Arabia's Eastern Province. The national mining company, Maaden, has a $12-billion joint venture with Alcoa for bauxite mining and aluminum production and a $7-billion joint venture with the leading American fertilizer firm Mosaic and SABIC to produce phosphate-based fertilizers.

Joint ventures almost always take the form of limited-liability partnerships, to which there are some disadvantages. Foreign partners in service and contracting ventures organized as limited-liability partnerships must pay, in cash or in kind, 100 percent of their contribution to authorized capital. SAGIA's authorization is only the first step for setting up such a partnership. Still, foreign investment is generally welcome in Saudi Arabia if it promotes economic development, transfers foreign expertise to Saudi Arabia, creates jobs for Saudis, and/or expands Saudi exports.

Professionals, including architects, consultants, and consulting engineers, are required to register with, and be certified by, the Ministry of Commerce and Industry, in accordance with the requirements defined in the Ministry's Resolution 264 from 1982. These regulations, in theory, permit the registration of Saudi-foreign joint-venture consulting firms. As part of its WTO accession commitments, Saudi Arabia generally allows consulting firms to establish an office in Saudi Arabia without a Saudi partner. However, offices practicing law, accounting and auditing, design, architecture, engineering, or civil planning or providing healthcare, dental, or veterinary services must have a Saudi partner, and the foreign partner's equity cannot exceed 75% of the total investment.

For additional analytical, business and investment opportunities information, please contact Global Investment & Business Center, USA at (202) 546-2103. Fax: (202) 546-3275. E-mail: ibpusa3@gmail.com Global Business and Legal Information Databank: www.ibpus.com

Privatization Program

In 2002, the Supreme Economic Council announced the approval of privatization procedures, open to domestic and foreign investors, and a timetable to transfer certain public services to the private sector. Twenty state-owned companies handling water supply and drainage, water desalination, telecommunications, mining, power, air transportation and related services, railways, some sectors of roadways, postal services, flour mills and silos, seaport services, industrial-cities services, government hotels, sports clubs, some municipality services, educational services, social services, agricultural services, health services, government portions of SABIC, banks, and local refineries were slated for privatization.

As a result of the privatization strategy, the Saudi Telecommunications Company (STC) floated a minority stake (approximately 20%) on the stock market in January 2003, netting close to $4 billion in proceeds. An additional 10% has since been offered for private ownership. The initial public offering (IPO) of 50% of the formerly state-owned National Company for Cooperative Insurance (NCCI) was completed in January 2005. The first SABIC offering went public on December 17, 2005, for 35% of the newly formed Yanbu National Petrochemical Company (YANSAB; to be capitalized at $1.5 billion). YANSAB is SABIC's largest petrochemical complex to date, and the IPO netted $533 million in capital.

In July 2003, the SAG took significant, long-awaited steps to lower the corporate tax rate on foreign investors to a flat 20%; however, separate rates apply to investments in hydrocarbons. The flat tax replaced a tiered system with tax rates as high as 45%. While this was a welcome step toward more balanced treatment of foreign and Saudi-owned capital, the tax structure still favors Saudi companies and joint ventures with Saudi participation. Saudi investors do not pay corporate income tax, but are subject to a 2.5% tax, or "zakat," on net current assets.

Screening of FDI

All foreign investment projects in the Saudi Arabia must obtain a license from SAGIA. Investments in specific sectors may require additional licenses from other government authorities, including, but not limited to, the Saudi Arabian Monetary Agency (SAMA), the Capital Market Authority (CMA), or the Communications and Information Technology Commission (CITC).

As noted above, SAGIA's Investor Service Center (ISC) offers detailed information on the investment process, provides licenses and support services to foreign investors, and coordinates with government ministries to facilitate investment. According to SAGIA's regulations, the ISC must grant or refuse a license within 30 days of receiving an application and supporting documentation from the prospective investor. SAGIA established and posted new licensing guidelines in 2012, but many companies looking to invest in Saudi Arabia work with local representation to facilitate the slow and often bureaucratic licensing process. Licenses in services and agriculture must be renewed after one year and in industry after two years. The periodic license reviews, with the possibility of cancellation, adds uncertainty for investors and can provide a disincentive to longer-term investment commitments.

Competition Law

SAGIA and the Ministry of Commerce and Industry review transactions for competition-related concerns. Concerns have arisen that allegations of price fixing for certain products may have been used on occasion as a pretext to control prices.

Investment Trends

Despite political upheaval across the Middle East and North Africa, and the transition to a new king upon the death of former King Abdullah in January 2015, Saudi Arabia's economy continues to expand at a healthy pace, with real GDP growth of 3.8% for CY2014, and inflation standing at a moderate 2.7% at the end of 2014. Oil revenues through Saudi Aramco accounted for 85% of the Saudi Arabian government's (SAG's) total export revenue in 2014. Notwithstanding the downturn in oil prices beginning in mid-2014, the Saudi government is committed to maintaining high levels of government spending and investment, particularly in health care, education, transportation/infrastructure, and housing.

Table 1

Measure	Year	Index or Rank	Website Address
TI Corruption Perceptions index	2014	55 of 175	transparency.org/cpi2014/results
World Bank's Doing Business Report "Ease of Doing Business"	2015	49 of 189	doingbusiness.org/rankings
Global Innovation Index	2014	38 of 143	globalinnovationindex.org/content.aspx?page=data-analysis
World Bank GNI per capita	2013	USD 26,260	data.worldbank.org/indicator/NY.GNP.PCAP.CD

INVESTMENT INCENTIVES

REGULATORY INCENTIVES

Saudi Arabia constantly improves investment environment, especially the logistic regulations in an effort to support foreign investment. In 2000, the Saudi government announced a new Foreign Investment Law, introducing major regulatory incentives including:

• The establishment of the Saudi Arabian General Investment Authority (SAGIA), to be the responsible authority for issuing investment licences to foreign investors and coordinating with other related governmental bodies for the approval.

• Accelerated investment application, business registration and set-up process, within thirty (30) days of submission to SAGIA.

• Foreign investors will benefit from incentives and guarantees that local and national investors receive according to laws and regulations.

• Limited Liability Companies are not required to Minimum Capital.
• Owning Direct Property for the licensed company including residence and employees allocations.
• Permissions of transferring capital and profit abroad.
• Flexibility of transferring/allocation of companies shares between shareholders according to regulations.

• The licensed company is sponsoring the investor and its employees (non-Saudis).
• The availability and eligibility to apply for loans from the Saudi Industrial Development Fund.

FINANCIAL INCENTIVES

• Benefit from corporative/collateral and massive agreements regarding taxation and investment with other countries.

• No personal income taxes.

• Taxes are 20% from total profits on companies.

• The ability to transfer losses for future years in regard to taxes.

• Foreign investors have access to generous regional and international financial programs and incubators, including:

o Saudi Industrial Development Fund
o Arab Fund for Economic and Social Development (AFESD): Participates in financing economic and social development projects in Arab countries.
o Arab Monetary Fund: Promotes the development of Arab financial markets and trade among member states; advises member states on investment of resources.
o Arab Trade Financing Program: Provides medium and long-term loans to individuals and organizations for private and commercial trade.
o Inter-Arab Investment Guarantee Corporation: Provides insurance coverage for inter-Arab investments and export credits against commercial and non-commercial risks.
o Islamic Development Bank: Participates in equity capital and grants loans for productive projects and enterprises. It accepts deposits to mobilize financial resources through Shari'a compatible avenues.

Other financial incentives the encourage investments in the Kingdom include:

o The Human Resources Development Fund to support activities related to qualifying, training and recruitment of Saudi labor.
o Competitive industrial utility rates for water, power and land.
o Large research and development endowments at King Abdullah University for Science and Technology (KAUST) and King Abdul Aziz City of Science and Technology (KACST).

Tax incentives (Specified Regions Only)

Saudi government offered tax incentives for training and recruitment of Saudi labor in some regions, including:

1. Ha'il
2. Jazan
3. Najran
4. Al-Baha
5. Al-Jouf
6. Northern Borders

**For additional analytical, business and investment opportunities information,
please contact Global Investment & Business Center, USA
at (202) 546-2103. Fax: (202) 546-3275. E-mail: ibpusa3@gmail.com
Global Business and Legal Information Databank: www.ibpus.com**

The tax incentives include the following:

Tax Reduction equal to 50% from annual expenses for recruiting and training of Saudis, tax reduction equal to 50% from Saudis annual salaries, plus tax reduction for industrial projects in these areas not exceeding 15% of non-Saudis' share in the capital.

CONVERSION AND TRANSFER POLICIES

Foreign Exchange

There is no limitation on the inflow or outflow of funds for remittances of profits, debt service, capital, capital gains, returns on intellectual property, or imported inputs, with the exception that bulk cash shipments greater than 60,000 riyals must be declared at the point of entry or exit. Since 1986, when the last devaluation occurred, the official exchange rate has been 3.75 Saudi riyals per USD. Transactions take place using rates very close to the official rate.

Remittance Policies

There are no restrictions on converting and transferring funds associated with an investment (including remittances of investment capital, earnings, loan repayments, and lease payments) into a freely usable currency at a legal market-clearing rate. There have been no recent changes, but press reports have quoted the Minister of Labor as saying the SAG intends to limit remittances by foreign workers at some point in the future. There are no delays in effect for remitting investment returns such as dividends, repatriation of capital, interest and principal on private foreign debt, lease payments, royalties and management fees through normal legal channels. There is no need for a legal parallel market for investor remittances.

Saudi Arabia is a member of Middle East and North Africa Financial Action Task Force (MENA-FATF).

3. Expropriation and Compensation

The Embassy is not aware of the SAG ever having expropriated property from foreign investors without adequate compensation. There have been no expropriating actions in the recent past or policy shifts that would suggest there the SAG will initiate such actions in the near future. Some small to medium-sized foreign investors, however, have complained that their investment licenses have been cancelled without justification, causing them to forfeit their investments.

DISPUTE SETTLEMENT

Legal System, Specialized Courts, Judicial Independence, Judgments of Foreign Courts

The Saudi legal system is derived from the legal rules of Islam, known as Sharia law. The Ministry of Justice oversees the Sharia-based judicial system, but most ministries have committees to rule on matters under their jurisdiction. Many disputes that would be handled in a court in the United States are handled through intra-ministerial administrative processes in Saudi Arabia. Generally, the Saudi Board of Grievances has jurisdiction over disputes with the government and over commercial disputes. The Board also reviews all foreign arbitral awards and foreign court decisions to ensure that they comply with Sharia law. This review process can take years, and outcomes are unpredictable. Currently, the Saudi Ministry of Commerce and

Industry is leading an ambitious project to overhaul commercial laws. This project entails drafting new laws while modernizing current ones, along with creating an arbitration center in cooperation with the Saudi Chambers of Commerce and Industry. In several cases, disputes have caused serious problems for foreign investors. For instance, Saudi partners have blocked foreigners' access to exit visas, forcing them to remain in Saudi Arabia against their will. In cases of alleged fraud, foreign partners may also be jailed to prevent their departure from the country while awaiting police investigation or adjudication of the case. Courts can impose precautionary restraint on personal property pending the adjudication of a commercial dispute. As with any investment abroad, it is important that U.S. investors take steps to protect themselves by thoroughly researching the business record of the proposed Saudi partner, retaining legal counsel, complying scrupulously with all legal steps in the investment process, and securing a well-drafted agreement.

Saudi commercial law is still in its developing stage. In 1994 Saudi Arabia ratified the 1958 New York Convention on the Recognition and Enforcement of Foreign Arbitral Awards. Saudi Arabia is also a member of the International Center for the Settlement of Investment Disputes (ICSID Convention). In 2012, the SAG revised its arbitration law to update certain provisions.

Dispute settlement and enforcement of foreign arbitral awards in Saudi Arabia continues to be time-consuming and uncertain, carrying the risk that Sharia principles can potentially trump any foreign judgments or legal precedents. Even after a decision is reached in a dispute, enforcement of a judgment can still take years. The Embassy recommends consulting with local counsel in advance of investing to review legal options and appropriate contractual provisions for dispute resolution.

The Committee for Labor Disputes (under the Ministry of Labor) and the Negotiable Instruments Committee, also called the Commercial Paper Committee) handle disputes involving private individuals. Judgments obtained in foreign courts, including arbitral awards, are not consistently enforced by Saudi courts, despite Saudi Arabia's ratification of the New York Convention. Monetary judgments are based on the terms of the contract—i.e., if the contract is calculated in USD, a judgment may be obtained in USD. If unspecified, the judgment is denominated in Saudi riyals. Non-material damages and interest are not included in monetary judgments.

In October 2007, King Abdullah issued a royal decree to overhaul the judicial system and allocated 7 billion Saudi riyals (approximately $1.9 billion) to train judges and build new courts. To date, few changes have been implemented, although the SAG has disbursed a portion of the funds allocated for constructing new appeals courts and sending judges abroad for legal seminars. In early 2010, Saudi Arabia started the process of codifying the sharia regulations that govern the Kingdom's courts in an effort to bring clarity and uniformity to judicial rulings.

Bankruptcy

A bankruptcy law was enacted by Royal Decree no. N/16, dated 4/9/1416H in the Islamic calendar (corresponding to January 24, 1996). Articles contained in the law allow debtors to conclude financial settlements with their creditors through committees in each municipal or regional Chamber of Commerce and Industry or through the Board of Grievances. Designated as the Regulation on Bankruptcy Protective Settlement, the law is open to ordinary creditors, except in the case of privileged debts, and debts which arise pursuant to the settlement procedures. The Ministry of Commerce and Industry is revising the bankruptcy law to update key provisions and address several deficiencies in the Saudi bankruptcy regime. Potential investors should note that the indicator that most negatively affects Saudi Arabia's World Bank "Doing Business" ranking is resolving insolvency, where it ranks 163rd out of 189 countries.

Investment Disputes

The use of any international or domestic dispute settlement mechanism within Saudi Arabia continues to be time-consuming and uncertain, as all outcomes are subject to a final review in the Saudi judicial system and carry the risk that principles of Sharia law may potentially trump a judgment or legal precedent. The Embassy recommends consulting with local counsel in advance of investing to review legal options and contractual provisions for dispute resolution.

International Arbitration

The United States and Saudi Arabia signed a Trade and Investment Framework Agreement in 2003. In 2012, the SAG revised their domestic arbitration law to update certain provisions. However, as noted above, dispute settlement and enforcement of foreign arbitral awards in Saudi Arabia continue to be time-consuming and uncertain, as all outcomes are subject to a final review in the Saudi judicial system and carry the risk that principles of Sharia law may potentially trump a judgment or legal precedent. Even after a decision is reached in a dispute, effective enforcement of the judgment can still take years.

ICSID Convention and New York Convention

The Kingdom of Saudi Arabia ratified the 1958 New York Convention on the Recognition and Enforcement of Foreign Arbitral Awards in 1994. Saudi Arabia is also a member state of the International Center for the Settlement of Investment Disputes (ICSID Convention), though under the terms of its accession it cannot be compelled to refer investment disputes to this system absent specific consent, provided on a case-by-case basis. Saudi Arabia has yet to consent to the referral of any investment dispute to the ICSID for resolution.

Duration of Dispute Resolution

Dispute resolution in Saudi Arabia is time-consuming and can last for months or years. Even after a decision is reached in a dispute, effective enforcement of the judgment can take additional years.

PERFORMANCE REQUIREMENTS AND INVESTMENT INCENTIVES

WTO/TRIMS

The Saudi Arabia is a member of the World Trade Organization (WTO). To date, the SAG has not notified the WTO of any measures inconsistent with the requirements of the Agreement on Trade-Related Investment Measures (TRIMs), nor does it maintain any measures that are alleged to violate the WTO TRIMs text.

Investment Incentives

The government does not impose conditions on investment, such as locating in a specific geographic area, committing to specific percentages of local content or local equity, substitution for imports, export requirements or targets, or financing only by local sources. Nonetheless, the SIDF will provide additional incentives and better loan terms to foreign investors who set up their manufacturing facilities in Jizan, Hail, and Tabuk.

The government uses its purchasing power to encourage foreign investment, requiring offsetting investments equivalent to 35% of a program's value for defense contracts exceeding 400 million Saudi riyals ($107 million). In addition to defense offsets, the SAG is also seeking FDI in various key sectors, such as oil, power generation, railways, and others, with the aim of fostering job creation.

Research and Development

American and other foreign firms are able to participate in SAG-financed and/or -subsidized research-and-development programs.

Performance Requirements

Investors are not currently required to purchase from local sources or export a certain percentage of output, and their access to foreign exchange is unlimited. While not required to procure from local sources, investors may avoid import duties on raw materials only if they can show that these are not available locally. There is no requirement that the share of foreign equity be reduced over time. Investors are not required to disclose proprietary information to the SAG as part of the regulatory approval process, except where issues of health and safety are concerned.

The government encourages recruitment of Saudi employees through a series of incentives and limits placed on the number of visas for foreign workers available to companies. The largest groups of foreign workers now come from Bangladesh, Egypt, India, Pakistan, the Philippines, and Yemen.

The SAG announced in 2002 it would ease restrictions on the issuance of visas to foreign businessmen to allow greater access and decreed in 2005 that sponsor requirements for business visas would be lifted. Difficulties remain regarding the Saudi visa procedures, however, despite the government's announcement that foreign business visitors will no longer need to provide invitation letters from Saudi businesses to receive visas. In November 2007, Saudi Arabia declared that it would begin issuing U.S. business visitors five-year, multiple-entry visas at Saudi embassies, consulates, and ports of entry, but it has not yet fully implemented this policy. One-year "business visas" are routinely issued to U.S. visitors who do not have an invitation letter from a Saudi company, and the visa applicants must provide proof that they are engaged in legitimate commercial activity. By contrast, "commercial visas" are issued by invitation from Saudi companies to applicants who have a specific reason to visit a Saudi company, and the maximum validity is five years if sponsored by Saudi Chamber of Commerce, rather than the company that issued the invitation letter.

Data Storage

Other than a requirement to retain records locally for ten years for tax purposes, there is no requirement regarding data storage or access to surveillance.

RIGHT TO PRIVATE OWNERSHIP AND ESTABLISHMENT

All entities with appropriate licenses have the right to establish and own business enterprises and engage in all forms of remunerative activity, except in those sectors on the SAG's "negative list" reserved for state monopolies and Saudi citizens. Private entities generally have the right to establish, acquire, and dispose of interests freely in business enterprises.

For additional analytical, business and investment opportunities information,
please contact Global Investment & Business Center, USA
at (202) 546-2103. Fax: (202) 546-3275. E-mail: ibpusa3@gmail.com
Global Business and Legal Information Databank: www.ibpus.com

PROTECTION OF PROPERTY RIGHTS

Real Property

The Saudi legal system protects and facilitates acquisition and disposition of all property, consistent with Islamic practice respecting private property. Non-Saudi corporate entities are allowed to purchase real estate in Saudi Arabia according to the foreign-investment code, and mortgages do exist, although the recording system is reportedly unreliable. Other foreign-owned corporate and personal property is protected, and the Embassy knows of no cases of government expropriation or nationalization of U.S.-owned assets in the Kingdom without adequate compensation. Saudi Arabia does have a system of recording security interests, and has plans to modernize an archaic land registry system. For more information, please refer to Saudi Arabia's data in the World Bank Group's "Doing Business 2015: Going Beyond Efficiency" publication: **http://www.doingbusiness.org/rankings**.

Intellectual Property Rights

Saudi Arabia undertook a comprehensive revision of its laws covering intellectual property rights to bring them in line with the WTO agreement on Trade Related Aspects of Intellectual Property Rights (TRIPs) and promulgated changes in coordination with the World Intellectual Property Organization (WIPO). The SAG updated its Trademark Law (2002), Copyright Law (2003), and Patent Law (2004) with the dual goals of TRIPs compliance and effective deterrence. In 2008, the Violations Review Committee created a website and has populated it with information on current cases. Although intellectual property right reforms are slow and inconsistent in some areas, the Kingdom is progressing overall.

The current Law on Patents, Layout Designs of Integrated Circuits, Plant Varieties and Industrial Designs has been in effect since September 2004. The patent office continues to build its capacity through training, has streamlined its procedures, hired more staff, and reduced its backlog. Patents are available for both products and processes. The term of protection was increased from 15 to 20 years under the new law, but patent holders can no longer apply for a routinely granted five-year extension. In December 2009, the Saudi Council of Ministers approved the Kingdom's accession to both the Intellectual Property Owners Association Patent Cooperation Treaty (PCT) and its Implementing Regulations and the Patent Law Treaty (PLT) adopted by the Diplomatic Conference in Geneva on June 1, 2000.

In September 2009, the King approved a mechanism to protect Exclusive Marketing Rights (EMR) for certain pharmaceutical products that had lost patent protection when Saudi Arabia transitioned to a new TRIPS-compliant patent law in 2004. EMR protection in Saudi Arabia expires on the same date the patent expires in the United States or the European Union, and companies report that they have received EMR protection for accepted applications.

The SAG has revised its Copyright Law and is seeking to impose stricter penalties on copyright violators. In January 2010, the Ministry of Culture and Information referred the first-ever copyright-violation case to the Board of Grievances for deterrent sentencing. The SAG has stepped up efforts to force pirated printed material, recorded music, videos, and software off the shelves of stores, including relatively frequent raids on shops selling pirated goods. However, many pirated materials are still available in the marketplace. The use of pirated software increases possible cyber-security vulnerability in some systems. An Islamic religious edict ("fatwa") stating that software piracy is "forbidden" has not been backed up by strong enforcement efforts. Some software utilized by the Saudi government is reportedly unlicensed or "underlicensed."

Comprehensive data on seizures of counterfeit goods is not available, but the SAG does make public announcements in local media when large seizures are made. Based on such announcements by Saudi Customs, the U.S. Embassy estimates that over $500 million in counterfeit goods are seized on average during one calendar year.

The Rules for Protection of Trade Secrets came into effect in 2005. Trademarks are protected under the Trademark Law. Saudi Arabia has one of the best trademark laws in the region, and the Saudi Customs Authority has significantly stepped up its enforcement efforts. Saudi Arabia received anti-counterfeiting and piracy awards from the World Customs Organization (WCO) in 2009 for organizing the first Pan-Arab conference on this issue, building the capacity of the Customs Authority, and translating WCO documents into Arabic. Saudi Arabia has not signed or ratified the WIPO internet treaties.

For additional information about treaty obligations and points of contact at local IP offices, please see WIPO's country profiles at **http://www.wipo.int/directory/en**/.

Resources for Rights Holders

Embassy point of contact: Economic Officer Mary Jo Pham; **PhamMJ@state.gov**

TRANSPARENCY OF THE REGULATORY SYSTEM

There are few aspects of the SAG's regulatory system that are transparent, although Saudi investment policy is less opaque than many other areas. Saudi tax and labor laws and policies favor technology transfer and the employment of Saudis rather than fostering competition. Saudi health and safety laws and policies are not used to distort or impede the efficient mobilization and allocation of investments. Bureaucratic procedures are cumbersome, but red tape can generally be overcome with persistence.

There are no informal regulatory processes managed by NGOs or private-sector associations. Proposed laws and regulations are not always published in draft form for public comment. Some government agencies permit public comments through their websites. Before introducing major regulatory changes, Saudi authorities are usually open to consultation with stakeholders, though the processes and procedures for doing so are not generally codified in law or regulations. There are no private-sector or government efforts to restrict foreign participation in the industry standards-setting consortia or organizations that are available.

EFFICIENT CAPITAL MARKETS AND PORTFOLIO INVESTMENT

Financial policies generally facilitate the free flow of private capital, and currency can be transferred in and out of Saudi Arabia without restriction. The Saudi Capital Market Authority is reportedly poised to open the stock market to qualified foreign investors in 2015; non-GCC foreign investors are currently only able to invest in the stock market through swap agreements and exchange-traded funds.

The Capital Markets Law, passed in 2003, allows for brokerages, asset managers, and other non-bank financial intermediaries to operate in the Kingdom. The law created a market regulator, the Capital Market Authority (CMA), which was established in 2004, and opened the stock exchange to public investment. As of the end of 2013, the CMA listed the number of licenses issued for various securities business activities at 514, with "Advising" activity accounting for the highest number of licenses at 83. There is an effective regulatory system governing portfolio investment in Saudi Arabia.

In 2003, the Saudi Arabian Monetary Agency (SAMA), the central bank, enhanced and updated its 1995 Circular on Guidelines for the Prevention of Money Laundering and Terrorist Financing. The enhanced guidelines are more compliant with the Banking Control Law, the Financial Action Task Force (FATF) 40 Recommendations, the nine Special Recommendations on Terrorist Financing, and relevant UN Security Council Resolutions. In 2014, King Abdullah ratified a new counter-terrorism law officially criminalizing acts of terrorism and the financing of terrorism.

Historically, credit was widely available to both Saudi and foreign entities from commercial banks and was allocated on market terms. The global financial crisis of 2008, followed by the default on $20 billion in debt by two Saudi business concerns and the debt restructuring in Dubai, substantially reduced this availability to all parties, resulting in the delay or cancellation of some projects. Credit became somewhat more available in 2011 and 2012, but extraordinary public spending limited the demand for private lending. In addition to large-scale supplemental programs, credit is available from several government institutions, such as the Saudi Industrial Development Fund, which allocate credit based on government-set criteria rather than market conditions. Companies must have a legal presence in Saudi Arabia in order to qualify for credit. The private sector has access to term loans, and there have been a number of issuances of sharia-compliant bonds, known as "sukuk," but there is no fully developed corporate bond market. There were six public securities offerings in 2014.

In 2012, the Council of Ministers issued five long-awaited new laws concerning mortgages and the wider financial sector—the Real Estate Finance Law, Financial Lease Law, Law on Supervision of Finance Companies, Real Estate Mortgage Law, and Execution/Enforcement Law. Private-sector contacts are generally optimistic about the laws' long-term potential to enhance mortgage penetration, attract additional investment to the private housing market, and increase overall lending, but the extent of their impact remains unclear. The eventual implementing regulations for the Execution/Enforcement Law will prove especially important, given that uncertainty about enforcement of lenders' rights has been cited as a major reason for anemic mortgage lending in the Kingdom.

As part of the economic reforms initiated for accession to the WTO, Saudi Arabia liberalized licensing requirements for foreign investment in financial services. In addition, the government increased foreign-equity limits in financial institutions from 40% to 60% to entice further foreign investment.

Money and Banking System, Hostile Takeovers

In the last few years, the SAG has taken steps to increase foreign participation in its banking sector by granting operating licenses to foreign banks. As of 2014, SAMA had granted 11 foreign banks licenses to operate in the Kingdom: BNP Paribas, Deutsche Bank, Emirates NBD, Gulf International Bank, J.P. Morgan Chase, Muscat Bank, National Bank of Bahrain, National Bank of Kuwait, National Bank of Pakistan, State Bank of India, and T.C. Ziraat Bankasi A.S. The Cabinet further approved the licensing of a branch of the Chinese Bank of Industry and Commerce, although according to SAMA's website the license "has not started yet."

The legal, regulatory, and accounting systems practiced in the banking sector are generally transparent and consistent with international norms. SAMA, which oversees and regulates the banking system, generally gets high marks for its prudent oversight of commercial banks in Saudi Arabia. SAMA is the only central bank in the Middle East other than Israel's that is a member and shareholder of the Bank for International Settlements in Basel, Switzerland.

COMPETITION FROM STATE-OWNED ENTERPRISES

State-owned enterprises (SOEs) play a leading role in the Saudi economy, particularly in water, power, oil, natural gas, and petrochemicals. Saudi Aramco, the world's largest producer and exporter of crude oil and a large-scale oil refiner and producer of natural gas, is 100% SAG-owned, and its revenues typically account for around 85-90% of the SAG's budget. Saudi Arabia's leading petrochemical company, Saudi Basic Industries Corporation (SABIC), is 70% owned by the SAG. SABIC's Chairman is a member of the royal family and also the chair of the Royal Commission of Jubail & Yanbu; four additional members of SABIC's seven-member board are SAG officials. The SAG tends to be similarly well-represented in the leadership of other SOEs. State-owned Saudi Arabian Airlines (Saudia) competes against Nas Air, a private, low-cost carrier, but enjoys substantial discounts on aviation fuel.

OECD Guidelines on Corporate Governance of SOEs

The Embassy is not aware of SOEs expressly exercising delegated governmental powers, though they are heavily involved in policy consultations. SOEs benefit from water, power, and feedstock sold below market rates and often receive free land from the SAG. Generally, private industries also get water, power, and feedstock at below-market prices, and the SAG often gives land as part of public-private partnerships, but fully private enterprises do not typically receive free land unless as part of a SAG effort to stimulate specific sectors. In principle, credit is equally available to private companies and SOEs. The Embassy does not believe Saudi SOEs to operate, in practice, under hard budget constraints. The detail and regularity of financial reporting by SOEs vary and do not consistently meet international financial reporting standards, including the OECD Guidelines on Corporate Governance for SOEs. It is likely that domestic courts would tend to resolve investment disputes in favor of SOEs, though there are examples of rulings in favor of private sector claimants against SAG entities.

Sovereign Wealth Funds

In 2008, the Kingdom established a sovereign wealth fund, the Saudi Arabian Investment Company (also known as Sanabil al-Saudia), a wholly SAG-owned entity within the Ministry of Finance's Public Investment Fund. The fund began with $5.3 billion of startup capital, but little information is available regarding the fund's organization or operations.

CORPORATE SOCIAL RESPONSIBILITY

There is a dawning awareness of corporate social responsibility (CSR) in Saudi Arabia. The SAG sees CSR primarily as a component of its competitiveness vis-à-vis global economies and has knit CSR promotion to its goal of becoming a top-ten economy. In July 2008, SAGIA, the King Khalid Foundation, and the international NGO AccountAbility jointly established the Saudi Arabian Responsible Competitiveness Index (SARCI), a ranking of companies' CSR contributions. The results led to the granting of the King Khalid Responsible Competitiveness Award in several categories at the annual Global Competitiveness Forum. The Embassy believes the SAG and major corporations are fully aware of CSR but does not believe CSR currently has a broad impact on consumer perception.

OECD Guidelines for Multinational Enterprises

The government encourages foreign and local enterprises to follow generally accepted CSR principles, including the OECD Guidelines for Multinational Enterprises.

POLITICAL VIOLENCE

The Department of State authorized the return of staff family members to U.S. Embassy Riyadh, U.S. Consulate General Jeddah, and U.S. Consulate General Dhahran in 2010, but continues to warn U.S. citizens about the security situation in Saudi Arabia and frequently reminds U.S. citizens of recommended security precautions. In the most recent Travel Warning for Saudi Arabia, the Department of State urges U.S. citizens to consider carefully the risks of traveling to Saudi Arabia. Significant enhancements in the capacity and capability of Saudi security and intelligence forces have greatly improved the security environment, but it is important to note that there is an ongoing security threat from transnational terrorist organizations such as the Islamic State and Al Qaida in the Arabian Peninsula (AQAP).

CORRUPTION

Saudi Arabia has limited legislation aimed at curbing corruption. The Tenders Law of Saudi Arabia, approved in 2004, has improved transparency in the government procurement process through the publication of tenders. Ministers and other senior government officials appointed by royal decree are forbidden from engaging in business activities with their ministry or organization while employed there. There are few cases of prominent citizens or government officials being tried on corruption charges.

Corruption has been identified by foreign firms as a barrier to investment in Saudi Arabia, nevertheless authorities have only taken modest steps toward combating it. In April 2007, King Abdullah established the National Authority for Combating Corruption that was to report directly to the king, but there was little tangible follow-through to empower this institution. The General Auditing Bureau is also charged with combating corruption. In 2011, King Abdullah reconstituted the Authority as the Anti-corruption Commission under new and more energetic leadership. Although little of its work has so far been publicized and many remain skeptical, some anecdotal evidence suggests the Commission has been active in its investigations and is not shying away from influential players whose indiscretions may previously have been ignored.

UN Anticorruption Convention, OECD Convention on Combatting Bribery

Saudi Arabia ratified the U.N. Convention against Corruption (UNCAC) in April 2013 and signed the G-20 Anti-Corruption Action Plan (ACAP) in November 2010.

Resources to Report Corruption

Options for reporting corruption to Nazaha, the National Anti-Corruption Commission:

The Anti-Corruption Committee's (ACC) physical address by post, telegram, or in person

For additional analytical, business and investment opportunities information,
please contact Global Investment & Business Center, USA
at (202) 546-2103. Fax: (202) 546-3275. E-mail: ibpusa3@gmail.com
Global Business and Legal Information Databank: www.ibpus.com

Anti-Corruption Committee
P.O. Box (Wasl)7667
Elalia-Hiaelghader
Riyadh 2525-13311
The Kingdom of Saudi Arabia.
ACC's Fax (012645555)

Through the "Complainant Service" on the website of the National Anti-Corruption
Commission: **http://www.nazaha.gov.sa/eServices/sso/User/Complaints/Pages/SendCompla
int.aspx**

BILATERAL INVESTMENT AGREEMENTS

Saudi Arabia has Investment Promotion & Protection Agreements with Austria, Belgium, China,
France, Germany, Italy, Malaysia, and Taiwan. The Kingdom has cooperation agreements of
varying scope with 36 countries, including an agreement on secured private investment with the
United States that has been in place since February 1975. The United States and Saudi Arabia
signed a Trade and Investment Framework Agreement in 2003.

Further information on the above, and on miscellaneous additional agreements, can be found
at**http://www.sagia.gov.sa/en/Investment-climate/Some-Things-You-Need-To-Know-
/International-agreements/**.

Bilateral Taxation Treaties

Saudi Arabia does not have a bilateral taxation treaty with the United States.

OPIC AND OTHER INVESTMENT INSURANCE PROGRAMS

OPIC stopped operating in Saudi Arabia in 1995 due to the government's failure to take steps to
adopt and implement laws that extend internationally recognized workers' rights to its labor force.
Saudi Arabia has been a member of the Multilateral Investment Guarantee Agency since April
1988.

LABOR

The Ministry of Labor and the Ministry of Interior regulate recruitment of expatriate labor, which
makes up a large majority of the private-sector workforce. The government encourages
recruitment of Saudi employees through a series of incentives and limits placed on the number of
visas for foreign workers available to companies. The largest groups of foreign workers come
from Bangladesh, Egypt, India, Pakistan, the Philippines, and Yemen. Westerners compose less
than 2% of the labor force.

Beginning with the 1969 Labor and Workman Regulations, Saudi Arabia has pursued a number
of localization schemes to combat unemployment among Saudis, which the CIA World Factbook
estimated at 10.5% for Saudi males in 2013, a rate believed to be much higher among women.
Local bank and other estimates put the unemployment rate at as high as 25%. The employment
schemes attempted to require blanket "Saudi-ization" percentages irrespective of sector or
company size, failing to account for fundamental differences in organization and the nature of
work. Enforcement was inconsistent. The SAG largely ignored violations by influential business

**For additional analytical, business and investment opportunities information,
please contact Global Investment & Business Center, USA
at (202) 546-2103. Fax: (202) 546-3275. E-mail: ibpusa3@gmail.com
Global Business and Legal Information Databank: www.ibpus.com**

owners and lacked resources to conduct sufficient inspections elsewhere, as a majority of firms were unable to meet the unreasonable requirements.

In 2011, however, the Ministry of Labor laid out a more sophisticated plan known as "Nitaqat," under which companies are divided into sectors, each with a different set of quotas for Saudi employment based on company size. Each company is determined to be in one of four strata based on actual percentage of Saudi employees, with platinum and green strata for companies meeting or exceeding the quota for their sector and size, and yellow and red strata for those failing to meet it. The Ministry of Labor set the quota for each sector so that 50% of companies were already platinum or green and the remaining 50% non-compliant. Expatriate employees in red and yellow companies can move freely to green or platinum companies, without the approval of their current employers, and green and platinum companies have greater privileges with regard to securing and renewing work permits for expatriates. The Ministry of Labor has announced the goal of reducing the expatriate population from approximately 30% currently to 20% of the total population.

Many elements of Nitaqat have garnered criticism from the private sector and parts of the government, but the SAG claims it resulted in the employment of 380,000 Saudis in its first ten months. In 2013, the Ministry of Labor and Ministry of Interior launched an ongoing campaign to deport illegal and improperly documented workers, which has resulted in higher labor costs for many businesses. In addition, all companies operating in the Kingdom, regardless of sector or size, are now obliged to pay SR 2,400 ($640) per year for each expatriate employee in excess of the number of the company's Saudi employees. Numerous employers, particularly in construction and other blue-collar services sectors, have vehemently criticized the SAG's new labor policies, but it appears the SAG will continue to enforce them.

Saudi labor law forbids union activity, strikes, and collective bargaining. However, the government allows companies that employ more than 100 Saudis to form "labor committees." By-laws detailing the functions of the committees were enacted in April 2002. Domestic workers are not covered under the provisions of the latest labor law, issued in 2005. The Saudi Majlis al-Shura, a consultative assembly with a role in the legislative process, has proposed a law covering domestic workers.

Overtime is normally compensated at time-and-a-half rates. The minimum age for employment is 14. The SAG does not adhere to the International Labor Organization's (ILO) convention protecting workers' rights. A July 2004 decree addresses some workers'-rights issues for non-Saudis, and the Ministry of Labor has begun taking employers to the Board of Grievances. Some of these penalties include banning these employers from recruiting foreign and/or domestic workers for a minimum of five years.

FOREIGN TRADE ZONES/FREE PORTS/TRADE FACILITATION

Saudi Arabia permits transshipment of goods through its ports in Jeddah, Dammam, and King Abdullah Economic City, and it has bonded re-export zones at the Jeddah and Dammam ports. Saudi Arabia is also a member of the Gulf Cooperation Council (GCC), which confers special trade and investment privileges among the six member states (Bahrain, Kuwait, Oman, Qatar, Saudi Arabia, and the UAE), and of the Arab Free Trade Zone, established in 2005.

FOREIGN DIRECT INVESTMENT AND FOREIGN PORTFOLIO INVESTMENT STATISTICS

Key Macroeconomic Data, U.S. FDI in Host Country/Economy

Economic Data	Host Country Statistical source*		USG or international statistical source		USG or International Source of Data: BEA; IMF; Eurostat; UNCTAD, Other
	Year	Amount	Year	Amount	
Host Country Gross Domestic Product (GDP) ($M USD)	2013	718,500	2013	$748,400	www.worldbank.org/en/country
Foreign Direct Investment	Host Country Statistical source*		USG or international statistical source		USG or international Source of data: BEA; IMF; Eurostat; UNCTAD, Other
U.S. FDI in partner country ($M USD, stock positions)	N/A		2013	$10,550	BEA
Host country's FDI in the United States ($M USD, stock positions)	N/A		2013	$0	BEA
Total inbound stock of FDI as % host GDP	N/A		2013	1.5%	BEA

Table 3: Sources and Destination of FDI

Direct Investment from/in Counterpart Economy Data					
From Top Five Sources/To Top Five Destinations (US Dollars, Millions)					
Inward Direct Investment			Outward Direct Investment		
Total Inward	169,206	100%	Total Outward	N/A	100%
Kuwait	16,761	10%			
France	15,918	9%			
Japan	13,160	8%			
United Arab Emirates	12,601	7%			
China, P.R.: Mainland	9,035	5%			

"0" reflects amounts rounded to +/- USD 500,000.

INSTITUTIONAL RAMEWORK

Formulation and implementation of Saudi Arabia's trade policy is the responsibility of the Ministry of Commerce and Industry (MCI), in coordination with other ministries, such as the Supreme Economic Council (headed by the King), and the Saudi Negotiating Team in charge of discussing and assessing WTO-related issues. The private sector provides inputs to trade policy formulation by communicating its views either directly to the MCI or through the chambers of commerce and industry on an *ad hoc* basis. Saudi Arabia is taking steps to boost its participation in the multilateral trading system, commensurate with its growing importance worldwide, including through the establishment of its WTO mission in June 2010.

The WTO Agreements and the GCC Treaty are the main factors underlying Saudi Arabia's trade policy. As part of its WTO accession negotiations, Saudi Arabia bound 100% of its tariff lines; made extensive commitments under the GATS; and became a signatory to the Information Technology Agreement (ITA) . Saudi Arabia has not been involved in any dispute under the WTO Dispute Settlement Mechanism directly, but has participated as a third party in six cases. Up to March 2011, Saudi Arabia had 15 notifications outstanding.

Saudi Arabia participates in two overlapping regional trade agreements, the GCC and the Pan-Arab Free Trade Area (PAFTA) . As a group, the GCC has concluded free-trade agreements with EFTA States and Singapore, which are in the process of ratification. The GCC is also involved in trade negotiations with Australia, China, EU, India, Japan, Korea, MERCOSUR, New Zealand, Pakistan, and Turkey. GCC Heads of States have agreed that any new preferential agreement concluded by a member would apply *pari passu* to all members, except for agreements with the United States.

TRADE POLICY INSTRUMENTS

Since 2003, Saudi Arabia has been aligning its tariff to the GCC common external tariff (CET) . Initially, a transition period of three years (31 December 2005) was envisaged to complete the CET alignment, but this was extended until the end of 2011. Saudi Arabia has a relatively simple MFN tariff; 98.6% of all rates are *ad valorem*, 19 tariff lines have mixed rates (on tobacco and tobacco-related products), and 81 lines correspond to products prohibited for religious reasons e.g. alcoholic beverages, live swine and swine products. There are no tariff quotas, no applied seasonal tariffs, and no other duties and charges on imports. Saudi Arabia does not impose VAT, excise duties or any other internal tax or charges on domestically produced or imported products.

Saudi Arabia's average MFN applied tariff is 5.2%. On the basis of the WTO definition, tariffs average 6.1% on agricultural products, and 5% on non-agricultural products. Upon its accession to the WTO, Saudi Arabia bound its tariff at rates ranging up to 200% (on tobacco and tobacco-related products) and averaging 10.9%, i.e. average bound rates of 15.4% on agricultural products, and 10.1% on non-agricultural goods. The overall average MFN applied tariff, at 5.7 percentage points lower than the bound rate, presents an element of uncertainty as it gives the authorities some margin for increasing applied MFN tariffs. Saudi Arabia also made seasonal tariff binding commitments on some fruits and vegetables.

On aggregate, Saudi Arabia's tariff displays positive escalation, from first-stage processed products, with an average tariff of 4.2%, to semi-finished goods, with an average rate of 5%, and fully processed products, on which tariffs average 5.5%. At a more disaggregate level, there are mixed results: tariff escalation is positive from the first to the final stage of processing in some industries (e.g. textiles and apparel, and wood products), thereby providing higher levels of effective protection to those industries than that reflected by the nominal rates; mixed (negative from the first to the second stage, and then positive) in the food, beverages, and tobacco industry (reflecting the high rates on tobacco) and non-metallic mineral products; and negative from the first to the final stage of processing in chemicals and plastics, partly because of duty-free imports of pharmaceuticals.

On the basis of commitments undertaken during its WTO accession negotiations, Saudi Arabia eliminated the requirement to authenticate import documentation, as of 31 December 2007. The use of a Saudi commercial agent is required only to import or export agricultural machinery. Import and export prohibitions and restrictions are maintained on a number of products, mainly for health, security, moral, and religious reasons, but also on SPS grounds. Saudi Arabia is harmonizing its regime on standards and technical regulations at the GCC level, and accepted the TBT Code of Good Practice in 2006.

Saudi Arabia has adopted the GCC Treaty provisions on contingency trade remedies, but has never imposed any anti-dumping, countervailing or safeguard measures. The GCC Ministerial Committee has not applied any trade remedy measures, although it initiated two safeguard investigations, both of which were terminated due to lack of injury.

Saudi Arabia applies only one export duty, to untanned hides and skins, which will be eliminated on 10 September 2013. It maintains export bans on 11 categories of products, including Arabian breeding horses and wood. Saudi Arabia continues its efforts to diversify its export base, including through various finance and credit insurance operations on exports.

In addition to import duty concessions, other general incentives available to all investors, include: no personal income tax; 20% tax on profits while losses may be transferred indefinitely; medium- or long-term loans from the Saudi Industrial Development Fund of up to 50% of the project cost with competitive interest rates; land at competitive rates; supply of electricity, fuel, water, and natural gas at competitive industrial prices; support activities related to qualifying, training, and recruitment of Saudi workforce under the Human Resources Development Fund; and large R&D endowments.

Saudi Arabia notified the WTO that it does not maintain any state-trading enterprises. Despite some privatizations, state ownership remains significant throughout the economy, with the public sector being one of the largest employers.

Saudi Arabia's government procurement regime does not apply to certain procurements, including weapons and military equipment; consultancy; and goods and services available only through one supplier. It also provides for price preferences of 10% and 5% for local and GCC products, respectively. Saudi Arabia has been an observer to the plurilateral Government Procurement Agreement (GPA) since December 2007; it has yet to begin negotiations for GPA membership.

Saudi Arabia's competition legislation applies to all establishments, with the exception of public and wholly state-owned corporations. It addresses agreements between Saudi and foreign companies or between foreign companies, even when the agreements are concluded outside Saudi Arabia. There are no free zones or free economic zones. Some goods and services are subject to price regulation, e.g. wheat flour, fuel, gas, electricity, energy transportation services, and pharmaceuticals (subject to profit regulation) . During the last few years, Saudi Arabia has made significant progress in enforcing IPR protection.

SECTORAL OLICIES

The mining and energy sector has underpinned Saudi Arabia's economic development. The simple average applied MFN tariff on mining and quarrying (major division 2 of ISIC, Revision 2) is 5%. Saudi Arabia is the world's largest exporter of oil and one of the biggest producers of oil and natural gas. It retains the largest additional oil production capacity within OPEC, and has invested to increase its total production capacity to 12.5 million barrels per day (mbpd) (current production is around 8.5 mbpd) . Recent years have seen a substantial increase in domestic and foreign investment in gas. Saudi Arabia is also encouraging a reduction in the domestic consumption of oil through gas replacement, and is trialling solar thermal and other sustainable electricity generation methods. The fully state-owned Saudi Arabian Oil Company (Saudi Aramco) benefits from certain concessionary rights and privileges with respect to the production of crude oil, for example on (upstream) oil extraction, and certain exclusive rights and privileges in gas.

Services constitute a crucial component in Saudi Arabia's overall policy of economic diversification. In 2010, the sector accounted for 50.6% of real GDP and employed about three quarters of the workforce. Several state-owned enterprises participate in the sector on the basis of commercial considerations, according to the authorities. These include the National Commercial Bank, Tawuniya, Saudi Arabian Airlines Company, and Saudi Telecom Company.

Financial services, notably banking and cooperative insurance, have expanded substantially since Saudi Arabia's accession to the WTO.

Manufacturing contributed 12.6% to Saudi Arabia's real GDP in 2010. The sector benefits from its relatively large endowment of hydrocarbons, which are used as inputs by industries producing cement, petrochemicals, metals, and fertilizers. The simple average applied MFN tariff on manufacturing (major division 3 of ISIC, Revision 2) is 5.3%. The Government is an important shareholder in key manufacturing companies, e.g. Saudi Arabian Basic Industries Corporation (SABIC) . Four economic cities are being constructed, focusing mainly on heavy industries, comprising petrochemical, copper refinery and smelter, and aluminium complexes.

Despite its relatively small share of total real GDP (4.6% in 2010), agriculture is of key importance in the economy because of Saudi Arabia's food security objective. This is to be achieved mainly through relatively low customs tariffs (3.5%, major division 1 of ISIC, Revision 2) . In order to increase food security, Saudi Arabia has encouraged private companies to invest in farm projects abroad. The private sector has played a major role in the development of Saudi agriculture, mostly due to government programmes that offer, *inter alia*, long-term, interest-free loans; low-cost water, fuel and electricity; and reduced duties on imports of raw materials and machinery.

INVESTMENT RAMEWORK

The promotion of private-sector (foreign and domestic) investment is an important part of Saudi Arabia's economic programme, in order to diversify its economy away from oil, foster GDP growth, and create job opportunities for its young labour force. Saudi Arabia is promoting local and foreign investment in most economic activities, particularly energy; transport and logistics; information and communication technologies; health; life sciences; education; and tourism.

Under the Foreign Investment Law of 2000 and its Implementing Regulations of 2002 [44], foreign investment may take the form of an enterprise owned by foreign and national investors (i.e. joint-ventures but with no requirement for minimum share for national investors); or an enterprise wholly owned by foreign investors (i.e. 100% foreign equity) . Foreign investment projects benefit from all of the incentives and privileges offered to local projects.

GCC nationals are treated as Saudi nationals for the purposes of investment. Companies or citizens from GCC countries may currently own land (except real estate investment in Makkah and Madina) and engage in internal trading and distribution activities.

The Foreign Investment Law permits foreigners to invest in all sectors of the economy, except for activities on the Negative List (Table II.2), which includes fisheries; oil exploration, drilling and production; and various services subsectors. The list is periodically revised and is subject to the approval by the Supreme Economic Council. [45]

Economic activities in which foreign investment is not permitted

Manufacturing
Oil exploration, drilling, and production, except mining services listed at 5115 and 883 in International Industrial Classification Codes
Manufacturing of military equipment, devices, and uniforms
Manufacturing of civilian explosives
Services
Catering to military sectors
Security and detective services
Real estate investment in Makkah and Madina

Tourist orientation and guidance services related to Hajj and Umrah
Recruitment and employment services, including local recruitment offices
Real estate brokerage
Printing and publishing, except:
- Pre-printing services internationally classified at CPC 88442
- Printing presses internationally classified at CPC 88442
- Drawing and calligraphy internationally classified at CPC 87501
- Photography internationally classified at CPC 875
- Radio and television broadcasting studios internationally classified at CPC 96114
- Foreign media offices and correspondents internationally classified at CPC 962
- Promotion and advertising internationally classified at CPC 871
- Public relations internationally classified at CPC 86506
- Publication internationally classified at CPC 88442
- Press services internationally classified at CPC 88442
- Production, selling and renting of computer software internationally classified at CPC 88
- Media consultancies and studies internationally classified at CPC 853
- Typing and copying internationally classified at CPC 87504 and 87904
- Motion picture and video tape distribution services internationally classified at CPC 96113
Commission agents internationally classified at CPC 621
Audio-visual and media services
Land transportation services, excluding intercity passenger transport by trains
Services provided by midwives, nurses, physical therapy services, and quasi-doctoral services internationally classified at CPC 93191

Other

Fisheries
Blood banks, poison centres, and quarantines

Source: Information provided by the Saudi authorities.

Any foreign investor has the right to transfer out of Saudi Arabia their share derived from selling their equity or profits, as well as any amounts required for the settlement of contractual obligations pertaining to the project. There is a flat 20% tax rate on profits; losses may be carried forward; and there are no taxes on personal income. Investments related to the foreign investor will not be confiscated without a court order. They may not be subject to expropriation except for reasons of public interest and in exchange for an equitable compensation according to regulations. A foreign facility licensed under the Foreign Investment Act is entitled to own any real-estate for practicing the licensed activity and for the housing of staff. The Real-Estate Regulation allows foreign investment in real-estate worth SAR 30 million or more.

In 2000, the Council of Ministers established the Saudi Arabian General Investment Authority (SAGIA) as a one-stop shop to provide information and assistance to foreign investors, and to foster investment opportunities in Saudi Arabia. SAGIA operates under the umbrella of the Supreme Economic Council, and its duties include formulating government policies on investment activities; proposing plans and regulations to enhance the investment climate in Saudi Arabia; and evaluating and licensing investment proposals.

Other entities that actively promote investment opportunities in Saudi Arabia, include the majority-government-owned Saudi Arabian Basic Industries Corporation (SABIC), the Saudi Industrial Development Fund (SIDF) and Saudi Arabia Industrial Property Authority (MODON) . Private investment companies that have promoted opportunities in Saudi Arabia's industrial cities and other regions, include National Industrialization Company, Saudi Venture Capital Group, Saudi Industrial Development Company, Royal Commission for Jubail and Yanbu, and Arriyadh Development Authority

All foreign investment has to be approved by SAGIA, except for activities on the Negative List or where the authority to license is assigned to an agency other than SAGIA, such as the Saudi Arabian Monetary Agency (SAMA), the Capital Market Authority (CMA), the Communication and Information Technology Commission (CITC) or the Presidency of Meteorology and Environment (PME) . Saudi (and GCC) investors do not require to obtain a licence from SAGIA to invest. The requirement for SAGIA approval for foreign investment is a national treatment limitation inscribed in Saudi Arabia's Schedule on Specific Commitments in Services. [47]

Foreign investors may obtain more than one licence in diverse activities, provided they are not the owner of or a shareholder in a project that is in financial default. SAGIA set up an Investor's Service Centre (ISC) to issue licences to foreign companies, provide support services to investment projects, offer detailed information on the investment process, and coordinate with government ministries in order to facilitate investment procedures. The ISC must decide to grant or refuse a licence within 30 days of receiving an application and supporting documentation from the investor.

A petition against any penalty may be brought by the investor before the Board of Grievances. Possible penalties include: withholding incentives offered to the foreign investor; a fine not exceeding SAR 500,000; and cancelling the licence in case of a continuing violation and after written notification by SAGIA to rectify the violation within a specified period.

11. Saudi Arabia has signed bilateral investment treaties with: Austria, Azerbaijan, Belarus, Belgium, Czech Republic, China, Egypt, France, Germany, India, Indonesia, Italy, Korea (Rep. of), Malaysia, Philippines, Singapore, Spain, Sweden, Switzerland, Chinese Taipei, Turkey, Ukraine, and Viet Nam. [48] Saudi Arabia is a member of the Multilateral Investment Guarantee Agency. Saudi Arabia has also signed agreements for the avoidance of double taxation and the prevention of tax evasion with: Austria, Bangladesh, Belarus, China, France, Greece, India, Italy, Japan, Korea (Rep. of), Malaysia, Netherlands, Pakistan, Russian Federation, Singapore, South Africa, Spain, Syria, Tunisia, Turkey, United Kingdom, and Uzbekistan.

MAIN TRADE-RELATED LEGISLATION

Issue

Customs tariffs	- Common Customs Law dated the GCC States (1999), ratified by Royal Decree No. M/41 dated 3/11/1423H (5 January 2003)
	- GCC Common Customs Law (1999), ratified by Royal Decree No. M/41 dated 3/11/1423H (5 January 2003), and its rules of implementation
	- Royal Decree No. 104 dated 20/4/1423H (30 June 2002) (applying GCC Common Customs Tariff)
	- Royal Decree No. 40 dated 12/12/1424H (3 February 2004) (tariff rates for sensitive items)
Import licensing	- Council of Ministers Decision No. 84 dated 1.4.1421H (3 July 2000) (Import Licensing Guide)
	- The Import Licensing Law, issued pursuant to Council of Ministers Decision No. 88 dated 6/4/1423H (16 June 2002) (Import Licensing Procedures)

Quantitative import restrictions	- Ministry of Commerce and Industry Decision No. 1308 dated 27/5/1424H (27July 2003)
Customs valuation	- Royal Decree No. 190 dated 16/12/1409H (19 July 1989)
	- Royal Decree M/41 dated 3/11/1423H (5 January 2003) (Common Customs Law of the GCC)
	- Council of Ministers Decree No. 162 dated 17/6/1423H (28 August 2002)
	- Ministerial Decision No. 1207 dated 9/5/1425H (27 June 2004)
Trade in transit	- Ministerial Decree No. 5618 dated 15/11/1424H (8 January 2004)
Technical barriers to trade	- Saudi Arabian Standards Organization (SASO) Technical Directive, Parts 1 through 4, issued 18 July 2000, as amended
	- Saudi Standards, Metrology and quality organization (SASO) Technical Directive part I through 4 issued 18 July 2000 as amended on 19 July 2005
Preshipment inspection	- Council of Ministers Decision No. 213 dated 3/8/1424H (30 September 2003) (cancelling the ICCP)
	- Ministerial Decision No. 6386 dated 21/6/1425H (8 August 2004) (establishing the ICCP Replacement Committee)
Sanitary and phytosanitary measures	- Shelf Life of Food Products, WT/ACC/SAU/27
	- Ministerial Decision No. 943 dated 1/5/1424H (1 July 2003) ("Sanitary and Phytosanitary Unified Procedures")
	- Council of Ministers Decision No. 109 dated 30/4/1424H (30 June 2003)
	- Council of Ministers Decision No. 85 dated 1/4/1421H (4 July 2000)
	- Council of Ministers Decree No. 207 dated 26/1/1396H (28 January 1976)
	- Royal Decree No. M/10 dated 3/3/1392H (16 April 1972)
	- Royal Decree No. M/3 dated 8/2/1423H (21 April 2002) (Law of Private Laboratories) and Implementing Regulations, issued pursuant to Ministerial Decision No. M/3 dated 21/2/1424H (23 April 2003)
	- Royal Decree No. M/4905 dated 1/6/1430H (26 May 2009) "Transferring SPS Responsibility from MCI to SFDA"
Framework for making and enforcing policies	- Basic Law of Governance, Royal Decree No. A/90 dated 27/8/1412H (1 March 1992)
	- Law of the Shoura Council, Royal Decree No. A/91 dated

	27/8/1412H (1 March 1992)
	- Law of the Council of Ministers, Royal Decree No. A/13 dated 27/3/1414H (20 August 1993)
	- Commercial Agencies Law, issued pursuant to Royal Decree No. M/11 dated 20/2/1382H (22 July 1962)
	- Combat of Commercial Fraud Law, Royal Decree No. M/11 dated 29/5/1404H (1 March 1984)
	- Negotiable instruments Law, Royal Decree No. M/37 dated 11/10/1383H (24 February 1964)
	- Board of Grievances Law, issued pursuant to Royal Decree No. M/51 dated 17/1/1402H (14 November 1981)
	- Council of Ministers Resolution No. 165 dated 24/6/1423H (1 September 2002) (implementing the Vienna Convention on the Law of Treaties)
Trading rights	- Law on Commercial Registration, issued pursuant to Royal Decree No. M/1 dated 21/2/1416H (19 July 1995)
	- Law on Commercial Names, issued pursuant to Royal Decree No. M/15 dated 12/8/1420H (20 November 1999) and the associated rules and regulations
	- Professional Companies Law, issued pursuant to Royal Decree No. M/4 dated 18/2/1412H (29 August 1991)
	- Commercial Agencies Law, issued pursuant to Royal Decree No. M/11 dated 20/2/1382H (22 July 1962)
	- Implementing Regulations for Commercial Agencies Law, Ministerial Resolution No. 1897 dated 24/5/1401H (29 March 1981)
Trade and environment	- General Environment Regulations and Rules for Implementation in the Kingdom of Saudi Arabia
Competition policies	- Law on Competition Policies, issued pursuant to Royal Decree No. M/25 dated 4/5/1421H (22 June 2004)
Pricing policies	-Council of Ministers Resolution No. 68 dated 29/5/1412H (1 December 1991)
	-Council of Ministers resolution No. 260 dated 23/10/1422H (7 January 2002) (cancelling Council of Ministers Resolution No. 68 dated November 1992)
	-Supreme Council for the Petroleum and Mineral Affairs Resolution No. 15 dated 11/3/1422H (3 June 2001)
	-Law of the Pharmaceutical Established and Pharmaceutical(Preparations) and its Executive Regulations, issued by the Royal Decree No. (M/31) dated 1/6/1424H
Privatization	- Council of Ministers Decision No. 219 dated 6/9/1423H (11 November 2002) (Privatization Strategy)
	- Supreme Economic Council Decision No. 1/23 dated

For additional analytical, business and investment opportunities information,
please contact Global Investment & Business Center, USA
at (202) 546-2103. Fax: (202) 546-3275. E-mail: ibpusa3@gmail.com
Global Business and Legal Information Databank: www.ibpus.com

	23/3/1423H (4 June 2002)
	- Council of Ministers Resolution No. 60 dated 1/4/1418H (5 August 1997)
	- Council of Ministers Resolution No. 257 dated 11/11/1421H (5 February 2001)
	- Royal Decree No. 7-B-16941 dated 6/11/1417H (15 March 1997)
	- Council of Ministers Resolution 169 dated 11/8/1419H (30 November 1998) (restructuring electricity sector)
Investment regime	- Foreign Investment Law, Royal Decree No. M/1 dated 5/1/1421H (9 April 2000) and implementing regulations issued 14/4/1423H (24 June 2002) (replacing the 1979 Foreign Capital Investment Law)
	- "Negative List", issued by Supreme Economic Council Decision No. 17/23 dated 1/12/1423H (22 May 1993)
	- Foreign Capital Investment Law, Royal Order No. M/4 dated 2/2/1399H (1 January 1979)
	- Capital Market Law, Royal Decree No. M/30 dated 2/6/1424H (13 July 2003)
	- Council of Ministers Decision No. 50 dated 21/4/1415H (27 September 1994)
	- Council of Ministers Bureau Letter 8/490 dated 28/6/1414H (13 December 1993)
Government procurement	- Standard Rules for Giving Priority in Government Purchases to National Products and Products of National Origin of Gulf Cooperation Council States
	- Government Purchases Law, issued pursuant to Royal Decree No. M/14 dated 7/4/1397H (27 March 1977)
Trade-related intellectual property	- Copyrights Law, issued pursuant to Royal Decree No. M/41 dated 2/7/1424H (30 August 2003), and Implementing Regulations, issued pursuant to Ministerial Decision No. 1688/1 dated 10/4/1425H (29 May 2004)
	- Law of Trademarks, issued pursuant to Royal Decree No. M/21 dated 29/5/1423H (7 August 2002) and Implementing Regulations, issued pursuant to Ministerial Order No. 1723 dated 26/7/1423H (4 October 2002)
	- Law of Trade Names, issued pursuant to Royal Decree No. M/15 dated 12/8/1420H (20 November 1999)
	- Law of Commercial Data, issued pursuant to Royal Decree No. M/15 dated 15/4/1423H (25 June 2002), and Regulations for the Protection of Confidential Commercial Information, issued pursuant to Council of Ministers Decision No. 50 dated 25/2/1426H (4 April 2005), as amended by Ministerial Decision No. 3218 dated 25/3/1426H (4 May 2005), and as further amended by Ministerial Decision No. 431 dated 1/5/1426H (8 June 2005)

	- GCC Patents Law
	- Law on Patents, Layout Designs of Integrated Circuits, Plant Varieties and Industrial Designs, issued pursuant to Royal Decree No. M/27 dated 29/5/1425H (17 July 2004), and Implementing Regulations, issued pursuant to Ministerial Decision No. 118828/M/10 dated 14/11/1425H (26 December 2004)
	- Border Measures Regulations, issued pursuant to Ministerial Decision No. 1277 dated 15/5/1425H (3 July 2004)
Agricultural policy	- Royal Decree No. 58 dated 3/12/1382H (6 May 1963) (founding the Saudi Arabian Agricultural Bank)
	- Royal Decree No. 184 dated 24/9/1419H (14 December 1998) (ending issuance by GSFMO of permits for importing or exporting any product)
	- Royal Decree No. 4/B/49434 dated 8/12/1423H (10 February 2003) (ending GFSMO receipt of domestic barley)
	- Council of Ministers resolution No. 335 dated 19/11/1428H "Phasing out local wheat production received by GFSMO within 8 years"
	- Royal Decree No. (M/9) dated 1/2/1430H/ The Agriculture Development Fund (ADF) replacing the Saudi Arabian Agriculture Bank (SAAB)
Industrial policy	- Rules for the coordination of Industrial Establishments in the GCC States
	- Saudi Industrial Development Fund Law, promulgated by Royal Decree No. M/3 dated 26/2/1394H (20 March 1974)
	- Law for the Protection and Encouragement of National Industries
	- Saudi Industrial Development Fund Law
Services	- Cooperative Insurance Companies Control Law, Royal Decree No. M/32 dated 2/6/1424H (31 July 2003), and Implementing Regulations, issued pursuant to Ministerial Decision No. 1/596 dated 1/3/1425H (20 April 2004), as amended by Royal Decree No. 3120/MB dated 4/3/1426H (13 April 2005)
	- Council of Ministers Decision No. 222 dated 12/8/1422H (29 October 2001) (Compulsory Auto Insurance Act)
	- Royal Decree No. M/10 dated 1/5/1420H (12 August 1999) (Law of Cooperative Health Insurance)
	- Royal Decree No. M/5 dated 17/5/1405H (18 January 1986) (establishment of National Company for Co-operative Insurance)
	- Banking Control Law

For additional analytical, business and investment opportunities information, please contact Global Investment & Business Center, USA at (202) 546-2103. Fax: (202) 546-3275. E-mail: ibpusa3@gmail.com Global Business and Legal Information Databank: www.ibpus.com

	- Labour and Workmen Law, Royal Decree No. M/21 dated 6/9/1389H (15 November 1969)
	- Credit Information Law, Royal Decree No. M/37 dated 5/7/1429H (9/7/2008)
	- Law of the Private Health Institution and its Executive Regulations, issued by the Royal Decree No. (M/40) dated 3/11/1423H
	- Law of Practice of Health profession and its Executive Regulations, issued by the Royal Decree No. (M/59) dated 11/4/1426H

Source: Information provided by the Saudi authorities/

For additional analytical, business and investment opportunities information,
please contact Global Investment & Business Center, USA
at (202) 546-2103. Fax: (202) 546-3275. E-mail: ibpusa3@gmail.com
Global Business and Legal Information Databank: www.ibpus.com

PRACTICAL AND LEGAL INFORMATION FOR STARTING BUSINESS

ENTERING THE MARKET REGULATIONS

MARKET OVERVIEW

To date, the accession of His Majesty King Salman has been relatively smooth with little disruption to the Saudi economy. Saudi Arabia is the only Middle Eastern country among the G-20 members of industrialized states, and had a 2014 real GDP of approximately USD 777.9 billion. The public sector dominates the Saudi economy with oil accounting for 45% of GDP and nearly 90% of government revenues. A nascent manufacturing sector accounts for less than 10% of GDP. Economists project a fiscal deficit of 13.3% of GDP due to lower oil revenues, the government's rising salary bill and the costs related to military action in the region. There have been cuts in certain capital expenditure areas such as stadium construction and certain future Aramco petrochemical and refinery projects, though most current projects are moving forward and there has not been significant deterioration in the business climate resulting from lower oil prices. In fact, from January – May 2015, contract awards in Saudi Arabia increased nearly 25% from the same period last year to $22 billion, while the value of awards in other Gulf countries has fallen. Given the continued drive towards economic diversification, there will be areas to increase off budget spending like programs to build affordable housing. Economic growth is forecast at 3% for 2015 and is expected to slow to 2.8% by 2019. Private sector growth continues to be driven by several major infrastructure projects including rail networks, housing, ports, and civil infrastructure.

The Saudi Government will continue towards economic diversification from oil, and improved living standards and expanded Saudi labor opportunities in the private sector will remain key Saudi priorities.

The United States exported USD 18.679 billion to Saudi Arabia in 2014, our second largest export market in the Gulf behind the UAE, and the Kingdom is America's 12th largest trading partner. Major U.S. exported products include passenger automobiles, trucks/buses, industrial machinery, construction/building equipment, civil aircraft, defense systems, IT, health care products.

MARKET CHALLENGES

Inflation:

Saudi inflation dropped to 2% year-on-year during first quarter 2015, which is the lowest inflation level in 9 years. The lowering of inflation was attributed to falling commodity prices and the strong U.S. Dollar. However, as Saudization and pressures for subsidy reform move forward, economists forecast inflation to hit 3.5% by 2017.

Commercial Disputes Settlements:

The enforcement of foreign arbitration awards for private sector disputes has yet to be upheld in practice. Furthermore, government agencies are not allowed to agree to international arbitration without approval from the Council of Ministers, which is rarely granted.

For additional analytical, business and investment opportunities information,
please contact Global Investment & Business Center, USA
at (202) 546-2103. Fax: (202) 546-3275. E-mail: ibpusa3@gmail.com
Global Business and Legal Information Databank: www.ibpus.com

Intellectual Property Protection:

Intellectual property protection has steadily increased in the Kingdom. Over the last seven years, Saudi Arabia has comprehensively revised its laws covering intellectual property rights to bring them in line with the WTO agreement on Trade Related Aspects of Intellectual Property Rights (TRIPs). The Saudi Government undertook the revisions as part of Saudi Arabia's accession to the WTO, and promulgated them in coordination with the World Intellectual Property Organization (WIPO). The Saudi Government updated its Trademark Law (2002), Copyright Law (2003), and Patent Law (2004), with the dual goals of TRIPs-compliance and effective deterrence against violators. In 2008 the Violations Review Committee created a website and has populated it with information on current cases. The patent office continues to build its capacity through training, has streamlined its procedures, hired more staff, and reduced its backlog.

In September 2009, the King approved a mechanism to protect Exclusive Marketing Rights (EMR) for certain pharmaceutical products which lost patent protection when Saudi Arabia transitioned to a new TRIPS-compliant patent law in 2004. The Saudi Ministerial Council in December 2009 approved the Kingdom's accession to both the Intellectual Property Owners Association Patent Cooperation Treaty (PCT) and its Implementing Regulations and the Patent Law Treaty (PLT) adopted by the Diplomatic Conference in Geneva on June 1, 2000. The Council of Ministers issued a resolution on 23/11/1428H (December 3, 2007) approving the Law of Trademarks for GCC countries.

Counterfeiting:

Although anti-counterfeiting laws exist, manufacturers of consumer products and automobile spare parts are particularly concerned about the availability of counterfeit products in Saudi Arabia. The Saudi Government remains committed to stopping counterfeit products from entering into the country.

Standards and labeling:

As part of the GCC Customs Union, the six Member States are working toward unifying their standards and conformity assessment systems. However, each Member State continues to apply its own standard or a GCC standard. The Government of Saudi Arabia mandates that a Certificate of Conformity must accompany all consumer goods exported to Saudi Arabia. Labeling and marking requirements are compulsory for any products exported to Saudi Arabia. Industrial standards and conformity assessment remains the most significant trade issue affecting U.S. manufacturers.

Travel Advisories:

Americans visiting Saudi Arabia are advised to check the U.S. State Department's website at http://travel.state.gov for the latest information on travel to Saudi Arabia.

MARKET OPPORTUNITIES

Saudi Arabia has the largest IT market in the Gulf region, projected at approximately USD4.6 billion. Particularly important growth sectors include cyber security, smart grid, and command/control of major infrastructure utilizing geospatial IT systems.

Saudi Arabia's ambitious rail plans are fuelling activity in the infrastructure sector, with USD 30 billion worth of contracts either under way or at the bidding stage. Major projects include the North-South railway, the Saudi Land Bridge, and the Mecca-Medina railway. In addition to both light rail and heavy rail, Saudi Arabia also seeks to expand intermodal connectivity of various transportation modes including maritime shipping, buses, rail and airport expansion.

The state-owned utility Saudi Electricity Company (SEC) intends to invest USD70 billion by 2018 to add 22MW to the nation's power-generating capacity in order to meet the growing demand from a rapidly increasing population. SEC's goal is to reach a power- generation capacity of 65,000 MW by the end of 2018. SEC will also invest in personnel training as it continues to evolve into a regional supplier and distributor of electricity.

Over the long term, Saudi Arabia is expanding minerals mining and diversification of downstream petrochemicals in order to develop a strong manufacturing base for entire automobiles, electronics and life science technologies. The purpose is to create highly technical and high paying jobs for Saudi nationals.

The Saudi healthcare market is expected to continue to provide excellent opportunities for U.S. firms. The government healthcare budget in 2015 increased almost 50% to $43 billion reflecting the high priority the sector plays in Saudi government planning. With a new dynamic, market-oriented Health Minister, the Saudi healthcare sector is expected to open up further to public-private partnerships. As Saudi Arabia implements a ten year plan to build five medical cities in the Kingdom, U.S. e-health and hospital management solutions and medical devices will continue to find solid opportunities.

MARKET ENTRY STRATEGY

Although American exporters are not required to appoint a local Saudi agent or distributor to sell to Saudi companies, we strongly recommend that all new-to-market U.S. companies consider partnering with a local company for the purposes of monitoring business opportunity, navigating import and standards testing regulations and identifying public sector sales opportunities. For complete information and regulations on registering a business in Saudi Arabia, please visit the Saudi Arabia Government Investment Agency (SAGIA) at www.sagia.gov.sa .

Although the Saudi Government encourages foreign investment, a U.S. firm is strongly encouraged to seek in-country legal counsel on the best approach. The U.S. Commercial Service can assist by providing a list of local attorneys, which may be associated with American law firms.

The U.S. Department of Commerce in Saudi Arabia assists U.S. exporters and service companies to identify market opportunity, business partners, and are regularly advocating greater transparency in commercial matters relating to industry standards, commercial rule of law, and public procurement.

Commercial and industrial rents

Inside industrial cities	SAR 1 - 2 per square meter per year [US$0.26]
Elsewhere	SAR 20 to SAR100 per square meter per year [US$5.33 to US$26.67]

Residential rents

Rentals for residential accommodation can vary immensely. Worker accommodation is usually the least expensive but the annual rental for senior management accommodation would likely exceed US$40,000 for a three bedroom furnished villa in a residential compound.

Utilities
Electricity

Rate of industrial consumption of loads (1000 KwH) or less

Time	Seasonal Rate (For plants with electromechanical counters)		Rate (For plants with digital counters)	
	Time period	Rate (KwH/H)	Time period	Rate (KwH/H)
Oct- April	all the times	12	all times	12
May - Sep	All the times	15	Off-peak time Sat-Thu : 08:00-00:00 Fri:09:00-00:00 21:00 - 00:00 -	10
			Peak time Sat-Thu :12:00- 17:00	26
			The other times	15

Rate of industrial consumption of loads (1000 KwH) or more

Time	Seasonal Rate (For plants with electromechanical counters)		Rate (For plants with digital counters)	
	Time period	Rate (KwH/H)	Time period	Rate (KwH/H)
Oct- April	all the times	14	all times	14
May - Sep	All the times	15	Off-peak time Sat-Thu : 08:00-00:00 Fri:09:00-00:00 21:00 - 00:00 -	10
			Peak time Sat-Thu :12:00- 17:00	26
			The other times	15

Water	Rising from SAR0.10 [US$0.027] over four further bands to a maximum of SAR6.00 [US$1.6] per cubic meter.

Employee costs

Employee incomes vary according to the status, position and experience of the employee as elsewhere in the world.

In addition 18% General Organization for Social Insurance (GOSI) contribution for annuities is payable (9% by the employer and 9% by the employee), for Saudis employed and 2% for occupational hazards: health insurance, transportation or compensation in lieu of cars for more senior personnel, return tickets to the country of origin and an end of service bonus payment.

BASIC LAWS AND REGULATIONS AFFECTING BUSINESS

MAIN CORPORATE AND COMMERCIAL LAWS

Royal Decree for the Regulation of Companies No. M6 of 1965 (as amended).
Royal Decree for the Regulation of Commercial Agencies No. 11 of 1962 (as amended). Implementation Rules for Commercial Agencies Regulations No. 1897 of 1981.

Foreigners wishing to conduct business in Saudi Arabia may do so by establishing a permanent presence in Saudi Arabia or by entering into an agency relationship for the distribution and sale of their products. Below is a summary of the business forms available under Saudi law:

LIMITED LIABILITY COMPANY (LLC)

This is the most common form for entering into joint ventures with Saudi partners; however, a Saudi partner is not required since there are no legal limitations on the percentage of foreign ownership.

The minimum capital investment required to establish an LLC is SR 500,000. An LLC must have between 2 and 50 shareholders and is managed and represented by one or more managers. There is no Board of Directors, although shareholders often provide for a Board and other management arrangements in the Memorandum of Association. The LLC must also have an auditor and, where it has more that twenty (20) partners, it must establish a Board of Controllers.

PARTNERSHIPS

Foreign companies seeking to do business in the Kingdom may enter into a limited partnership. The limited partnership, or "sharikat tawsiya baseetah", is a separate business entity comprised of several individuals or companies, including general (at least one) and limited partners. The general partners are liable for partnership debts to the full extent of their personal assets while the limited partners are liable only to the extent of their capital contributions.

JOINT STOCK CORPORATION

A Joint Stock Corporation ("JSC") is an entity with at least five shareholders holding transferable shares. The minimum capital requirements are SR 2 million for a private JSC and SR 10 million for a public JSC. Liability of shareholders is limited to the par value of each shareholder's share capital. The JSC must be approved by license or Royal Decree published in the Saudi Official Gazette. Additionally, it must be registered with the MOC Companies Department and the MOC Commercial Registry.

BRANCH OFFICES

Foreign companies may register a wholly foreign-owned Saudi branch office, provided that they obtain the requisite license. The branch office may engage in any government contract or private sector work within the scope of its license. Branch offices are subject to the requirements of the Government Tenders Regulations, where applicable. Branch office registration follows the same general procedure as for the registration of an LLC.

For additional analytical, business and investment opportunities information,
please contact Global Investment & Business Center, USA
at (202) 546-2103. Fax: (202) 546-3275. E-mail: ibpusa3@gmail.com
Global Business and Legal Information Databank: www.ibpus.com

SPONSORSHIP AND TEMPORARY COMMERCIAL REGISTRATION

As an alternative to forming one of the above entities, foreign contractors have in the past performed isolated private sector projects under the sponsorship of their Saudi customer and, in contracts with the Saudi government, the foreign contractor may perform its obligation under a temporary commercial registration (TCR).

With respect to sponsorships, they can be in two forms. The first is where the foreign contractor obtains a business visa, sponsored by the Saudi customer. The second form of sponsorship is where the foreign contractor 'seconds' its employees to the employment and sponsorship of the Saudi customer.

If a foreign contractor is awarded a project with the Saudi government and it does not have a registered presence in Saudi in one of the above-discussed forms, it must obtain a TCR (Commerce Ministry Resolution No. 680 dated 10 October 1978). An application for TCR must be filed within 30 days of obtaining the contract, along with a copy of the contract. Additionally, a 'service agent' must be identified pursuant to the Saudi Service Agent Regulations. TCRs are limited in scope and duration to the substance and term of the government contract for which they are issued.

COMMERCIAL AGENCIES

Agencies and distributorships are governed by the Commercial Agencies Regulations and the related Implementing Rules (Royal Decree No. M/11, as amended by Royal decree No. M/32; Ministry of Commerce Decision No. 1897). The rules and regulations reserve a monopoly for Saudi nationals and wholly owned Saudi entities on 'trading' activities. Trading activities include the import and local purchase of goods for resale. Therefore, foreign companies engaging in such activities must use Saudi commercial agents and distributors, who must register their Agency Agreements with the MOC Agency Register. The agent must hold a valid Saudi commercial registration permitting him to act as an agent or distributor and the directors and authorized representatives of the agent must be Saudi nationals. The Commercial Agency Regulations bar appointment of shell agents indirectly owned or controlled by the foreign principal, therefore, the Saudi agent must be independent from the foreign principal.

Agencies do not have to be exclusive, although MOC will not normally register more than one agreement for the same principal.

The Regulations do specify requirements for compensation of a terminated agent. The MOC Model agency contract provides for "reasonable compensation" of the agent upon termination for "activities that may have resulted in the apparent success of the business". Shari'a law, which is applied by both the arbitration and the Grievance Board, excludes indirect or consequential damages.

MOC will not register a new agency agreement with the same foreign principal before the old one has been deregistered. This normally requires a letter of consent by the old agent or administrative cancellation by MOC upon the expiry of the contract.

INDUSTRIAL PROJECTS

All industrial projects, whether Saudi or foreign, and joint ventures whose fixed capital exceeds SR 1million (US $267,000), excluding the value of land and buildings, must be licensed. Licenses

For additional analytical, business and investment opportunities information,
please contact Global Investment & Business Center, USA
at (202) 546-2103. Fax: (202) 546-3275. E-mail: ibpusa3@gmail.com
Global Business and Legal Information Databank: www.ibpus.com

are granted pursuant to either the National Industries Protection and Encouragement Act, which applies to projects by Saudi citizens with full Saudi capital, or the New Foreign Investment Law, which applies to projects with full foreign capital or mixed Saudi/foreign capital (see discussion above).

Industrial establishments are entitled to the following incentives and exemptions under Saudi law:

- Certain tariff exemptions;

- Subsidized industrial land, housing and utilities;

- Subsidies for training Saudi employees and other forms of assistance for partially foreign owned Saudi businesses;
- Export assistance for locally manufactured products; and
- Public procurement preference for majority Saudi owned joint venture companies.

COMMERCIAL AGENCIES

The underlying statutory framework concerning commercial agencies, distributorships and franchises in Saudi Arabia is set out in the Commercial Agency Regulation, Royal Decree No. 11 of 20th Safar 1382 Hejra corresponding to 22nd July 1962 Gregorian, and the Rules for the Implementation of the Commercial Agency Regulations of 1981. The application of these two statutes to franchises arises from Ministerial Order No. 1012 of 1992 of the Minister of Commerce. For ease of reference, we shall refer below to commercial agencies, distributorships and franchises collectively as agencies, unless the context requires otherwise.

Article 6 of the Implementing Rules provides that no entity may act as an agent without being registered in the commercial agents' register of the Ministry of Commerce and Industry, and requires agency agreements to be registered with the Ministry of Commerce and Industry within three months from the agreement coming into effect, the ostensible reason being consumer protection, namely that after-sales service and the provision of spare parts is guaranteed.

The Service Agency Regulation of 1978 required that foreign parties who are not already licensed to conduct business in Saudi Arabia cannot perform contracts for the Saudi Arabian government or government agencies without having a registered service agent in the country, but that Regulation was repealed by Royal Decree No. M/22 of 16th Jumada Awal 1422 Hejra corresponding to 6th August 2001 Gregorian. Historically, registration of agency agreements was not crucial where only private sector sales were contemplated, because there are no Saudi Arabian laws which provide that a foreign party selling foreign goods to a Saudi Arabian private sector entity must have an agent or distributor in Saudi Arabia. In particular, until very recently there was no requirement that only a registered distributor may import specific brand goods into Saudi Arabia. However, in line with a tightening-up of trademark protection following Saudi Arabia's accession to the World Trade Organisation on 11th December 2005, in recent months the Ministry of Commerce and Industry has made the import of high profile brand goods conditional upon the importer being the registered distributor, to prevent the import of pirated goods. To date, the application of this rule appears to be flexible, and determined by whether or not the concerned Ministry of Commerce and Industry officials are familiar with a given brand.

Articles 10 and 11 of the Implementing Rules provide that agency agreements must satisfy certain minimum requirements by setting out, inter alia:
the rights and obligations of each of the parties;

the obligations of both parties vis-a-vis consumers as regards the provision of maintenance and spare parts;
the capacity and nationality of each of the parties;
the subject of the agency;
the area covered by the agreement;
the services, works and goods covered by the agreement;
the duration and method of renewal of the agency; and
the mode of termination or lapse of the agency.

In 1982 the Ministry of Commerce and Industry first issued a recommended form of agency agreement, commonly referred to as the "model agency agreement", which was recommended to be used in agency and distributorship relations with foreign principals. The terms of this model agreement have been amended from time to time. Similarly, together with Ministerial Order No. 1012 was issued a model franchise agreement "for the guidance of franchise contractors". The use of any of these model agreements has never been mandatory, provided that the minimum requirements laid down by Articles 10 and 11 of the Implementing Rules are met. Apart from these formal requirements, the validity, effect and interpretation of agency agreements is governed by Islamic Law, which grants considerable freedom of contract to the parties to a contract. In general, the Saudi Arabian courts will give effect to the parties' common intention set out in the agreement.

It is the agent's duty to register the agreement. The principal has no actual involvement in the process. Registration of an agency does not afford an agent particular protection vis-a-vis the principal. The Saudi Arabian courts are not concerned with the registration of contracts and will, ordinarily, give effect to the common intention of the parties expressed in their written agreements, whether registered or not. The only context where registration of an agency agreement gives the agent some advantage in Saudi Arabia is that, until a dispute between a terminated agent and the principal is finalized, in principle no new agent can be registered, thus depriving the principal of the opportunity to effect government sales in Saudi Arabia. However, a newly appointed agent can still effect private sector sales in the meantime, and, in appropriate circumstances, a newly appointed agent can apply to the Ministry of Commerce and Industry for a temporary registration of the agency, particularly if he can demonstrate that sale of the principal's products or services is in the public interest.

A new commercial agencies regulation has been under discussion since 1995, and has gone through numerous drafts in the meantime. Government sources have indicated that a final draft may now be ready. While earlier drafts were more restrictive on the principal's and agent's freedom of contract than under the current regime, current indications are that the parties to agency agreements may enjoy even greater freedom of contract under the new legislation.

COMPANIES REGULATIONS

Formation and operation of business firms and companies is regulated by companies Law promulgated by Royal Decree No. M/6 dated 22 Rabi I 1385 H., (1965). Royal Decree No. M/5 dated 12 Safar 1387 H. (1967) and Royal Decree No. M/23 dated 28 Jumada II 1402 H. (1982) amended the regulations for companies. Under Article 1 of the Companies Law, a company has been defined as a contract pursuant to which each of two or more persons undertake to participate, in an enterprise aiming at profit, by offering in specie or as work a share, for sharing in the profits or losses resulting from such enterprise.

Following are some of its important provisions:

**For additional analytical, business and investment opportunities information,
please contact Global Investment & Business Center, USA
at (202) 546-2103. Fax: (202) 546-3275. E-mail: ibpusa3@gmail.com
Global Business and Legal Information Databank: www.ibpus.com**

- Under article 2, companies can take any of the following forms:

  - General Partnerships.
  - Limited partnerships.
  - Joint Ventures.
  - Corporations.
  - Partnerships Limited by Shares.
  - Limited Liability Partnerships.
  - Variable Capital Companies.
  - Cooperative Companies.

- Without prejudice to the companies acknowledged by the Islamic "Shari'ah" Law, any company not having any of the legal forms as given in Article 2 of the Companies Law shall be null and void.
- Partner's contribution may consist of a certain sum of money (a contribution in cash), or of a capital asset (a contribution in kind). It may also comprise services except in the cases where the provisions of the Companies' Regulations imply otherwise, but it may not consist (solely) of the partner's reputation or influence.
- Every partner shall be considered indebted to the company for the contribution he has undertaken to make. If he fails to surrender it on the date set therefore, he shall be liable to the company for any damages arising from such delay.
- Save in the case of a joint venture, a company's memorandum of association and any amendment thereto must be recorded in writing in the presence of a registrar. Otherwise, such memorandum or amendment shall not be valid vis-à-vis third parties.
- With the exception of joint ventures, any company incorporated in accordance with these Regulations shall establish its head office in the Kingdom. It shall be deemed to have Saudi nationality, but this shall not necessarily entail its enjoyment of such rights as may be restricted to Saudis.

For details pertaining to formation and operation of companies, please contact Companies Department, Ministry of Commerce (see here for address).

THE TAX SYSTEM:

The Kingdom of Saudi Arabia has a very liberal tax system; there are few taxes payable by an individual or a company and they are also at very low rates.

1. Zakat

The Zakat (a form of tithe) is paid annually by Saudi individuals and companies within the provisions of Islamic law as laid down by Royal Decree No. 17/2/28/8634 dated 29/6/1370 H. (1950). The Zakat is an annual flat rate of 2.5 percent of the assessable amount.

2. Personal Income Tax

For individual employees, both national and expatriate, there is no income tax in the Kingdom.

For additional analytical, business and investment opportunities information, please contact Global Investment & Business Center, USA at (202) 546-2103. Fax: (202) 546-3275. E-mail: ibpusa3@gmail.com Global Business and Legal Information Databank: www.ibpus.com

Self-employed expatriates such as doctors, accountants, lawyers, etc. pay taxes on their net annual income at the following rates:

Net Income (per year)	Tax Rate (percent)
First 6,000	Exempted
From SR 6,001 - 10,000	5
From SR 10,001 - 20,000	10
From SR 20,001 - 30,000	20
Over SR 30,000	30

A slab system is followed to calculate such taxes.

3. Tax on Business Income:

A company, under the tax regulations, means a company or partnership having material gain as the basic objective. The taxable incomes of companies include:

* profits of a foreign company;
* shares of non-Saudi sleeping partners in the net profits of partnership companies.

All legitimate business expenses and costs, including business losses and depreciation, are deductible in computing net profits. Any reasonable method of depreciation may be adopted by the company but the same must be adhered to from year to year. Capital gains are included in the profits of the company. The following tax rates, on a slab basis, are now in force:

Net Profit Level	Tax Rate (percent)
First SR 100,000	25
From SR 100,001-500,000	35
From SR 500,001-1,000,000	40
Over SR 1,000,000	45

Income tax is charged at different rates for companies engaged in the production of petroleum and hydrocarbons in the Kingdom.

Every company is required to submit a financial statement on an official form and to pay the tax not later than the 15th day of the third month of the year following the Saudi Arabian fiscal year, which commences on the 10th of Capricorn (December 31).

Companies formed under the provisions of the Foreign Capital Investments Regulations with participation of Saudi capital of not less than 25 percent are exempt for up to ten years from payment of income tax.

For further details, please contact the Ministry of Finance and National Economy, Directorate of Zakat and Income, Companies Department, (see here for address). Note the New Amendments according to the new Foreign investment Law below:

1. For purpose of the State bearing 15% of taxes imposed on companies' profits that exceed one hundred thousand Riyals. this percentage shall be calculated out of the tax brackets values provided for in Article (11) dated 21/1/1370(H). This shall include all capital companies subject to tax with the exception of companies operating in the field of oil, gas and hydrocarbon production.
2. The State's bearing this tax percentage is limited only to profits which exceed one hundred thousand Riyals per year. Accordingly, this shall be carried out when collecting taxes from the capital companies as follows:

1. First bracket: 1 - 100,1000 SR.   value 25%

2. Second Bracket: 100,001 - 500,000   value 20% in lieu of 35%

3. Third bracket: 500,001 - million Riyals value 25% in lieu of 40%

4. Fourth bracket: Over million Riyals   value 30% in lieu of 45%

3. Net losses which may be carried forward shall be determined by the legally amended operational losses without regard to book losses. Operational losses shall mean expenses which are legally deductible in accordance to Article 14 of the Tax Law and which are in excess of the income subject to tax during the taxable year.
4. All subject who keep regular account and who are subject to Income Tax pursuant to the aforementioned Royal Decree shall benefit from the principle of reallocating losses.
5. Subjects exempted from tax shall not benefit from the principle of subsequent to the issuance of the aforementioned Resolution of the Council of Ministers and shall not include the accounts of previous fiscal years whether such accounts were submitted to the department or not, or by tax Dispute Committee or Appellate Committees.
6. This Resolution is applicable on fiscal years which end at dates that are subsequent to the issuance of the aforementioned Resolution of the Council of Ministers and shall not include the accounts of previous fiscal whether such accounts were submitted to the department or not, or by Tax Dispute Committees or Appellate Committees.

Amendments:

JEDDAH, 29 April 2003 — Saudi businessmen have welcomed yesterday's Shoura Council decision to cut taxes on profits of foreign companies from 45 percent to a maximum of 25 percent, saying the move will boost foreign investment   more...

TRADE MARKS REGULATIONS:

The Trade Marks Regulations were originally issued by Royal Decree No. 8762 dated

28-7-1358 H. (1938). It contained 43 Articles. However, Articles 41, 42 and 43 were subsequently repealed by Royal Decree No. 8/M of 20 Rabi II, 1393 H. (1973). Thereafter these were reviewed and promulgated by Royal Decree No. M/5 dated 4-5-1404 H. (Jan. 7, 1984). Rules for Implementation of the Trade Marks Regulations were issued by the Minister of Commerce Resolution No. 94 dated 5.8.1404 H. (May 6, 1984).

Provisions of the new Regulations included: definitions of trade marks, registration, announcement, renewal and deletion thereof in addition to the transfer of ownership of marks, mortgage, seizure, and licensing thereof together with definition of fees due on registration, etc.

They define crimes and penalties regarding trade marks to protect public and private rights and formulation of procedural rules to decide on their crimes and impose penalties thereon.

The fees due under the provisions of these Regulations were defined by Article 47 in the following manner:

a) SR 1,000 (one thousand) on any part of the following:

1. Application to register a trade mark for one category.
2. Application to register a collective trade mark for one category.
3. Request to examine a trade mark for one category.
4. Viewing the Register for one trade mark in respect of one category.
5. Every photocopy taken from the records of the Register in respect of one trade mark for one category.
6. Application to enter transfer or assignment of ownership for one trade mark in respect of one category.
7. Application to license the use of a mark for one category as well as entering its mortgage in accordance with article 36 and 40 of these regulations.
8. Each amendment or addition to a mark for one category as well as entering its mortgage in accordance with Article 22 of the Regulations.
9. Application to add or to alter any statement for which no fee is specified in respect of a mark for one category.

b) SR 3,000 (three thousand) on any part of the following:

b) SR 3,000 (three thousand) on any part of the following:

1. Application for temporary protection for a trade mark of one category.
2. Registration of trade mark.
3. Renewal of registration of one trade mark for one category.
4. Renewal of registration of a collective trade mark for one category.

These fees may be amended by a resolution of the Council of Ministers.

For further details, please contact the Department of Internal Trade, Ministry of Commerce (see here for address).

PATENTS LAW:

The Patents Law was promulgated by Royal Decree No. M/38 dated 10/6/1409 (January 17, 1989). The Law contains 62 articles with the main objective of providing adequate protection of inventions inside the Kingdom of Saudi Arabia.

Applications for patents shall be submitted to the Directorate of Patents at King Abdul Aziz City for Science and Technology on the form designed for such purpose (see here for address). The patent's term shall be fifteen years from date of grant and it may be extended for five more years.

For additional analytical, business and investment opportunities information, please contact Global Investment & Business Center, USA at (202) 546-2103. Fax: (202) 546-3275. E-mail: ibpusa3@gmail.com Global Business and Legal Information Databank: www.ibpus.com

Patents' disputes shall be resolved by an ad hoc Committee at the King Abdul Aziz City for Science and Technology. Appeal against the Committee decision may be made to the Board of Grievances within sixty days from the date of notification.

Patents fees as referred to in Article 59 of this law are as follows:

Type of Fee	Individuals	Companies
Patent Application	SR 400	SR 800
Issuance/Publication of Patent	SR 500	SR 1,000
Annual Fees per Patent	SR 400	SR 800
Amendment or Addition	SR 100	SR 200
Change of Ownership	SR 200	SR 400
Obtain Patent Copy/Other documents	SR 50	SR 100
Grant of Forcible Licensing	SR4,000	SR 8,000
Registration of Licensing Contracts	SR 400	SR 800
Application for Patent Extension	SR 400	SR 200

For further information, please contact the Patents Department, King Abdul Aziz City for Science and Technology

MERGERS AND ACQUISITIONS REGULATIONS

The Mergers and Acquisitions Regulations apply in any situation where there is restricted purchase of, or a restricted offer for, the shares of any listed company, or where there is a takeover offer or a reverse takeover relating to any listed company. The Regulations ensure that offerors and offerees act in the best interests of their shareholders, and grant them sufficient information and advice in order to reach a properly informed decision.

A restricted purchase of shares comprises the purchase of voting shares listed on the Exchange when as a result, 10% or more of such class of the relevant company shares is owned by, or under the control of, the purchaser. A restricted offer for shares is achieved through a public announcement where the announcer offers to purchase voting shares of a particular class listed on the Exchange if the amount of shares to be acquired by the offering party would increase its ownership or the shares under its control to 10% or more of the shares of the relevant company.

A takeover offer is that which is made to the holders of the securities of the offeree company which aims to acquire control of the offeree company. A reverse takeover comprises an arrangement where a listed company makes an offer for an unlisted company on terms that (a) the listed company will offer new shares in itself to the shareholders of the unlisted company in exchange for their shares and (b) the number of shares to be issued by the listed company under this arrangement is so large that the shareholders of the unlisted company acquire between them more than 50%. The Regulations apply to Exchange participants including issuers, shareholders and the directors of the companies which are subject thereto.

The Mergers and Acquisitions Regulations set out detailed provisions concerning the situations in which a public announcement is required to be made including where a company is considering a potential takeover and an approach to a potential offeree company has been made and the parties have reached an understanding that an offer will be made or where there have been stipulated minimum price movements, above the lowest share price since the time of approach, of the shares of the relevant company following a bid approach. Following certain announcements, the offeror must submit to the CMA, for its approval, a takeover timetable including shareholders' approval of the takeover, the delivery of the final offer document to it, the publication of the offer document and making it available to the board of directors of the offeree company, the earliest permitted first closing date of the offer and the last date on which it is no longer unconditional as to acceptances.

The offer document must include:
01. a heading stating that an independent financial adviser authorised by the CMA must be consulted if there is any doubt about the offer;
02. the date when the document is published, the name and address of the offeror and of any person making the offer on behalf of the offeror;
03. details of the securities for which the offer is made, including whether they will be transferred with dividends;
04. the total payment proffered;
05. the closing market price for the securities to be acquired and securities offered, for the first day in each of the six months immediately before the date of the publication of the offer document, for the last day before the commencement of the offer period and for the latest available date before the publication of the offer document (quotations stated in respect of securities listed on the Exchange should be taken from the official list and, if any of the securities are not so listed, any information available as to the number and price of transactions which have taken place during the preceding six months should be stated together with the source, or an appropriate negative statement);

06. in the case of a securities exchange offer, particulars of the first dividend or interest payment in which the new securities will participate and how the securities will rank for dividends or interest, capital and redemption and a statement indicating the effect of acceptance on the capital and income position of the offeree company's shareholders; and
07. in the case of a securities exchange offer, the effect of full acceptance of the offer upon the offeror's assets, profits and business which may be significant for a proper appraisal of the offer.

The offer document must be submitted by the offeror to the CMA for its approval prior to publication; the time frame for the granting of approval by the CMA is thirty days from receiving the requisite information and documents. The CMA has the discretion to accept the offer document and grant its approval to the offer if it is satisfied that the offer is in the interests of investors and that it does not breach the Capital Market Regulation or the Implementing Rules.

SAUDI ARABIA BUSINESS FORMS AND STRUCTURES

Business associations are governed by the Regulations for Companies (issued in 1982, and amended in 1992). The Regulations list business forms and structures, of which joint stock companies and limited liability partnerships are the most attractive to foreign investors. Additionally, there are certain business forms and structures, such as liaison and technical/scientific offices, which are not specifically dealt with by the Regulations but are nevertheless subject to them.

Establishments, or sole proprietorships, although required to register with the Ministry of Commerce, are not subject to the Regulations. Such enterprises are of marginal interest to foreigners since a foreigner is not allowed to conduct business in Saudi Arabia as a sole proprietor. In addition, Saudi law forbids foreigners from engaging in business in the Kingdom under the name of a Saudi national.

Although not provided for in the Companies Law, the Ministry of Industry and Electricity and the Ministry of Commerce have issued administrative fiats that have allowed the creation of wholly foreign owned branches. Such branches do not require a local sponsor and may enter into and do business in Saudi Arabia under their own names.

COMPANIES LAW

The Regulations define a company as a joint undertaking to participate in an enterprise with a view to profit. Thus, a registered company is deemed to be a commercial entity, whatever its objectives may be. Upon registration, the company acquires legal personality. If it is not fully owned by Saudis, it may not enjoy certain rights but would still be as a Saudi company.

Every industrial or commercial establishment must be registered in the Commercial Register. Saudi participants in foreign companies and foreign branches need to obtain the consent of the Foreign Capital Investment Committee prior to registration.

JOINT STOCK COMPANIES

A joint stock company is owned by five or more individuals or entities. Capital is apportioned into negotiable shares of an equal amount, and shareholders are liable only to the extent of the value of their holdings. The minimum capital requirement is two million Saudi Riyals (SR) or no less than ten million SR if its shares are offered for public subscription. The par value of each share cannot be less than SR 50, and upon incorporation, its issued paid-up capital must be no less than one-half of the authorized capital. A recent change to the Regulations allows a joint stock company to issue non-voting preferred shares in an amount up to 50 percent of its capital.

Prospective joint stock companies involving businesses such as minerals exploitation, administration of public utilities, banking and finance require authorization by Royal Decree prior to incorporation.

The management is composed of a board of directors. This board, appointed by the shareholders, must have a minimum of three members. Directors must own at least 200 shares of the joint stock company.

Limited Liability Companies

Generally, a company with foreign participation would incorporate as a limited liability company, meaning a privately held company used to set up industrial, agricultural, contracting or services projects having Saudi and foreign partners. Limited liability companies are specifically not permitted to conduct banking, insurance or savings operations. These entities may not offer subscriptions to the public to raise capital, and partners cannot transfer their interest without the unanimous consent of the other partners.

Limited liability companies may also be established in the form of partnerships limited by share, in which the limited partner is liable to the partnership's debts only to the extent of his capital contributions reflected in fully tradable share certificates. In practice, partnerships limited by shares are relatively rare.

A limited liability company must be registered under the Regulations for Companies as well as under the foreign capital investment regulatory regime. The various regulations do not specify minimum capital requirements for regular limited partnerships. A minimum capital of 1,000,000 SR, however, is required for the establishment of a partnership limited by shares. Contribution stipulations, as well as other mandatory information, must be registered with the Ministry of Commerce.

PARTNERSHIPS

General Partnerships

A general partnership is an association of two or more persons who are jointly liable for the debts of the partnership to the extent of their personal fortunes. As a separate legal entity it can transact business in its own name. Partners are forbidden to transfer interests without the unanimous consent of the other partners. No minimum capital is required, and contribution terms are set forth in the partnership agreement which must be registered with the Ministry of Commerce.

Limited Partnerships

Limited partnerships are composed of general partners who are liable for the partnership's debts to the extent of their personal fortunes and limited partners who are liable for partnership's debts only to the extent of their investment. Participation by limited partners in the management of the partnership might expose them to joint individual liability with the general partners. Registration requirements are the same as for general partnerships.

The name of the firm must include the name of at least one general partner. For reasons of liability, limited partners should avoid having their names included in the firm name.

Professional Partnerships

As of 1991, foreign 'free professionals' such as lawyers, engineers and medical practitioners, may establish joint practices with partnerships that are locally licensed. The establishment of a professional partnership requires approval from the Ministry of Commerce, which sets conditions that concern the reputation of the foreign firms, transfer of interests and minimum participation of Saudi partners (25 percent). Profits of foreign partners from such professional partnership will presumably be taxable, unlike salaries earned by foreign professionals working for local firms.

JOINT VENTURES

Foreign investment in joint ventures with Saudi partners has advantages. While foreign partners in a joint venture entity may hold 100 percent of the equity in some Gulf Cooperation Council (GCC) countries, there are advantages in having a local Saudi partner own 50 percent of the equity or more. For example, if a Saudi holds 50 percent of the equity in a joint venture company it enables the company to obtain an interest-free loan for up to 50 percent of the project cost, which is repayable over a period of ten years. In addition, majority Saudi-owned joint ventures are entitled to preference after wholly Saudi-owned companies in the allotment of government contracts. Trading and marketing activities aimed at Saudi individuals or wholly Saudi-owned companies, however, are forbidden to mixed Saudi-foreign joint ventures by Royal Decree M/11 of 1962.

BRANCH OFFICES

Foreign companies carrying out industrial or contracting works essential to the goals of economic development in Saudi Arabia may apply to the Foreign Capital Investment Committee for a license to establish a branch in the Kingdom. Upon receiving the license, the company may complete its registration process under the Regulation. It may be noted that, unlike a limited liability joint venture, a branch of a foreign entity is not entitled to a tax holiday. In practice, relatively few branch licenses have been issued, consistent with a general government policy of insulating the local market from direct competition by foreign companies.

In recent years, however, the concept of branches has been expanded to cover companies that are not involved in industrial and contracting works although the granting of such licenses is rare.

SAUDI SERVICE AGENTS

Foreign companies operating exclusively for the purpose of implementing government contracts are required to obtain temporary commercial registration. Such registration is available only to contractors operating in the public sector. If a foreign contractor is engaged in a governmental contract and does not have a Saudi partner, it must engage a Saudi national as an agent. In cases of certain military contracts an exception to this general rule may sometimes be made. Agents may receive compensation not exceeding 5 percent of the contract value. The agency agreement should be submitted to the Ministry of Commerce along with the application for temporary commercial registration within 30 days of signing the contract.

COMPANY REGISTRATION[2]

REGISTRATION REQUIREMENTS

	Procedure	Time to complete:	Cost to complete:
1	Register at the Unified Registry/ Ministry of Commerce and Industry	2-5 days	SR 1200 registration fee + SR 2,100 Chamber of Commerce fee+ SR 2,250 publication
*2	Open bank account	1 day (simultaneous with previous	no charge

---

[2] The World Bank Materials

For additional analytical, business and investment opportunities information, please contact Global Investment & Business Center, USA at (202) 546-2103. Fax: (202) 546-3275. E-mail: ibpusa3@gmail.com Global Business and Legal Information Databank: www.ibpus.com

		procedure)	
3	Register with the Department of Zakat and Income Tax (DZIT) to obtain a file number and a certificate of commencement of business	1 day	no charge
4	Register employer and employees for the General Organization of Social Insurance (GOSI) contributions online	1 day	no charge

* Takes place simultaneously with another procedure.

REGISTRATION REQUIREMENTS DETAILS

Procedure 1.
   Register at the Unified Registry/ Ministry of Commerce and Industry
Time to complete:
   2-5 days
Cost to complete:
   SR 1200 registration fee + SR 2,100 Chamber of Commerce fee+ SR 2,250 publication
Name of Agency:
Comment:
   The applicant completes all required forms and submits them to the new one-stop Unified Office at the Ministry of Commerce in Riyadh. The Unified Office includes representatives from: Companies Department, Commercial Names Department, Commercial Registration Department, Chamber of Commerce, Private Bank, Publication Office, and Notary Public. In addition, the Company registration with the Chamber of Commerce is done through the Chamber of Commerce desk at the MoCI.
   -The registration fees for LCC is SAR 1200 as stated in the Council of Minister's resolution No.163 dated 23/6/1429 (16/6/2008) and SAR for 2,100 Chamber of Commerce fee. The requirement to publish summary Articles of Association in the Official Gazette cost SR 1500-3000, depending on the length.
Procedure 2.
   Open bank account
Time to complete:
   1 day (simultaneous with previous procedure)
Cost to complete:
   no charge
Name of Agency:
Comment:
Procedure 3.
   Register with the Department of Zakat and Income Tax (DZIT) to obtain a file number and a certificate of commencement of business
Time to complete:
   1 day
Cost to complete:
   no charge
Name of Agency:
Comment:
   Zakat, a religious wealth tax, is assessed on taxable income and on certain assets.
Procedure 4.
   Register employer and employees for the General Organization of Social Insurance (GOSI) contributions online
Time to complete:

For additional analytical, business and investment opportunities information,
please contact Global Investment & Business Center, USA
at (202) 546-2103. Fax: (202) 546-3275. E-mail: ibpusa3@gmail.com
Global Business and Legal Information Databank: www.ibpus.com

1 day
Cost to complete:
    no charge
Name of Agency:
Comment:
    To register for social security insurance, the employer must open a file with the General Organization of Social Insurance (GOSI). This action will register the employer and the employee with the organization's two branches, the Pension Fund and the Industrial and illness Fund (Occupational Hazards Fund). Employers must contribute 11% of employee salary (Saudi employees) and employees must contribute 9%.

REGISTERING PROPERTY

Procedure	Time to complete:	Cost to complete:
1 Legal representatives of the parties appear before the notary public for the transfer of the title deeds	1 day	no cost
2 Legal representative of the buyer signs receipt and obtains the title deed from the notary public	1 day	no cost

REGISTRATION REQUIREMENT DETAILS

Procedure 1.
    Legal representatives of the parties appear before the notary public for the transfer of the title deeds
Time to complete:
    1 day
Cost to complete:
    no cost
Name of Agency:
    First Notary Public Department
Comment:
    The legal representatives of the buyer and the seller attend at the First Notary Public Department in Riyadh. The receptionist at the First Notary Public Department will give the legal representatives a transfer note for presentation to one of the notaries public within the Notary Public Department. Copies of the articles of association of the buyer and seller have to be presented to the notary public to ensure that the parties are authorized to sell and purchase real property. The First Notary Public Department in Riyadh has adopted in June 2007 a comprehensive electronic system of registering title deeds. The responsible notary public (i) reviews the original deed, (ii) reviews the copies of articles of association of the seller and the buyer to ensure that the parties are authorized to sell and purchase real property, (iii) reviews the documents evidencing the authorities of the legal representatives of the seller and the buyer, and (iv) reviews the original check showing the value of the plot. Once the responsible notary public is satisfied that all documents are available, he will transfer internally the transfer to the Records Department.
    The original title deed must be submitted to the notary public by the seller.

    The details of the transactions are copied into the title register internally. The Records Department then prepares a new title deed showing the buyer as the owner of the property (the "New Title Deed"). The new title deed is now included electronically in the comprehensive records of all title deeds in the city of Riyadh. The legal representatives will appear again before the responsible notary public, who will print a copy of the new title deed and ask the legal representatives along with two witnesses to sign a standard form, sale agreement. The new title deed will be given to the legal representative of the

buyer. The sale agreement will be scanned and saved in the comprehensive record file and the original sale agreement will be retained by the responsible notary public. The whole procedure will take approximately between 1 and 2 hours.
Procedure 2.
Legal representative of the buyer signs receipt and obtains the title deed from the notary public
Time to complete:
1 day
Cost to complete:
no cost
Name of Agency:
First Notary Public Department
Comment:
The legal representative of the buyer will then obtain from the notary public the original new title deed which contains the full details of the transaction, stating the buyer as the owner of the property. The buyer will simply be required to appear before the notary, sign a confirmation of receipt of the title deed and receive the title deed. The whole procedure will take approximately two hours.

SELLING PRODUCTS AND SERVICES IN SAUDI ARABIA REGULATIONS

USING AN AGENT OR DISTRIBUTOR

American exporters are not required to appoint a local Saudi agent or distributor to sell to Saudi companies, but commercial regulations restrict importing for resale and direct commercial marketing within the Kingdom to Saudi nationals, wholly Saudi-owned companies, and Saudi-foreign partnerships where the foreign partner holds 25% equity. Nationals from the Gulf Cooperation Council (GCC) countries, which include Saudi Arabia, Kuwait, Qatar, Oman, Bahrain, and the UAE, are also allowed to engage in trading and retail activities, including real estate. Agent/distributor relations are governed by the Commercial Agency Regulations of the Kingdom of Saudi Arabia that is administered by the Ministry of Commerce and Industry. Saudi business people cannot act as commercial agents unless their names are entered into the Register maintained by the Ministry of Commerce and Industry.

In July 2001, the Council of Ministers cancelled a decree compelling foreign companies with government contracts to appoint a Saudi service agent. The old decree also specified a maximum commission of 5%. Some government contracts, however, still require a minimum participation by a Saudi entity. In addition, government contracts typically include a clause requiring training programs for Saudis. Even though it is no longer legally required, we recommend that U.S. companies seeking to do business with Saudi government agencies appoint a Saudi service agent. The sales commission paid to the Saudi service agent is justified by the relatively quick and easy access to the appropriate government decision-maker. The U.S. Commercial Service in Saudi Arabia can help U.S. companies find a reputable Saudi account executive (service agent).

Sales commissions are entirely negotiable between the U.S. party and the Saudi agent or distributor, but typically range from 3 to 10 percent, depending on the product or

service and the duties required of the service agent. Whether or not sales commissions are to be paid, and the percentage thereof, should carefully be spelled out in any agency or distribution contract.

For additional analytical, business and investment opportunities information, please contact Global Investment & Business Center, USA at (202) 546-2103. Fax: (202) 546-3275. E-mail: ibpusa3@gmail.com
Global Business and Legal Information Databank: www.ibpus.com

Terminating an agent/distributor agreement can be difficult even though Saudi policy has changed to permit registration of a new agreement over the objections of the existing distributor. While most prospective Saudi agents and/or distributors generally prefer exclusive agency contracts, these are by no means required. Given the close-knit nature of business circles in Saudi Arabia, replacing an agent or distributor could damage a U.S. firm's reputation if not handled sensitively. A U.S. company should at all costs avoid being viewed as lacking adequate commitment to its Saudi business relationships. Saudi agents may request "parting compensation" in the event the foreign exporter decides to dissolve a business relationship. Since this is a common practice in this market, U.S. companies should address this eventuality prior to executing a contract.

U.S. firms interested in the Saudi market are cautioned against trying to use lists of importers for "cold calls" on prospective agents. Saudis prefer to do business with someone only when they have been properly introduced and have met face-to-face. To help dispel reluctance on the Saudi side, an introduction by a "go-between" typically serves to vouch for the reliability of both parties. The U.S. Commercial Service in Saudi Arabia performs just this sort of introduction for U.S. companies as part of its "Gold Key " matching service (available to U.S. companies *exclusively*). Other appropriate third parties for such introductions include other Saudi firms, U.S. companies that have successfully done business in Saudi Arabia, banks, trade associations, and chambers of commerce.

The Saudi legal system, known as *Shari'a,* is based on the Koran and Hadith (sayings of the Prophet) and differs considerably from U.S. practice. The Saudi Government has earmarked nearly $2 billion to overhaul its judicial system and court facilities in an effort to streamline the legal process. Royal Decree M/78 dated October 1, 2007, approved the Charter of the Judiciary System and the Charter of the Board of Grievances, and implemented relevant mechanisms.

American firms contemplating an agency or distribution agreement are strongly urged to consult with a local attorney and have a legally binding contract drawn up, setting forth in detail the rights and obligations of all parties, how and when sales commissions are to be paid, and how and in what venue any disputes are to be settled. A list of local law firms is available on the website of the U.S. Embassy in Riyadh , Saudi Arabia.

The U.S. Commercial Service, through its domestic U.S. Export Assistance Centers and overseas offices in Embassies and Consulates, offers a variety of services to assist American firms in selecting a reputable and qualified representative. In Saudi Arabia, the U.S. Commercial Service maintains offices in the capital, Riyadh, and in the regional business centers of Jeddah and Dhahran. CS Saudi Arabia's Gold Key Matching Service is a personalized and targeted matchmaking service that combines an orientation briefing, a profile of each Saudi prospect, interpreter services for meetings, a Commercial Specialist from the Embassy to escort you to your meetings, and assistance in developing follow-up strategies. The International Company Profile provides background information on potential partners. These services are available to U.S. companies exclusively.

ESTABLISHING AN OFFICE

The procedures to establish an office in Saudi Arabia differ according to the type of business undertaken. The most common and direct method is simply to appoint an agent/distributor who can set up the office under its own commercial registry. The agent/distributor agreement should be registered with the Ministry of Commerce and Industry . The Commercial Agency regulations govern the agent/distributor agreement.

For additional analytical, business and investment opportunities information,
please contact Global Investment & Business Center, USA
at (202) 546-2103. Fax: (202) 546-3275. E-mail: ibpusa3@gmail.com
Global Business and Legal Information Databank: www.ibpus.com

Technical and Scientific Service Office: The office requires a license from the Ministry of Commerce and Industry. This approach preserves the independence and identity of the foreign company and provides for more leeway in managing and marketing the company's products or services. Technical and scientific service offices are not allowed to engage directly or indirectly in commercial activities, but they may provide technical and advisory support to Saudi distributors, as well as conduct market surveys and product research.

Branch Office: Saudi Arabia's Foreign Investment Law allows international companies the possibility of 100% ownership of projects and property required for the project itself, while enabling them to retain the same incentives given to national companies. A branch office involves a more direct presence than a commercial agent. Branch offices are largely restricted to an administrative role and may not engage in trading activities. Nevertheless, a branch office can be very useful as a liaison presence for a U.S. company. A branch office offers the benefits of a physical presence without the formal requirements of a joint venture company. An U.S. company can open an independent branch office without a Saudi partner. Its parent company must accept full responsibility for all work undertaken by the branch office in Saudi Arabia.

Independent Office: To establish an office in Saudi Arabia, a foreign company needs to submit to related Saudi authorities a copy of its articles of association as incorporated in the country of origin, a copy of its commercial registration, a written approval by the board of directors of the company, its chief executive officer/president or a similar entity related to their decision to open a subsidiary office stating the name of the city and the name of the subsidiary's manager. All aforementioned documents are to be attested as required. The authorization to the applicant has to be attested by the Saudi Embassy in Washington, D.C.

Liaison Office: A liaison office is normally granted only for companies that have multiple contracts with the Government and require a local office to oversee contract implementation. Representative offices are not allowed to engage in direct or indirect commercial activity in the Kingdom. Founding a business establishment requires a license from the Ministry of Commerce and Industry.

Joint Venture: A company can establish a joint venture with a Saudi firm. Usually, the Saudi business community refers to limited liability partnerships as joint ventures. These partnerships must be also registered with the Ministry of Commerce and Industry and the partners' liabilities are limited to the extent of their investment in the partnership.

Finally, foreign companies can get a license from the Saudi Arabian General Investment Authority (SAGIA) to set up an industrial or a non-industrial project in Saudi Arabia.

SAGIA will license projects under the new Foreign Investment Act, which allows for 100% foreign ownership. In addition, foreign investors can open a sales/administration/ marketing office to complement their industrial or non-industrial project. SAGIA has a broad mandate on all matters relating to foreign investments in industry, services, agriculture, and contracting.

The Companies Law is the principal body of legislation governing companies. Saudi company law recognizes eight forms of companies. The most common forms are limited- liability companies (LLC), joint stock companies, general partnerships and limited partnerships. The less common company forms are partnerships limited by shares and joint ventures. Apart from the above, *Shari'a* law specifies a number of other types of companies, which cannot, however, be used by foreign investors. In practice, foreign companies usually establish LLCs. Partnerships and joint stock companies are only established in exceptional cases.

LLCs are a popular corporate vehicle among foreign investors in Saudi Arabia because they are simple to establish and administer and the personal liability of each of the partners is limited to the individual partner's contribution to the company's share capital.

Costs of doing business in Saudi Arabia are substantially lower than those in the West. Commercial and industrial rents average is $5.33 to $26.67 per square meter per year. The rate is much lower in industrial cities, where it is at $0.021 per square meter per year. Rentals for residential accommodation can vary immensely depending on location and quality of housing. With respect to utilities, electricity costs are at $0.027 per KwH for industrial use. Water costs range from $0.027 to $1.6 per cubic meter depending on the number of bands. Employee costs vary based on the employee's status, position, and relevant experience.

FRANCHISING

Franchising is a popular and successful approach to establish consumer-oriented businesses in Saudi Arabia. The franchise market is rapidly expanding in a variety of business sectors. According to a local study, the Saudi franchise market is expected to grow an average of 10-12% annually over the next three years. The same study projects the value of paid fees and royalties at more than SR 1.2 billion ($323 million). The growth in this sector is based on Saudis' desire to own their own business and a widely held appreciation for western methods of conducting business. American franchises dominate the market and more U.S. brands have recently obtained a foothold here, including Gap, Krispy Kreme, TGIF and Curves. American companies face growing competition from local and foreign companies in the following sectors: car rental agencies, fast food and business services. Franchising opportunities are known to exist in many business categories, including apparel, laundry and dry cleaning services, automotive parts and servicing, restaurants, mail and package services, printing, and convenience stores. There are more than 300 foreign companies that have founded franchises in Saudi Arabia. Kuwaiti investors own a disproportionately high number of U.S. franchises in Saudi Arabia.

To establish a franchise in Saudi Arabia, a foreign franchisor must select a franchisee and register the franchise. The franchisor must be the original one, and may not be a third-country franchisor. All franchise agreements follow the Saudi Commercial Law and must be approved by the Ministry of Commerce and Industry. A foreign company is strongly urged to consult with an attorney familiar with Saudi law before establishing,

changing, or terminating a franchise agreement.

DIRECT MARKETING

Direct marketing is not widely used in Saudi Arabia. Personal relations between vendors and customers play a more important role than in the West. Furthermore, many forms of direct marketing practiced in the United States are unacceptable due to Islamic precepts regarding gender segregation and privacy at home. Limitations in the Saudi postal system are also a constraint, though. A new mail delivery system called *Wasel* delivers mail and parcels to residences. The Saudi Post set up a company named *Naqel,* which is a joint project with the private sector and aims to upgrade Saudi Post's competitive capabilities and develop its services.

Direct marketing has been conducted on a very limited basis using unsolicited mail campaigns and fax, catalog sales (with local pick-up or delivery arranged), and commercials on satellite television providing consumers with a local telephone number to arrange delivery. Extensive

For additional analytical, business and investment opportunities information, please contact Global Investment & Business Center, USA at (202) 546-2103. Fax: (202) 546-3275. E-mail: ibpusa3@gmail.com Global Business and Legal Information Databank: www.ibpus.com

consumer surveys are being undertaken, mainly on behalf of multi-national manufacturers and particularly in the consumer goods sector.

JOINT VENTURES/LICENSING

Under the Foreign Investment Law , a foreign investor may either set up his/her own project or do so in association with a local investor. If the latter option is chosen, foreign investors may structure their enterprise as a limited-liability company, which is the most commonly used approach. By law, the minimum capital of an LLC with foreign participation is SAR 500,000. The required amount is increased to SAR 1,000,000 for industrial projects and SAR 25,000,000 for agricultural projects. The Board of Directors of SAGIA may reduce the minimum invested capital requirement in projects established in specified areas, in export projects or those which require considerable technical experience. Limited-liability companies must have at least two, but not more than fifty shareholders. The Ministry of Commerce and Industry must approve formation of all joint ventures.

Most foreign companies prefer to establish a limited-liability company (LLC) because it is simple to incorporate and manage. Limited-liability companies can be owned 100% by foreign investors or have a mixed ownership. Licenses should be obtained from the Saudi Arabian General Investment Authority (SAGIA). Foreign companies may qualify for a favorable tax treatment or other economic incentives from the Saudi Government, especially if Saudi investors join in the newly formed company's capital.

According to Article 52 of the Company Law, the establishment of a joint-stock company generally requires an authorization from the Minister of Commerce and Industry after reviewing a proposed company's "feasibility" study. The law requires the authorization through a Royal Decree based on the approval of the Council of Ministers for the formation of any joint-stock companies with concessions, undertaking public sector projects, receiving assistance from the State, in which the State or other public institutions participate, or for joint-stock companies engaging in a banking business. In general, the provisions applicable to the administration of joint-stock companies are more detailed than those applicable to limited liability companies.

The Investors Service Center (ISC) at the Saudi Arabian General Investment Authority (SAGIA) oversees all matters related to foreign investor licensing and registration process. The ISC is intended as a one-stop shop that will assist foreign investors and minimize lengthy procedures. Another very significant change in the Foreign Investment Act is the reduction in the corporate tax rate for foreign companies with profits in excess of $26,000 a year. It lowers the maximum rate from 45 to 20% and allows companies to carry forward corporate losses for an unspecified number of years.

Depending on the nature of the foreign investment, the Saudi Arabian Standards Organization (SASO) may be involved. SASO is the Saudi authority for establishing product standards for imports and locally manufactured goods. The Communications and Information Technology Commission (CITC) also has authority on imported telecommunications and IT products and services. Recently, the CITC has taken a more proactive role and has published a number of specifications relating to various products and services within its jurisdiction.

The Saudi Industrial Development Fund (SIDF) may be engaged to provide up to 50% financing for approved industrial projects, and payback period could be up to 15 years. Market intelligence also is available through the SIDF for prospective investors.

Other Saudi Arabian Government entities that may be involved in the process include the Ministry of Foreign Affairs (visas), the Ministry of Interior (residence permits and industrial safety and security approvals), the Royal Commission for Jubail and Yanbu (if the project is in those industrial cities), the General Organization for Social Insurance (social insurance and disability payments for Saudi employees), and the Technical and Vocational Training Corporation (training programs for Saudis).

SELLING TO THE GOVERNMENT

In 2001, the Saudi Council of Ministers repealed a 25 year-old decree requiring foreign contractors to have a Saudi agent in order to bid for contracts. Under the new decree, foreign companies interested in operating in Saudi Arabia without a Saudi agent can open offices and appoint representatives to pursue business opportunities directly with various government agencies and departments.

There is no central tender board in Saudi Arabia. Every government agency has full contracting authority. Foreign companies interested in bidding on a government project must make themselves known to that specific government agency/ministry offering the project. When a project becomes available, the government agency/ministry selects bidders from a list of prequalified/known companies and invites them to bid for that particular project. The law states that all qualified companies and individuals will be given opportunities in dealing with the Government and will be treated equally. The law also states that locally manufactured products and those of a non-Saudi origin of equal quality will have priority in dealing with the Government. Saudi Government Contacting and Procurement Law also affirms that all government bids be announced in the official gazette *Umm al-Qoura* (Arabic), in two local newspapers, as well as in the electronic media. Projects which do not have a contractor must be advertised both inside and outside Saudi Arabia.

Foreign companies can provide services to the Saudi Arabian government directly without a Saudi service agent, and can market their services to other public entities through an office that has been granted temporary registration. Foreign suppliers

working only for the government, if not already registered to do business in Saudi Arabia, are required to obtain a temporary registration from the Ministry of Commerce and Industry within 30 days of contract signing. Foreign investment regulations also allow foreign companies to establish a branch office. In 2003, the Saudi Council of Ministers required increased transparency in government procurement. The contract information to be made public includes: parties, date, financial value, brief description, duration, place of execution, and point of contact information.

Several royal decrees that strongly favor GCC nationals apply to Saudi Arabia's government procurement. (However, most Saudi defense contracts are negotiated outside these regulations on a case-by-case basis.) Under a 1983 decree, contractors must subcontract 30% of the value of any government contract, including support services, to firms majority-owned by Saudi nationals. An exemption is granted where no Saudi-owned company can provide the goods and services necessary to fulfill the procurement requirement.

The tender regulations require that preferences be given in procurements to Saudi individuals and establishments and other suppliers in which Saudi nationals hold at least 51% of the supplier's capital. The tender regulations also give a preference to products of Saudi origin that satisfy the requirements of the procurement. In addition, Saudi Arabia gives priority in government purchasing to GCC products. These items receive up to a 10% price preference over non-GCC products in all government procurements in which foreign suppliers participate. Foreign suppliers that participate in government procurement are required to establish a training program for Saudi nationals.

As a practical matter, American companies seeking sales of goods and services to the Saudi Government are encouraged to appoint a reputable agent or distributor with experience in the field. American firms considering sales to the Government should request a briefing from the U.S. Commercial Service in Riyadh, Jeddah, or Dhahran on the latest situation on payments and how U.S. firms can protect and secure timely disbursements.

DISTRIBUTION AND SALES CHANNELS

There are three major distribution and sales regions in Saudi Arabia: the Western Region, with the commercial center of Jeddah; the Central Region, where the capital city of Riyadh is located; and the Eastern Province, where the oil and gas industry is heavily concentrated. Dammam is the capital city of the Eastern Province, and its metropolitan area includes the contiguous cities of Dhahran and Al-Khobar. Each city has a distinct business community and cultural flavor, and there are only a few truly "national" companies dominant in more than one region.

American exporters may find it advantageous to appoint different agents or distributors for each region having significant market potential. Multiple agencies and distributorships may also be appointed to handle diverse product lines or services. Multiple agencies and distributors can present logistical and management difficulties, so U.S. firms, particularly in the franchise sector, often choose to appoint a master franchisor or distributor for states of the Gulf region, which includes Saudi Arabia, Kuwait, Qatar, Bahrain, Oman, and the UAE.

While there is no statutory requirement that distributorships be granted on an exclusive basis, it is clearly the policy of the Saudi Ministry of Commerce and Industry that all arrangements be exclusive with respect to either product line or geographic region.

SELLING FACTORS/TECHNIQUES

Expatriate managers have had a strong influence in introducing advanced selling techniques into a market that relied heavily on word-of-mouth and established buying patterns until a few years ago. Saudi consumers are increasingly becoming more discerning and sophisticated. Although details of a transaction can be handled electronically, no serious commitment is likely to be made without a face-to-face introduction. Business cards are usually printed in English on one side and Arabic on the other.

Saudis are gracious hosts and will try to put a visitor at ease, even during arduous business dealings. A large portion of upper and middle class Saudis were educated in the United States or in Europe.

Financing and credit facilities may be offered as part of a sales proposal, usually after a solid relationship has been established. Passed in 2003, the Capital Market Law (CML) created the Saudi Stock Exchange (Tadawul), as well as the Capital Market Authority (CMA) charged with overseeing and regulating the Exchange. The law established a new regulatory framework designed to encourage greater participation in the financial market. It also established Tadawul as the exclusive securities market in Saudi Arabia. The Capital Market Authority was created to ensure that Saudi Arabia's capital markets operate fairly, transparently, and efficiently.

For additional analytical, business and investment opportunities information,
please contact Global Investment & Business Center, USA
at (202) 546-2103. Fax: (202) 546-3275. E-mail: ibpusa3@gmail.com
Global Business and Legal Information Databank: www.ibpus.com

The CML provides for the establishment of two committees to settle securities disputes, the Committee for the Resolution of Securities Disputes (CRSD) and the Appeals Panel. The CRSD has jurisdiction over disputes falling under the provisions of the Capital Market Law, the rules and regulations issued by the CMA, and the Stock Exchange. The Appeals Panel, which was formed by the Council of Ministers, will hear appeals against decisions issued by the CRSD. A decision issued by the CRSD may be appealed to the Appeal Panel within thirty days of the notification date. CML also created the Securities Deposit Center (SDC), which is operated by Tadawul, the Saudi Stock Exchange Company. SDC is in charge of managing deposits, transfers, settlements, clearing, and registration of all Saudi securities on the exchange. Other entities created by the CML include the Department of Authorization and Inspection; and Corporate Finance, Enforcement and Market Supervision.

The Government has liberalized the wholesale, retail, and franchise sectors, allowing foreign investors to establish joint ventures and retain a 51% share. The foreign partner's capital requirement is set at $5.3 million and his equity share can be increased to 75% after 3 years from the contract date. All industrial enterprises are open to non-Saudis, and they can also trade in the products they manufacture. Restrictions on individual professions also are in force, such as who can practice law, medicine, accounting and financial services, architect and engineers, and other similar professions. A Saudi joint- venture partner is a requirement for any entity or individual to practice the above-mentioned professional services.

Many Saudi companies handle numerous product lines (sometimes even competing

product lines), making it difficult to promote all products effectively. Saudi agents typically expect the foreign supplier to assume some of the market development costs, such as hiring of dedicated sales staff (especially for high-tech or engineered products), setting up workshops and repair facilities, and funding local advertising. Foreign suppliers often detail a sales person to the Saudi distributor to provide marketing, training, and technical support. Absent such an arrangement, American firms should expect to make frequent, periodic visits each year to support their Saudi distributor.

ELECTRONIC COMMERCE

Electronic Commerce in Saudi Arabia is projected to reach USD 13 billion in sales by 2015, according to industry projections. Approximately one in four Saudi Internet users are already aware of and use e-commerce sites. There are nearly 70 million web site hits per month. User growth continues to expand at an estimated 9.3 percent per annum. Current e-commerce market share shows that souq.com is the largest entity in the Kingdom with a 13 percent market share. Sukar.com (8 percent), Namshi (7 percent), and MarkaVIP (5 percent) dominate the b2c market space.

E-commerce still has inherent difficulties in growing even more quickly. Saudi consumers continue to favor cash on delivery as the most common method of payment. Saudi e-commerce b2c websites would need to grow in credit card payment methods or pay pal in order to significantly increase e-commerce market potential. Payment gateways are being developed to address this issue. With Saudi Arabia being the second largest market for spam e-mail, improved cyber security will afford greater consumer trust in e-commerce transactions.

Internet users in Saudi Arabia increased to over 13 million, which accounts for over 49% if the total population. Almost half of all Saudi Internet users reported that they purchased products and services online and through their mobile handsets. The Saudi Government has already passed a

For additional analytical, business and investment opportunities information, please contact Global Investment & Business Center, USA at (202) 546-2103. Fax: (202) 546-3275. E-mail: ibpusa3@gmail.com Global Business and Legal Information Databank: www.ibpus.com

number of regulations to control and monitor electronic transactions, *i.e.,* regulations for e-transactions and cybercrime.

Additionally, the government has allocated close to $800 million to implement the e- government initiative. A published report has mentioned that in order to drive Saudi Arabia's e-government initiative forward, the YESSER program (an Arabic word meaning "to facilitate") was launched by the government to develop the first National e- Government Strategy and Action Plan which will be implemented within the next five years. The YESSER program's role is to enable the implementation of individual e- government services by ministries and other government agencies, on the one hand, by building the national infrastructure and defining common standards which these agencies can use; and on the other hand by providing best practice examples and accompanying implementation of pilot services. Moreover, YESSER will ensure an appropriate level of coordination and collaboration between implementing agencies. The vision for Saudi Arabia's e-government initiative is user-centric and aims at providing better government services to the user. It is understood that users are individuals (citizens and expatriates), businesses and government agencies.

TRADE PROMOTION AND ADVERTISING

The U.S. Commercial Service in Saudi Arabia organizes a number of annual trade events, including the recruitment of official Saudi buyer delegations to International

Buyer Program events in the United States as well as Trade Missions, promotion of trade events in Saudi Arabia, the USA and in other countries, *etc.*

Advertising: Companies seeking to develop an advertising and/or a promotional campaign will find highly experienced advertising agencies in Jeddah and Riyadh that can prepare a full campaign whether in print media, radio, or television. Already resident in Saud Arabia are Porter Novelli, Akeel Saatchi and Saatchi, Hill and Knowlton Strategies, Asda'a Burson-Marsteller, and TERAACS Saudi Arabia.

Advertising, especially on satellite television, is rapidly expanding, but commercials have to conform to religious and ethical codes. With some minor exceptions, the female human form is not culturally or religiously acceptable in the media. The Saudi monopoly on television broadcasting was broken with the introduction of satellite television, which also forced TV advertising rates to come down.

Saudi companies have opted to run commercials through international satellite TV channels such as the Middle East Broadcasting Corporation (MBC) and Arab Radio and Television. Other Arabic satellite channels that also have proved to be popular in the Arab world include LBC, Future Television, Dubai One TV, Dubai TV, New TV, Channel 2, MBC 2 and MBC 4. Many Saudi companies place commercials on these channels as well as on two pan-Arab news channels, Al-Arabiya and Al-Jazeera channels. In addition, two encrypted TV networks each provide approximately 30 channels for an average subscription of $1,000 per year. The networks include Orbit Communications and ShowTime.

Newspaper advertising is carried in both the local English and Arabic press, but its effectiveness is somewhat limited by relatively low readership rates. The two local English dailies, Arab News and the Saudi Gazette , have an average circulation in the range of 35,000 copies. The leading Arabic newspapers, with nationwide distribution, have circulations in the range of 70,000 to 100,000: Al-Hayat, Al-Riyadh, and Okaz.

Other relevant newspapers have lower circulations, and some have only regional distribution. The principal papers are Al-Bilad, Al0Jazirah, Al-Madina, Al-Nadwa, Al-Yaum, Um Al-Qoura, Al-Watan, Al-Riyadiya (sports only). The economic daily Al-Eqtisadiah has rapidly earned a loyal readership of executives and government officials.

Trade promotion events take place from September through June, with most of exhibitions held in the modern exhibit centers in Saudi Arabia's three major cities, Riyadh , Jeddah and Dhahran . Smaller exhibition facilities are also located in regional centers, and often operate in cooperation with or under the sponsorship of a local chamber of commerce.

Most chambers have a proactive approach to promotion and trade, organizing shows and presentations for individual companies or groups, and have been eager to attract American and other Western suppliers.

PRICING

The government maintains a free-trade approach and, since 1981, the Saudi Arabian Monetary Agency (SAMA, the Central Bank), has pegged the Saudi riyal to the U.S. dollar to facilitate long term planning and minimize exchange risk for the private sector. As such, Saudi importers expect American producers to practice a more stable pricing policy than their foreign competitors. In the last couple years, there have been numerous speculations that the Saudi Government would revalue the riyal, but SAMA has consistently stated that it has no intention to do so, and given SAMA's huge stock of

foreign assets, there does not appear to be a need.

Products are usually imported on a CIF basis, and mark-ups depend almost entirely on what the vendor feels the market will bear relative to the competition. There is no standard formula to come up with the mark-up rates for all product lines at different levels in the relatively short distribution chain.

Contrary to popular belief, pricing is very important to the average Saudi. Therefore, where there are competitive products, Saudi buyers frequently will compare prices before making a decision. For the American supplier, some give-and-take is expected in preliminary negotiations.

SALES SERVICE/CUSTOMER SUPPORT

Saudi Arabia is a relatively open market, which makes it highly competitive. Brand loyalty and established preferences are less developed than in some other countries. Consequently, sales service and customer support is indispensable to win and maintain new clients.

Saudis view a foreign firm's physical presence in the Kingdom as a tangible sign of a long-term commitment. Prompt delivery of goods from available stock and the presence of qualified support technicians have become more important, and they influence repeat business much more now than ten or even five years ago. Government agencies usually require equipment suppliers to commit to providing maintenance and spare parts for an average of three years.

PROTECTING YOUR INTELLECTUAL PROPERTY

Protecting Your Intellectual Property in Saudi Arabia

For additional analytical, business and investment opportunities information, please contact Global Investment & Business Center, USA at (202) 546-2103. Fax: (202) 546-3275. E-mail: ibpusa3@gmail.com Global Business and Legal Information Databank: www.ibpus.com

Several general principles are important for effective management of intellectual property ("IP") rights in Saudi Arabia. First, it is important to have an overall strategy to protect your IP. Second, IP may be protected differently in Saudi Arabia than in the United States. Third, rights must be registered and enforced in Saudi Arabia, under local laws. For example, your U.S. trademark and patent registrations will not protect you in Saudi Arabia. There is no such thing as an "international copyright" that will automatically protect an author's writings throughout the entire world. Protection against unauthorized use in a particular country depends, basically, on the national laws of that country. However, most countries do offer copyright protection to foreign works under certain conditions, and these conditions have been greatly simplified by international copyright treaties and conventions.

Granting patents registering are generally is based on a first-to-file [or first-to-invent, depending on the country], first-in-right basis. Similarly, registering trademarks is based on a first-to-file [or first-to-use, depending on the country], first-in-right basis, so you should consider how to obtain patent and trademark protection before introducing your products or services to the Saudi Arabia market. It is vital that companies understand that intellectual property is primarily a private right and that the U.S. government cannot enforce rights for private individuals in Saudi Arabia. It is the responsibility of the rights' holders to register, protect, and enforce their rights where relevant, retaining their own counsel and advisors. Companies may wish to seek advice from local attorneys or IP

consultants who are experts in Saudi Arabia law. The U.S. Commercial Service can provide a list of local lawyers upon request http://photos.state.gov/libraries/saudi-arabia/231771/pdfs/list-of-law-firms-040714.pdf .

While the U.S. Government stands ready to assist, there is little we can do if the rights holders have not taken these fundamental steps necessary to securing and enforcing their IP in a timely fashion. Moreover, in many countries, rights holders who delay enforcing their rights on a mistaken belief that the USG can provide a political resolution to a legal problem may find that their rights have been eroded or abrogated due to legal doctrines such as statutes of limitations, laches, estoppel, or unreasonable delay in prosecuting a law suit. In no instance should U.S. Government advice be seen as a substitute for the responsibility of a rights holder to promptly pursue its case.

It is always advisable to conduct due diligence on potential partners. A good partner is an important ally in protecting IP rights. Consider carefully, however, whether to permit your partner to register your IP rights on your behalf. Doing so may create a risk that your partner will list itself as the IP owner and fail to transfer the rights should the partnership end. Keep an eye on your cost structure and reduce the margins (and the incentive) of would-be bad actors. Projects and sales in Saudi Arabia require constant attention. Work with legal counsel familiar with Saudi Arabia laws to create a solid contract that includes non-compete clauses, and confidentiality/non-disclosure provisions.

It is also recommended that small and medium-size companies understand the importance of working together with trade associations and organizations to support efforts to protect IP and stop counterfeiting. There are a number of these organizations, both Saudi Arabia or U.S.-based. These include:

* The U.S. Chamber and local American Chambers of Commerce
* National Association of Manufacturers (NAM)
* International Intellectual Property Alliance (IIPA)
* International Trademark Association (INTA)

* The Coalition Against Counterfeiting and Piracy
* International Anti-Counterfeiting Coalition (IACC)
* Pharmaceutical Research and Manufacturers of America (PhRMA)
* Biotechnology Industry Organization (BIO)

IP Resources

A wealth of information on protecting IP Is freely available to U.S. rights holders. Some excellent resources for companies regarding intellectual property include the following:

* For information about patent, trademark, or copyright issues -- including enforcement issues in the US and other countries -- call the STOP! Hotline: 1-866-999-HALT or visit www.STOPfakes.gov .

* For more information about registering trademarks and patents (both in the U.S. as well as in foreign countries), contact the U.S. Patent and Trademark Office (USPTO) at: 1-800-786-9199, or visit www.uspto.gov .

* For more information about registering for copyright protection in the United States, contact the U.S. Copyright Office at: 1-202-707-5959, or visit http://www.copyright.gov/

* For more information about how to evaluate, protect, and enforce intellectual property rights and how these rights may be important for businesses, please visit the "Resources" section of the STOPfakes website at http://www.stopfakes.gov/resources.

* For information on obtaining and enforcing intellectual property rights and market-specific IP Toolkits visit: www.stopfakes.gov /businesss-tools/country-ipr-toolkits. The toolkits contain detailed information on protecting and enforcing IP in specific markets and also contain contact information for local IPR offices abroad and U.S. government officials available to assist SMEs.

* The U.S. Department of Commerce has positioned IP attachés in key markets around the world. You can get contact information for the IP attaché who covers Saudi Arabia at:

Aisha Y. Salem
Middle East and North Africa
American Embassy P. O. Box 77 Safat 13001, Kuwait
Office Phone: +965 2259 1455
Email: aisha.salem@trade.gov

DUE DILIGENCE

The U.S Commercial Service in Saudi Arabia prepares the International Company Profile (ICP) report, which provides detailed information on a specific Saudi company and comments based on information from the U.S. Embassy's Commercial Section.

LOCAL PROFESSIONAL SERVICES

There are service providers in Saudi Arabia offering professional services to foreign and domestic firms alike. The U.S. Commercial Service maintains a list of such Business Service Providers on its website; these local "BSPs" pay a nominal fee for an annual listing.

The websites of the U.S. Embassy in Riyadh and the U.S. Consulates General in Dhahran and Jeddah provide access to various business-support networks, including lawyers, translators, and a representative group of other service providers that offer their professional services to U.S. exporters and investors interested in Saudi Arabia:

U.S. Embassy – Riyadh
U.S. Consulate General – Dhahran
U.S. Consulate General – Jeddah

WEB RESOURCES

KACST http://www.kacst.edu.sa/en/
Saudi Arabian General Investment Authority (SAGIA) http://www.sagia.gov.sa/
Saudi Arabian Standards Organization (SASO) http://www.saso.gov.sa/en/
Saudi Industrial Development Fund http://www.sidf.gov.sa/en/
Saline Water Conversion Corporation http://www.swcc.gov.sa/
Water and Electricity Company http://www.wec.com.sa/
Saudi Telecommunications Company http://www.stc.com.sa/
Foreign Credit Insurance Association
http://www.greatamericaninsurancegroup.com/Insurance/FCIA/
Saudi Aramco http://www.saudiaramco.com/en/home.html
Saudi Arabian Monetary Agency (SAMA) http://www.mci.gov.sa/en/
Al-Harithy Company for Exhibitions (Jeddah) http://acexpos.com/
GCC Patent Office http://www.gccpo.org/
Ministry of Commerce and Industry http://www.mci.gov.sa/en/
Dhahran International Exhibitions Company www.arabianbusiness.com

MARKETING PRODUCTS AND SERVICES REGULATIONS

MARKETING AND SALES STRATEGY

There are very good prospects for U.S. companies who want to export their products to the Saudi Arabian market. However, there are certain marketing procedures and sales techniques which have to be observed in order to develop and sustain business relationships over a long period of time.

- The Saudi market should be constantly reviewed for product adaptation and change.
- Exporters should ensure regular supplies as per specifications, at the specified time and place already agreed upon and at the stipulated prices.
- Any subsequent and sudden price changes, even pertaining to after-sales services, should be avoided.
- Exporters' contacts with importers in Saudi Arabia should be direct and regular.
- Complete product lines, rather than single products, should be introduced into the Saudi market whenever possible in order to benefit from greater demand stimulation and cost reductions.

For additional analytical, business and investment opportunities information,
please contact Global Investment & Business Center, USA
at (202) 546-2103. Fax: (202) 546-3275. E-mail: ibpusa3@gmail.com
Global Business and Legal Information Databank: www.ibpus.com

- Exporters are required to check with Saudi importers or directly with the Saudi Arabian Standards Organization, (see appendix I for address) on the precise implementation of Saudi Arabian Standards pertaining to their exported products to the Kingdom. Saudi Standards can be purchased from SASO or the American National Standards Institute, ANSI (11 West 42nd Street, New York City, NY 10036, telephone number (212)642-4900 or fax number (212)302-1286).
- Exporters to Saudi Arabia should display their products regularly in the major commercial urban centers of the Kingdom. Necessary permission is obtained by writing or contacting directly the Director, Exhibitions Department, Ministry of Commerce (see appendix I for address).
- Efforts should be made to improve the appearance of exported commodities by means of attractive packaging.
- Products to be exported should be properly branded and labeled both in English and Arabic.
- In the case of machinery and equipment; after-sales service, including warranties, maintenance and the provision of spare parts, should be prompt and efficient.

BUSINESS OPPORTUNITIES IN THE KINGDOM

In pursuit of the policy of free market enterprise, economic diversification, structural shift from building the infrastructure to the production of goods and services and the subsequent increasing reliance on the private sector as the major economic force, the Kingdom of Saudi Arabia invites American companies to participate in the following areas which are essential to its current and future economic growth:

- Import-substitution and export-oriented joint ventures.
- Projects contributing to technological progress in the Kingdom and the development of established factories through improvement of production methods and minimization of production costs.
- Projects directly related to the current economic development in the Kingdom which include, but are not limited to, the following:

> a) Industries utilizing locally abundant raw materials from petrochemical or petroleum products.
> b) Food industries utilizing locally abundant agricultural products.
> c) Specialized industries in the fields of maintenance and the manufacturing of spare parts and equipment.

In most of the industrial joint ventures, the foreign partner supplies the management, technical expertise, and part of equity resources, if they are desired, depending on the collaboration arrangements. The Saudi partner provides local supervision, local skilled and unskilled labor, and handles local business contacts, apart from participating in the equity resources. For further details on establishing joint ventures in the Kingdom, see Chapter 5, Industrial Licensing Regulations and Procedures.

With a foothold in the Saudi Arabian market, there will be numerous business opportunities for:

- Companies providing labor-saving equipment and services.
- Training services either directly delivered or as part of a product package.
- Managerial services either directly delivered or as part of a product package.
- Nearly all areas of health, personnel, and services.

In addition to the section on growth targets during the sixth development plan that we discussed in Chapter Two of this guide, the following list of principal growth areas of the Saudi Arabian economy provides tips on prospective commercial opportunities in the Kingdom:

- Industry: Most industrial activities in the Kingdom are carried out by the energetic Saudi private sector. The structure of the Saudi Arabian industrial sector is composed of three distinct sub-sectors: petrochemicals, oil refining, and other manufacturing. The main objectives of the Kingdom's industrialization are:

> a) To reduce the Kingdom's dependence on the export of crude oil as the major source of income
> b) To increase Saudi Arabian private sector participation in the economic development of the country
> c) To create new job opportunities.
> d) To establish an advanced industrial and technological base.

Export oriented industries such as petrochemical, papers, glass plastics, etc. are expected to do well during the sixth plan period. Over the next few years the petrochemical industry is expected to grow at an average rate of more than 8 percent annually. Thus foreign investors are invited to join the Saudi Arabian private sector to invest in new industries that utilize modern technology, and to expand investment in import substitution and export-oriented industries including basic, supporting and downstream metal and petrochemical industries

- Mining and quarrying: The Saudi government has prioritized the diversification of the Kingdom's economy and the utilization of the country's extensive mineral wealth. The mining industry is promising in the next few years, especially with the initiative of the Ministry of Petroleum and Mineral Resources to develop new mines to produce phosphate, iron, bauxite and other precious and non-precious metals. In 1993 Petromin extracted 189,353 tons of ore. Net gold production amounted to around 670,000 ounces between 1989-1993. The Directorate General of Mineral Resources (see appendix I for address) is currently pursuing the exploitation of the mineral fields throughout the Central and Western regions of the Kingdom. The government's investment in this sector has already exceeded seventeen billion Saudi Riyal (more than U.S. $4.5 billion). Foreign investors are offered tax exemption, long term extraction concessions and other incentives to invest or establish joint ventures in this growing Saudi industry.
- Transportation, telecommunications and information technology: During the fifth development plan (1990-1994) the Kingdom's main road network increased by about 2,100 kms, to about 43,000 kms. Rail freight volume grew by 36 percent to about 2.1 million tons. Air passenger volume grew from 20.3 million departure and arrival to 25.1 million. The cargo handled in the Kingdom's major ports rose from 63.7 million tons to 83 million tons.

In addition to upgrading the road network and domestic airports in the Kingdom during the sixth development plan, the government is planning to link Dammam and Jubail Industrial City with a new railroad. Furthermore, to enhance and modernize the fleet of Saudi Arabian Airlines, the government has already purchased from two American companies (Boeing and Mcdonnell Douglas) commercial airplanes worth more than six billion dollars. The Saudi Ministry of Post, Telephone and Telegraph awarded the U.S. firm of AT&T four billion dollars contract to upgrade and expand the telephone network in the Kingdom.

- Electricity: Saudi per capita consumption of gas, water and electricity is one of highest in the world. Over the past two decades electricity consumption rate increased by more than 20 percent annually. Power generation expanded from 4,214 megawatts in 1979 to 18,238 megawatts in 1994. Over the sixth development plan period (1995-1999) electric generation capacity will be raised by more than seven thousand megawatts.
- Other important areas of growth prospects during the sixth development plan (1995-1999), include banking and insurance, leasing, travel, and consumer products such as food and beverages, clothing, soap, cosmetics, etc.

A further consideration for business opportunities is the procurement of government contracts. Government contracts are often offered through tenders. There is no central tenders' board in Saudi Arabia, and every government agency may extend contracts. Bids for tenders must be applied for by local agents. In most cases, government contracts awarded to foreign companies require 30 percent of the total work to be subcontracted to a Saudi Arabian contractor.

The pending application of Saudi Arabia to the WTO could have profound implications for the way one does business in the Kingdom. Until accession occurs, the following describes the present state of affairs.

DISTRIBUTION AND SALES CHANNELS

There are three major marketing regions in Saudi Arabia: The Western Region, with the commercial center of Jeddah; the Central Region, where the capital city Riyadh is located; and the Eastern Province, where the oil and gas industry is most heavily concentrated. Each has a distinct business community and cultural flavor, and there are few truly "national" companies dominant in more than one region.

Many companies import goods solely for their own use or for direct sale to end-users, making the number and geographical pattern of retail outlets a factor of potential significance. U.S. exporters may find it advantageous to appoint different agents or distributors for each region having significant market potential. Multiple agencies and distributorships may also be appointed to handle diverse product lines or services.

In considering the socio-cultural differences between Saudi Arabia and the United States, in particular, the relative segregation of men and women, it should not be overlooked that the number of Saudi businesses owned and managed by women is significant, and growing rapidly.

According to official statistics, Saudi women own and run about 15,000 companies, about 4.3 percent of registered Saudi businesses. In addition, women account for about ten percent of the Saudi workforce. That percentage is expected to reach 11.9 percent by the end of the year 2000. The Saudi Government projects that more Saudi women will enter the labor market, and their number will increase to 240,000 based on a recent report published by the Jeddah Chamber of Commerce.

While there is no requirement that distributorships be granted on an exclusive basis, it is clearly the policy of the Saudi Ministry of Commerce that all arrangements be exclusive with respect to either product line or geographic region.

Many Saudi companies handle numerous product lines making it difficult to promote all products effectively. Saudi agents typically expect the foreign supplier to assume many of the market development costs, such as hiring of dedicated sales staff. Foreign suppliers often detail a sales person to the Saudi distributor to provide marketing, training, and technical support. Absent such an arrangement, U.S. firms should expect to make at least four visits per year to support their Saudi distributor.

PRODUCT PRICING STRUCTURES

A rate of exchange of the dollar to the riyal has been set at 3.7450 since 1987, a competitive dollar value compared to the Japanese and European currencies, and reasonable interest rates have greatly facilitated market penetration. Thanks to this, Saudi importers expect U.S. producers to practice a more stable pricing policy than their foreign competitors.

Products are usually imported on a CIF basis, and mark-ups depend almost entirely on what the vendor feels that the market will bear relative to the competition. There is no standard formula to come up with the mark-up rates for all product lines at different levels of the relatively short distribution chain.
Pricing is very important to the average Saudi. Therefore, where there are competitive products, Saudi buyers frequently will compare prices before making a buying decision.

Stability of prices has been a policy of the Saudi Government for years, and after rising to five percent in 1995 as a result of the utility and gas rates hikes, inflation was down 0.4 percent for the 12-month period ending in December 1997. The cost of living index fell by 0.2 percent in 1998 reflecting price stability in the market.

For the U.S. supplier, some give-and-take is expected in preliminary negotiations. The asking price is usually lowered slightly to attract the client.

FINDING A PARTNER

The Saudi Government is currently reviewing a new agency law and related regulations with the aim of improving and further promoting commercial exchanges as the Kingdom prepares to join the World Trade Organization (WTO).

U.S. exporters are not required to appoint a local Saudi agent or distributor to sell to Saudi companies, but commercial regulations restrict importing and direct commercial marketing within the Kingdom to Saudi nationals and wholly Saudi-owned companies. Agent/distributor relations are governed by the Commercial Agency Regulations of the Kingdom of Saudi Arabia, administered by the Ministry of Commerce.

Obtaining a business visa for Saudi Arabia requires sponsorship by a Saudi national, and Saudi nationals receive strong preference in sales to Government agencies and parastatal corporations. Consequently, U.S. firms may find it advantageous to establish local representation, especially for product lines requiring strong sales and service efforts.

Foreign contractors wishing to bid for Government contracts must appoint a local service agent, and consultants must be represented by a Saudi consulting agency.

The compensation payable to a local service agent is limited to five percent of the total contract price as per the Service Agency Regulations. However, that percentage is not adhered to at all times.

Terminating an agent/distributor agreement can be difficult even though Saudi policy has changed to permit registration of a new agreement over the objections of the existing distributor. Time is better spent in making the proper initial selection than in attempting to end an unsatisfactory relationship at a later date. The U.S. Commercial Service, through its U.S. District Offices, Export Assistance Centers, and overseas posts, offers a variety of services to assist U.S. firms in selecting a reputable and qualified representative. A complete "Guide to Agency/Distributor Regulations in Saudi Arabia" is available through the National Trade Data Bank in CD-ROM format (Tel: (202) 482-1986 for details).

FRANCHISING

Franchising is a popular and growing approach for local firms to establish additional consumer-oriented business in Saudi Arabia. Although the franchise market is small relative to that in the United States, it is rapidly expanding in several business sectors.

Franchising opportunities exist in the following business categories: apparel, laundry and dry cleaning services, automotive parts and servicing, mail and package services, printing, and convenience stores.

Success in franchising in the Saudi market is often attributed to finding the appropriate franchisor and location. Non-food franchises account for 55 percent to 65 percent of the franchise market.

Franchising remains a growing sector in Saudi Arabia. This is in part due to a desire among Saudis to own their own business, and an appreciation for Western methods of conducting business. Competition is particularly fierce between U.S. franchisors and local and third country competitors in the following sectors: car rental agencies, laundry and dry cleaning services, and auto maintenance. Moreover, some local fast food outlets are already making inroads, being more successful and more accommodating to the Saudi tastes.

DIRECT MARKETING

Direct marketing is not widely used in Saudi Arabia. Personal relations between vendors and customers play a more important role than in the West; furthermore, many forms of direct marketing practiced in the United States are unacceptable due to Islamic precepts regarding gender segregation and privacy in the home. Limitations in the Saudi postal system are also a constraint: no home delivery or postal insurance is available yet; however, as part of the privatization of the Post, Telecommunications, and Telegraph Ministry, it is highly likely that mail and parcel home deliveries could begin by the end of 1999.

Direct marketing has been conducted on a very limited basis using unsolicited mail campaigns and fax, catalog sales (with local pick-up or delivery arranged), and commercials on satellite television providing consumers in many nations (including Saudi Arabia) with a local telephone number to arrange delivery.

The advent of the Internet in the Saudi market will increasingly have a profound effect on Saudi shopping behavior, providing increased possibilities and accessibility for Saudi consumers.

JOINT VENTURE/LICENSING

The Saudi Government is currently reviewing the foreign investment code to encourage more Saudi-foreign joint ventures in Saudi Arabia. Foreign investment is generally welcomed in Saudi

Arabia if it promotes economic development, transfers foreign expertise to the Kingdom, involves Saudis in ownership and management, creates jobs for Saudis, and expands Saudi exports.

Foreign investment is regulated under the Foreign Capital Investment Law administered by the Ministry of Industry and Electricity (MIE), which must approve all investments except banks, which are licensed by the Ministry of Finance and National Economy. The Ministry of Petroleum and Mineral Resources handles investments involving mineral extraction.

Foreign investment is normally limited to joint ventures in which the Saudi partner holds at least 25 percent up to a majority share. There are no restrictions on the use of currency accounts or on the entry or repatriation of capital, profits, dividends, or salaries, provided tax requirements have been satisfied and clearance provided by the Department of Zakat and Income Tax.

Foreign ownership is not permitted in a few sensitive areas or in well-developed sectors where it is believed sufficient local investment and expertise already exist.

A variety of incentives may be available to foreign investors upon approval of the Ministry of Industry and Electricity (MIE). These include tax holidays for five years (ten years for industrial and agricultural projects), duty free importation of capital equipment, spare parts and raw materials for the duration of the project, and access to low cost financing, industrial land, and utilities.

Local products receive price preferences of 10-20 percent in Government tenders. Most incentives are only available to joint ventures with at least 25 percent Saudi ownership.

Licensing is an appropriate method of doing business in the Kingdom under some circumstances, but the tax implications should be considered. Royalties, license fees, and certain management fees are deemed to be 100 percent profit, and the full amount will be taxed at the normal corporate tax rate for non-Saudi companies.

The process for establishing a joint venture is as follows:

First, the Ministry of Industry and Electricity (MIE) and its constituent parts must review and process all applications for industrial projects. Within the MIE, the Industrial Licensing Department (ILD) and Foreign Capital Investment Bureau (FCIB) are responsible for evaluating and licensing industrial projects. Non-industrial projects are handled unilaterally by the FCIB.

The MIE's Industrial Protection and Encouragement Department (IPED) studies the project's potential impact on domestic industry and determines any tariff protection that may apply. The MIE's Industrial Cities Department (ICD) evaluates requests for sites in Saudi Arabia's industrial cities.

In addition, an application must be made to the Foreign Capital Investment Committee (FCIC) for a foreign investment license. The FCIC is an inter-ministerial committee that receives recommendations forwarded by the MIE/FCIB, and after study makes its recommendation for final approval to the MIE. Following the issuance of the investment license, an application for commercial registration is made to the Ministry of Commerce (MOC).

In this process, the MOC will approve the joint venture's Articles of Association, register the company under the MOC's Companies Regulations, and assign a commercial registration number.

Depending on the nature of the foreign investment, the Saudi Arabian Standards Organization (SASO) may be involved. SASO is the Saudi authority for establishing product standards for imports and locally-manufactured goods, and will examine products or processes to be used to ensure they meet existing or planned Saudi standards.

The Saudi Industrial Development Fund (SIDF) may be engaged to provide up to 50 percent financing for approved industrial joint venture projects. Market intelligence also is available through the SIDF for prospective investors.

Other Saudi Arabian Government entities that may be involved in the process include the Ministry of Foreign Affairs (visas), the Ministry of Interior (residence permits and industrial safety and security approvals), the Ministry of Labor and Social Affairs (work permits for foreigners), the Royal Commission for Jubail and Yanbu (if the project is sited at the Saudi industrial cities of Jubail or Yanbu), the General Organization for Social Insurance (social insurance and disability payments for Saudi employees), and the General Organization for Technical Education and Vocational Training (training programs for Saudis).

Foreign investors may structure their enterprise as a limited liability company (the most commonly used approach), as a joint-stock company, or as a joint venture. By law, limited liability companies must not have less than two nor more than fifty shareholders and must be capitalized with at least SR. 500,000 ($133,333). Limited liability companies are forbidden to deal in insurance or financial enterprise. Joint stock companies are a variety of the limited liability company that can be held either privately or publicly. They resemble U.S. corporations in structure and function.

Joint ventures are unincorporated associations in which each party to the venture holds title to his mutually agreed contribution. They resemble general partnerships. The Ministry of Commerce approves formation of all joint ventures.

Applications must include the venture's objectives, rights and liabilities, as well as the manner in which profits are to be divided. A detailed "Guide to Establishing Joint Ventures in Saudi Arabia" is available in CD-ROM format on the National Trade Data Bank. A few major U.S. accounting firms with Saudi offices also publish very useful guides to the tax and legal aspects of doing business in Saudi Arabia.

STEPS TO ESTABLISHING AN OFFICE

The procedures to follow in establishing an office in Saudi Arabia differ according to the type of business undertaken. The most common and direct method of establishing an office is simply to appoint an agent/distributor, who can set up the office under their own commercial registry and obtain residency visas for any necessary expatriate personnel. The agent/distributor agreement should be registered with the Ministry of Commerce as previously described.

A second method might be to establish a technical and scientific service office, which requires a license from the Ministry of Commerce. This approach preserves the independence and identity of the foreign company's local office as a separate entity from the Saudi agent/distributor.

Technical and scientific service offices are not allowed to engage directly or indirectly in commercial activities, but they may provide technical support to the Saudi distributor as well as conduct market surveys and product research.

A third method is to establish a branch office, which is normally permitted only for foreign defense contractors. The establishment of branch offices is open to wholly foreign-owned entities, and requires approval of the Ministry of Industry and Electricity's Foreign Capital Investment Committee (FCIC).

An essential element in the FCIC's approval process is that the branch office contributes to the Kingdom's economic development. FCIC approval also requires the foreign company submit a certified copy of its charter and bylaws, accompanied by an Arabic translation, as well as the company name, address, date of establishment, type of business and amount of capital. The company's board of directors must also provide a resolution authorizing the establishment of a Saudi branch office.

Following FCIC approval, the branch office must establish and register with the Commercial Register of the Ministry of Commerce. The registration process requires representation by a Saudi attorney.

A fourth method is to establish a representative (or liaison) office. This is normally granted only for companies that have multiple contracts with the Government and require a local office to oversee contract implementation. Representative offices are not allowed to engage in direct or indirect commercial activity in the Kingdom. Establishment requires a representative office license from the Ministry of Commerce.

Finally, foreign companies may establish an office by entering into a joint venture with a Saudi firm, as described in the previous section.

Costs associated with setting up an office in Saudi Arabia can vary considerably. As a general guide, the following are current costs of housing and office rental, as well as costs for employee salaries, taxes, and transportation. Most of these costs have remained relatively unchanged from the previous year. Typical rent per year for a one-bedroom furnished apartment is $13,200, and $16,134 for a two-bedroom apartment.

A one-bedroom furnished villa in a Western-standard residential compound will rent per year for $22,000 to $23,650; two bedrooms, $27,866 to $29,333; three bedrooms, $33,733 to $36,666; four bedrooms, $42,533 to $54,266. Residential compounds in Saudi Arabia often include a swimming pool, tennis courts, a club house, and eating facilities.

Typical management, maintenance, and use charges are usually included in the rental price, and security deposits are in the range of $2,970. Rental terms are for one year payable in advance. Office rental costs are variable, and are governed largely by the city and business location.

Typical rental costs in a modern commercial center are approximately $220 per square meter, inclusive of maintenance and utility charges. A 12-month rental is the minimum and advance payment is required.

Saudi law requires that Saudi nationals make up 75 percent of a company's work force and 51 percent of its payroll in all businesses. However, due to a shortage of qualified Saudis, in practice much of the work force is made up of non-Saudi Arabs, Europeans, Americans and Asians. In 1996, the Saudi Government implemented a regulation requiring each company employing over 20 workers to include a minimum of five percent Saudi nationals. Companies not complying with the five percent rule (which will increase in annual increments of five percent) will not be given visas for expatriate workers.

For additional analytical, business and investment opportunities information, please contact Global Investment & Business Center, USA at (202) 546-2103. Fax: (202) 546-3275. E-mail: ibpusa3@gmail.com Global Business and Legal Information Databank: www.ibpus.com

An employee's nationality and level of experience, as well as the nature and location of the business will create variations in pay, but a typical manager's yearly salary (base) is approximately $30,000 to 40,000. Mid-level office workers are paid approximately $20,000 to 30,000 per year. A clerical worker's base yearly salary is in the range of $8,000 to 10,000. A support worker (driver, caretaker) earns in the range of $6,000 to 7,000 yearly. Saudi Arabia's six million expatriates include 4.7 million laborers employed in various sectors, who annually transfer close to $16 billion.

Local Saudi employee taxes are 15 percent of base or combined with benefits. From base salary and housing, companies withhold five percent and pay 10 percent.

It is customary to provide non-Saudi workers with furnished accommodations or a housing allowance as well as round-trip air fare to their country of origin on a yearly basis.

Regarding transportation, four-door sedans rent monthly for approximately $960, and yearly for about $11,500. A new GMC Suburban can be purchased for approximately $30,373. It is important to note that, law forbids females in Saudi Arabia, regardless of nationality, to drive motor vehicles.

Additional monies, along the lines mentioned above, should be included in an office budget to provide sufficient cars and drivers for transportation of female family members and staff.

Business travelers coming to Saudi Arabia to explore business opportunities are eligible for a visitor's visa, which currently is a single-entry visa for up to three months' duration. However, there is hope that the Saudi Government will very soon agree to two-year, multiple-entry visas for U.S. citizens.

Currently, the visitor's visa application requires the U.S. company's representative to submit to Saudi visa authorities a letter of invitation issued by a Saudi company that has agreed to serve as his sponsor. The letter, which must be in Arabic, must be on the Saudi company's letterhead, in the original, and must bear an authenticating stamp from the Saudi company's local chamber of commerce.

The U.S. company's representative must apply for the visa prior to departing the United States at either the Saudi Embassy in Washington, D.C., or at one of the Saudi Consulates in Houston, Los Angeles or New York City. Saudi visa authorities strictly enforce these requirements. The Saudi Government announced in late May of 1999 a new and simplified procedure for the issuance of entry visas to foreign businessmen, but full details have not been published.

SELLING FACTORS/TECHNIQUES

Expatriate managers have had a strong influence in introducing advanced selling techniques into a market that relied heavily on word-of-mouth and established buying patterns until a few years ago. Advertising and public relations firms are multiplying in Saudi Arabia, and the Saudis themselves have become a discerning, sophisticated clientele.

Although details of a transaction can be handled by facsimile, now in widespread use, no serious commitment is likely to be made without a face-to-face introduction. Business cards are usually printed in English on one side and Arabic on the other.

Saudis are gracious hosts and will try to put a visitor at ease, even during arduous business dealings. A large portion of upper and middle class Saudis were educated in the United States or in Europe.

The positive aspect of the Saudis' familiarity with the United States is that most importers are very receptive to American products because of the U.S. reputation for state-of-the-art technology, durability, and stable prices.

Of course, this goodwill can be used only as an introduction, since a product must be competitively priced and readily available to make a sale.

Financing may also be offered as part of a sales proposal, usually after a solid relationship has been established. Financing is increasingly becoming an important facet of business dealings with Saudi Government agencies. Likewise, the Government has begun to experiment with Build-Operate-Transfer (BOT) financing schemes.

Foreigners need to find a Saudi partner before they are allowed to engage in trade within the Kingdom, but direct sales can be made to Saudi private clients without having to use a local agency. Saudi Ministries will purchase only from local agents or distributors, and contracts for major projects are usually awarded to joint ventures linking foreign and Saudi partners.

An irrevocable letter of credit (L/C) is the instrument normally used for Saudi imports; open account, cash in advance and documentary collection are also acceptable if both parties agree. Maximum or minimum credit terms are not required. Export Credit Insurance for political and commercial risk is available from the Foreign Credit Insurance Association (F.C.I.A) of the U.S. Export-Import Bank in Washington, D.C. (Tel: 202-566-8990 or 212-306-5084).

The Government maintains a free trade approach to exchange transactions: no exchange restrictions apply; exchange for payments abroad is obtained freely; and there are no taxes or subsidies on foreign currency transactions.

With the advent of the Internet, industry sources expect that such access will boost regional and international business. For that matter, the Ministry of Commerce is forming a team to establish regulations regarding electronic commerce that is expected to expand.

Since 1981, the Saudi Arabian Monetary Agency (SAMA) has pegged the riyal to the dollar, to facilitate long term planning and minimize exchange risk for the private sector. The rate has remained stable at $1 = SR 3.7450 since 1987.

ADVERTISING AND TRADE PROMOTION

Advertising, once a relatively secondary aspect of sales, has come into its own, especially with the recent lifting of a ban on televised commercials. Most companies' advertising budgets now cover the complete array of media, such as TV, newspapers, trade magazines and billboards, in addition to trade promotion events. Saudis receive preferential rates.

Bright colors such as red, blue, green and black dominate ads. Pink, cream and other soft colors are not as popular. With some modest exceptions, the female human form is not culturally or religiously acceptable in the media. Landscapes and other non-human images are commonly featured. Ads, packages, literature, etc. are frequently in English and Arabic.

A recent study by a local research firm indicated that advertising expenditures in the Gulf Cooperation Council (GCC) countries are expected to rise 12 percent from $817 million in 1998 to $913 million in 1999.

Advertising is critical in gaining retail sales and market share. Most companies' advertising budgets now cover the complete array of media, including: television, newspapers, magazines, billboards, and trade promotion events. Some televised commercials are broadcast on the two Saudi channels (Secam color system) during limited periods of the day. One TV channel is in Arabic; the second is in English, with broadcasting covering the entire Kingdom.

Cost of a time slot varies considerably, depending on timing, and is usually less costly for Saudis than foreign firms. Contents are thoroughly screened to conform with strict moral and religious standards.

A new approach to presenting products is advertising through international TV channels such as CNN and MBC (Middle East Broadcasting Corporation in London). In 1997, two new satellite channels broadcasting from Beirut, Lebanon, went on the air, the Lebanese Broadcasting Company (LBC) and Future Television. Many analysts rate the two channels as the most popular pan-Arab stations, and most major Saudi companies place commercials on these two channels as well as on the MBC channel.

Arab satellite TV stations are expected to have an increasing share of advertising spending which is projected to reach $439 million in 1999, a 22 percent rise over 1998.

In addition, two encrypted TV networks each provide approximately 30 channels for an average subscription of $1000 per year. The networks include Orbit Communications and ShowTime. Other Arabic satellite channels that have been launched, such as Arab Radio and Television, are also attracting numerous advertisers. These TV channels have succeeded in introducing several new products to the market.

There are no signs that the cable television network will be launched in the foreseeable future. The first of its kind in the Kingdom, SARA Cable is an offshoot of a large, Riyadh-based, media and production company, ARA International. Print advertising is also important. In recent years, several magazines have appeared on the local market. Popular magazines are: Al-Wasat, Al-Majallah, Al-Yamamah, and Sayidati. Advertising rates for publications vary greatly; however their level is well below the U.S. norm, in keeping with the reduced readership.

Newspaper advertising is carried out in both the local English and Arabic press, but its effectiveness is somewhat limited by the relatively low readership rates. The three local dailies published in English have circulation in the 20,000 to 50,000 copies range: Arab News (London); Saudi Gazette (Jeddah); Riyadh Daily (Riyadh). The leading Arabic newspapers, with nationwide distribution, have circulation in the 70,000 to 100,000 range: Al-Hayat, Al-Shark Al-Awsat, Okaz. Other relevant newspapers have lower circulation, and some have only regional distribution: Al Bilad, Al Jazira, Al Madina, Al Nadwa, Al Riyadh, Al Youm, Um Al Qura, Al-Riyadiya (sports only). Another economic daily, Al Iqtisadiah, has rapidly earned a loyal readership of executives and Government officials.

Numerous trade promotion events take place from September through June, with most of them held in the modern exhibit centers in the Kingdom's three major cities:
Riyadh Exhibitions Co., Ltd.
PO Box 56101

Riyadh 11554, Saudi Arabia
Tel: (01) 454-1448, Fax: (01) 454-4846
Tlx: 406359 EXHB SJ
Contact: Akram Al-Masri, Director of Exhibition Services

Al-Harithy Co. for Exhibitions, Ltd.
PO Box 40740
Jeddah 21511, Saudi Arabia
Tel: (02) 654-6384, Fax: (02) 654-6853
Tlx: 602784 EXPO SJ
Contact: Saeed Haider, General Manager

Dhahran International Exhibition
PO Box 7519
Dammam 31472, Saudi Arabia
Tel: (03) 857-9111, Fax: (03) 857-2285
Contact: Najeeb Abdul Rahman Al-Zamil, General Manager

Each exhibit center organizes five to ten events a year, and even though the programs have varied over time, the recurrent themes cover most industries of interest for U.S. exporters: agriculture, automotive, computers, medical and lab equipment, construction, production technology, electrical and A/C-heating, and communications. Smaller exhibit facilities are also located in regional centers, and often operate in cooperation with or under the sponsorship of the local chamber of commerce.

Most chambers have a proactive approach to promotion and trade, organize shows and presentations for individual companies or groups, and have been eager to attract American and other Western suppliers.
The main Chambers are:

Council of Saudi Chambers of Commerce and Industry
PO Box 16683
Riyadh 11474, Saudi Arabia
Tel: (01) 405-3200, Fax: (01) 402-4747

Riyadh Chamber of Commerce and Industry
PO Box 596
Riyadh 11421, Saudi Arabia
Tel: (01) 404-0044, Fax: (01) 402-1103

Jeddah Chamber of Commerce and Industry
PO Box 1264
Jeddah 21431, Saudi Arabia
Tel: (02) 651-5111, Fax: (02) 651-7373

Dammam Chamber of Commerce and Industry
PO Box 719
Dammam 31421, Saudi Arabia
Tel: (03) 857-1111, Fax: (03) 857-0607

For additional analytical, business and investment opportunities information,
please contact Global Investment & Business Center, USA
at (202) 546-2103. Fax: (202) 546-3275. E-mail: ibpusa3@gmail.com
Global Business and Legal Information Databank: www.ibpus.com

Makkah Chamber of Commerce and Industry
PO Box 1086
Makkah, Saudi Arabia
Tel: (02) 534-3838, Fax: (02) 534-2904

Medina Chamber of Commerce and Industry
PO Box 443
Medina, Saudi Arabia
Tel: (04) 822-5380, Fax: (04) 826-8965

Taif Chamber of Commerce and Industry
PO Box 1005
Taif, Saudi Arabia
Tel: (02) 736-6800, Fax: (02) 738-0040

NOTE: Add country code 966 if dialing from the United States or other locations outside Saudi Arabia, and drop the zero before the first digit of the telephone or fax numbers above, which are the city codes.

PRODUCT PRICING

A rate of exchange of the dollar to the riyal has been set at 3.7450 since 1987, a competitive dollar value compared to the Japanese and European currencies, and reasonable interest rates have greatly facilitated market penetration. Thanks to this, Saudi importers expect U.S. producers to practice a more stable pricing policy than their foreign competitors.

Products are usually imported on a CIF basis, and mark-ups depend almost entirely on what the vendor feels that the market will bear relative to the competition. There is no standard formula to determine the mark-up rates for all product lines at different levels of the relatively short distribution chain. Pricing is very important to the average Saudi.

Therefore, where there are competitive products, Saudi buyers frequently will compare prices before making a buying decision. Stability of prices has been a policy of the Saudi Government for years, and after rising to five percent in 1995 as a result of the utility and gas rates hikes, inflation was negative 0.2 percent for the 12-month period ending December 1998. The Embassy forecasts a 1 to 2 percent rise in prices during 1999, based on the latest hike in gasoline prices and depending on when the consolidation of the electric company takes place, with a resulting jump in costs for high volume users. For the U.S. supplier, some give-and-take is expected in preliminary negotiations. The asking price is usually lowered a bit, to entice the client and to bow to the old-fashioned Saudi penchant for bargaining and personal exchange.

Financing has become a leading consideration in purchasing, especially for investment goods and repeat orders. As leveraged transactions become the norm, Saudis have come to understand that an attractive financial package can be even more interesting than an up-front low price.

The support and services provided by the U.S. Export-Import Bank attract the Saudis' keen interest, and are being considered for several major projects.

SALES SERVICE/CUSTOMER SUPPORT

Saudi Arabia is a relatively open market, which makes it highly competitive. Brand loyalty and established preferences are less developed than in other countries. Consequently, above average sales service and customer support are indispensable to win and maintain new clients.

As the Saudi market matures, this will become more and more the norm, and the recent economic slowdown is adding to the competitive pressure; the sell-and-forget techniques still common in the 1980s are definitely out.

Saudis view a foreign firm's physical presence in the Kingdom as a tangible sign of a long-term commitment.

Prompt delivery of goods from available stock and the presence of qualified support technicians have become more important, and they influence repeat business much more now than ten or even five years ago. Government agencies usually require equipment suppliers to commit to providing maintenance and spare parts for an average period of three years.

SELLING TO THE GOVERNMENT

Government spending accounted for approximately 38 percent of GDP in 1998, but was expected to drop to 30 percent in 1999 and to remain as such in 2000. A sign that the Saudi private sector is again assuming an increasingly major role in the Kingdom's economic performance.

U.S. firms considering sales to the Government should request a briefing from the Embassy concerning the latest situation on payments and how U.S. firms can protect themselves.

As a practical matter, U.S. companies seeking sales of goods and services to the Saudi Government should appoint a reputable agent or distributor with experience in the field. Foreign contractors operating solely for the Government, if not already registered to do business in Saudi Arabia, are required to obtain temporary registration from the Ministry of Commerce within 30 days of contract signing and to select a Saudi national as an officially registered agent (weapons sales are exempt from this agency requirement). Compensation for agents is limited to a maximum of 5 percent of contract value; however, the rate may vary depending on the agreement.

Foreign companies also may be allowed to establish a branch office by obtaining a foreign capital investment license from the Ministry of Industry and Electricity.

Branch offices are usually approved only for foreign defense contractors. For others, a liaison office may be established to supervise work in the Kingdom and to facilitate coordination between the Government and home offices.

This requires approval of the Ministry of Commerce. Liaison offices are prohibited from conducting commercial business in Saudi Arabia.

Foreign contractors involved in public works projects are required to subcontract at least 30 percent of the contract value to 100 percent Saudi-owned companies. This requirement also applies to limited liability partnerships with less than 51 percent Saudi ownership.

For additional analytical, business and investment opportunities information,
please contact Global Investment & Business Center, USA
at (202) 546-2103. Fax: (202) 546-3275. E-mail: ibpusa3@gmail.com
Global Business and Legal Information Databank: www.ibpus.com

The subcontractor must be qualified to perform the work and may not further subcontract any portion of it. Purchases of Saudi products and services and of imported products from Saudi distributors may count toward the 30 percent requirement.

PROTECTING PRODUCT FROM IPR INFRINGEMENT

Saudi Arabia has a patent office, but has only issued a few patents, and has an enormous backlog of patents pending. Saudi Arabia has made Important strides in improving intellectual property rights (IPR) protection, including a series of well-publicized raids on stores selling pirated material and the release of a fatwa by the late Grand Mufti of Saudi Arabia confirming that piracy is theft, and therefore forbidden under Islamic law. However, piracy remains a problem in Saudi Arabia and the Kingdom remains on the U.S. Trade Representative's "Watch List" of countries that need to improve IPR protection.

U.S. firms that wish to sell products in Saudi Arabia should work through their local representative to register their trademarks with the Ministry of Commerce and copyrighted products with the Ministry of Information, which are responsible for IPR protection in these areas, and report any suspected incidents of piracy or infringement to the Ministry.

During the first six months of 1999, the Ministry of Information imposed fines worth $347,000 on violators of copyright laws. During that period, the Ministry also destroyed 125,000 counterfeit computer programs and videos and about 44,000 audio cassettes.

Despite the backlog of patent applications, the Embassy recommends that if a U.S. company is concerned about the possibility of patent infringement, it should "file" a patent application request with the Saudi Patent Office.

To learn more about the procedure, we recommend interested companies consult a local attorney who specializes in this area. The Embassy can provide a representative list of qualified attorneys.

NEED FOR A LOCAL ATTORNEY

Saudi law is based on the Islamic Shari'a and differs considerably from U.S. practice. U.S. firms contemplating a joint venture, licensing, or distribution agreement are advised to consult with a local attorney. The American Embassy and Consulates can provide a list of attorneys.

PERFORMING DUE DILIGENCE/CHECKING BONA FIDES OF BANKS/AGENTS/CUSTOMERS

In 1995, the Commercial Service in Saudi Arabia ceased to offer regular International Company Profile (ICP) reports. Nonetheless, CS Saudi Arabia will provide bona fides checks in support of a U.S. company's due diligence process, if requested.

Dun and Bradstreet's local agent, Amer Research Company, can produce complete background and credit reports. The company can be reached at:
(966 1) 406-5050 ext. 4118, Fax: (966 1) 403-7491, Attention: Mr. Salah Ibrahim. E-mail:mikebaulch@zajil.net.

TRADE AND PROJECT FINANCING

FINANCIAL RESOURCES

A sound, efficient and liberal financial system is essential for the Kingdom's economic development process and the attraction of foreign investment into the country. Therefore, the Saudi government has created a well-structured financial system made of the following:

(1) Saudi Arabian Monetary Agency (SAMA):

Saudi Arabian Monetary Agency is the Central Bank of the Kingdom. SAMA monitors the operations of commercial banks and the Saudi stock market, issues the currency, determines the money supply, and manages the country's financial reserves (See appendix I for address).

(2) Commercial Banks:

Commercial banks in Saudi Arabia evolved through branches of foreign banks. The National Commercial Bank is the first Saudi bank in the Kingdom, (see ad., page ---). It was established in 1953 followed by the opening of Riyadh Bank in 1957 (see ad., page ---). Saudization of the banking system began in the mid 1970's and was accomplished in the early 1980s. There are twelve commercial banks now operating in the Kingdom. Some of these banks are totally owned by Saudis and some are joint ventures with foreign banks with hundreds of branches in major cities of the Kingdom (for names and addresses, see appendix VI).

(3) Government Specialized Investment Funds:

These funds, mentioned above, were established by the government and are financed through budgetary appropriations. Their main function is to provide medium and long-term loans to private and public projects (see listing in appendix I).

(4) The Non-Bank Financial Institutions:

These financial institutions function mainly in investment, insurance, and money exchange. Listings of these institutions can be obtained from the Saudi Chambers of Commerce and Industry (see appendix IV for address).

Regulations affecting foreign investment in Saudi Arabia are provided in the next chapter.

- The banking system

The Saudi banking system posted excellent results in 2000. New regulations allowing for foreign ownership of certain mutual funds boosted the results at Saudi banks. Moreover, there has been a steady and growing shift to retail lending, which provided comparatively higher margins and lower risk factors. The extension of consumer credit was directly enhanced by the developments in electronic banking, which facilitated direct-deposit of salaries and thus collections.

Both the local stock market and share prices of the commercial banks saw a significant rise after the announcement of the new regulations, with the Saudi stock market registering a large 43.6 percent gain for 1999. In 2000, the stock market gained a mere 11.3 percent, less than expected given the historically close correlation between Saudi share and oil price movements.

The Saudi American Bank led other banks announcing an exceptional rise in profits, from $240.6 million in 1999 to $534.7 million in 2000, more than 122 percent increase. Saudi Arabia's commercial banks have enjoyed steady profits for the last five years. In January 1999, the United Saudi Bank (USB), owned by Prince Al-Waleed Bin Talal, merged with the Saudi-American Bank (SAMBA). Today the banking community is composed of ten Saudi banks and a GCC bank, the Bahrain-based Gulf International Bank, licensed in 2000. In 1999, the National Commercial Bank (NCB), largest in Saudi Arabia in terms of assets, sold 50 percent of its shares to the government-run Public Investment Fund (PIF) as part of a change of management and ownership. The SAG has stated its intent to sell back the shares as the local capital markets are able to absorb them.

If the Saudi government follows the opening of mutual funds to foreigners with a similar opening of stock ownership, share values may be boosted further. The stock market should also receive a boost from the adoption of a new capital markets law, which is expected to establish an independent regulator and provide greater transparency. Although the Saudi stock market is the largest in the region in absolute terms (about $60 billion), its capitalization to GDP ratio lags several other Middle Eastern markets. Only 76 firms are traded, with banks and SABIC dominating total capitalization. Greater privatization in the Saudi economy, including the creation of partial savings accounts in the two major pension systems of the country, would greatly enhance the capitalization of the stock exchange, and make it a more important engine for economic growth.

The Saudi Arabian Monetary Agency (SAMA), the Saudi central bank, regulates and controls the Saudi banking sector. Financing is available to Saudi and non-Saudi businessmen and entities. Offshore banking and trust operations do not exist in Saudi Arabia, and there is no legislation to permit the establishment of these operations.

The securities market is still not highly developed, but continues to mature. Banks are the sole entities that may act as stockbrokers for publicly traded shares or for joint stock companies. The most significant recent development is SAMA's approval to allow foreigners to buy and trade shares of Saudi companies within a closed-end fund listed in the United Kingdom.

Commercial banks operating in Saudi Arabia ranked by total assets:

1) The National Commercial Bank 6) Saudi French Bank
2) Saudi American Bank 7) Arab National Bank
3) Riyadh Bank 8) Saudi Hollandi Bank
4) Al-Rajhi Banking & Investment Corporation 9) Saudi Investment Bank
5) Saudi British Bank 10) Bank Al-Jazira

- Foreign Exchange Controls Affecting Trade

Saudi Arabia imposes no foreign exchange restrictions on capital receipts or payments by residents or nonresidents, beyond a prohibition against transactions with Israel. Although officially linked to the IMF's Special Drawing Rights, Saudi Arabia in practice pegs its currency, the riyal, to the U.S. dollar.

Saudi Arabia last devalued the Riyal in June 1986 when it set the official selling rate at SR 3.745 = $1. The Saudi Arabian Monetary Agency and all residents may freely and without license buy, hold, sell, import, and export gold, with the exception of gold of 14 karats or less.

- General Financing Availability and Terms of Payment

For additional analytical, business and investment opportunities information, please contact Global Investment & Business Center, USA at (202) 546-2103. Fax: (202) 546-3275. E-mail: ibpusa3@gmail.com Global Business and Legal Information Databank: www.ibpus.com

Saudi policies facilitate the free flow of financial resources. Credit from the commercial banks is allocated on market terms, and foreign investors can obtain credit on the local market. The private sector has access to a variety of credit instruments.

"Soft" term financing is available from specialized credit institutions: the Saudi Agricultural Bank, the Saudi Credit Bank, the Public Investment Fund, the Saudi Industrial Development Fund (SIDF), and the Real Estate Development Fund. The Saudi banking system is well capitalized and well provisioned. SIDF loans are available to finance foreign-owned businesses in Saudi Arabia under the new foreign investment law.

The Embassy is not aware of any "cross-shareholding" or "stable shareholder" arrangements being used by private firms to restrict foreign investment through mergers and acquisitions. Nor is the Embassy aware of any laws or regulations that specifically authorize private firms to adopt articles of incorporation/association which limit or prohibit foreign investment, participation, or control. Foreign participation in the Saudi Arabian Standards Organization (SASO) is not possible, although a number of foreign advisors from OECD countries (including the US National Institute of Standards and Technology) assist and provide counsel to SASO.

- Availability of GSM Credit Guarantees

GSM credit guarantees are not available in Saudi Arabia.

- Availability of Loan Guarantees, Insurance, and Project Financing from the Export-Import Bank of the United States, OPIC and the IFIs

The U.S. Export-Import Bank has been involved in Saudi Arabia supporting trade with private Saudi companies. OPIC does not provide coverage in Saudi Arabia. The Government of Saudi Arabia may use the facilities of International Financial Institutions to support major infrastructure projects.

The Islamic Development Bank fosters the economic development and social progress of member countries and Muslim communities. It participates in equity capital and grants loans for productive projects and enterprises, besides providing financial assistance to member countries in other forms for economic and social development.

Project financing is available in Saudi Arabia for longer-term loans by the local commercial banks and Saudi specialized credit institutions such as the Saudi Industrial Development Fund or the Public Investment Fund. The Saudi Government does not receive project financing from multilateral institutions such as the World Bank. The U.S. Export-Import Bank has not, so far, engaged in any project finance activities in Saudi Arabia.

Financing schemes were arranged in 2000 for a number of Saudi entities, including:

1) Saudi Telecommunications Company ($666.6 million)
2) Arabian Industrial Fibers Company ($1,050 million)
3) Arab Petroleum Investments Corporation ($200 million)
4) Arabian Petrochemicals Company ($600 million)
5) Islamic Development Bank ($84 million)

The International Finance Corporation (IFC), the private sector lending arm of the World Bank Group, is participating in a Saudi Government project, the Saudi Orix Leasing Corporation (SOLC), which will help finance short and medium-sized projects by making asset-backed

For additional analytical, business and investment opportunities information,
please contact Global Investment & Business Center, USA
at (202) 546-2103. Fax: (202) 546-3275. E-mail: ibpusa3@gmail.com
Global Business and Legal Information Databank: www.ibpus.com

financing more accessible. SOLC is the IFC's first joint venture in Saudi Arabia. In addition, the Council of Saudi Chambers of Commerce and Industry is assisting with the set up of a Saudi-Japanese company to finance small and medium-sized companies in Saudi Arabia.

- Financing and Methods of Payment to Export from the Local Economy to Another Market, Including U.S. Import

Recently, the Saudi Fund for Development began to offer financing for Saudi exports to countries where there is no commercial bank coverage, no correspondent banks and/or high risk country/bank.

The Islamic Corporation for the Insurance of Investment and Export Credit (ICIEC) provides Export Credit guarantees on exports to member states and to companies owned/partly owned by member states. In addition, the corporation provides investment insurance and guarantees against country risks to member states.

- List of Banks with Correspondent U.S. Banking Arrangement

Because of their ownership structure, Saudi American Bank (Citibank) and Saudi Investment Bank (Chase Manhattan) have direct correspondent relationships with U.S. banks. Other Saudi banks also have correspondent relationships with the U.S. institutions, whether the home office in the United States or branches in Europe or Bahrain.

- List of U.S. Financial/Lending Institutions Operating in Saudi Arabia

There are no U.S. financial/lending institutions operating independently in Saudi Arabia.

- Contact Information for Locally or Regionally Based MDB or Other IFI Offices

Islamic Development Bank

Contact: Dr. Ahmed Mohammad Ali, President
PO Box 5925 Jeddah 21432, Saudi Arabia
Phone: (966 2) 636-1400, Fax: (966 2) 636-6871

The World Bank
Contact: Edgar Saravia, Resident Representative
P.O. Box 5900 Riyadh 11432, Saudi Arabia
Phone: (966 1) 483-4956, Fax: (966 1) 488-5311

BUSINESS AND LEGAL CONTACTS

Contact for More Information

Economic Section and Foreign Commercial Service Offices
Embassy of the United States of America
P. O. Box 94309
Riyadh 11693, Saudi Arabia
Phone: +966 11 488-3800
Fax: +966 11 488-3237
E-mail: **office.riyadh@trade.gov**

LAW FIRMS

The Riyadh Consular District includes central Saudi Arabia and portions of the Northern Province. This list contains only the names of firms with offices in the city of Riyadh. The firms are listed in no particular order. Unless otherwise indicated, these firms will take cases throughout the Consular District.

The Saudi legal system, Sharia law, is based on the Koran and Hadith. This system differs considerably from other legal systems - in particular, the U.S. legal system. Therefore, the services of an attorney schooled in Sharia law is advisable when dealing with legal matters within the Kingdom.

Law offices generally follow Saudi working hours (9:00 - 13:00 and 16:30 - 20:30). Attorneys do not normally perform notarial services. All of the firms on the list have attorneys who speak English.

THE LAW FIRM OF MOHAMED AL-SHARIF **THE LAW FIRM OF MOHAMED AL-SHARIF**
Website:**Website:** http://www.alshariflaw.comhttp://www.alshariflaw.com
Email:Email: johnsonch51@gmail.comjohnsonch51@gmail.com and and chris@alshariflaw.comchris@alshariflaw.com
Phone:**Phone: 011-462-5925** 011-462-5925
Fax:**Fax:** 011-464-4898 011-464-4898

Street Address:**Street Address:** Al-Musa Commercial Center, Tower 2, 5th Floor, Office No. 259, Main Olaya St. RiyadhAl-Musa Commercial Center, Tower 2, 5th Floor, Office No. 259, Main Olaya St. Riyadh Mailing Address:**Mailing Address:** P.O. Box 9170, Riyadh 11423 P.O. Box 9170, Riyadh 11423

Specialties:Specialties: Corporate, business, finance and intellectual property law, including contracts, Corporate, business, finance and intellectual property law, including contracts, joint ventures, disputes and representing foreign companies in their trade and joint ventures, disputes and representing foreign companies in their trade and investment activities in the Kingdom. investment activities in the Kingdom.

PRIME LEGAL SUPPORT **PRIME LEGAL SUPPORT**
Website:**Website:** http://www.primesupport.com.sahttp://www.primesupport.com.sa
E-mail:**E-mail: faiza@primesupport.com.sa**faiza@primesupport.com.sa

Phone:Phone: 011-2816635 / 4831877 011-2816635 / 4831877
Fax:Fax: 011-4826266 011-4826266

Street Address:Street Address: Diplomatic Quarters, Al Fazari Plaza, Riyadh Diplomatic Quarters, Al Fazari Plaza, Riyadh

Specialties: Specialties: Banking, Energy, Litigation, Emerging companies, Government / Commercial Banking, Energy, Litigation, Emerging companies, Government / Commercial contracts, Employment law International contracts, Employment law International

ABDULAZIZ ALASSAF LAW FIRM **ABDULAZIZ ALASSAF LAW FIRM**
Web Site:**Web Site:** http://www.aaafirm.comhttp://www.aaafirm.com
E-mail:**E-mail:** aalmasoud@aaafirm.comaalmasoud@aaafirm.com
Phone:**Phone:** 011-211-2000 011-211-2000
Fax:**Fax: 011-211-2727** 011-211-2727
Street Address:**Street Address:** Kingdom Center, 24th floor, King Fahad Road Kingdom Center, 24th floor, King Fahad Road, ,
Mailing Address: **Mailing Address: P.O. Box 90217, Riyadh 11613** P.O. Box 90217, Riyadh 11613

Specialties:**Specialties:** Employment and Labor Disputes; Contract; Mergers and acquisitions; Private Employment and Labor Disputes; Contract; Mergers and acquisitions; Private equity; Joint ventures; Corporate restructuring; Capital markets and regulatory equity; Joint ventures; Corporate restructuring; Capital markets and regulatory advice; Company law and corporate governance; Structuring foreign advice; Company law and corporate governance; Structuring foreign investments; Formation of Saudi, GCC and foreign owned companies. investments; Formation of Saudi, GCC and foreign owned companies.

Agency, distribution and franchises; Procurement contracts; Litigation; Agency, distribution and franchises; Procurement contracts; Litigation; Arbitration and mediation; Risk management; Enforcement and debt recovery; Arbitration and mediation; Risk management; Enforcement and debt recovery; Regulatory enforcement; and Alternative dispute resolution. Regulatory enforcement; and Alternative dispute resolution.

LAW OFFICE OF OMAR AL BORAIK **LAW OFFICE OF OMAR AL BORAIK**
Website:**Website:** www.omarlawfirm.comwww.omarlawfirm.com
E-mail:**E-mail:** omar@omarlawfirm.comomar@omarlawfirm.com ; ; omarlawfirm@hotmail.comomarlawfirm@hotmail.com
Phone:**Phone:** 011-200-1766 011-200-1766
Fax:**Fax:** 011-229-4181 011-229-4181
Street Address:**Street Address:** King Fahad Road, P O Box: 66133 Riyadh 11576 King Fahad Road, P O Box: 66133 Riyadh 11576
AL-JOUFI LAW FIRM **AL-JOUFI LAW FIRM**
Website:**Website:** http://www.aljoufilaw.comhttp://www.aljoufilaw.com
E-mail:**E-mail:** info@aljoufilaw.cominfo@aljoufilaw.com
Phone:**Phone: 011-464-1304** 011-464-1304
Fax:**Fax: 011-464-2104** 011-464-2104
Street Address:**Street Address: First Floor, The Plaza Complex, Olaya Street, Olaya** First Floor, The Plaza Complex, Olaya Street, Olaya
Mailing Address:**Mailing Address: P.O. Box: 84421, Riyadh 11671** P.O. Box: 84421, Riyadh 11671

Specialties: Specialties: Banking & Financial, foreign investment, Corporate and Commercial, Real Estate Banking & Financial, foreign investment, Corporate and Commercial, Real Estate & Mortgage, Energy, Power & Infrastructure, Dispute Resolution, Litigation & & Mortgage, Energy, Power & Infrastructure, Dispute Resolution, Litigation & Arbitration. Arbitration.

KHALID A. AL-THEBITY LAW FIRM **KHALID A. AL-THEBITY LAW FIRM**

Website:Website: http://www.dl.comhttp://www.dl.com
E-mail:E-mail: kal-thebity@dl.comkal-thebity@dl.com
Phone:Phone: 011-416-9990 / 01-416-9991 / 01-416-9992 011-416-9990 / 01-416-9991 / 01-416-9992
Fax:**Fax: 011-416-9980** 011-416-9980
Street Address:**Street Address: 8th Floor, Sky Towers, King Fahad Road, Riyadh** 8th Floor, Sky Towers, King Fahad Road, Riyadh
Mailing Address:**Mailing Address: P.O. Box: 300807, Riyadh 11372** P.O. Box: 300807, Riyadh 11372

Specialties: **Specialties:** Energy, corporate, financial services, international trade and investment, Energy, corporate, financial services, international trade and investment, boundary disputes, privatization, environmental, litigation, real estate, and boundary disputes, privatization, environmental, litigation, real estate, and technology/intellectual property. technology/intellectual property.

MOHAMMED S. Al-GHAMDI LAW FIRM IN ASSOCIATION WITH FULBRIGHT & JAWORSKI **MOHAMMED S. Al-GHAMDI LAW FIRM IN ASSOCIATION WITH FULBRIGHT & JAWORSKI L.L.P L.L.P**

Website:**Website:** http://www.fulbright.com/mal-ghamdihttp://www.fulbright.com/mal-ghamdi
E-mail:**E-mail:** mal-ghamdi@fulbright.commal-ghamdi@fulbright.com ; ; mohammed.al-ghamdi@nortonrosefulbright.commohammed.al-ghamdi@nortonrosefulbright.com
Phone:**Phone:** 011-279-5401 011-279-5401
Fax:**Fax:** 011-419-8278 011-419-8278
Street Address:**Street Address:** Mawhiba Center, 3rd Floor, Olaya Main Street, Riyadh Mawhiba Center, 3rd Floor, Olaya Main Street, Riyadh
Mailing Address:**Mailing Address:** P.O. Box 52681, Riyadh 11573 P.O. Box 52681, Riyadh 11573

Specialties:Specialties: Corporate, commercial transactions, banking, company formation, government Corporate, commercial transactions, banking, company formation, government contracting including defense contracts, labor law, litigation, taxes, licensing and contracting including defense contracts, labor law, litigation, taxes, licensing and distribution issues. distribution issues.

SAUD M.A. SHAWWAF LAW OFFICE **SAUD M.A. SHAWWAF LAW OFFICE**

Web Site:**Web Site:** http://www.smas-ip.comhttp://www.smas-ip.com
E-mail:**E-mail:** saudi@smas-ip.comsaudi@smas-ip.com
Phone:**Phone:** 011-412-7711 011-412-7711
Fax:**Fax: 011-412-8585** 011-412-8585
Street Address:**Street Address:** Office no # 2, 2nd floor Gulf Real Estate building Prince Abdulaziz bin Mosaad Office no # 2, 2nd floor Gulf Real Estate building Prince Abdulaziz bin Mosaad
Dabab Street, Riyadh , Riyadh

Specialties:**Specialties:** Complex international transactions; advising clients with respect to large Complex international transactions; advising clients with respect to large financial transactions; corporate matters; litigation; international trade; financial transactions; corporate matters; litigation; international trade; mergers; acquisitions; labor disputes; and intellectual property. mergers; acquisitions; labor disputes; and intellectual property.

OMAR ALRASHEED & PARTNERS LAW FIRM **OMAR ALRASHEED & PARTNERS LAW FIRM**
Website:**Website:** www.alrasheedlaw.comwww.alrasheedlaw.com
Phone:**Phone:** 011-464-6777 011-464-6777
Fax:**Fax:** 011-464-6096 011-464-6096
E-mail:**E-mail:** omar@alrasheedlaw.comomar@alrasheedlaw.com
Street Address:**Street Address:** 2nd floor 2nd floor Siricon Buildings, Bldg. No.8-Back Entrance, Mousa Bin Nossaiar St., Olaya, Siricon Buildings, Bldg. No.8-Back Entrance, Mousa Bin Nossaiar St., Olaya, RiyadhRiyadh
Mailing Address:**Mailing Address: P.O. Box 300294, Riyadh 11372** P.O. Box 300294, Riyadh 11372

Specialties: **Specialties:** Banking and finance, commercial transactions, companies law, Saudi Banking and finance, commercial transactions, companies law, Saudi government contracts, joint ventures, licensing, agencies, IPOs, taxation, government contracts, joint ventures, licensing, agencies, IPOs, taxation, trademarks and litigation. trademarks and litigation.

THE LAW FIRM OF SALAH AL-HEJAILAN **THE LAW FIRM OF SALAH AL-HEJAILAN**
Web page:**Web page:** http://www.hejailanlaw.com/http://www.hejailanlaw.com/
E-mail:**E-mail:** Robert.thoms@hejailanlaw.comRobert.thoms@hejailanlaw.com ; ; Lfshriyadh@hejailanlaw.comLfshriyadh@hejailanlaw.com
Phone:**Phone: 011-479-2200** 011-479-2200
Fax:**Fax:** 011-479-1717 011-479-1717
Street Address:**Street Address: Al-Dahna Center, 54 Al-Ahsaa Street, Malaz District, Riyadh** Al-Dahna Center, 54 Al-Ahsaa Street, Malaz District, Riyadh
Mailing Address:**Mailing Address:** P.O. Box 1454, Riyadh 11431 P.O. Box 1454, Riyadh 11431

Specialties:**Specialties: General international practice, including corporate, financial, tax, litigation and** General international practice, including corporate, financial, tax, litigation and arbitration, investment, joint venture, real estate, construction, commercial, arbitration, investment, joint venture, real estate, construction, commercial, civil, maritime, intellectual property, criminal and administrative, international civil, maritime, intellectual property, criminal and administrative, international matrimonial and child custody law. matrimonial and child custody law.

KEY GOVERNMENT AGENCIES, FINANCIAL INSTITUTIONS AND JOINT VENTURES PARTNERS AFFECTING FOREIGN INVESTMENT IN THE KINGDOM OF SAUDI ARABIA

1) Ministry of Industry and Electricity:

a. **Foreign Capital Investment Committee:**
   This is an inter-ministerial committee which passes judgment on joint ventures recommended by the Foreign Capital Investment Bureau.

b. **Foreign Capital Investment Bureau, FCIB:**
Relevant information on foreign capital investment regulations can be obtained from FCIB. The bureau evaluates and licenses non-industrial joint ventures on its own, and industrial projects in association with the Industrial Licensing Department.

c. **Engineering and Projects Department:**
Engineering drawings for proposed joint ventures are evaluated by this department.

d. **Industrial Protection and Encouragement Department:**
This department grants tariff protection for national industries.

e. **Industrial Cities Department:**
This department assigns plots of land in industrial cities.

2) Ministry of Commerce:

The Companies Department approves the joint venture's Article of Association, registers the companies under Companies Regulations and assigns Commercial Registration numbers (CR).

3) Saudi Consulting House:

Conducts market research and industrial feasibility studies for proposed joint ventures (for a fee). In addition, SCH prepares and publishes data on industrial development.

4) Investment Funds:

There are a number of specialized credit institutions established by the Government which provide credit to Saudi individuals and companies in all sectors of the economy.

(a) The Saudi Industrial Development Fund (SIDF) is the most important of these credit institutions. The fund is linked to the Ministry of Industry and Electricity and has particular relevance for joint ventures. Its objective is to encourage Saudis in the private sector to establish small and medium size industrial projects by providing low-cost medium and long-term capital for these projects. In addition the Fund provides marketing, technical and financial advice to all Fund-financed projects to enhance their chances of success.

(b) The Public Investment Fund, a government institution linked to the Ministry of Finance and National Economy, was established in 1971 to provide medium and long-term loans to the large scale government and private industrial projects that Saudi commercial banks fail to finance.

(c) The Real Estate Development Fund provides medium or long-term loans to individuals or organizations for private or commercial housing projects.

(d) The Saudi Arabian Agricultural Bank works under the umbrella of the Saudi Arabian Ministry of Agriculture and Water. Its purpose is the provision of loans and credit facilities to farmers with the overall objective of developing and promoting agriculture and related activities. Loans are granted to those projects licensed under the Ministry of Agriculture and Water.

For additional analytical, business and investment opportunities information,
please contact Global Investment & Business Center, USA
at (202) 546-2103. Fax: (202) 546-3275. E-mail: ibpusa3@gmail.com
Global Business and Legal Information Databank: www.ibpus.com

5) Major Joint Ventures' Partners:

In addition to being the major joint ventures' partners with several international industrial corporations in oil, gas, and petrochemicals, the activities of **Petromin**, **Saudi Aramco** and Saudi Basic Industries Corporation cover the development of national human resources and research and development.

6) The National Industrialization Company of Saudi Arabia:

NIC (P.O. Box 26707, Riyadh 11496, Saudi Arabia, Telex. No. 406662 TAWSAT SJ., Fax. No. 477-0898, Phone No. 476-7166) has been organized to stimulate approximately $10 billion of private industrial development in the Kingdom. It is a holding company with 12 percent of its paid-in capital to be owned by the Saudi government and the balance to come from private individual investors. NIC is seeking joint venture project proposals from companies who may be interested in 20-40 percent equity participation in new industrial joint ventures in Saudi Arabia.

GRANT OF LICENSES TO FOREIGN COMPANIES TO ESTABLISH OFFICES IN THE KINGDOM

The Ministerial Resolution No. 680 dated 9 Thul Qa'dah 1398 H. (January 1978) issued by the Minister of Commerce stipulates the following:

- Directors of foreign companies that enter into contract with Ministries and government agencies, or companies that receive sub-contracts from such companies with government approval, should request from the Ministry of Commerce, within 30 days of the date of signing the contract, a license to open an office in the Kingdom in order to undertake implementation of the works assigned to them, in accordance with such contracts.
- Branches and offices of foreign companies operating in the Kingdom should prepare a statement of their financial positions and activities annually showing, in particular, all works that have been completed and are under completion. Copies of these documents should be sent to the Companies Department, Ministry of Commerce within one month of their preparation.
- The said branches and offices should facilitate the task of the representatives of the Ministry to gain access to such documents, books, and registers and to provide data and information they require.

The Ministerial Order No. 1502 of 8 Rabi I 1400 H. (1980) stipulates terms and conditions governing a foreign company which enters into a contract with any government authority and which may be licensed to establish a representative office in the Kingdom to supervise its activities and to facilitate liaison with its head office.

IMPORTANT LAWS AND REGULATIONS AFFECTING BUSINESS

BASIC LAW OF THE KINGDOM (CONSTITUTION)

The Basic Law, which incorporates the arrangements for the Consultative Council and for regional government, established in written form both a description of the essential structure and organization of government and, in effect, a bill of rights for the citizen.

The Basic Law sets out the general principles on which the Kingdom of Saudi Arabia is founded.

The Basic Law set out, with remarkable clarity, the basis on which the Kingdom is governed, and the rights and obligations of both the state and the citizen. As the processes of consultation are extended, it becomes necessary to formalize the principles underlying the traditions which have enabled the Kingdom to pass through periods of extraordinary change with an equally extraordinary degree of stability.

The promulgation of the Basic Law; the formation of the Majlis Al-Shoura (Consultative Council) and the restructuring of the Kingdom's regional government - all form part of this necessary process.

BASIC LAW: GENERAL PRINCIPLES

Article 1:

The Kingdom of Saudi Arabia is a sovereign Arab Islamic State.
Religion: Islam
Constitution: The Holy Qur'an and the Prophet's Sunnah (traditions)
Language: Arabic
Capital: Riyadh
Article 2:
Its national holidays:
- Eid Al-Fitr (a religious feast celebrated on the 1st of Shawal, the 10th month of the Islamic calendar)
- Eid Al-Ad-ha (a religious feast celebrated on the 10th of Dhul-Hijjah, the 12th month of the Islamic calendar)
- Calendar: Hijira (Lunar)

Article 3:

Its national flag:
- Green in color
- Width equal to two thirds of length

- Article of faith (translated as "There is no God but Allah, Muhammad is Allah's Messenger") inscribed in the center with a drawn sword underneath.

Article 4:

For additional analytical, business and investment opportunities information,
please contact Global Investment & Business Center, USA
at (202) 546-2103. Fax: (202) 546-3275. E-mail: ibpusa3@gmail.com
Global Business and Legal Information Databank: www.ibpus.com

The State's emblem consists of two intersecting swords with a datepalm in the upper space between them. Both the national anthem and the decorations awarded by the State shall be determined by the law.

SYSTEM OF GOVERNMENT

Article 5:

 (a) The system of government in Saudi Arabia shall be monarchical.

 (b) The dynasty right shall be confined to the sons of the Founder, King Abdul Aziz bin Abdul Rahman Al Saud (Ibn Saud), and the sons of sons. The most eligible among them shall be invited, through the process of "bai'ah", to rule in accordance with the Book of God and the Prophet's Sunnah.

 (c) The King names the Crown Prince and may relieve him of his duties by Royal Order.

 (d) The Crown Prince shall devote full time to his office and to any other duties which may be assigned to him by the King.

 (e) The Crown Prince shall assume the powers of the king on the latter's death pending the outcome of the "bai'ah".

Article 6:

 Citizens shall pledge allegiance to the King on the basis of the Book of God and the Prophet's Sunnah, as well as on the principle of "hearing is obeying" both in prosperity and adversity, in situations pleasant and unpleasant.

Article 7:

 The regime derives its power from the Holy Qur'an and the Prophet's Sunnah which rule over this and all other State Laws.

Article 8:

 The system of government in the Kingdom of Saudi Arabia is established on the foundation of justice, "Shoura" and equality in compliance with the Islamic Shari'ah (the revealed law of Islam)

CONSTITUENTS OF SAUDI SOCIETY

Article 9:

 The family is the nucleus of Saudi society. Its members shall be brought up imbued with the Islamic Creed which calls for obedience to God, His Messenger and those of the nation who are charged with authority; for the respect and enforcement of law and order; and for love of the motherland and taking pride in its glorious history.

Article 10:

For additional analytical, business and investment opportunities information, please contact Global Investment & Business Center, USA at (202) 546-2103. Fax: (202) 546-3275. E-mail: ibpusa3@gmail.com Global Business and Legal Information Databank: www.ibpus.com

The State shall take great pains to strengthen the bonds which hold the family together and to preserve its Arab and Islamic values. Likewise it is keen on taking good care of all family members and creating proper conditions to help them cultivate their skill and capabilities.

Article 11:

The Saudi society shall hold fast to the Divine Rope. Its citizens shall work together to foster benevolence, piety and mutual assistance; and it avoids dissension.

Article 12:

The State shall foster national unity and preclude all that may lead to disunity, mischief and division.

Article 13:

Education aims at the inculcation of the Islamic creed in the young generation and the development of their knowledge and skills so that they may become useful members of society who love their homeland and take pride in its history.

ECONOMIC PRINCIPLES

Article 14:

All God-given resources of the country, both under and above ground, or in territorial waters, or within terrestrial and maritime limits to which the State jurisdiction extends, as well as the revenues accruing therefrom shall be owned by the State as specified by the law. Likewise the law shall specify the means to be employed for the utilization, protection and development of these resources in a manner conducive to the promotion of the State's interest, security and economy.

Article 15:

No concessions shall be awarded or permission given for the utilization of the country's natural resources, except as permitted by the law.

Article 16:

Public property is sacrosanct. It shall be protected by the State and preserved by both citizens and foreign residents.

Article 17:

Ownership, capital and labor are the fundamentals of the Kingdom's economic and social life. They are private rights that serve a social function in conformity with Islamic Shari'ah.

Article 18:

The State shall guarantee the freedom and inviolability of private property. Private property shall be not be expropriated unless in the public interest and the confiscatee is fairly compensated.

Article 19:

Collective confiscation of properties shall be prohibited. Confiscation of private properties shall only be effected in accordance with a judicial verdict.

Article 20:

Taxes and fees shall be imposed only on the basis of fairness and when the need arises.

They shall only be imposed, amended, abolished or remitted in accordance with the law.

Article 21:

Zakat (poor-due) shall be levied and dispensed to its legitimate beneficiaries.

Article 22: Economic and social development shall be achieved in accordance with a methodical and equitable plan.

RIGHTS AND DUTIES

Article 23:

The State shall protect the Islamic Creed and shall cater to the application of Shari'ah. The State shall enjoin good and forbid evil, and shall undertake the duties of the call to Islam.

Article 24:

The State shall maintain and serve the Two Holy Mosques. It shall ensure the security and safety of all those who call at the Two Holy Mosques so that they may be able to visit or perform the pilgrimage and "Umrah" (minor pilgrimage) in comfort and ease.

Article 25:

The State shall be keen to realize the aspirations of the Arab Muslim nations with regard to solidarity and unity while enhancing its relations with friendly states.

Article 26:

The State shall protect human rights in accordance with Islamic Shari'ah.

Article 27:

The State shall guarantee the right of its citizens and their families in an emergency of in case of disease, disability and old age. Likewise it shall support the social security system and encourage individuals and institutions to contribute to charitable pursuits.

Article 28:

The State shall provide job opportunities to all able-bodied people and shall enact laws to protect both the employee and the employer.

Article 29:

The State shall foster sciences, arts and culture. It shall encourage scientific research, shall preserve Arab and Islamic heritage and shall contribute to Arab, Islamic and human civilization.

Article 30:

The State shall provide public education and shall commit itself to the eradication of illiteracy.

Article 31:

The State shall be solicitous for promoting public health and shall provide medical care to every citizen.

Article 32:

The State shall seek to conserve, protect and develop the environment and prevent pollution.

Article 33:

The State shall build and equip the armed forces to defend the Islamic faith, the Two Holy Mosques, the society and the homeland.

Article 34:

Defending the Islamic faith, the society and the homeland shall be the duty of each and every citizen. Rules of military service shall be spelled out by the law.

Article 35:

The rules which govern the Saudi Arabian nationality shall be defined by the law.

Article 36:

The State shall ensure the security of all its citizens and expatriates living within its domains. No individual shall be detained, imprisoned or have his actions restricted except under the provisions of the law.

Article 37:

Houses are inviolable. They shall not be entered without the permission of their owners, nor shall they be searched except in cases specified by the law.

Article 38:

Punishment shall be restricted to the actual offender. No crime shall be established as such and no punishment shall be imposed except under a judicial or law provision. No punishment shall be imposed except for acts that take place after enaction of the law provision governing them.

Article 39:

Mass media, publication facilities and other means of expression shall function in a manner that is courteous and fair and shall abide by State laws. They shall play their part in educating the masses and boosting national unity. All that may give rise to mischief and discord, or may compromise the security of the State and its public image, or may offend against man's dignity and rights shall be banned. Relevant regulations shall explain how this is to be done.

Article 40:

All forms of correspondence, whether conveyed by telegraph, post or any other means of communication shall be considered sacrosanct. They may not be confiscated, delayed or read, and telephones may not be tapped except as laid down in the law.

Article 41:

Foreign residents in the Kingdom of Saudi Arabia shall abide by its regulations and shall show respect for Saudi social traditions, values and feelings.

Article 42:

The State shall grant political asylum, if so required by the public interest. The law and international agreements shall define the procedures and rules for the extradition of common criminals.

Article 43:

The "Majlis" of the King and the "Majlis" of the Crown Prince shall be open to all citizens and to anyone who may have a complaint or a grievance. Every individual shall have the right to communicate with public authorities regarding any topic he may wish to discuss.

POWERS OF THE STATE

Article 44:

The powers of the State shall comprise:
- The Judicial Power
- The Executive Power
- The Organizational Power

All these powers shall cooperate in performing their duties according to this Law and other regulations. The King is the ultimate source of all these authorities.

Article 45:

For additional analytical, business and investment opportunities information,
please contact Global Investment & Business Center, USA
at (202) 546-2103. Fax: (202) 546-3275. E-mail: ibpusa3@gmail.com
Global Business and Legal Information Databank: www.ibpus.com

The source of Ifta (religious ruling) in the Kingdom of Saudi Arabia is the Holy Qur'an and the Prophet's Sunnah. The law shall specify the composition of the Senior Ulema Board and of the Administration of Religious Research and Ifta and its jurisdictions.

Article 46:

The judicial authority is an independent power. In discharging their duties, the judges bow to no authority other than that of Islamic Shari'ah.

Article 47:

Both citizens and foreign residents have an equal right to litigation. The necessary procedures are set forth by the law.

Article 48:

Courts shall apply the provisions of Islamic Shari'ah to cases brought before them, according to the teachings of the Holy Qur'an and the Prophet's Sunnah as well as other regulations issued by the Head of State in strict conformity with the Holy Qur'an and the Prophet's Sunnah.

Article 49:

Subject to the provisions of article 53 of this law, the courts shall have jurisdiction to deal with all kinds of disputes and crimes.

Article 50:

The King, or whomsoever he may deputize, shall be concerned with the implementation of the judicial verdicts.

Article 51:

The law specifies the formation of the supreme judicial council and its functions as well as the organization and jurisdiction of the courts.

Article 52:

Judges are appointed and their service is terminated by a Royal Order upon a proposal by the supreme judicial council as specified by the law.

Article 53:

The law defines the structure and jurisdiction of the Court of Grievances.

Article 54:

The law shall specify the reference, organization and jurisdictions of the Board of Investigation and Public Prosecution.

For additional analytical, business and investment opportunities information, please contact Global Investment & Business Center, USA at (202) 546-2103. Fax: (202) 546-3275. E-mail: ibpusa3@gmail.com Global Business and Legal Information Databank: www.ibpus.com

Article 55:

The King shall undertake to rule according to the rulings of Islam and shall supervise the application of Shari'ah, the regulations, and the State's general policy as well as the protection and defense of the country.

Article 56:

The King shall be the Prime Minister and shall be assisted in the performance of his duties by members of the Council of Ministers according to the rulings of this law and other laws. The Council of Ministers Law shall specify the Council's Powers with regard to internal and external affairs, organizing government bodies and co-ordinating their activities. Likewise the Law shall specify the conditions which the Ministers must satisfy, their eligibility, the method of their accountability along with all other matters related to them. The Council of Ministers' law and jurisdiction shall be modified with this Law.

Article 57:

(a) The King shall appoint the Deputy Prime Minister and Cabinet Ministers and may relieve them of their duties by a Royal order.

(b) The Deputy Prime Minister and Cabinet Ministers shall be jointly responsible before the King for the applications of Islamic Shari'ah, the laws and the State's general policy.

(c) The King shall have the right to dissolve and re-form the Council of Ministers.

Article 58:

The King shall appoint ministers, deputy ministers and officials of the "excellent grade " category and he may dismiss them by a Royal order in accordance with the rules of the law.

Ministers and heads of independent authorities shall be responsible before the Prime Minister for their ministries and authorities.

Article 59:

The law shall prescribe the provisions pertaining to civil service, including salaries, bonuses, compensation, privileges and retirement pensions.

Article 60:

The King shall be the Supreme Commander of the armed forces and shall appoint military officers and terminate their service in accordance with the law.

Article 61:

The King shall have the right to declare a state of emergency and general mobilization as well as war.

Article 62:

If danger threatens the safety of the Kingdom, the integrity of its territory, the security of its people and their interests, or impedes the performance of State institutions, the King shall take necessary and speedy measures to confront this danger. If the King feels that these measures may better be permanent, he then shall take whatever legal action he deems necessary in this regard.

Article 63:

The King receives Kings and heads of state, appoints his representatives to other countries and accepts accreditation of the representatives of other countries to the Kingdom.

Article 64:

The King awards medals in the same manner as specified by the law.

Article 65:

The King may delegate parts of his authority to the Crown Prince by a Royal order.

Article 66:

In the event of his traveling abroad, the King shall issue a Royal Order deputizing the Crown Prince to run the affairs of the State and look after the interests of the people as stated in the Royal Order.

Article 67:

Acting within its term of reference, the Organizational Power shall draw up regulations and by-laws to safeguard public interests or eliminate corruption in the affairs of the State in accordance with the rulings of the Islamic Shari'ah. It shall exercise its powers in compliance with this law and the two other laws of the Council of Ministers and the Majlis Al-Shoura (Consultative Council).

Article 68:

The Majlis Al-Shoura shall be constituted. Its law shall determine the structure of its formation, the method by which it exercises its special powers and the selection of its members. The King shall have the right to dissolve the Majlis Al-Shoura and re-form it.

Article 69:

The King may call the Council of Ministers and Majlis Al-Shoura to hold a joint meeting to which he may invite whomsoever he wishes for a discussion of whatsoever issues he may like to raise.

Article 70:

Laws, treaties, international agreements and concessions shall be issued and modified by Royal Decrees.

Article 71:

Laws shall be published in the official gazette and they shall take effect as from the date of their publication unless another date is stipulated.

FINANCIAL AFFAIRS

Article 72:

(a) The law shall determine the management of State revenues, and the procedures of their delivery to the State Treasury.

(b) Revenues shall be accounted for and expended in accordance with the procedures stated on the law.

Article 73:

No obligation shall be made to pay funds from the State Treasury except in accordance with the provisions of the budget. Should the provisions of the budget not suffice for paying such funds, a Royal Decree shall be issued for their payment.

Article 74:

State property may not be sold, leased or otherwise disposed of except in accordance with the law.

Article 75:

The regulations shall define the provisions governing legal tender and banks, as well as standards, measures and weights.

Article 76:

The law shall determine the State's fiscal year. The budget shall be issued by a Royal Decree which shall spell out revenue and expenditure estimates for the year. The budget shall be issued at least one month before the beginning of the fiscal year. If, owing to overpowering reasons, the budget is not issued on time and the new fiscal year has not yet started, the validity of the old budget shall be extended until a new budget has been issued.

Article 77:

The concerned authority shall prepare the State's final accounts for the expired fiscal year and shall submit it to the Prime Minister.

Article 78:

The budgets and final accounts of corporate authorities shall be subject to the same provisions applied to the State budget and its final accounts.

For additional analytical, business and investment opportunities information,
please contact Global Investment & Business Center, USA
at (202) 546-2103. Fax: (202) 546-3275. E-mail: ibpusa3@gmail.com
Global Business and Legal Information Databank: www.ibpus.com

CONTROL AND AUDITING AUTHORITIES

Article 79:

All State revenues and expenditures shall be kept under control, so shall its fixed and liquid (mobile) assets which will be checked to ascertain that they are properly utilized and maintained. An annual report thereon shall be submitted to the Council of Ministers.

The law shall name the control and auditing authority concerned, and shall define its terms of reference and accountability.

Article 80:

Government bodies shall be monitored closely to ensure that they are performing well and applying the law properly. Financial and administrative violations shall be investigated and an annual report thereon shall be submitted to the Council of Ministers.

The law shall name the authority to be charged with this task and shall define its accountability and terms of reference.

GENERAL PROVISIONS

Article 81:

The implementation of this law shall not violate the treaties and agreements the Kingdom has signed with other countries or with international organizations and institutions.

Article 82:

Without prejudice to the provisions of article 7 of this law, none of the provisions of this law shall, in any way, be obstructed unless it is a temporary measure taken during the time of war or in a state of emergency as specified by the law.

Article 83:

No amendments to this law shall be made except in the same manner in which it has been issued

COUNCIL OF MINISTERS STATUTE[3]

[Part 1 General Provisions]

Article 1
The Council of ministers is an organizational body headed by the King.

[3] Adopted on: 20 Aug 1993

Article 2
The headquarters of the Council of Ministers will be in the city of Riyadh. It would be possible for its sessions to be held in other parts of the country.

Article 3
Membership of the Council of Ministers will have to meet the following conditions:
(a) Must be of Saudi nationality by origin and upbringing.
(b) Must be known to be of propriety and competence.
(c) Must not be convicted of a crime in violation of religion and honor.

Article 4
Members of the Council of Ministers will not assume their posts until they have made the following oath: I swear by Almighty God that I will be loyal to my religion and then to my King and country, and that I will not divulge any secrets of state and that I will safeguard its (the State's) interests and rules and carry out my duties sincerely, honestly and loyally.

Article 5
Membership of the Council of Ministers must not be combined with any other governmental post unless the Chairman of the Council of Ministers deems it necessary.

Article 6
While in office, a member of the Council of Minister's will not be allowed to buy or rent any state property directly, through a third party or in a State auction. He will also not be allowed to sell or rent out any of his properties to the government. He must not undertake any commercial of financial work, nor must he accept membership of the board of directors of any company.

Article 7
The sessions of the Council of Ministers are held under the chairmanship of the chairman of the Council of Ministers- the King or any of the deputies of the chairman. Its decisions are final after the King approves them.

Article 8
The appointment of the members of the Council of Ministers or to relieve them of their posts or to accept their resignations will be by royal order. Their responsibilities will be defined in accordance with Article 57 and 58 of the Basic Law of Government. The internal statute of the Council of Ministers defines their rights.

Article 9
The term (in office) of the Council of Ministers will not exceed four years during which it can be reformed by a royal order. In the event of the period expiring before it is reformed, it will continue to perform its work until it is reformed.

Article 10
The minister is regarded as the direct head and the final point of reference of the affairs of his ministry. He exercises his duties in accordance with the provision of this statue and other rules and regulations.

Article 11
(a) Only another minister can deputize for a minister at the Council of Ministers and (it has to be) in accordance with an order which is issued by the chairman of the Council.
(b) The deputy minister takes over the exercise of the powers of the minister during his absence.

For additional analytical, business and investment opportunities information, please contact Global Investment & Business Center, USA at (202) 546-2103. Fax: (202) 546-3275. E-mail: ibpusa3@gmail.com Global Business and Legal Information Databank: www.ibpus.com

Article 12
The Council of Ministers is composed of:
(a) Chairman of the Council
(b) Deputy Chairman of the Council
(c) Ministers
(d) Ministers of State who are appointed as members of the Council of Ministers by Royal order.
(e) Advisers to the King who are appointed as members of the Council of Ministers by Royal order.

Article 13
Attending the meeting of the Council of Ministers is a right that belongs to its members only and to the secretary-general of the Council. At the request of the chairman or a member of the Council of Ministers and after the approval of the Chairman of the Council an official or expert may be permitted to attend sessions of the Council of Ministers and to present information, and explanations he may have. However, the voting shall remain exclusive to members only.

Article 14
The session of the Council of Ministers will not be considered proper except when two thirds of its members attend the session. Its decisions will not be effective unless they are adopted by the majority of those attending the meeting. In the event of a tie, the chairman will have the casting vote. In extraordinary cases the convening of the Council of Ministers will be proper when half its members attend. Its decisions will not be legal in this case accept with the agreement of two thirds of the members who are present and the chairman has the right to evaluate the extraordinary cases.

Article 15
The Council of Ministers shall not take a decisions on a matter that concerns the work of one of the ministries except in the presence of the minister in charge of that ministry or any one else that acts for him. if necessary.

Article 16
The deliberations of the Council of Ministers take place behind closed doors. As for its decisions they are basically public except for those which are considered to be secret by the Council.

Article 17
Members of the Council of Ministers will be put on trial for offenses they may commit in their official duties, in accordance with a special statute that contains the statement of the offices and defines the procedures of the charges, the trial and the manner in which the body of the court is formed.

Article 18
The Council of Ministers can form committees that include its members or others to discuss a matter that is included on the agenda so that they (the committees) submit a special report on it. The internal statute of the Council of Ministers will decide size and composition of the committee and the work procedure.

[Part 2] The Jurisdiction of the Council

Article 19
Taking into consideration the stipulations of the basic law of government and the statute of the Consultative council, the Council of Ministers will plan the internal, external, financial, economic,

educational and defence policies and all the public affairs of the state, and oversee their implementation. It will look into the decrees of the Consultative council. It will have executive power and it will be the point of reference for financial and administrative affairs in all the ministries and other governmental bodies.

[Part 3] Organizational Affairs

Article 20
Taking into consideration the stipulations of the statute of the Consultative council, statutes, international treaties, and agreements and franchises will be issued and amended in accordance with Royal Decrees after having been studied by the Council of Ministers of Ministers.

Article 21
The Council of Ministers will study draft rules and regulations submitted to it and vote on each article and then vote on the whole draft in accordance with the measures stipulated in the internal statute of the council.

Article 22
Every minister will have the right to propose a draft statute or rule pertaining to his ministry's work. Every member of the Council of Ministers will have the right to propose whatever he believes to be of benefit for discussion at the Council of Ministers after the approval of the chairman.

Article 23
All decrees must be published in the official gazette. They will come into effect as from the date of their publication unless another date is stipulated.

[Part 4] Executive Affairs

Article 24
As the direct executive power, the council will have full control over executive and administrative affairs. The following will come under its executive jurisdictions:
(1) Monitoring the implementation of statutes, rules and decrees.
(2) Creation and organization of public services.
(3) Following up the implementation of the overall development plan.
(4) Establishment of committees that will investigate the progress of the work of ministries and other governmental bodies or a specific issue. These committees will submit the outcome of their investigations to the council at a time set for them . The council will look into the outcome of their investigations, and may set up committees to investigate (further) in light of the outcome and make a decision regarding the outcome after taking into consideration the stipulations of the statutes and rules. Financial Affairs

Article 25
The government will not be able to sign a loan (agreement) without the approval of the Council of Ministers and the issuance of a pertinent Royal Decree.

Article 26
The Council of Ministers will study the state budget and vote on it chapter by chapter, and it will be issued in accordance with a Royal Decree.

For additional analytical, business and investment opportunities information, please contact Global Investment & Business Center, USA at (202) 546-2103. Fax: (202) 546-3275. E-mail: ibpusa3@gmail.com Global Business and Legal Information Databank: www.ibpus.com

Article 27
Any increase required in the budget can only be made in accordance with a Royal Decree.

Article 28
The Minister of Finance and National Economy will submit the states final accounts of the previous financial year to the Chairman of the Council of Ministers to be referred to the Council of Ministers for approbation.

[Part 5] Chairmanship of the Council

Article 29
The King as Chairman of the Council of Ministers will steer the overall policy of the state. He will be steering, coordinating and (ensuring the) cooperation of the various government bodies, and ensure harmony, continuity and uniformity in the work of the Council. He has the authority to supervise the Council, ministries, and governmental bodies. He will monitor the implementation of statutes, rules and decrees. All the ministries and other governmental bodies have to submit to the chairman of the Council of Ministers within 90 days of the beginning of every financial year a report on the achievements they have made in comparison with what had been stated in the overall development plan during the previous financial year, the difficulties they had faced and their proposals for improved operations in them.

Article 30
The following machinery is included in the administrative formations of the Council:
(1) The office of the chairman of the Council
(2) The general secretariat of the Council
(3) The panel of experts
The internal statute of the Council of Ministers explains the formations and the specializations of these organs and the manner in which they carry out their duties.

Article 31
The internal statute of the Council of Ministers is issued by a royal order.

Article 32
This statute can be amended only by the method in which it was issued.

CONSULTATIVE COUNCIL LAW

The Consultative Council, or Majlis Al-Shoura (established by Royal Decree No. A/91, dated 27-8-1412) marked a significant move towards the formalization of the participative nature of government in Saudi Arabia. The Consultative Council was inaugurated by King Fahd himself in December, 1993. The announcement of the establishment of the Council, which coincided with the tenth anniversary of the accession of King Fahd and which was accompanied by details of a new "basic law", clearly marked the first steps towards a more broadly based involvement in the Kingdom's political processes.

The primary function of the broadly-based Majlis Al-Shoura is to provide the King with advice on issues of importance in the Kingdom.

The Consultative Council, when set up, consisted of a speaker and 60 members selected by the King. The Royal Decree establishing the Council made it clear, first and foremost, that the Council was set up and would operate:

"in compliance with [the existing system of government in the Kingdom] and in adherence to the Book of God and the tradition of His Messenger."

The term of the Majlis Al-Shoura is set at four years (Hijira Calendar), with a clear stipulation that, when a new Shoura Council is formed, at least half of those appointed must be new members.

(The setting of fixed terms in this instance may indicate a shift away from past policy of indefinite tenure of political office.)

The scope of matters on which the Council may deliberate was very widely defined. The members of the initial Council were chosen to represent a wide mix of clan and religious leaders, business and professional men, as well as government officials. Academics formed the largest group, however, and there is an impressive number of members with advanced degrees.

Members of the new majlis will meet regularly in Riyadh in full session. Council members are expected to devote themselves

"to serve the common interest, preservation of the unity of the people, the entity of the state and the interests of the nation".

In practice, members of the Council are able to initiate legislation and review the domestic and foreign policies of the government. Any government action not approved by the Council will have to be referred back to the King. The King therefore remains the final arbiter of state affairs. The King also retains the power to appoint and dismiss both Ministers and Council members and has the power to dissolve the Council, restructure it, and appoint a new one at any time.

In 1997, King Fahd increased membership of the Consultative Council to 90 members.

By 1998, the Council was well established and operating effectively. In addition to its defined role in the political process, it had established a library containing more than 25,000 volumes, together with 305 periodicals in a number of languages as well as Arabic, and a total of more than 6,000 slides.

In grasping the significance of these measures, it is important to understand that the Kingdom's purpose in establishing the Majlis Al-Shoura and in introducing other planned reforms is to provide an institutional framework through which the traditional form of Saudi Arabian government, based on consultation within the context of the tenets and requirements of Islam, can be most effectively expressed in today's increasingly complex and interdependent world.

The reforms can be seen as marking an important new chapter in the life of the Kingdom and King Fahd's desire to hasten the pace of modernization within the religious and cultural traditions of the Kingdom. The oil wealth has transformed the economy and infrastructure of Saudi Arabia in the past three decades. These measures mark the start of a cumulative process facilitating the modernization of Saudi Arabian government.

For additional analytical, business and investment opportunities information, please contact Global Investment & Business Center, USA at (202) 546-2103. Fax: (202) 546-3275. E-mail: ibpusa3@gmail.com Global Business and Legal Information Databank: www.ibpus.com

The reforms do not, however, mean that the Kingdom has moved away from its Islamic traditions. King Fahd himself stressed that his reforms were based on Islamic principles of fairness, decency and popular consultation.

In essence, the Consultative Council should be seen, not as a modest move towards Western-style democracy, but as an organic development of the consultative processes on which the Kingdom has been governed since its inception, processes which arose from a tradition that goes back to the life of the Prophet (peace be upon him).

LAW OF REGIONS

Article 1:

This law shall aim at improving the standard of administrative work and development in the Kingdom. It shall also aim at the preservation of law and order, the rights of citizens and their freedom within the framework of Islamic Shari'ah.

Article 2:

The Kingdom's regions and the headquarters of the administrative body "Imarah" of each shall be organized by a Royal Order upon the recommendation of the Minister of the Interior.

Article 3:

In respect to administration, each region shall be made up of a number of governorates (Class A and Class B) and centers (Class A and Class B). This division shall take into consideration the population, geography, security, environment and means of transportation. The governorates shall report to the Governor of the region and shall be organized by a Royal Order upon the recommendation of the Minister of the Interior. Centers meanwhile, shall be set up and their accountability specified by a resolution from the Minister of the Interior on the basis of a proposal by the Governor of the region.

Article 4:

Each region shall have a Governor with the rank of "Minister" and shall have a Vice-Governor at the "excellent grade", who shall assist the Governor in the discharge of his duties and substitute for him during his absence. Governors and their Vice-Governors shall be appointed and relieved by a Royal decree upon the recommendation of the Minister of the Interior.

Article 5:

The Governor of the region shall answer to the Minister of the Interior.

Article 6:

The Governor and the Vice-Governor shall take the following oath before the King prior to their assumption of their duties:

"I swear by Almighty God that I shall be loyal to my religion, then to my King and country; shall not divulge any secrets of the state, shall uphold its interests and respect its laws, shall perform my duties in good faith, honesty, sincerity and equity".

Article 7:

Each Governor shall administer his region according to the State's general policy, the provisions of this law and other laws and regulations. He shall be required in particular to:

(a) Preserve law and order and stability and take the necessary measures in this connection according to laws and regulations.

(b) Implement the judicial rules after their final endorsement.

(c) Protect the rights of individuals and their freedoms, and desist from any act that may compromise these rights and freedoms except within limits prescribed by the law.

(d) Work for the development of the region in social, economic and urban terms.

(e) Work for the development of the public services in the region and enhancement of their efficiency.

(f) Manage the governorates and centers and supervise the governor of governorates and directors of centers, to ascertain their competence to perform their duties.

(g) Preserve the State's assets and property and prevent encroachment.

(h) Supervise government departments and their personnel in the region to ascertain their performance of their duties properly, honestly and with diligence. Employees of different ministries and government departments, who work in the region, shall be answerable to their own ministries and departments.

(i) Make direct contact with ministers and heads of government departments for the discussion of affairs of the region with a view to promoting the performance of the bodies answerable to them. The Minister of the Interior shall be acquainted with these contacts.

(j) Submit annual reports to the Minister of the Interior on, among other things, the efficiency of public utilities in the region according to the executive rules of this Law.

Article 8:

An annual meeting shall be held by regional Governors under the chairmanship of the Minister of the Interior to discuss issues related to regions.

The Minister of the Interior shall submit a report hereon to the Prime Minster.

Article 9:

The Governor of each region shall hold bi-annual meetings for the governors of governorates to discuss matters of interest to the region. The region's Governor shall submit a report thereon to the Minister of the Interior.

Article 10:

(a) One or more deputy governors shall be appointed for each region at a grade not less than "14". The appointment shall be by a cabinet resolution upon the recommendation of the Minister of the Interior.

(b) Each class "A" governorate shall have a governor at a grade not less than "14". He shall be appointed upon order of the Prime Minister as recommended by the Minister of the Interior. Each governorate shall have a deputy at a grade not less than "12". He shall be appointed by the Minister of the Interior upon the recommendation of the regional Governor.

(c) Each class "B" governorate shall have a governor at a grade not less than "12". He shall be appointed by the Minister of the Interior upon the recommendation of the regional Governor.

(d) Each class "A" center shall have a director at a grade not less than "8". He shall be appointed by the Minister of the Interior upon the recommendation of the regional Governor.

(e) Each class "B" center shall have a director at a grade not less than "5". He shall be appointed by the regional Governor.

Article 11:

Regional Governors, governors of governorate and directors of centers shall reside at their place of work and shall not leave it without the permission of their immediate superiors.

Article 12:

Governors of governorate and directors of centers shall perform their duties within the administrative framework of their respective authorities, and within the limits of the powers vested in them.

Article 13:

Governors of governorate shall run their governorates within the framework of the functions outlined in article (7) with the exception of its provisions (f, i, j). They shall monitor the work of the heads of centers answerable to them to ascertain their ability to handle their duties efficiently, and shall submit periodical reports to the Governor of the region on the performance of public services and other matters with which the governorate is concerned in accordance with what is stipulated under the executive regulations of this Law.

Article 14:

Each Ministry or government agency providing services to the region shall appoint an official at the head of its bodies in the region with a rank not less than grade 12. He shall report directly to the parent ministry or agency and shall operate in close co-ordination with the Governor of the region.

Article 15:

Each region shall have a region council with its offices installed at the headquarters of the region's governorate.

Article 16:

The "regional council" shall consist of:

(a) The Governor as Chairman
(b) The deputy Governor as Vice-Chairman.
(c) Governorate "wakil".
(d) Heads of the region's official bodies which shall be specified in a resolution to be passed by the Council of Ministers on the recommendation of the Governor and approval by the Minister of the Interior.

(e) A number of locals (not less than 10) judged as eligible in terms of learning, experience and specialization and appointed by order of the Prime Minister upon the Governor's recommendation and the approval of the Minister of the Interior with a renewable four-year membership term.

Article 17:

A Council member shall satisfy the following:

(a) To be a Saudi National both by descent and upbringing.
(b) To be of proven integrity and ability.
(c) Not to be less than 30 years of age.
(d) To have his place of residence in the region.

Article 18:

A member may submit in writing to the chairman of the region's council any proposals falling within the council's jurisdiction. The chairman shall place each proposal on the council's agenda for discussion.

Article 19:

A member of the region's council shall not attend council deliberations or the deliberations of any of its committees when dealing with a matter of personal interest to him or to anyone whose testimony in his favor is unacceptable, or if the Member is a guardian or agent of one who has a stake therein.

Article 20:

If a member wishes to resign he shall submit an application to this end to the Minister of the Interior through the region Governor. The resignation shall not be considered valid unless endorsed by the Prime Minister on recommendation from the Minister of the Interior.

Article 21:

In all cases other than those specified in this Law, a nominated member may not be dismissed during his term of membership unless by order of the Prime Minister on recommendation from the Minister of the Interior.

Article 22:

If the seat of a nominated member is rendered vacant for any reason, a substitute shall be appointed within three months from the vacancy date. The new member shall hold office for a period equal to the remainder of his predecessor's term in accordance with what is prescribed in item "e" of Article 16 of this Law.

Article 23:

The regional council shall have the competence to discuss all that is conducive to improving service standards in the region, and shall be entitled in particular to :

 (a) Determine the needs of the region and propose their inclusion into the State's development plan.

 (b) Determine what projects are useful, arrange them in order of priority and propose their adoption as part of the annual State budget.

 (c) Study the region's urban and rural organizational layouts and follow up their implementation after being adopted.

 (d) Follow up the implementation and co-ordination of those parts of the development and budget plans related to the region.

Article 24:

 The region's council shall propose and submit to the Minister of the Interior any move calculated to serve the general good of the region's resident population and shall encourage citizens' contribution thereto.

Article 25:

 The region's council may not overstep its area of competence as determined under this Law, otherwise its resolutions shall be considered null and void and a resolution to this end shall be issued by the Minister of the Interior.

Article 26:

 The region's council shall hold a three-month ordinary session at the invitation of its chairman who may also invite the council to convene an extraordinary meeting if he deems that necessary.

Article 27:

 The members of the region's council specified in items "c" and "d" of Article 16 of this Law shall attend the meetings of the council ex-officio. They shall attend the meetings in person, or by proxy in case of being absent from work. As to the members specified in item "e" of the said

Article, failure by one of them to attend two successive sessions without an acceptable excuse shall be considered good reason for his dismissal from the council. In this case the dismissed member may not be eligible for re-appointment except after the lapse of two years from the date of issue of the decision of his dismissal.

Article 28:

Meetings of the region's council shall be considered in order only if attended by at least two thirds of council members. Council resolutions shall be issued by absolute majority of the votes. Should the votes be equally divided, the chairman shall have the casting vote.

Article 29:

The region's council may set up, when the need arises, special committees to study any matter falling within its jurisdiction, and it may seek the help of people of experience and specialists. Likewise it may invite whomever it wishes to attend council meetings and participate in the deliberations without having the right to vote.

Article 30:

The Minister of the Interior shall have the right to call the council to meet under his chairmanship in any place he may choose. Likewise he shall have the right to preside at any meeting he may attend.

Article 31:

The region's council may convene only at the request of its Chairman or Vice-Chairman or by order of the Minister of the Interior.

Article 32:

The chairman of the council shall submit a copy of its resolutions to the Minister of the Interior.

Article 33:

The Chairman of the council shall inform the ministries and governmental agencies of council's resolutions which have a direct bearing on them.

Article 34:

Ministries and government agencies shall pay due regard to what is stated in items "a" and "b" of Article 23 of this Law. If the Ministry or governmental agency concerned finds any such resolution unacceptable, it shall have to explain to the region's council the reasons on which its objection is based. Should the region's Council remain unimpressed, it may refer the matter to the Minister of the Interior to put it before the Prime Minister.

Article 35:

Each ministry or governmental agency which maintains services of its own in the region shall inform the region's council, the moment the State budget is issued, of the projects allocated to it in the said budget and also of what has been decided for it to obtain under the development plan.

Article 36:

Each minister and governmental agency head may sound out the region's council on any matter pertaining to its area of competence and the council shall give its opinion as requested.

Article 37:

The Prime Minister, acting upon a proposal from the Ministry of the Interior, shall fix the bonuses of the Chairman and members of the region's council. In the assessment of these bonuses due regard shall be paid to transportation and dwelling costs.

Article 38:

The region's council shall not be dissolved except by order of the Prime Minister, based on a proposal from the Minister of the Interior. The Council shall be re-constituted within three months from the dissolution date. In the interim the members specified in items "c" and "d" of Article 16 of this Law shall exercise the council's authority under the chairmanship of the region Governor.

Article 39:

The council shall have a secretariat installed in the region's governorate and entrusted with the duty of drawing of the agenda, sending out invitations on time, keeping record of the deliberations which take place at meetings, separating votes, drawing up the minutes of meetings, editing resolutions, taking the necessary measures to maintain discipline at council meetings and noting down the council's resolutions.

Article 40:

The Minister of the Interior shall issue the necessary regulations for the implementation of this Law.

Article 41:

This Law shall not be amended except in the manner in which it was issued.

MAJLIS AL-SHOURA LAW

Article 1:

In line with the Almighty Allah's words:

It is part of the Mercy
Of Allah that thou dost deal
Gently with them.
Wert thou severe

Or Harsh-hearted,
They would have broken away
From about thee: so pass over
(Their faults), and ask
For (Allah's) forgiveness
For them; and consult
Them in affairs (of moment).
Then, when thou hast
Taken a decision,
Put thy trust in Allah.
For Allah loves those
Who put their trust (in Him).
And, with Allah's words:"
38
Those who respond
To their Lord, and establish
Regular prayer; who (conduct)
Their affairs by mutual
Consultation;
Who spend out of what
We bestow on them
For Sustenance;

Then, following the example of God's Prophet (peace be upon him) in consulting his companions and urging the nation to do the same; The Majlis Al-Shoura shall be set up to undertake appropriate tasks in compliance with this law and the Basic law of Government, in adherence to the Book of God and the Prophet's Sunnah and in fostering the bonds of brotherhood as well as in co-operation in righteousness and piety.

Article 2:

The Majlis Al-Shoura shall be established on the Qur'anic injunction calling on Muslims to hold fast by the Rope of God, and on strict adherence to the sources of Islamic Legislation. The Members of the Majlis shall be keen to uphold the general good and to preserve the unity of the community as well as the entity of the State and the interests of the Nation.

Article 3:

The Majlis shall consist of a Chairman and sixty well-educated and qualified members to be selected by the King. The rights and duties of the members and all their affairs shall be determined by a Royal Decree.

Article 4:

A member of the Majlis shall be:

(a) A Saudi National by birth and descent.
(b) Of proven integrity and efficiency.
(c) Not less than 30 years old.

Article 5:

The member of the Majlis may submit a request to the Chairman that he be relieved from his post, and, in turn, the Chairman shall forward the matter to the King.

Article 6:

If a member of the Majlis plays his duties false, an investigation shall be conducted, and he shall be prosecuted in accordance with rules and procedures issued by a Royal Order.

Article 7:

If, for any reason, the seat of a Majlis member becomes vacant, the King shall name a substitute by a Royal Order.

Article 8:

The member of the Majlis may not exploit his membership to serve his own interests.

Article 9:

The member of the Majlis may not be combined with a government post or a senior administrative job with a company unless the King sees a need for this.

Article 10:

The Chairman of the Majlis, his deputy and the Majlis' Secretary-General shall be appointed and may be relieved from their posts by a Royal Order.

Their grade, rights and duties as well as other affairs shall be determined by a Royal Order.

Article 11:

The Chairman, members and the Secretary-General of the Majlis shall take the following oath before reporting to work with the Majlis:

"I swear by Almighty God that I will be loyal to my Religion, then to my King and country; shall not divulge any secrets of the State; will uphold its interests and laws; and will perform my duties in good faith, honesty, sincerity and fairness."

Article 12:

The city of Riyadh shall be the headquarters of the Majlis. However, the Majlis may meet in any other place inside the Kingdom if approved by the King.

Article 13:

The Majlis term shall be four Hijira calendar years beginning as of the date set in the Royal Order by which the Majlis was established. The new Majlis shall be set up at least two months before the expiration of the term of its predecessor. If the term ends before a new Majlis is formed, the old Majlis shall continue to discharge its duties until a new Majlis has been set up. When a new

For additional analytical, business and investment opportunities information,
please contact Global Investment & Business Center, USA
at (202) 546-2103. Fax: (202) 546-3275. E-mail: ibpusa3@gmail.com
Global Business and Legal Information Databank: www.ibpus.com

Majlis is established, its new members shall account, at least, for one half of the total number of members.

Article 14:

The King, or whomever he may deputize, shall deliver a Royal speech before the Majlis on a yearly basis dealing with State domestic and foreign policies.

Article 15:

The Majlis may express its opinion on the general policies of the State referred to it by the Prime Minister. It may in particular:

(a) discuss and express its opinion of the general economic and social development plan.

(b) study laws, regulations, treaties, international agreements and concessions, and offer its comments thereon.

(c) interpret Laws.

(d) discuss and make suggestions concerning the annual reports submitted by various ministries and other government bodies.

Article 16:

A meeting of the Majlis shall be valid only if attended by at least two thirds of its members, including the Majlis Chairman or whomever he may deputize. Resolutions shall not be legal unless approved by the majority of the Majlis members.

Article 17:

Resolutions passed by the Majlis shall be submitted to the Prime Minister, who shall refer them to the Council of Ministers for consideration. If the Majlis and the Council are of the same opinions, Royal endorsement shall be issued; but if their opinions are at variance, the King may take whatever he may deem proper.

Article 18:

Laws, international agreements, treaties and concessions shall be issued and amended by Royal Decree, after being reviewed by the Majlis.

Article 19:

The Majlis shall form specialized committees, from among its members, to carry out its various functions. The Majlis shall also have the right to set up special committees, from among its members, to discuss any item on its agenda.

Article 20:

The Majlis affiliated committees may, with the Chairman's approval, seek the help of anyone they consider suitable from among non-members.

Article 21:

The Majlis shall set up its panel comprising the Chairman of the Majlis, his deputies, and heads of the Majlis specialized committees.

Article 22:

The Chairman of the Majlis shall submit to the Prime Minister a request to call any government official to attend the Majlis sessions, while the Majlis is discussing matters within the area of competence of this official who shall have the right to take part in the discussions but not the right to vote.

Article 23:

Every group of ten members of the Majlis may make a motion for the enactment of a new regulation or the amendment of one already in effect and present it to the Chairman who shall forward it to the King.

Article 24:

The Chairman of the Majlis shall submit an application to the Prime Minister requesting access to governmental documents and statements deemed necessary by the Majlis for the pursuit of its activities.

Article 25:

The Chairman of the Majlis shall submit an annual report to the King detailing the activities carried out by the Majlis in accordance with its internal by-laws.

Article 26:

Civil Service regulations shall be applied to the personnel of the Majlis, unless its internal by-law stipulates otherwise.

Article 27:

The Majlis shall have a special budget endorsed by the King, and dispensed in accordance with rules issued by a Royal Order.

Article 28:

The Majlis financial affairs, financial control and final accounts shall be organized in accordance with special rules issued by a Royal Order.

Article 29:

The Majlis internal by-law shall organize the duties of the Chairman, the Vice-Chairman, and the Secretary-General. It also organizes the Majlis bodies, the manner in which its sessions are run, the way the Majlis and its committees go about their work and its method of voting. Likewise it organizes the rules of debate, rejoinder and other matters that could enhance order and discipline in the Majlis and enable it to perform its duties in an manner that is beneficial to the Kingdom and the well-being of its people. This by-law shall be issued by a Royal Order.

Article 30:

This law shall be amended in the same manner in which it has been issued.

ROYAL DECREE ON FOREIGN INVESTMENT CODE
Royal Decree Number: M/1
Dated: Muharram 1, 1421 A.H. corresponding to April 10, 2000 A.D.

Article (1)

The following terms shall have the meanings stated herein unless the context requires otherwise:

(i)The Council: the Supreme Economic Council, (SEC);

(ii)The Commission: the General Commission for Investment, (GCI);

(iii)The Board of Directors: the GCI board of directors;

(iv)The Chairman: the chairman of the GCI board of directors;

(v)The Governor: the governor and Chairman of GCI;

(vi)Foreign Investor: a natural person who is not a Saudi citizen or a legal entity all of whose partners are not Saudi citizens;

(vii)Foreign Investment: investment of Foreign Capital in an activity licensed pursuant to this Decree;

(viii)Foreign Capital: foreign capital in this law includes (by way of example, not limitation) the following assets and rights owned by the foreign investor (a) money and securities; (b) profits of the Foreign Investment if used to increase the capital, expand existing projects or establish new projects; (c) machinery, equipment, spare parts, means of transportation and production requirements pertaining to the Foreign Investment; (d) rights like licenses, intellectual property rights, technical knowledge, administrative skills and means of production;

(ix)Entities of Commodities: projects of industrial, agricultural, vegetable and animal products;

(x)Services – Installations: services and contracts;

(xi)The Code: the Foreign Investment Decree;

(xii) The Regulations: the executive regulations of this Decree.

Article (2)

Without violation of any law or agreement, the Commission will issue foreign investment licenses on a temporary or permanent basis.

The Commission should decide on the application of the investment within 30 days, effective from the date of receipt of the required documents as stipulated in the Code.

If the Commission denies the application within the fixed time, then such decision should be reasoned and justified.

The Investor whose application has been rejected has the right to appeal the decision, according to the law.

Article (3)

The Council is empowered to issue a list of the activities, which are excluded from Foreign Investment.

Article (4)

In consideration of Article (2), the Foreign Investor has the right to obtain more than one license in various activities. The Regulations determine the required restrictions.

Article (5)

The licensed Foreign Investment should either be in installations owned by a national investor and a Foreign Investor, or installations wholly owned by the Foreign Investor. The legal form for the installation is to be consistent with this Decree and instructions.

Article (6)

A project licensed in accordance with this Decree shall enjoy all privileges, incentives and guarantees that are enjoyed by a national project according to law.

Article (7)

The Foreign Investor has the right to remit abroad his share either from selling his portion of the profit or surplus from the dissolution of the project or of the profits earned by the project. He also has the right to use it in any legal manner. And he also has the right to remit the necessary sums to meet any contracting obligations pertaining to the project.

Article (8)

The licensed foreign firm has the right to own real estate needed to practice the licensed activity or to house some or all of the firm's personnel in accordance with real estate regulations for non-Saudis.

Article (9)

The licensed firm is empowered to sponsor the Foreign Investor and his non-Saudi employees.

Article (10)

The Commission will provide to whoever is interested in investments the required information, clarification, and statistics as well as the required services and procedures to facilitate all matters pertaining to investments.

Article (11)

The investments of the Foreign Investor are not allowed to be confiscated either partially or entirely without a judicial verdict, and his property is also not allowed to be expropriated, either partially or entirely, except for public interest and in return for fair compensation in accordance with the law and regulations.

Article (12)

The Investment Commission shall notify the Foreign Investor of any violation of this Decree or its Regulations in writing within a reasonable period of time that is to be fixed by the Commission. This process is intended to eliminate the violation within its Regulations.

  (i)If the violation remains uncorrected, the Foreign Investor will be subject to one of the following actions:

   (a) deprivation of all or some of the incentives and privileges,

   (b) payment of a fine not to exceed SR 500,000, or

(c) loss of his investment license.

  (ii)The above-mentioned actions will be carried out by a decision issued by the Board of Directors.

  (iii)The Foreign Investor has the right to appeal the action taken against him to the Grievances Committee in accordance with its Regulation.

Article (13)

Without violation of the agreements to which the Kingdom of Saudi Arabia is a party, settlement of disputes between the Saudi government and the Foreign Investor or between the Saudi partner and the Foreign Investor concerning the latter's licensed investment in accordance with this Decree is to be settled in an amicable manner, but if such settlement is not reached, the dispute will be settled in accordance to the Saudi laws.

Article (14)

For additional analytical, business and investment opportunities information, please contact Global Investment & Business Center, USA at (202) 546-2103. Fax: (202) 546-3275. E-mail: ibpusa3@gmail.com Global Business and Legal Information Databank: www.ibpus.com

All licensed Foreign Investments will be treated in accordance with the tax law and its amendments implemented in the Kingdom of Saudi Arabia.

Article (15)

The Foreign Investor shall adhere to the laws, regulations and instructions implemented in the Kingdom of Saudi Arabia and to the international agreements to which the Kingdom is a party.

Article (16)

The implementation of this Decree does not contravene the acquired rights of foreign investments that exist prior to the implementation of this Decree; nonetheless, the practice of these investment projects or the increase of their capital will be subject to the rules of this Decree.

Article (17)

The Commission shall issue regulations and publish them in the Official Gazette, and they will be implemented effective upon their date of publication.

Article (18)

This Decree shall be published in the Official Gazette and be effective 30 days after its publication. The Foreign Investment Decree, issued by the Royal Decree Number M/4 dated 2.2.1399 shall be annulled and it will also annul all provisions that contradict with its rules.

LABOR AND WORKERS LAW

The Labor and Workmen Law of the Kingdom has been approved by the Council of Ministers on his Decision No 745 dated 24 Sha'ban 1389 H. (4 November 1969) and issued under Royal Decree No. M/21 of 6 Ramadan 1389 H. (6 November 1969). Labor disputes are governed by this law. Under Article 2, the provisions of this Law shall apply to the following:

1.   a- Any contract under which any person undertakes to work for the account of an employer under the latter's direction or control in consideration of wage.
2.   Contracts of Apprenticeship (industrial indentures).
3.   Workmen of the government, local authorities, charitable institutions, and public organizations.

Article 147 of the law states that "a workman shall not be employed for more than eight actual working hours in any one day, or forty-eight hours a week, in all months of the year, with the exception of the month of Ramadan when actual working hours shall not exceed six hours a day or thirty-six hours a week, exclusive of the intervals reserved for prayer, rest, and meals. The number of working hours maybe raised to nine hours a day in respect of certain categories of workmen or in certain industries and operations where the workman does not work continuously, such as seasonal establishments, hotel, snack bars, restaurants, etc. The number of daily working hours may be reduced for certain categories of workmen, industries, and operations referred to in this Article, these to be determined by decision of the Minister of Labor." Articles 148-159 (Chapter IX) of the said law deal with some other aspects of working hours and weekly holidays.

For additional analytical, business and investment opportunities information,
please contact Global Investment & Business Center, USA
at (202) 546-2103. Fax: (202) 546-3275. E-mail: ibpusa3@gmail.com
Global Business and Legal Information Databank: www.ibpus.com

Article 151 defines the wage for additional work hours to be the workman's normal wage plus fifty percent. Article 153 stipulates that the workman who has completed one year in service of the employer shall be entitled to an annual vacation of fifteen days with full wages payable in advance. This vacation shall be increased to 21 days when the workman completes ten continuous years in service of the employer.

Chapter XI of the said law concerned with Labor Commissions and Settlement of Disputes. The Law States that the Labor and Settlement of Disputes Commissions shall be as follows:

1.   The Primary Commissions for Settlement of Disputes.
2.   The Supreme Commissions for Settlement of Disputes.

Article 174 defines the exclusive jurisdiction of "The Primary Commission for Settlement of Disputes" as:

1- To render final decisions on:

a) Labor disputes, the value of which does not exceed three thousand Riyals.
b) Disputes relating to the stay of execution of decisions to terminate workmen, which are filed in accordance with the provisions of this law.
c) Disputes relating to the imposition of fines or requests for exemption from such fines.

2- To render decisions of first instance on:

a) Labor disputes, the value of which exceeds three thousand Riyals.
b) Disputes pertaining to labor injuries whatever the amount involved may be.
c) Disputes pertaining to termination of service.

Article 176 states that "the Supreme Commission shall have exclusive jurisdiction to render final and definitive decisions in all disputes referred to it on appeal and shall likewise be competent to impose upon the violators of the provisions of this Law the penalties prescribed herein".

For further details pertaining to the Labor and Workmen law and attached procedures, contact the Ministry of Labor and Social Affairs, Labor Affairs Agency (see appendix I for address).

REAL ESTATE LAW

As a corollary to the Foreign Investment Law, enacted in April 2000 to encourage non-Saudi investment in the Kingdom, the government announced a new Real Estate Law seven months later. The new law, with eight basic articles, was aptly named "The system of real estate ownership and investment of non-Saudis." This law entitled resident non-Saudis to own real estate for their private residence with the permission of the Interior Ministry. It also allowed ownership of real estate by foreign investors to conduct their business activities and own properties required for their accommodation and that of their employees. The law also entitled investors to rent their properties. It is anticipated that the new law will encourage major international companies and property developers to enter and influence the Saudi real estate market.

The law, however, makes provisions for preventing artificial price hikes and real estate speculation. To ensure this, it stipulates retaining ownership for at least five years. Previous laws

For additional analytical, business and investment opportunities information,
please contact Global Investment & Business Center, USA
at (202) 546-2103. Fax: (202) 546-3275. E-mail: ibpusa3@gmail.com
Global Business and Legal Information Databank: www.ibpus.com

permitted investors to keep properties only for three years before selling. The law also states that at least SR 30 million should be invested for receiving the license for purchasing land and buildings for selling and renting purposes. This law prevents foreigners from owning properties in the holy cities of Makkah and Madinah, except through inheritance and endowments. Renting within the two cities is, however, permitted for not more than two years. The application of the new law does not cancel the rights of foreigners and GCC citizen to own properties as per previous regulations.

On 8/4/1421 H, The Council of Ministers endorsed a new Saudi Real Estate Law to allow foreigners to own, sell and invest in the Real Estate Market.

The following is an overview of the new Law:

FIRST:

 (A) Non-Saudi Investors, either Persons Or Companies, may own the required Real Estate for their licensed businesses provided the approval of the Licensing Authority is obtained. This includes property for personal residences and workmen's housing. The property may also be leased to other entities.

(B) If the concerned License allows for the purchase of Real Estate or land for construction, investment, and sale or leasing, the total cost of the project, both land and construction, will not be less than SR 30 million. The Investment will have to be carried out within the first five years of ownership.

SECONDLY:

Non-Saudi expatriates enjoying normal legal residence status in Saudi Arabia may own Real Estate for housing purposes, provided they acquire a License from the Ministry of Interior.

THIRDLY:

Foreign accredited missions in the Kingdom may, on the basis of reciprocity, own the property where the Chancery and the official residence are based. International and Regional Organizations may also own property where their Headquarters are based within the limits of the Agreements that govern their operations. A License from the Minister of Foreign Affairs is conditional in this case.

FOURTHLY:

With the exception of inheritances, non-Saudis may not own Real Estate in Mecca or Medinah unless the estate is endowed to a particular Saudi Institution in accordance with the Regulations of Shari'a (Islamic Law). However, non-Saudis may lease property In Mecca And Medinah for a two-year renewable period.

FIFTHLY:

The enforcement of these Regulations will not override the following:
(A) Property ownership privileges acquired by citizens of GCC countries by virtue of GCC Ownership Regulations;
(B) Acquisition of ownership rights or rights in term of property by Inheritance;

(C) Regulations, Cabinet Resolutions, and Royal Decrees prohibiting Real Estate Ownership in certain locations.

INVESTMENT PROMOTION AND PROTECTION AGREEMENTS

These agreements aim to promote and protect the investments of the nationals and enterprises of one contracting party in the territory of the other contracting party by providing an appropriate legislative environment to stimulate and increase investment, trade and industrial activity. The agreement also provides adequate guarantees to nationals or enterprises of the other contracting party to transfer their profits, dividends and other current income. The investment will not be subject to expropriation except for a public purpose and against prompt and adequate compensation.

The Kingdom has signed Investment Promotion & Protection Agreements with the following eight countries:

- Italy
- Germany
- Belgium
- Taiwan
- China
- France
- Malaysia
- Austria

Avoidance of Double Taxation Agreements
These agreements aim primarily to eliminate the double payment of taxes by nationals and enterprises of a Contracting State in the territory of the other. It also aims to create an appropriate economic environment to attract capital between the two contracting parties.

○○○○○Economic, Trade and Technical cooperation Agreements
These agreements aim to develop economic, trade and technical cooperation in accordance with the laws of each contracting party, and create appropriate conditions to develop cooperation on the basis of reciprocal interests. This allows the free inflow of goods, capital, and services and the free movement of individuals and investment between the two contracting party.

Country	Type of Agreement	Date of Signing
Algeria	Economic, Cultural, Technical	21/3/1407 H
Argentina	Economic, Technical	12/10/1401 H
Australia	Economic, Technical	6/5/1400 H
Austria	Economic, Technical	11/8/1408 H
Azerbaijan	Economic, Investment, Cultural, Sports, Technical, Trade	2/2/1415 H
Bangladesh	Economic, Trade	20/1/1399 H
Belgium/Luxemburg	Economic, Technical	3/6/1398 H
Canada	Economic, Trade	12/2/1408 H
China	Economic, Trade, Investment, Technical	11/5/1423 H

Denmark	Economic, Industrial, Scientific, Technical	1/8/1394 H
Egypt	Economic, Trade, Investment	10/8/1410 H
Finland	Economic, Technical	6/5/1396 H
France	Economic	15/7/1395 H
Germany	Economic, Industrial, Technical	10/2/1397 H
Greece	Economic, Technical	13/1/1407 H
Holland	Economic, Technical	12/8/1404 H
India	Economic, Technical	10/6/1401 H
Indonesia	Economic, Trade	15/7/1410 H
Iraq	Economic, Trade	11/4/1404 H
Ireland	Economic, Technical	14/1/1404 H
Italy	Economic, Technical, Financial	21/2/1395 H
Japan	Economic, Technical	18/2/1395 H
Jordan	Economic	2/6/1382 H
Korea	Economic, Technical	10/6/1394H
Lebanon	Economic, Trade	23/9/1391 H
Malaysia	Economic, Trade	17/1/1395 H
Morocco	Cultural, Media, Trade	20/5/1386 H
Pakistan	Economic, Technical, Trade	10/6/1413 H
Philippines	Economic, Investment, Trade, Technical	12/5/1415 H
Russia	Economic, Investment, Trade, Technical	17/6/1415 H
Syria	Economic, Trade	19/2/1392 H
Tunisia	Trade	21/7/1408 H
Turkey	Economic, Technical, Trade	18/5/1394 H
USA	Secured Private Investment	10/2/1395 H
Uzbekistan	Economic, Investment, Cultural, Sports, Technical, Trade	25/6/1416 H
Yemen	Cultural, Trade, Technical	11/8/1408 H

OTHER AGREEMENTS:

In addition to the above, the Kingdom of Saudi Arabia is party to a number of trade and economic agreements with GCC and Arab League countries. These agreements aim at promoting trade and economic development in the respective countries.

- The Coordinated Gulf Efforts
- The GCC Joint Economic Accord
- Undertaking economic activities in the kingdom by GCC citizens
- The GCC countries' joint strategy for industrial development
- The Integrated Statutes Regulating Foreign Investment in the GCC Countries
- The Foundations for Economic Integration in the GCC Countries
- The Integrated Regulations for Protecting Industrial Products
- Trade Facilitation and Development Agreement Between the Arab Countries
- The Integrated Agreement on Investing Arab Capital Funds in the Arab Countries

- Transit Agreement Between Arab League Countries

The Agreement on Mutual Exemptions from Taxes and Administrative Charges the Activities and Equipment of Arab Airlines

GRANT OF LICENSES TO FOREIGN COMPANIES TO ESTABLISH OFFICES IN THE KINGDOM

The Ministerial Resolution No. 680 dated 9 Thul Qa'dah 1398 H. (January 1978) issued by the Minister of Commerce stipulates the following:

- Directors of foreign companies that enter into contract with Ministries and government agencies, or companies that receive sub-contracts from such companies with government approval, should request from the Ministry of Commerce, within 30 days of the date of signing the contract, a license to open an office in the Kingdom in order to undertake implementation of the works assigned to them, in accordance with such contracts.

- Branches and offices of foreign companies operating in the Kingdom should prepare a statement of their financial positions and activities annually showing, in particular, all works that have been completed and are under completion. Copies of these documents should be sent to the Companies Department, Ministry of Commerce within one month of their preparation

- The said branches and offices should facilitate the task of the representatives of the Ministry to gain access to such documents, books, and registers and to provide data and information they require.

The Ministerial Order No. 1502 of 8 Rabi I 1400 H. (1980) stipulates terms and conditions governing a foreign company which enters into a contract with any government authority and which may be licensed to establish a representative office in the Kingdom to supervise its activities and to facilitate liaison with its head office.

GRANT OF LICENSES TO PRACTICE VARIOUS PROFESSIONS

Accountants, auditors, lawyers and legal consultants, engineers and engineering consultants, translators and translation bureaus must be licensed by the Ministry of Commerce. Individuals wishing to obtain a license should possess the prerequisite qualifications and experience and establish contact with the appropriate authorities. The following Ministerial Resolutions are available on the subject:

1- Ministerial Resolution No. 346 dated 1 Ramadan 1397 H. (1977) related to "Organization of Translation Profession". Following are the main points:

- To practice translation, one should be on file with the Ministry of Commerce which keeps a register for this purpose.
- A license is issued to non-Saudis under the following conditions:

-Applicant should have a recognized university degree in his chosen language and six years general experience as a translator.
-Applicant should establish residency in the country three months prior to acquiring a license to practice translation.

2- Ministerial Resolution No. 1190 dated 16 Safar 1401 H. (1982) pertaining to "Organization for Practicing Legal Consultancy". Following are the main points:

- Only Saudi nationals are allowed to practice legal consultancy.
- Licensed legal consultants may hire one or more foreign legal consultants as long as they accept supervisory responsibility for them. Foreign consultants should be confined to preparing memoranda in the name of the Saudi consultant, providing legal advice, and assisting in office work.
- Previously licensed foreign legal consultants may temporarily continue practicing law provided they are working full time and available for at least nine months a year of uninterrupted service in the country.

3- Ministerial Resolution No. 264 dated 16 Ramadan 1402 H. (July 7,1982) which regulates the "Profession of Engineering Consultants". Following are the main points:

- Licenses shall be issued to those who hold Bachelor of Science degrees in the following engineering areas: 1)Architecture and Planning, 2)Civil Engineering, 3)Electrical Engineering, 4)Mechanical Engineering, 5)Mining Engineering, 6)Petroleum Engineering (Exploration), 7)Chemical Engineering, 8)Agriculture Engineering, 9)Industrial Engineering, 10)Systems Engineering and 11)Project Management Engineering.
- Licenses shall be granted to Saudi Engineers, general consulting bureaus, and Saudi professional general partnership (consulting engineers).
- The bureau owner of the partners must be Saudi engineers.
- License applications should be submitted to the Department of Internal Trade on a prescribed form accompanied by original documents which will be returned to the applicant after review.
- The license shall be valid for three years and may be renewed at least two months before expiration.
- Non-Saudi engineers may be licensed under certain specified conditions if Saudi engineers are not available in sufficient numbers.
- A foreign bureau or company with prior experience shall be licensed to engage in consulting engineering in its field in the country subject to the following conditions:

-The head office, bureau, or company must be licensed in the same work.
-The bureau or company must have at least ten years of experience in its field.
-The head office, bureau or company must submit an endorsed certificate pledging to support the bureau or company to carry out work in its name in the Kingdom. It must also agree to assume all responsibilities and commitments as indicated in the relevant rules and instructions in the Kingdom.
-A certificate from a bank acceptable to the Saudi Arabian Monetary Agency testifying to the company's capabilities, financial reputation, and commercial dealings must be submitted.
-A certified statement on work performed by the company outside the Kingdom of Saudi Arabia in the project area which the company proposes to undertake in the Kingdom should also be submitted.
-A photocopy of the company's balance sheet and profit and loss statement for the last two years duly certified by an accredited accountant must be submitted.
-Certificates showing the company's performance in relation to its operations inside or outside the

For additional analytical, business and investment opportunities information,
please contact Global Investment & Business Center, USA
at (202) 546-2103. Fax: (202) 546-3275. E-mail: ibpusa3@gmail.com
Global Business and Legal Information Databank: www.ibpus.com

Kingdom are also required.
-The license is valid for two years and may be renewed for an additional two years provided a request for renewal is received at least two months before expiration of the license.

4- Ministerial Resolution No. 595 dated 13 Thul Q'adah 95 H.(1975) covering the practicing of Chartered Accountants. Following are the main points:

- An individual wishing to register as a Chartered Accountant in Saudi Arabia must be a member of an internationally recognized chartered accountant's society.
- Prescribed forms must be used and accompanied by the necessary documents.

TRADE AND COMEMRCE ACTIVITY REGULATIONS

Saudi Arabia pursues a liberal trade policy with no quantitative or price restrictions for importers. However, there are a number of regulations and procedures governing business and trade in the Kingdom and adherence thereto could be very helpful for those intending to do business in Saudi Arabia.

CUSTOMS DUTIES

According to Royal Decree No. M/13 dated 10/5/1408 H., corresponding to 12/30/1987, and to the Saudi Council of Ministers order No. 86 dated 10/5/1408 H. (12/19/87) the following customs duties' rates have been in effect since 13/5/1408 H. (corresponding to January 2, 1988):

- Most of the basic consumer products are duty free, e.g., sugar, rice, tea, unroasted coffee, cardamom, barley, corn, livestock and meat (fresh or frozen).
- Customs duties of 20% are imposed on some imported commodities for the purpose of protecting the national infant industries.
- Import duty on other items is 12% ad valorem on the c.i.f. (cost, insurance, and freight) value.
- A limited number of items are subject to customs duties calculated on the basis of metric weight or capacity, rather than ad valorem. However, the rates for these items are fairly low.
- Members of the Arab League who are signatories to the Agreement to Facilitate Trade and Exchange and to Organize Transit between the Arab League States are granted special concessions.
- Imports from the Arab states with which Saudi Arabia has bilateral trade agreements are entitled to further reductions of duty.

Royal Decree No. M/56 dated 19/10/1407 H., corresponding to June 15, 1987, has approved the international Brussels agreement of 14 June 1983 on the Harmonized Commodity Description and Coding System (HS). According to the Minister of Finance and national Economy Order No. 3/1805 dated 19/10/1410 H., corresponding to May 14, 1990, the Kingdom has been implementing the Harmonized System since 15/6/1411 H., corresponding to 1/1/1991. For details, contact Customs Department

SHIPPING DOCUMENTS

The documents required for **all commercial shipments** to the Kingdom of Saudi Arabia, **irrespective of value or mode of transportation**, are: **a commercial invoice, a certificate of** origin, **a bill of lading** (or an airway bill), **a steamship or an airlines company certificate, an insurance certificate** (if goods are insured by the exporter) and **a packing list**. Depending on the nature of goods being shipped, or upon certain requests from the Saudi importer or in a letter of credit (L/C), or according to clauses in a contractual agreement, specific additional documents may also be required (see "Special Documents" below).

It is important to note that **authentication of the certificate of origin, the commercial invoice, and any special document is the responsibility of the exporter, who must make sure that they are certified in the following specified order:**

(1) Notarized by a Notary Public.
(2) Sealed and certified by a local U.S. Chamber of Commerce.
(3) Sealed and certified by an approved U.S.-Arab Chamber of Commerce (see appendix V for names and addresses).
(4) Legalized by one of the Consulates General of Saudi Arabia in the U.S.

The Saudi Arabian Consulates legalize only one copy. Additional copies will be legalized upon request. The Saudi Arabian Consulates will legalize the respective documents for $8.50 per document or page (an original or a copy). All fees must be submitted in the exact amount. No cash or personal checks will be accepted. Payments should be made by a company's check, a cashier's check, or a money order payable to the Royal Embassy of Saudi Arabia, or to the relevant Saudi Arabian Consulate. Companies' checks, money orders or cashier's checks must be signed.

Each document should be prepared in (at least) one original and one copy. The certifying U.S.-Arab Chamber of Commerce will retain the copy. The original is legalized and returned. All documents (originals or copies) should bear the handwritten signature of the person issuing the document. Facsimile signatures are not accepted.

All documents sent in by mail must include a self-addressed stamped envelope. Saudi Arabian Consulates will not return any documents without a self-addressed stamped envelope. Documents presented by hand will only be released upon presentation of the consular receipt.

DESCRIPTION OF SHIPPING DOCUMENTS:

Commercial Invoice:

All commercial invoices must be on the letterhead of the exporting company. The invoice should contain names and addresses of consignor and consignee, **accurate description of goods and components** (trademarks, name of the vessel or airlines) and the date of sailing, port of loading and port of discharge, net and gross weight, quantity, unit price and extended price of each type of goods, total value of the shipment, contents of each package and container, currency, number of L/C (if applicable) and freight and insurance.

As of 1/1/1417 H., corresponding to May 18, 1996, the Saudi customs authorities have emphasized that commercial invoices issued by exporters should contain accurate description of goods being exported to the Kingdom, for example:

A) For equipment:

- Line, number, and size of exported item.
- Model number.
- Trade marks.
- Manufacturer's complete name.
- Any other information helpful in identifying the exported equipment.

B) For other exported products:

- Complete material description including type, size, weight, and percentage of its components if possible.
- Complete name(s) of manufacturer(s) or producer(s).
- Trade marks.
- Any other information pertaining to the type of the exported item to the Kingdom of Saudi Arabia.

In addition, all commercial invoices should be certified by a responsible official of the exporting firm as follows:

"I certify this invoice to be true and correct and in accordance with our books, also that the goods referred to are of ....origin."

Certificate of Origin:

This certificate must be issued by the manufacturer (or the exporting firm). In addition to the name of the vessel (airlines) and the date of sailing, name(s), nationality(ies), and full street address(es) of the manufacturer(s) of all items to be shipped to Saudi Arabia, and components thereof, must be declared. Furthermore, the origin of each item or component must be specified. A signed statement to the effect that the document is true and correct must be given.

If the merchandise to be shipped to Saudi Arabia **is not** solely and exclusively originated in the U.S., then a notarized "**appended declaration to certificate of origin**" (available at any Saudi Consulate), must be attached to the certificate of origin.

In addition, the certificate of origin must include name and address of the Saudi importer, description of the goods, and address of the shipping company.

The Bill of Lading (or Airway bill):

One non-negotiable copy of the bill of lading is to be presented to a Saudi Arabian Consulate. The bill of lading should agree with the commercial invoice and show description, value, net and gross weight of shipped goods. Likewise, volume and measurement, marks, number of packages, name and address of consignee (Saudi importer) and consignor, name and address of shipping company and/or shipping agent, name of vessel and date of sailing, port of loading and port of discharge, etc., should be mentioned. Marks and numbers should agree with those on invoice and containers.

Steamship (or airlines company) certificate:

This certificate (**which is an appended declaration to bill of lading or the airway bill**) should be issued by the steamship (or airlines) company in at least one original. It **must be notarized**

For additional analytical, business and investment opportunities information,
please contact Global Investment & Business Center, USA
at (202) 546-2103. Fax: (202) 546-3275. E-mail: ibpusa3@gmail.com
Global Business and Legal Information Databank: www.ibpus.com

and contain the following information about the vessel (or plane), named in the Bill of Lading or the airline company certificate:

(1) Name of vessel (plane), and previous name (if applicable).
(2) Nationality of vessel (plane).
(3) Owner of vessel (plane).
(4) Name(s) of ports (airports) that Vessel (plane) will call on en route to the Kingdom of Saudi Arabia

A- Port (airport) of loading ....
B- ....
C- ....
    Port (airport) of discharge.................

Further, the steamship (airlines) company certificate should declare that said vessel (plane) shall not anchor or call on any other ports (airports) than those mentioned in it, and that all information provided in the certificate is true and correct. The standard form of the Appended Declaration to the Bill of Lading or airway bill is available at any Saudi Arabian Consulate.

Insurance Certificate:

This certificate (issued by an insurance company in at least one original) must contain the following information: actual amount of insurance, description and value of insured goods, name of vessel, port of loading and Saudi port of discharge, and name and address of beneficiary. Moreover, **the appended declaration to insurance policy** (form of which is available at any Saudi Arabian Consulate) should state that the insurance company has a duly qualified and appointed agent or representative in the Kingdom of Saudi Arabia, giving his name and full address.

Note: If the shipment is insured by an insurance company in Saudi Arabia, the exporter, on his letterhead, must state the name and address of said company.

Packing List:

This includes names and addresses of consignor and consignee, description and value of the exported goods, net and total weight, number of packages and their contents, number of containers and contents, numbers of seals, and number of L/C (if applicable).

For additional analytical, business and investment opportunities information,
please contact Global Investment & Business Center, USA
at (202) 546-2103. Fax: (202) 546-3275. E-mail: ibpusa3@gmail.com
Global Business and Legal Information Databank: www.ibpus.com

SPECIAL DOCUMENTS:

As mentioned earlier, depending on the nature of exported goods to Saudi Arabia, or according to a request from the Saudi importer, certain documents may be required in addition to the standard set of six shipping documents. Special certificates or documents are also required to be authenticated in accordance with the procedure for authentication of shipping documents delineated above. The most important of these certificates or documents are the following:

A. FOOD PRODUCTS' EXPORT DOCUMENTS:

Requirements for labeling of food and food products sold in the Kingdom of Saudi Arabia are determined by the Saudi Arabian Standards Organization (SASO). Exporters of these products should comply (among other SASO standards) with Mandatory Standards SSA 1/1984, whether for sample demonstration or for commercial shipments, and must provide the following certificates:

1. Food Manufacturer's Ingredients Certificate: This certificate should include description of exported food products (contents and percentage of each ingredient), chemical data, microbiological standards, storage, and life of product (date of manufacturing and date of expiration). When products contain any animal fats, the certificate must confirm the kind of animal from which it is taken, or state that no pork meat or its artificial flavor nor its animal fat is being used. This certificate must be obtained from your local health department and must be signed.

2. Consumer Protection Certificate: This certificate must confirm the healthiness of the various ingredients of the exported food products to Saudi Arabia, their safety and fitness for human consumption. This certificate must be obtained from the USDA or one of its local offices, and must be signed.

3. Price List: The price list should be issued by the exporter on his letterhead, and should indicate that the prices of the exported products to the Kingdom of Saudi Arabia are the standard local market prices.

B. MEAT IMPORTED INTO SAUDI ARABIA

The Kingdom of Saudi Arabia imports only (male) beef or lamb meats, fresh or frozen. In addition to the above-mentioned shipping documents, all meat shipments must be accompanied by the following certificates:

1) A certificate of "Halal" meat: This certificate indicates that slaughtering has taken place in an officially licensed slaughter-house and in accordance with Islamic "shari'ah," i.e., procedures. The "Halal" meat certificate should be legalized by a recognized Islamic Center in the United States. It must also accompany shipments of poultry into Saudi Arabia.

2) An Official Health Certificate: This certificate should indicating the date of slaughtering, kind of animals and their average age, in each shipment. The health certificate must also indicate that animals were examined within twelve hours before being slaughtered, and directly after, by a licensed veterinarian, and were found free from disease and suitable for human consumption.

For additional analytical, business and investment opportunities information,
please contact Global Investment & Business Center, USA
at (202) 546-2103. Fax: (202) 546-3275. E-mail: ibpusa3@gmail.com
Global Business and Legal Information Databank: www.ibpus.com

Note: The HEALTH CERTIFICATE is required for all exports to Saudi Arabia of all kinds of meat (including poultry and seafood), meat products, livestock, vegetables, fruits, human blood, etc., attesting that they are free from pests and/or diseases.

Slaughtered animals must be stamped by the concerned health authority on several parts. Age of animal, when slaughtered, should not exceed three years for lamb and five years for beef. Exporters should comply with prevailing Saudi rules and regulations regarding the procedure of cutting, shipping, storing, etc., of meat shipped to the Kingdom.

C. IMPORTATION OF SEEDS AND GRAINS INTO SAUDI ARABIA

Exporters of seeds and grains must clearly write in Arabic and English on each package or sack the following information:

Barley or Sorghum for animal Fodder:

1. Barley or Sorghum for animal fodder.
2. .Name of exporter.
3. Weight of sack.
4. Country of production.
5. Date of production.
6. Expiration date.

Grains used as Seeds:

1. Barley, Sorghum, or wheat as seeds.
2. Name of exporter.
3. Country of production.
4. The Phrase: (Poisonous for both human and/or animals), and sign of danger or "skull and crossbones" must be shown in red on each package or sack.
5. Date of production.
6. Expiration date.

In addition to shipping documents, the exporter of seeds or grains must provide the following authenticated certificates:

1- Certificate of Inspection:

Issued by a specialized company for inspection of seeds. The most important information the certificate must include are the following:

* Name and address of buyer.
* Name and address of seller.
* Kind and amount.
* Seed Class.
* Name of shipping vessel.
* Type of packing.
* The written information on sacks, bags and each package.
* Results of inspection and percentage of germination, purity, impurity, moisture, etc.
* Method of chemical treatment of the seeds.

* Confirmation that the seeds are free from insects, epidemic, diseases and weed seeds (their number and species in a sample of two kilograms must be mentioned).

2- PHYTOSANITARY CERTIFICATE:

The purpose of this certificate is to verify that the seeds or grains to be exported to the Kingdom of Saudi Arabia are free from agricultural diseases. It is obtainable from the U.S. Department of Agriculture (USDA), or from any of its local offices. This certificate is required to accompany all shipments of flour, rice, grains, agricultural seeds, lumber, plants, plant material, etc.

3- SEED ANALYSIS CERTIFICATE:

This certificate is to prove the degree of purity of the seeds shipped to Saudi Arabia. It is issued by the USDA or one of its local offices.

4- Certificate of Weight:

This certificate should be issued by the exporting company indicating the name and address of the Saudi importer, the name of the shipping vessel, the number of the bill of lading, the number of seals and containers, and net weight and total weight of shipment.

D. ANIMAL FODDER ADDITIVE:

In addition to the above-detailed shipping documents, the following certificates or documents are required:

1. Certificate of Free Sale.
2. Product Registration Certificate.
3. Certificate of Analysis.
4. Product Safety Data Sheet.

E. SHIPMENT OF LIVESTOCK TO THE KINGDOM:

Besides the standard set of six shipping documents, the following documents are required:

1. Certificate of Weight: This must show the average weight of the exported livestock.
2. Health Certificate: This must verify that the livestock are free from diseases. It is issued by the U.S.D.A. or one of its local offices.
3. Health Certificate issued by a veterinarian.
4. Pedigree Certificate issued by USDA.
5. Production records.
6. Declaration of Inspection and Acceptance.

F. CERTIFICATES REGARDING THE SHIPMENT OF PETS:

The additional required documents are the following:

1. A Health Certificate issued by a veterinarian and approved by the U.S.D.A. confirming that the animals are free from diseases.Animal Vaccination Certificate.
2. Only guard, hunting, and seeing-eye dogs are allowed into Saudi Arabia.

G. IMPORTATION OF HORSES TO THE KINGDOM:

The Saudi importer should submit an application to the President of the Saudi Equestrian Club, indicating the number of horses, exporting country, and customs center at the port of entry to the Kingdom. The application should be accompanied by the following documents:

1.   A certificate of origin, issued by the company raising and breeding the horses, with a color picture of each horse affixed to it. The certificate must be authorized by the USDA, U.S. Department of State and approved by a Saudi Arabian Consulate.

2.   A Health certificate, confirming that the horses are free from diseases, approved by a veterinarian and authenticated as in (1) above. It should be noted, however, that only Saudis are allowed to import horses into the Kingdom.

H. VEGETABLE AND FRUIT HEALTH CERTIFICATE:

This certificate must accompany all shipments of vegetables and fruits to the Kingdom certifying that such exports are free from pests, insects, and other agricultural diseases, and that they have not been exposed to ionizing radiation (but can be treated with aluminum phosphide). This certificate can be obtained from U.S.D.A. or any of its local offices.

I. Certificate of Free Sale:

This certificate should accompany all shipments of pharmaceutical and medicinal products to Saudi Arabia. It is obtainable from the U.S. Department of Health and Human Services and should be presented to a Saudi Arabian Consulate with other documents.

Moreover, imports of pharmaceuticals and medicinal products require a certificate issued by the U.S. Department of Health and Human Services. This certificate must state that the medicines are actually used by the public in the U.S. under the same trade name and formula and must include the name of each product, the formula, and the date and number of the permit to manufacture them if one is required. The certificate must be certified by the Department of State in Washington D.C., and be authenticated by a Saudi Arabian Consulate. This certificate must be filed with the Ministry of Health in Riyadh, Saudi Arabia, prior to any shipment of pharmaceutical or medicinal products to Saudi Arabia, and must be renewed every two years (see registration of medicines and pharmaceutical products below).

J. SASO Certificates of conformity for imported electrical appliances, equipment, a and accessories into Saudi Arabia:

There are two types of certificates:

a) Certificate of Conformity for electrical appliances and equipment.
b) Certificate of Conformity for electrical accessories.

The relevant certificate (the standard form is available at any Saudi consulate) must be issued by the manufacturer on their official letterhead, notarized by a notary public, certified by a local chamber of commerce, and then sent to SASO in Riyadh, Saudi Arabia (see appendix I for address) at least two months before shipment date, to be verified. Upon approval, the certificate will be returned to the manufacturing company which must attach a stamped copy with each shipment to Saudi Arabia of the commodity mentioned therein. These certificates are only required for commodities mentioned in the List of Imported Electrical Products issued by SASO.

For additional analytical, business and investment opportunities information,
please contact Global Investment & Business Center, USA
at (202) 546-2103. Fax: (202) 546-3275. E-mail: ibpusa3@gmail.com
Global Business and Legal Information Databank: www.ibpus.com

K. SASO MOTOR VEHICLES CONFORMITY CERTIFICATES:

Three months at least before dispatching the first consignment of any type of motor vehicles in any year, the manufacturer must send to SASO this certificate in English or Arabic for their approval. Individuals must obtain this certificate from the manufacturer prior to the shipment of any car for their personal use in the Kingdom (a personal used car of a Saudi student or diplomat is exempted).

ARRANGEMENT OF SHIPPING DOCUMENTS:

Shipping documents must be presented to any of the Saudi Arabian Consulates in the following manner or they will be rejected: Commercial Invoice, Certificate of Origin, Insurance Certificate, Bill of Lading (or airway bill), Steamship (or airline company certificate), Packing List and any of the special documents, all stapled together.

In addition, **an Export Information Sheet, EIS** (available at any U.S.-Arab Chamber of Commerce) must be *filled out, signed by an official of the exporting or shipping company and presented to a Saudi Arabian consulate along with the rest of the required shipping documents.* The EIS does not require authentication.

COMMERCIAL LEGAL DOCUMENTS:

All companies' documents, i.e. joint venture agreements, commercial agency agreements, collaboration agreements, authorization by proxy, etc., must be legalized in the following manner:

1. Notarized by a Notary Public.
2. Certified by the County Clerk of the respective county where the Notary Public is commissioned.
3. Certified under the seal of the Office of the Secretary of the State where the documents originated.
4. Authenticated by the Authentication Office of the U.S. Department of State
5. Legalized by one of the Royal Saudi Consulates in the U.S.A., for addresses and phone numbers). Please refer to the certification of shipping documents detailed above for fees and procedures.

Note: Please refer to the certification of shipping documents detailed above for fees and procedures.

GENERAL NOTES:

- Imports of plants, fruits, vegetables, seeds, live animals and poultry must have the prior approval of the appropriate Saudi Arabian authorities and must be accompanied by a phytosanitary or health certificate stating that they are free from pests and other diseases. All shipments of plants will be inspected upon arrival in Saudi Arabia.
- Shipment of hazardous materials must have the prior approval of the Ministry of Interior in Riyadh, Saudi Arabia.
- According to Royal Decree No. 5/E/27748 dated 24/11/1402 H. (corresponding to September 12, 1982), the country of origin must be mentioned on all products imported into Saudi Arabia, except when it is not feasible, as in the following list of examples:

(a) Small spare parts, nails, pins, nuts, etc. In this case, the country of origin should be mentioned on the package or box.

(b) Barbed wires, metal sheets, unfinished boards of glass, wood, marble, etc. In this case, the country of origin should be mentioned on the band.

(c) Raw materials or semi-finished products used as an input by national industries.

Carpet manufacturers and suppliers must indicate in Arabic the following data which is to be applied on each 5 meters along the carpet roll length:

(a) Thickness or weight of each square meter.

(b) Pile weight.

(c) Country of Origin.

(d) Type: Indicate whether made of nylon, wool, acrylic or polypropylene.

All carpet manufacturers, suppliers and distributors have to show the captioned data on the sales invoice.

- Shaving brushes and other articles made of raw hair should be accompanied by a recognized official certificate showing the consignment to be free from anthrax germs.
- Importing used clothing requires an official disinfection certificate. These goods will be subject to inspection by the Saudi Arabian quarantine officials.
- Islamic Law strictly forbid the importation, sale and use of pork and its products, liquor and narcotics.
- Saudi laws forbid the importation of firearms. Arms for hunting and similar sports arms need special permission.
- Books, publications, audio and video materials are subject to inspection and approval by customs for entry into the Kingdom. In particular, obscene literature and Communist propaganda will not be allowed entry.
- Medical drugs for personal use in small quantities are allowed. Travelers should be ready to show the inspectors the necessary documents to identify the drugs and the medical documents (e.g. doctor's prescription) to prove that the medicine is for personal use.
- Non-commercial shipments of less than 10,000 Saudi Riyals (about $2,600) and cars imported into the Kingdom for personal use, regardless of their value, do not require shipping documents.
- Commercial samples are subject to the payment of customs duty and surcharge either by a deposit equal to the duty at the time of import or by a bank guarantee. A refund is made if the goods are re-exported within 12 months. In the event of samples being sold, neither deposit nor guarantee will be refunded.

Prior permission to import samples must be obtained from the Director General of Customs, Customs Department (see appendix I for address), who should be furnished with lists of samples, prices and catalogues. A non-refundable duty of 12% is levied for imports of samples of jewelry and watches. *Authenticated shipping documents are required for all shipments of commercial samples.*

REGULATIONS FOR COMPANIES:

Formation and operation of business firms and companies is regulated by companies Law promulgated by Royal Decree No. M/6 dated 22 Rabi I 1385 H., (1965). Royal Decree No. M/5 dated 12 Safar 1387 H. (1967) and Royal Decree No. M/23 dated 28 Jumada II 1402 H. (1982)

amended the regulations for companies. Under Article 1 of the Companies Law, a company has been defined as a contract pursuant to which each of two or more persons undertake to participate, in an enterprise aiming at profit, by offering in specie or as work a share, for sharing in the profits or losses resulting from such enterprise.

Following are some of its important provisions:

- Under article 2, companies can take any of the following forms:

- General Partnerships.
- Limited partnerships.
- Joint Ventures.
- Corporations.
- Partnerships Limited by Shares.
- Limited Liability Partnerships.
- Variable Capital Companies.
- Cooperative Companies.

- Without prejudice to the companies acknowledged by the Islamic "Shari'ah" Law, any company not having any of the legal forms as given in Article 2 of the Companies Law shall be null and void.
- Partner's contribution may consist of a certain sum of money (a contribution in cash), or of a capital asset (a contribution in kind). It may also comprise services except in the cases where the provisions of the Companies' Regulations imply otherwise, but it may not consist (solely) of the partner's reputation or influence.
- Every partner shall be considered indebted to the company for the contribution he has undertaken to make. If he fails to surrender it on the date set therefore, he shall be liable to the company for any damages arising from such delay.
- Save in the case of a joint venture, a company's memorandum of association and any amendment thereto must be recorded in writing in the presence of a registrar. Otherwise, such memorandum or amendment shall not be valid vis-à-vis third parties.
- With the exception of joint ventures, any company incorporated in accordance with these Regulations shall establish its head office in the Kingdom. It shall be deemed to have Saudi nationality, but this shall not necessarily entail its enjoyment of such rights as may be restricted to Saudis.

For details pertaining to formation and operation of companies, please contact Companies Department, Ministry of Commerce

FOREIGN INVESTMENT POLICY & COMPANIES REGULATIONS

MARKETING AND SALES STRATEGY

There are very good prospects for Foreign companies who want to export their products to the Saudi Arabian market. However, there are certain marketing procedures and sales techniques which have to be observed in order to develop and sustain business relationships over a long period of time.

- The Saudi market should be constantly reviewed for product adaptation and change.

For additional analytical, business and investment opportunities information,
please contact Global Investment & Business Center, USA
at (202) 546-2103. Fax: (202) 546-3275. E-mail: ibpusa3@gmail.com
Global Business and Legal Information Databank: www.ibpus.com

- Exporters should ensure regular supplies as per specifications, at the specified time and place already agreed upon and at the stipulated prices.
- Any subsequent and sudden price changes, even pertaining to after-sales services, should be avoided.
- Exporters' contacts with importers in Saudi Arabia should be direct and regular.
- Complete product lines, rather than single products, should be introduced into the Saudi market whenever possible in order to benefit from greater demand stimulation and cost reductions.
- Exporters are required to check with Saudi importers or directly with the Saudi Arabian Standards Organization, on the precise implementation of Saudi Arabian Standards pertaining to their exported products to the Kingdom. Saudi Standards can be purchased from SASO or the American National Standards Institute, ANSI (11 West 42nd Street, New York City, NY 10036, telephone number (212)642-4900 or fax number (212)302-1286).
- Exporters to Saudi Arabia should display their products regularly in the major commercial urban centers of the Kingdom. Necessary permission is obtained by writing or contacting directly the Director, Exhibitions Department, Ministry of Commerce.
- Efforts should be made to improve the appearance of exported commodities by means of attractive packaging.
- Products to be exported should be properly branded and labeled both in English and Arabic.
- In the case of machinery and equipment; after-sales service, including warranties, maintenance and the provision of spare parts, should be prompt and efficient.

BUSINESS OPPORTUNITIES IN THE KINGDOM

In pursuit of the policy of free market enterprise, economic diversification, structural shift from building the infrastructure to the production of goods and services and the subsequent increasing reliance on the private sector as the major economic force, the Kingdom of Saudi Arabia invites Foreign companies to participate in the following areas which are essential to its current and future economic growth:

- Import-substitution and export-oriented joint ventures.
- Projects contributing to technological progress in the Kingdom and the development of established factories through improvement of production methods and minimization of production costs.
- Projects directly related to the current economic development in the Kingdom which include, but are not limited to, the following:

a) Industries utilizing locally abundant raw materials from petrochemical or petroleum products.
b) Food industries utilizing locally abundant agricultural products.
c) Specialized industries in the fields of maintenance and the manufacturing of spare parts and equipment.

In most of the industrial joint ventures, the foreign partner supplies the management, technical expertise, and part of equity resources, if they are desired, depending on the collaboration arrangements. The Saudi partner provides local supervision, local skilled and unskilled labor, and handles local business contacts, apart from participating in the equity resources. For further details on establishing joint ventures in the Kingdom, Industrial Licensing Regulations and Procedures.

With a foothold in the Saudi Arabian market, there will be numerous business opportunities for:

- Companies providing labor-saving equipment and services.
- Training services either directly delivered or as part of a product package.
- Managerial services either directly delivered or as part of a product package.
- Nearly all areas of health, personnel, and services.

In addition to the section on growth targets during the sixth development plan that we discussed in Chapter Two of this guide, the following list of principal growth areas of the Saudi Arabian economy provides tips on prospective commercial opportunities in the Kingdom:

- Industry: Most industrial activities in the Kingdom are carried out by the energetic Saudi private sector. The structure of the Saudi Arabian industrial sector is composed of three distinct sub-sectors: petrochemicals, oil refining, and other manufacturing. The main objectives of the Kingdom's industrialization are:

a) To reduce the Kingdom's dependence on the export of crude oil as the major source of income
b) To increase Saudi Arabian private sector participation in the economic development of the country
c) To create new job opportunities.
d) To establish an advanced industrial and technological base.

Export oriented industries such as petrochemical, papers, glass plastics, etc. are expected to do well during the sixth plan period. Over the next few years the petrochemical industry is expected to grow at an average rate of more than 8 percent annually. Thus foreign investors are invited to join the Saudi Arabian private sector to invest in new industries that utilize modern technology, and to expand investment in import substitution and export-oriented industries including basic, supporting and downstream metal and petrochemical industries

- Mining and quarrying: The Saudi government has prioritized the diversification of the Kingdom's economy and the utilization of the country's extensive mineral wealth. The mining industry is promising in the next few years, especially with the initiative of the Ministry of Petroleum and Mineral Resources to develop new mines to produce phosphate, iron, bauxite and other precious and non-precious metals. In 1993 Petromin extracted 189,353 tons of ore. Net gold production amounted to around 670,000 ounces between 1989-1993. The Directorate General of Mineral Resources is currently pursuing the exploitation of the mineral fields throughout the Central and Western regions of the Kingdom. The government's investment in this sector has already exceeded seventeen billion Saudi Riyal (more than U.S. $4.5 billion). Foreign investors are offered tax exemption, long term extraction concessions and other incentives to invest or establish joint ventures in this growing Saudi industry.
- Transportation, telecommunications and information technology: During the fifth development plan (1990-1994) the Kingdom's main road network increased by about 2,100 KM, to about 43,000 KM. Rail freight volume grew by 36 percent to about 2.1 million tons. Air passenger volume grew from 20.3 million departure and arrival to 25.1 million. The cargo handled in the Kingdom's major ports rose from 63.7 million tons to 83 million tons.

In addition to upgrading the road network and domestic airports in the Kingdom during the sixth development plan, the government is planning to link Dammam and Jubail Industrial City with a new railroad. Furthermore, to enhance and modernize the fleet of Saudi Arabian Airlines, the government has already purchased from two American companies (Boeing and McDonnell Douglas) commercial airplanes worth more than six billion dollars. The Saudi Ministry of Post, Telephone and Telegraph awarded the U.S. firm of AT&T four billion dollars contract to upgrade and expand the telephone network in the Kingdom.

For additional analytical, business and investment opportunities information, please contact Global Investment & Business Center, USA at (202) 546-2103. Fax: (202) 546-3275. E-mail: ibpusa3@gmail.com Global Business and Legal Information Databank: www.ibpus.com

- Electricity: Saudi per capita consumption of gas, water and electricity is one of highest in the world. Over the past two decades electricity consumption rate increased by more than 20 percent annually. Power generation expanded from 4,214 megawatts in 1979 to 18,238 megawatts in 1994. Over the sixth development plan period (1995-1999) electric generation capacity will be raised by more than seven thousand megawatts.
- Other important areas of growth prospects during the sixth development plan (1995-1999), include banking and insurance, leasing, travel, and consumer products such as food and beverages, clothing, soap, cosmetics, etc.

FOREIGN INVESTMENT POLICY

The Kingdom of Saudi Arabia realizes that achieving its ambitious economic goals requires a steady flow of technology and expertise into the country. Therefore, its policy is to welcome foreign capital and invite it to participate in economic development projects in cooperation with Saudi business. The government's established policy is not to impose any restrictions on the movement of capital into and out of the Kingdom and always to respect private ownership.

In addition, foreign investment that fulfills the requirements of the Foreign Capital Investment Code enjoys all privileges of national capital and is entitled to the same treatment, protection, and incentives accorded to national capital. The Code requires that foreign capital be invested in economic development projects (which, under the Code, do not include petroleum and mineral projects) and that it be accompanied by technical knowledge. Development projects are defined by the Ministry of Industry and Electricity.

Provided that the share of national capital is at least 25 percent, industrial or agricultural projects that fulfill the above requirements enjoy the following benefits:

- An income tax holiday of up to 10 years from the commencement of commercial production.
- Ownership of land according to the regulations governing land ownership by non-Saudis.
- For industrial projects, the same privileges as those enjoyed by Saudi capital under the National Industries Protection and Encouragement Regulations. These include:

a. Exemption from customs duties on machinery, equipment, tools and spare parts imported for industrial products.
b. Exemption from customs duties on primary raw materials, semi-finished goods, containers, etc., necessary for industrial projects (provided that similar items are not sufficiently available locally).
c. Provision by the government of plots of land at a nominal rate for factories and residential quarters for workers.
d. Low electricity and water rates.
e. No restriction on repatriation of profits.
f. Preferential treatment for local products in government procurement in addition to preferential treatment accorded to national products by Arab League and Saudi Arabian bilateral trade agreements.
Saudia-Online.

A further consideration for business opportunities is the procurement of government contracts. Government contracts are often offered through tenders. There is no central tenders' board in Saudi Arabia, and every government agency may extend contracts. Bids for tenders must be

For additional analytical, business and investment opportunities information,
please contact Global Investment & Business Center, USA
at (202) 546-2103. Fax: (202) 546-3275. E-mail: ibpusa3@gmail.com
Global Business and Legal Information Databank: www.ibpus.com

applied for by local agents. In most cases, government contracts awarded to foreign companies require 30 percent of the total work to be subcontracted to a Saudi Arabian contractor.

RELATIONSHIP BETWEEN A FOREIGN CONTRACTOR AND HIS SAUDI AGENT

The relationship between a foreign contractor and his Saudi Agent was regulated by Royal Decree No. M/2 of 21 Muharram 1398 H. (January 1978). This regulation applies to both, the Saudi agent and the foreign contractor who is contracting with the government of Saudi Arabia. It also applies to all contracts and agreements to which the foreign contractor and the government of Saudi Arabia are signatories.

Some of the salient features of this regulation are:

- A foreign contractor who does not have a Saudi partner, should have a Saudi services agent.
- The agent should be a Saudi national residing in the Kingdom of Saudi Arabia and should be registered in the Commercial Register of the Ministry of Commerce authorizing him to act as an agent.
- The relations between a Saudi agent and a foreign contractor should be governed by an Agency Agreement defining the obligations of both parties.
- A foreign contractor is required to pay the Saudi agent fees in return for the services he renders to the contractor. Such fees as determined by an agreement between both parties should not exceed 5 percent of the cost of the contract executed by the foreign contractor.
- A foreign contractor performing different types of work may have more than one Saudi agent so as to match each type of work.

THE TAX SYSTEM

The Kingdom of Saudi Arabia has a very liberal tax system; there are few taxes payable by an individual or a company and they are also at very low rates.

1. ZAKAT

The Zakat (a form of tithe) is paid annually by Saudi individuals and companies within the provisions of Islamic law as laid down by Royal Decree No. 17/2/28/8634 dated 29/6/1370 H. (1950). The Zakat is an annual flat rate of 2.5 percent of the assessable amount.

2. PERSONAL INCOME TAX

For individual employees, both national and expatriate, there is no income tax in the Kingdom.

Self-employed expatriates such as doctors, accountants, lawyers, etc. pay taxes on their net annual income at the following rates:

Net Income (per year)	Tax Rate (percent)
First 6,000	Exempted

From SR 6,001 - 10,000	5
From SR 10,001 - 20,000	10
From SR 20,001 - 30,000	20
Over SR 30,000	30

A slab system is followed to calculate such taxes.

3. TAX ON BUSINESS INCOME:

A company, under the tax regulations, means a company or partnership having material gain as the basic objective. The taxable incomes of companies include:

* profits of a foreign company;
* shares of non-Saudi sleeping partners in the net profits of partnership companies.

All legitimate business expenses and costs, including business losses and depreciation, are deductible in computing net profits. Any reasonable method of depreciation may be adopted by the company but the same must be adhered to from year to year. Capital gains are included in the profits of the company. The following tax rates, on a slab basis, are now in force:

Net Profit Level	Tax Rate (percent)
First SR 100,000	25
From SR 100,001-500,000	35
From SR 500,001-1,000,000	40
Over SR 1,000,000	45

Income tax is charged at different rates for companies engaged in the production of petroleum and hydrocarbons in the Kingdom.

Every company is required to submit a financial statement on an official form and to pay the tax not later than the 15th day of the third month of the year following the Saudi Arabian fiscal year, which commences on the 10th of Capricorn (December 31).

Companies formed under the provisions of the Foreign Capital Investments Regulations with participation of Saudi capital of not less than 25 percent are exempt for up to ten years from payment of income tax.

For further details, please contact the Ministry of Finance and National Economy, Directorate of Zakat and Income, Companies Department

For additional analytical, business and investment opportunities information,
please contact Global Investment & Business Center, USA
at (202) 546-2103. Fax: (202) 546-3275. E-mail: ibpusa3@gmail.com
Global Business and Legal Information Databank: www.ibpus.com

TRADEMARKS REGULATIONS

The Trade Marks Regulations were originally issued by Royal Decree No. 8762 dated

28-7-1358 H. (1938). It contained 43 Articles. However, Articles 41, 42 and 43 were subsequently repealed by Royal Decree No. 8/M of 20 Rabi II, 1393 H. (1973). Thereafter these were reviewed and promulgated by Royal Decree No. M/5 dated 4-5-1404 H. (Jan. 7, 1984). Rules for Implementation of the Trade Marks Regulations were issued by the Minister of Commerce Resolution No. 94 dated 5.8.1404 H. (May 6, 1984).

Provisions of the new Regulations included: definitions of trade marks, registration, announcement, renewal and deletion thereof in addition to the transfer of ownership of marks, mortgage, seizure, and licensing thereof together with definition of fees due on registration, etc. They define crimes and penalties regarding trade marks to protect public and private rights and formulation of procedural rules to decide on their crimes and impose penalties thereon.

The fees due under the provisions of these Regulations were defined by Article 47 in the following manner:

a) SR 1,000 (one thousand) on any part of the following:

1. Application to register a trade mark for one category.
2. Application to register a collective trade mark for one category.
3. Request to examine a trade mark for one category.
4. Viewing the Register for one trade mark in respect of one category.
5. Every photocopy taken from the records of the Register in respect of one trade mark for one category.
6. Application to enter transfer or assignment of ownership for one trade mark in respect of one category.
7. Application to license the use of a mark for one category as well as entering its mortgage in accordance with article 36 and 40 of these regulations.
8. Each amendment or addition to a mark for one category as well as entering its mortgage in accordance with Article 22 of the Regulations.
9. Application to add or to alter any statement for which no fee is specified in respect of a mark for one category.

b) SR 3,000 (three thousand) on any part of the following:

1. Application for temporary protection for a trade mark of one category.
2. Registration of trade mark.
3. Renewal of registration of one trade mark for one category.
4. Renewal of registration of a collective trade mark for one category.

These fees may be amended by a resolution of the Council of Ministers.

For further details, please contact the Department of Internal Trade, Ministry of Commerce.

PATENTS LAW

The Patents Law was promulgated by Royal Decree No. M/38 dated 10/6/1409 (January 17, 1989). The Law contains 62 articles with the main objective of providing adequate protection of inventions inside the Kingdom of Saudi Arabia.

Applications for patents shall be submitted to the Directorate of Patents at King Abdul Aziz City for Science and Technology on the form designed for such purpose. The patent's term shall be fifteen years from date of grant and it may be extended for five more years.

Patents' disputes shall be resolved by an ad hoc Committee at the King Abdul Aziz City for Science and Technology. Appeal against the Committee decision may be made to the Board of Grievances within sixty days from the date of notification.

Patents fees as referred to in Article 59 of this law are as follows:

Type of Fee	Individuals	Companies
1. Patent Application	R 400	SR 800
2. Issuance/Publication of Patent	SR 500	SR 1,000
3. Annual Fees per Patent	SR 400	SR 800
4. Amendment or Addition	SR 100	SR 200
5. Change of Ownership	SR 200	SR 400
6. Obtain Patent Copy/Other documents	R 50	SR 100
7. Grant of Forcible Licensing	R4,000	SR 8,000
8. Registration of Licensing Contracts	R 400	SR 800
9. Application for Patent Extension	R 200	SR 400

For further information, please contact the Patents Department, King Abdul Aziz City for Science and Technology

THE LAW FOR THE PROTECTION OF COPYRIGHTS

The Copyright Protection Law, approved by the Council of Ministers Resolution No. 30 dated 2512/1410H., corresponding to September 25, 1989 was enacted by Royal Decree No. M/11 dated 19/5/1410H, corresponding to December 17, 1989, to take effect on 15/6/1410, corresponding to January 12, 1990.

The Law's objective is to afford protection to authors of classified creative works in science, literature, and arts without regard to the type of classified work, its mode of expression, its significance or the purpose of composition. It contains definition of the following: classified work, author, publishing, creation, copying and national folklore and falls into the following seven chapters:

Chapter One: Copyright of Classified Works, Articles 2 through 6.
Chapter Two: Copyrights of Authors, Articles 7 through 15.
Chapter Three: Transfer of Copyrights, Articles 16 through 22.
Chapter Four: Scope and Duration of Copyrights, Articles 23 through 25.
Chapter Five: Filing Regulations, Articles 26 and 27.
Chapter Six: Penalties, Articles 28 through 31.
Chapter Seven: General Provisions, Articles 32 through 34.

For additional analytical, business and investment opportunities information, please contact Global Investment & Business Center, USA at (202) 546-2103. Fax: (202) 546-3275. E-mail: ibpusa3@gmail.com Global Business and Legal Information Databank: www.ibpus.com

COMMERCIAL REGISTRATION SYSTEM:

The Statute of Commercial Registration System as contained in the Council of Ministers Resolution No. 54 dated 29 Rabi II 1375 H. (1955) and No. 112 dated 13 Shawwal 1375 H. (1955) requires every industrial or commercial establishment, local and foreign, to be registered with the commercial registration offices of the Ministry of Commerce established in all the major towns of the kingdom. Some of the salient features of the system are:

- Branches of foreign business establishments or Saudi agents representing them must obtain prior approval of the Foreign Capital Investment Committee, Ministry of Industry and Electricity, after which they must register with the Ministry of Commerce within one month of the commencement of their business.
- All additional units or branches should also be registered within one month of commencement of business.
- All subsequent changes in particulars must be reported within one month of their occurrence.
- The prescribed application forms to be filled out require information such as names of the establishment and owners, their nationalities, the amount of capital and shares in the capital of each owner, etc

COMMERCIAL AGENCY REGULATIONS:

The Commercial Agency Regulations were promulgated by Royal Decree No. 11 dated 20 Safar 1382 H. (July 1962). Following are some of its salient features:

- Non-Saudis shall not be permitted to act as commercial agents in Saudi Arabia.
- No person may act as commercial agent unless his name has been entered in the Register maintained for that purpose by the Ministry of Commerce.
- The fees for registration in the agency register shall be SR 50 for an individual trader and SR 100 for a company, payable only once.

Further Implementation Rules for "Commercial Agencies Regulations" were issued under Minister of Commerce Order No. 1897 dated 24-5-1401 H. (March 30, 1981). A sample of the "CONTRACT OF AGENCY" prepared by the Ministry of Commerce according to Royal Decree No. M/32 issued on 10 Sha'ban 1400 H. (1980), amending the above-mentioned Royal Decree, has been included as appendix XIII to this Guide.

TENDERS REGULATIONS AND RULES FOR IMPLEMENTATION:

There is no central tenders board and every government agency is empowered to enter into contracts. The Kingdom supplemented the existing tenders regulations through Royal Decree No. M/14 issued on 7 Rabi II, 1397 H. (March 27, 1977). These regulations contain 14 Articles and govern bid submission, methods of procurement and performance, contract award, bid award and contracting authority, contract conditions, advance payments, delay fine, contract forms, etc. Article 14 stipulates that these regulations shall cancel and supersede all contradictory rules. Further, Rules for Implementation of Tenders Regulations were issued under ministerial Resolution No. 2131/97 dated 5 Jumada I 1397 H. (April 23, 1977). These rules contain 40 Articles and govern advertisement of tenders, manner in which they are submitted, bid evaluation process, time for acceptance of contract award, etc.

Council of Ministers Resolution No. 124 dated 29/5/1403 H. (March 14, 1983) requires that not less than 30 percent of contracts of "public works contracts" that require the performance of works, such as construction contracts generally, as well as maintenance and operations contracts, won by a foreign contractor or any Saudi-foreign joint venture prime contractor (with less than 51% Saudi capital), must be sub-contracted to contractors who are at least 51 percent Saudi owned and sponsor their own workers.

For details, please contact the Ministry of Finance and national Economy (see appendix I for address).

THE RELATIONSHIP BETWEEN A FOREIGN CONTRACTOR AND HIS SAUDI AGENT

The relationship between a foreign contractor and his Saudi Agent was regulated by Royal Decree No. M/2 of 21 Muharram 1398 H. (January 1978). This regulation applies to both, the Saudi agent and the foreign contractor who is contracting with the government of Saudi Arabia. It also applies to all contracts and agreements to which the foreign contractor and the government of Saudi Arabia are signatories.

Some of the salient features of this regulation are:

- A foreign contractor who does not have a Saudi partner, should have a Saudi services agent.
- The agent should be a Saudi national residing in the Kingdom of Saudi Arabia and should be registered in the Commercial Register of the Ministry of Commerce authorizing him to act as an agent.
- The relations between a Saudi agent and a foreign contractor should be governed by an Agency Agreement defining the obligations of both parties.
- A foreign contractor is required to pay the Saudi agent fees in return for the services he renders to the contractor. Such fees as determined by an agreement between both parties should not exceed 5 percent of the cost of the contract executed by the foreign contractor.
- A foreign contractor performing different types of work may have more than one Saudi agent so as to match each type of work.

INDUSTRIAL LICENSING REGULATIONS AND PROCEDURES FOR FOREIGN CAPITAL:

Industrial projects involving foreign capital are governed by Foreign Capital Investment Act promulgated under Royal Decree No. M/4 dated 2 Safar 1399 H. (January 1, 1979). Under Article 2 of this Act, foreign capital can enjoy the concessions allowed in the Act only if it meets the following three conditions:

- The foreign capital is for investment in economic development projects.
- The foreign capital is accompanied by foreign technical expertise.
- An industrial license has been obtained from the Ministry of Industry and Electricity, upon the recommendation of the Foreign Capital Investment Committee.

The Ministry of Industry and Electricity Resolution No. 11/G/O dated 17/7/1410 H., corresponding to 12 February 1990 (replacing Resolution No. 952 of 4 Zhul al Qa'dah, 1400 H.) considered the following five categories of development projects as qualifying for foreign investment:
a) Industrial Development projects.
b) Agricultural Development Projects.
c) Projects for the Development of Health Services.
d) Projects for the Provision of Services.
e) Projects for Undertaking Contracts.
However, Article Seven of the Resolution states the possibility that projects not mentioned in the list of development projects (detailed above) may be accepted on the proposal of the Foreign Capital Investment Committee.

Further, under this law, foreign investors can set up a project either exclusively on their own or in collaboration with Saudi partners (joint ventures). The rules of procedure for the implementation of the Law were issued by the Minister of Industry and Electricity Resolution No. 323 of 10th Jumada II, 1399 H., (1979).

The procedure for establishing industrial projects under Foreign Capital Investment Law requires that foreign investors planning to establish an industrial project in the Kingdom of Saudi Arabia should submit an application to the Evaluation and Licensing of Industrial Project Department at the Ministry of Industry and Electricity (see appendix I for address). This application should provide information about the proposed project's product, production capacity, capital, location, etc. If the Department considers the project feasible, it will provide the applicant with a License Application form. The License Application form should be completed with all required data and documents. A copy of the initial partnership contract between the Saudi and the foreign investor must be attached to it. This is to prove that the foreign partner has the required experience in the manufacturing and marketing of the proposed products. The License Application form should be signed by the applicants or their authorized agents and submitted to the Foreign Capital investment Committee as follows:

A. INDUSTRIAL PROJECTS:

1. The potential investor should indicate briefly the nature of the proposed project in terms of proposed products, output capacity, investment, etc. by writing to or visiting the Industrial Licensing Department of the Ministry of Industry and Electricity to inquire into the possibility of the project being considered for licensing.
2. If there is a possibility that a license may be issued (depending on considerations such as the installed capacity of established industries, market situation, etc.), the potential investor will be provided with the necessary forms by the Industrial Licensing Department to submit an application.
3. In the event that there is no possibility of the proposed project being considered for a license, due to lack of market, or for any other reason, a letter will be sent by the Industrial Licensing Department to the applicant informing him that the license application will not be considered and giving the reasons.
4. If the project can be considered for a license, the foreign investor, and in the case of joint venture the foreign or local partner (as authorized by the other), or the legally authorized representative, should submit the license application to the Foreign Capital Investment Bureau, with the appropriate documents.

B. TRANSPORTATION PROJECTS:

1.   Land and Maritime transportation projects (as listed in Article Five of the Ministerial Resolution on Development Projects).
2.   Such projects require a license under the Foreign Capital Investment Law (FCIL), before the company is registered and incorporated under the Companies Law.
3.   The foreign investor, and in the case of joint ventures, the foreign or local partner (as authorized by the other) or the legally authorized representative, should submit the license application to the Foreign Capital Investment Bureau, with the appropriate documents.

C. PROJECTS FOR THE PROVISIONS OF SERVICES OR UNDERTAKING CONTRACTS:

1.   The types of projects for the provision of services or for undertaking contracts which involve foreign investment and for which licenses could be considered are indicated in Articles 5 and 6 of the Ministerial Resolution on Development Projects under FCIL.
2.   All such projects require a license before the company is registered and incorporated under the Companies Law for such activities.
3.   Companies which are already licensed under the FCIL and are registered and incorporated for certain services or contract work, and wish to undertake new or additional services or contract work require an amendment to the license previously issued.
4.   Foreign companies without a license under the FCIL, but which have obtained temporary registration from the Ministry of Commerce for a particular period to undertake a contract awarded by a Ministry or other Government Agency, require a license under the FCIL to establish themselves in the Kingdom for further contract work.
5.   In all such cases indicated above, the foreign investor, and in the case of joint venture the foreign or local partner (as authorized by the other) or the legally authorized representative, should submit the license applications to the Foreign Capital Investment Bureau, with the appropriate documents.

   If the application is approved, the applicant will receive the original license and a copy thereof will be sent to the Ministry of Commerce (Department of Commercial Registration) where further action for commercial registration of the company will be taken when the licensee submits all the required documents including the Articles of Association.

For further details, please contact the Foreign Capital Investment Bureau, Ministry of Industry and Electricity (see appendix I for address).

TRADE IN AGRICULTURAL MACHINERY

Regulations for trade in agricultural machinery were issued by council of Ministers Resolution No. 96 dated 21/5/1405 H. (Feb. 11, 1985).Its important features are:

- Agricultural machines in these Regulations shall be taken to cover all machinery and equipment used in agricultural purposes.
- Trade in agricultural machinery shall not be permissible unless such machinery conform to Saudi standard specifications.
- The Minister of Agriculture and Water shall, by a decision from him, specify the type, quantity or ratio of spare parts that should be imported along with the agricultural machine or that should be available in the markets.
- If a defect or a damage, regardless of its type, appears in the agricultural machine during the warranty period, which is one year from the date of delivery of the machine to the

buyer, the trader shall be obliged to repair it free of charge, replace it, or refund its price to the buyer in case repair or replacement is impossible unless the damage or defect is the result of improper use by the buyer, and in this case the trader shall have to prove it.

- The Ministry of Agriculture and Water shall have full and direct supervision over premises selling agricultural machinery and spare parts thereof as well as workshops for its repair and maintenance to ascertain smooth performance.
- The profit margin for an agricultural machine shall not exceed 15 percent of the machine's CIF price and 20 percent for spare parts which are not accessories to the machine.
- These regulations shall replace and supersede the Council of Ministers' Resolution No. 77 dated 28/1/1395 H. (1975).

MINING REGULATIONS

In case of industries using mineral resources including quarry materials, and planning to extract their own raw materials, necessary concessions (excluding those for petroleum, natural gas, pearls, coral, and radio-active materials) must be obtained under the revised Mining Code promulgated by Royal Decree No. M/21 of 20/5/1392 H. (1973). For further information, contact the Ministry of Petroleum and Mineral Resources

REGISTRATION OF MEDICINES AND PHARMACEUTICALS

Under the existing regulations medicines and pharmaceutical products are not admitted to the Kingdom unless a prior registration is made with the Ministry of Health.

The applications supported by the required certificates duly legalized by a Saudi Arabian Consulate in the applicant's country are examined and the samples analyzed by the Ministry of Health to ensure that the samples correspond to the specifications. If the Ministry is satisfied with the results, a license is issued.

For further information, contact the Ministry of Health, Department of Registration of Medicines and Pharmaceuticals

SUPPLY AND CONSUMER PROTECTION

The Saudi Government is committed to assist the private sector in handling domestic and foreign trade. In pursuit of its efforts to contain inflation, the Ministry of Commerce regularly checks the supply and prices of basic commodities such as flour, rice, sugar, milk and milk products, vegetable oil and ghee substitute, frozen meat and the imported animal feeds (barley, sorghum and millet).

SUPPLY POLICY:

The Government has formulated a supply policy to achieve the following specific objectives:

- Procuring essential commodities continuously and in sufficient quantities for all markets.
- Providing supply items at reasonable quantities and prices.
- Expanding consumer choice.
- Reinforcing fair competition among suppliers.

- Encouraging the establishment of distribution chains and upgrading the level of commercial services in general.
- Promoting better understanding and cooperation between the private commercial sector and the government.

Further, the supply policy inspired by the country's socio-economic conditions is based on the following principles:

- Reliance on the private enterprise system under normal conditions.
- Government intervention only under abnormal conditions and when it is absolutely necessary.
- Fixation of local ceiling prices for a selected number of basic supply and food items in order to make these available to the majority of consumers and also to protect the consumers from volatile international market prices of commodities. At the same time, an appropriate subsidy scheme is in force to compensate importers of supply commodities when the cost of importation exceeds local ceiling prices.
- Fixation of ceiling profit margins in the trade of another group of essential supply commodities.
- Monitoring and regulation by government of import storage and warehousing operations carried out by the private sector with respect to supply commodities.

CONSUMER PROTECTION OBJECTIVES AND FUNCTIONS:

Main objectives are:

- To protect the consumer from all kinds of commercial fraud and to keep him well-informed.
- To prevent the rise of monopolies.
- To contribute to price and cost of living stability.
- To achieve better quality control in locally produced and imported foods and other consumer products by checking on specifications and standards adopted by the Saudi Arabian Standards Organization or internationally. This is also done by examining the product's conformity to the religious requirements of Islam.
- To ensure the commercial application of standardization rules with respect to volumes, weight, and measures.
- To ensure the commercial application of precious metal specifications with respect to gold, silver, platinum, etc.

Major functions are:

- Product and Price control.
- Quality control.
- Standardization and Hallmarking.

For further details on supply and consumer protection regulations and other connected matters, contact the Directorate-General of Supply or Directorate-General of Quality Control and Inspection, Ministry of Commerce (see appendix I for address).

SETTLEMENT OF COMMERCIAL DISPUTES

- Establishment and conduct of commercial courts is regulated by Royal Decree No. 32 issued on 15 Moharram 1350 H. (1930). Under this law, all commercial disputes, except for those related to insurance business, are settled by a "Committee for Commercial Disputes" comprising two "Shari'ah" Judges and one Legal Adviser. The disputes related to insurance business are referred to the Ministry of Commerce for decision.

- Arbitration Law, promulgated by Royal Decree No. M/46 dated 12/7/1403 H. (April 25, 1983) canceled and superseded the previous arbitration provisions contained in the above-mentioned Royal Decree No. 32.

- Since December 31, 1987, Commercial Disputes have been within the competence of the Grievances Court (Diwan Al-Mazalem), Commercial Circuit, instead of the Committee for Commercial Disputes.

- The disputes pertaining to negotiable instruments are governed by Negotiable Instruments Regulations approved by the Council of Ministers Resolutions No. 692 dated 26 Ramadan 1383 H. (1963) and issued under Royal Decree No. 37 dated 11 Shawwal 1383 H. (1963). These regulations supersede Chapters VI, VII, VIII and IX of Commercial Court Regulations issued under Royal Decree No. 32 of 1350 H. (1930).

- To settle commercial disputes related to negotiable instruments, committees in Riyadh, Jeddah, and Dammam have been constituted. The decisions of these committees are not binding. Any of the two parties can appeal against the decisions of these Committees to the Ministry of Commerce within 15 days of their issuance.

- Any of the two parties to the dispute can refer their dispute, pertaining to the negotiable instruments, directly to the Chairman of any of these Committees.

- Cases involving commercial fraud are governed by Regulations for the Control of Commercial Fraud issued under Royal Decree No. 45 dated 14 Sha'ban 1381 H. (1961). Under these regulations, the Ministry of Commerce shall issue special decisions for setting up a Central Tripartite Committee in Dammam, Jeddah, and Riyadh. Each committee shall be headed by a representative from the Ministry of Commerce. These committees shall carry out the necessary investigations and issue punishments provided for in these regulations. The decisions of these Committees are not binding except after being confirmed by the Ministry of Commerce. There is, however, permission to appeal to the Ministry of Commerce against these decisions within 15 days from the date of their issuance.

- The Commercial Office of the Royal Embassy of Saudi Arabia in Washington, D.C. (see appendix II for address) mediates commercial disputes between Saudi and American companies only when both parties are willing to reach an amicable out-of-court compromise. Since Arabic is the official language of the Kingdom of Saudi Arabia, translation of documents and related material into Arabic is recommended.

KINGDOM OF SAUDI ARABIA: ARBITRATION RULES AND CODES

Royal Decree: M 46
Date: 12-7-1403
(April 25, l983)

We Fahad Bin Abdul Aziz Al Saud, King of the Kingdom of Saudi Arabia.

After having reviewed Article (19) and Article (20) of the Council of Ministers Resolution issued by Royal Decree No. 38 dated 22-10-1377H.

And after having reviewed the Commercial Court Regulations, issued by Royal Decree No. 32 dated 15-1-1350H and the Council of Ministers Resolution No. 164 dated 21-6-1403 H.

Hereby issue the following Decree:

First: Approval of Arbitration Regulations in the form hereto attached.

Second: Deletion of the provisions relating to Arbitration contained in the Commercial Court Regulations, issued by Royal Decree No. 32, dated 15-1-1350H.

Third: His Royal Highness the Vice-President of the Council of Ministers, and the Ministers, each within his jurisdiction, shall cause this Decree to be implemented.

(Sgd.) Fahad Bin Abdul Aziz

NOTE: Published In Official Gazette (Umm Al-Kuraa No. Z969 dated 22-8-1404H (3-6 1983).

RESOLUTION NO. 164

The Council of Ministers,

After having reviewed the attached documents which were originally attached to the letter by the Presidency of the Council of Ministers, No. 7/Y/12084 dated 29-5-1399H, addressed to His Majesty the King with the letter of His Excellency the Minister of Commerce No. 410/F dated 11-5-1399, including the draft of Arbitration Regulations which has been prepared by their honors, the Minister of Justice, the Minister of Commerce, the President of the Grievances Board and the President of the Board of Experts;

And after having reviewed the Commercial Court Regulations which was issued by Royal Decree No. 32 dated 15-1-1350H .

The Labor Law issued by Royal Decree No. M/21 dated 6-9-1389H, the Council of Ministers Resolution No. 58 dated 17-1-1383 and the Memorandum of the Board of Experts No. 40 dated 25-4-1403.

Resolves as follows:

1. Approval of Arbitration Regulations in the form hereto attached.
2. Deletion of the provisions relating to Arbitration contained in the Commercial Court Regulations issued by Royal Decree No. 32 dated 15-1-1350H.
3. Preparation of a draft Royal Decree in the form hereto attached.

ARBITRATION RULES

Article (1):

An agreement may be made to refer any existing dispute to arbitration. It may also be agreed, in advance, to refer to arbitration any dispute which may arise as a results of performance of any particular contract.

Article (2):

Arbitration shall not be accepted in matters in respect of which settlement is prohibited. An agreement, with respect to arbitration, shall not be valid unless it is made by the person enjoying legal capacity.

Article (3):

Government agencies may not have recourse to arbitration for settlement of their disputes with third parties except with the approval of the President of the Council of Ministers. This provision may be amended by a resolution of the Council of Ministers.

Article (4):

The arbitrator must be selected from amongst experts and must be of good conduct and of full legal capacity. If more than one arbitrator is appointed, their number must be odd.

Article (5):

Parties to a disputed shall lodge the arbitration document with the Authority having original jurisdiction to consider the dispute. This document shall have been signed by the litigants or their duly authorized representatives and by the arbitrators and must show the subject matter of the dispute, name of litigants, names of arbitrators and their approval to consider the dispute. Copies of relevant documents must also be attached.

Article (6):

The Authority having original jurisdiction to consider the dispute shall cause the application for arbitration to be entered into the proper register and make a formal declaration accepting the arbitration document.

Article (7):

If the litigants have agreed to arbitration prior to the dispute and if a formal declaration, accepting the arbitration documents relevant to a particular dispute, has been made, the subject matter of such dispute shall not be considered except in accordance with the provisions of these Regulations.

Article (8):

The Clerk of the Authority, having original jurisdiction to consider the dispute shall issue all summons and notices herein provided for.

Article (9):

The dispute shall be decided within the period to be fixed by the Arbitration Board unless otherwise extended. If the litigants have not fixed a date for decision of the disputes in the Arbitration Document, the Arbitrators shall pass their award within ninety days from the date of approval of the Arbitration Document. Otherwise, any of the litigants may bring the matter to the attention of the Authority having original jurisdiction to consider the dispute to decide whether to consider the dispute or to extend the period.

For additional analytical, business and investment opportunities information, please contact Global Investment & Business Center, USA at (202) 546-2103. Fax: (202) 546-3275. E-mail: ibpusa3@gmail.com Global Business and Legal Information Databank: www.ibpus.com

Article (10):
If the litigants fail to appoint the arbitrators or if any of them fail to appoint its arbitrator or arbitrators, or if any one or more of the ar-bitrators has refused or is stopped to act as an arbitrator of has become disabled or has been dismissed, and if the litigants have not agreed otherwise, the Authority having original jurisdiction to consider the dispute shall appoint the necessary arbitrators upon request by the expediting litigant provided that it be in the presence of the other party or, if he is absent after he has been invited to attend a meeting to be held for this purpose. The number of arbitrators to be appointed shall be equal to the number agreed upon by the litigants or complementary thereto and the decision in this respect shall be final.

Article (11):
The arbitrator shall not be dismissed except with the consent of litigants. An arbitrator who has been dismissed my claim compensation for any work done by him prior to his dismissal, provided that the cause for dismissal was not attributed to him. He may not be prevented from giving his award except for events which happen or appear after the submission of the Arbitration Document.

Article (12):
The arbitrator shall be stopped for the same reasons of estoppel of the Magistrate. The application for estoppel shall be addressed to the Authority having original jurisdiction to consider the dispute within five days from the date of notifying the other party of the appointment of the arbitrator or from the date of the event or the occurrence which justify the estoppel. A request for estoppel shall be decided upon after the litigants and the arbitrator to the estopped have been called to a meeting to be held for this purpose.

Article (13):
The arbitration shall not be terminated by death of one of the parties but the period fixed for the award shall be extended by 30 days unless the arbitrators decide to extend this period further.

Article (14):
If an arbitrator has been appointed in place of the arbitrator who has been dismissed or who has declined to act as an arbitrator, the date originally fixed for the award shall be extended for a period of thirty days.

Article (15):
The arbitrators may by a resolution adopted by majority vote extended the date originally fixed for the award for circumstances relevant to the matter in dispute.
Article (16):
The award of the arbitrators shall be passed by majority vote, but if it is within their authority to reach settlement, the award shall be passed by unanimous vote.

Article (17):
The award shall, in particular; include the Arbitration document, a summary of the examination of the parties, the evidence submitted by each of them, reasons for the award, the date on which the award is passed, the signatures of arbitrators and the dissent of any one or more of the arbitrators.

Article (18):
All directives to be issued by arbitrators, even if relative to investigation procedures, shall be submitted within five days to the Authority haying original jurisdiction to consider the dispute with a copy thereof to the conflicting parties. The conflicting parties may, within fifteen days from the

date of their notification of the award, submit their objection to such award to the Authority with which the award has been filed. Other wise, the award shall be deemed final.

Article (19):
If the litigants or any of them submits an objection to the award within the period provided for in Article 18 above, the Authority having original jurisdiction to consider the dispute shall either reject such objection and issue an order for execution of the award, or accept the objection and take the action it deems appropriate.

Article (20):
The award of the arbitrators shall be executed when it has became final pursuant to an order by the Authority having original jurisdiction to consider the dispute. This order shall be passed upon request by an interested party after ensuring that it is not contrary to Shariatic principles.

Article (21):
When the order for execution of the award has been passed pursuant to the provisions of Article 20 above, such award shall have the same force and effect as if it has been passed by the Authority which passed the order for execution.

Article (22):
Fees of the Arbitrators shall be fixed by mutual consent of the conflicting parties and, unless paid to them, shall be deposited within five days from the date of the decision approving the Arbitration Document with the Authority having original jurisdiction to consider the dispute and shall be paid within one week from the date of the execution order.

Article (23):
If the arbitrators fees have not been upon and a dispute arose with respect thereto, such dispute shall be decided by the Authority having original jurisdiction to consider the dispute and its decision shall be final.

Article (24):
Decisions necessary for the implementation of these Regulations shall be issued by the President of the Council of Ministers upon a recommendation by the Minister of Justice in consultation with the Minister of Commerce and the President of the Grievances Board.

Article (25):
These Regulations shall be published in the Official Gazette and be implemented thirty days after the date of publication thereof.

CODES FOR THE IMPLEMENTATION OF THE ARBITRATION
CHAPTER ONE ARBITRATION, ARBITRATORS AND PARTIES

Article (1):
Arbitration in matters wherein conciliation is not permitted such as Hudoud(1) Laan(2) between spouses, and all matters relating to the public order, shall not be accepted.

Article (2):
An agreement to arbitrate shall only be valid if entered into pay persons of full legal capacity. A Guardian of minors, appointed guardian or endowment administrator may not resort to arbitration unless being authorized to do so by the competent court.

Article (3):

The arbitrator shall be a Saudi National or Muslim expatriate form the private Sector or others. The Arbitrator may also be an employee of the State, provided, approval of the department to which he belongs is obtained. In the case of more than one arbitrator, the Chairman of the arbitration panel shall have a knowledge of Shariah rules, commercial regulations, customs and traditions applicable in Saudi Arabia.

Article (4)
Any persons having an interest in the dispute or having being sentenced to a (HUD)(3) or penalty in a crime of dishonor, or being from a public position following a disciplinary order, being a judicated as bankrupt, unless being relived, shall not act as arbitrator.

Translator's Notes:
(1) Hudoud, are the crimes of murder, injury, adultery, drunkenness, theft and robbery which are specifically provided for in the Muslim Holy Book, the Quran.
(2) Laan, is a court procedure under which a confrontation between spouses takes place and through which they terminate their marital relationship after either spouse directs an accusation of adultery against the other.
(3) Hud is the singular of Hudoud (1) above.
Article (5):
Subjects to the provisions of articles (2) and (3) above, a list containing the names of arbitrators shall be prepared by agreement between the Minister of Justice, the Minister of Commerce, and the Chairman of the Grievance Board. The Courts, Judicial Committees and Chambers of Commerce and Industry shall be informed of such lists and the respective and industry shall be informed of such lists and the respective parties my select. arbitrators from these lists or from others.

Article (6):
The appointment of an arbitrator or arbitrators shall be completed by agreement between the disputing parties in an arbitration instrument which shall sufficiently outline the dispute and the names of the ar-bitrators. Agreement to arbitration may be concluded by a condition in a contract in respect of disputes that may arise from the execution of such contract.

Article (7):
The authority originally competent to hear the dispute shall issue a decision for approval of the arbitration instrument within fifteen days and shall notify the arbitration panel of the same.

Article (8):
In disputes where a government authority is a party with others, such government authority shall prepare a memorandum with respect to arbitration in such dispute, stating its subject matter, the reasons for arbitration and the names of the parties, the reasons for arbitration and the names of the parties. Such memorandum shall be submitted to the President of the Council of Ministers for approval of arbitration. The Prime Minister may, by a prior resolution, authorize a government authority to settle the disputes arising from a particular contract, through arbitration. In all cases the Council of Ministers shall be notified of the arbitration awards adopted.

Article (9):
The clerk of the authority originally competent to hear the dispute shall act as secretary for the arbitration panel, establish the necessary records for registration of the arbitration application and shall submit the same to the concerned authority for approval of the arbitration instrument. Such clerk shall also be in charge of the summons and notices provided for in the arbitration regulations and any other assignments as may be decided by the relevant Minister. The concerned authorities shall make the necessary arrangements regarding the above.

Article (10):

The arbitration panel shall fix the date of the hearing for consideration of the dispute within a period not exceeding five days form the date on which approval of the arbitration instrument had been notified to the arbitration panel and shall notify the disputed parties of the same through the clerk of the authority originally competent to hear the dispute.

CHAPTER TWO

NOTIFICATION OF PARTIES, APPEARANCE, DEFAULT, AND PROXIES IN ARBITRATION

Article (11):

Every summons or notice relating to the subject matter of arbitrations made through the clerk of the authority originally competent to hear the dispute, shall be made through the messenger or the official authorities, whether the said proceeding is requested by the disputing parties or initiated by the arbitrators. Police or Mayors are required to assist the relevant authority in performing its duties within their prescribed jurisdiction.

Article (12):

The summons or notice shall be written in the Arabic language and shall consist of two or more copies, according to the number of disputing parties and shall contain the following:

The date, day, month and year in which the summons of notice was made.
The first name, surname, title, profession and domicile of the party requesting the summons or notice, and the first name, surname, title, profession and domicile of his representative, if he is working for another personl.

The name of messenger who forwarded the summons of notice, his employer and his signature on the original and copy of the summons of notice.
The first name, surname, profession and domicile of the person to be summoned or notified, and if his domicile is not known at the time of issuance of the summons, then his latest, domicile.

Title of the person to whom copy of the summons has been served, and his signature on the original indicating receipt, or indication of his refusal to take receipt of the summons when returned to the concerned authority.
Name and place of the arbitration panel, the subject matter of procedure, and the date specified therefore.

Article (13):

The papers to be served on summons shall be delivered to the respective person, or to his place of domicile, and my be delivered to a chosen place of domicile determined by the concerned parties.

In case such person is not present at his place of domicile, the summons papers shall be delivered to any person who declares that he is an agent or responsible for the business of the person to be summoned, or his employee or that he or she is living with him such as spouses, relatives or others.

Article (14):

If the messenger did not find the proper person to whom the papers are to be delivered pursuant to the preceding section, or it the person mentioned therein refrained from accepting the papers, the messenger shall state that in the original copy and deliver the same that day to the Police Commissioner or Mayor or the representative of any of them, if the residence of the person summoned falls within their authority.

Also, the messenger shall within twenty four (24) hours send the person summoned at his original or chosen domicile a registered letter, informing that the copy was delivered to the administration and stating all such details in the original copy of the summons. The summons or notice shall be valid and effective from the time of delivery thereof as a aforementioned.

Article (15):
Except as provided for in special regulations, the copy of the summons or notice shall be delivered in the following manners:

matters relating to the state, it shall be delivered to the Ministers, District Governors, Directors of Government Departments or their representatives.
In matters relating to public persons, it shall be delivered to the person acting on its behalf according to the law, or his representative.

In matters relating to companies, societies and private establishments, it shall be delivered to the head offices, as indicated in the commercial registration, to the Chairman, Managing Director or his representative, from among the employees. With respect to foreign companies having branches or agents in Saudi Arabia, the papers shall be delivered to the branch of the agent.

Article (16):
The official in charge shall submit the arbitration file to the authority originally competent to hear the dispute, for approval of the arbitration instrument. The clerk of such authority shall notify the parties and the arbitrators of the decision taken with respect to approval of the arbitration instrument within one week from the date of adoption of such decision.

Article(17):
One the day fixed for arbitration the parties shall appear by themselves or through their representatives, by virtue of a notarized power of attorney, or by proxy issued by any official authority or certified by on of the Chambers of Commerce and Industry. A copy of the power of attorney shall be kept in the file of the claim after the original has been reviewed by the arbitrator, without prejudice to the right of the arbitrator or arbitrators to require the personal appearance of the respective party if the circumstances so require.

Article (18):
In the event of default by one of the parties in appearing at the first hearing, and if the arbitration panel is satisfied that such defaulting party had been properly served notice, the arbitration panel my decide on the dispute as long as the respective parties have filed their statements of claim, defenses and documentation. The award adopted shall, in such case, be considered a decision made in the presence of the parties.

However, if the defaulting party was not property served a summons, the hearing shall be adjourned to another hearing so that the defaulting party is properly notified. If the defendant parties are many and are only partially served a personal summons, and if they have all, or those who are not served notice, defaulted to appear, the arbitration panel in other than urgent matters shall adjourn the hearing so that the defaulting parties are properly served notice, and the award adopted in such other hearing shall be deemed as if made in the presence of all defaulting parties.

Also, the award of arbitration shall constructively be deemed made in the presence of the presence of the party who appears personally or by proxy in any of the hearings, or filed his statement of defense in the claim or a document relating thereto. However, if the defaulting party

For additional analytical, business and investment opportunities information,
please contact Global Investment & Business Center, USA
at (202) 546-2103. Fax: (202) 546-3275. E-mail: ibpusa3@gmail.com
Global Business and Legal Information Databank: www.ibpus.com

appeared prior to the end of the hearing, any award or decision adopted therein shall be deemed null and void.

Article (19):
If the arbitration panel discovers that a summons published to a defaulting party in a newspaper is not proper, it shall adjourn arbitration of the dispute to another hearing and such defaulting party shall be properly served a summons in respect thereto.

CHAPTER THREE

HEARINGS, TRIAL, AND RECORDING OF CLAIM

Article (20):
The claim shall be tried openly unless the arbitration panel decides, by it own motion, or if one of the parties requests that the hearing be held in camera for reasons appreciated by the arbitration panel.

Article (21):
The arbitration of the claim shall not, without an acceptable reason, be adjourned more than once for a reason attributed to one of the parties.

Article (22):
The arbitration panel shall reasonably allow each party to make his remarks and defenses either orally or in writing in the times specified 3y the arbitration panel. The defendant party shall be the last to make his submission and the panel shall complete the case and prepare the award.

Article (23):
The Chairman of the arbitration panel shall control and mange the hearings, direct questions to the parties or witnesses, and shall have the right to dismiss from the hearing any one in contempt of the hearing. However, if any one present commits a violation, the Chairman of the arbitration panel shall record the incident and transfer it to the concerned authority. Each arbitrator shall have the right to direct questions and examine the parties or witnesses through the Chairman of the arbitration panel.

Article (24):
The parties may request the arbitration panel at any stage of the claim to record their agreement in the minutes of the hearing as related to admission, conciliation, waiver or otherwise, and the arbitration panel shall make an award of the same.

Article (25):
The Arabic language shall be the official language to be used before the arbitration panel, whether in the discussion or in writing. The arbitration panel and the parties may not speak other than the Arabic Language and any party who does not speak Arabic shall be accompanied by an accredited translator who shall sign with him the minutes of the hearing, approving the statements made.

Article (26):
Any party may request adjournment of the proceeding for a reasonable period, that period to be decided by the arbitration panel, so that such a party can submit any documents, papers, or remarks which may be productive or have a material effect on the case. The arbitration panel may allow further adjournments if there is justification therefore.

Article (27):

The arbitration panel shall record the facts and proceeding which take place in the hearing. in minutes written by the secretary of the arbitration panel under its supervision. The minutes shall contain the date and place of the hearing, names of arbitrators, the secretary and the parties. It shall also contain statements of the respective parties, the minutes shall be signed by the Chairman of the arbitration panel, arbitrations, and the secretary.

Article (28):
The arbitration panel may, by its own motion, or pursuant to a request from one of the parties, require the other party to produce any document which he may possess and which may have material effect on the proceedings, in the following cases:

If such document is a joint document between the parties. Such document will be deemed joint if in particular, it is in favor of both parties or if it proves their mutual rights and obligations.

If one of the parties invoked such document in any phase of the claim.
If the Regulations permit demand for delivery or release of such a document.

The application must state the following:

Description of the document requested.
Contents of the document, with as much details as possible.

The fact in issue for which such document is called.

The evidence and circumstances proving that the document is under possession of the other party.

The reason for obligating the other party to present the said document.

Article (29):
The arbitration panel may designate the effective means of inquiry in the claim whenever the facts to be proven are proximate to the dispute and are admissible.

Article (30):
The arbitration panel may disregard the evidentiary procedure it has ordered, provided that reasons for such disregard shall be stated in the minutes of the hearing. The arbitration panel may not consider the result of such procedures and shall state its reasons in the award.

Article (31):
They party requesting testimony of witnesses shall specify the facts to be proved in the testimony either orally or in writing, and shall accompany his witness in the specified hearing. Admission of witnesses and hearing of their statements shall be conducted before the arbitration panel pursuant to Shariah rules, and the other party may refute such testimony in the same manner.

Article (32):
The arbitration panel may cross-examine the parties at the request of either party or on its own motion.

Article (33):
The arbitration panel may, if necessary, seek the assistance of one or more experts to provide technical report regarding a technical or material matter which may have effect on the claim. The arbitration panel shall mention in its award an accurate statement of the experts' mission and the urgent arrangements which he is permitted to take.

The arbitration panel shall estimate the fees of the said expert, the party who shall pay them, and the deposit is not made by the party required to do so or by the other parties to the arbitration, the expect will not be bound to perform his duty, and the right to adhere to the decision made for the appointment of the expert shall be void, if the arbitration panel finds that the reasons given are unacceptable. In performing his duty, the expert may hear the statements of both parties or others and shall submit a report of his opinion on the specified date.

The arbitration panel may cross-examine the expert in the hearing concerning the result of his report. If there is more than one expert, the panel shall specify the manner of their performance whether severally or collectively.

Article (34):
The arbitration panel may request the expert to provide a complementary report to overcome any default or omissions in his previous report and the parties may submit advisory reports to the panel. However, in all cases the arbitration panel shall not be bound by the expert's opinions.

Article (35):
The arbitration panel may, on its own motion or at the request of either party, decide to move for inspection of some facts or matters which were disputed and have material effect on the claim and shall make make a report of the inspection proceedings.

Article (36):
The arbitration panel shall observe the principles of litigation, so as to include confrontation in proceedings, and to permit either party to take cognizance of the claim proceedings, to have access to its material papers and documents in reasonable periods of time, and to give him a sufficient opportunity to present his documentation, defenses and arguments in the hearing, either orally or in writing, and to record them in the minutes.

Article (37):
If a preliminary issue of a matter falling outside the jurisdiction of the arbitration panel arose during the process of arbitration, or if a document had been claimed to have been forged or if criminal proceedings had been instituted for the forgery or for any other criminal act, the arbitration panel shall suspend proceedings and the date fixed for the award until a final decision is issued from the concerned authority in relation to that matter which had arisen.

CHAPTER FOUR

AWARDS, OBJECTIONS, AND EXECUTION

Article (38):
When the arbitration panel is ready to render a decision the panel shall close the case for review and deliberations. Deliberations shall be held in camera and shall only be attended collectively by the arbitration panel who attended the hearings. The panel shall fix, at the time the case is closed or in another hearing, a date for issuance of the award subject to the provisions of articles (9), (13), (14), and (15) of the arbitration regulations.

Article (39):
The arbitrators shall issue their awards without being bound by legal procedures except as provided for in the arbitration regulations and its rules of implementation. Awards shall follow the provisions of Islamic Shariah and the applicable regulations.

Article (40):

When the case is closed for review and deliberation, the arbitration panel may not hear further submissions from either of the parties or their representative except in the presence of the other party, and shall not accept any memoranda or document without the document being reviewed by the other party; if such explanation, memoranda or document is deemed material, the panel may extend the date fixed for the award and reopen the proceedings by virtue of a decision stating the reasons and justifications therefore, and shall notify the parties of the date fixed for continuation of the proceedings.

Article (41):
Subject to articles 16 and 17 of the arbitration regulations, awards shall be adopted by the opinion of the majority of the arbitrators. The award shall be pronounced by the Chairman of the arbitration panel in the specified hearing. The award shall contain the names of the members of the respective panel, the date, place, and subject matter of the award, first names, surnames, description, domicile, appearance and absence of the parties, a summary of the facts of the claim, requests of the parties, summary of their defenses, substantial defenses, and the reasons and text of the award. The arbitrators and the clerk shall, within seven days form the filing of the draft, sign the original copy of the award which comprises the above contents and which Shall kept in the file of the claim.

Article (42):
Without prejudice to provisions of articles 18 and 19 of the arbitration regulations, the arbitration panel shall certify any material typing or arithmetical errors that may occur in its awards, by virtue of a decision to be issued on its own motion, or at the request of either party without pleading procedures. Such ratification shall be made on the original copy of the award and duly signed by the arbitrators. The decision for rectification of the award may be objected to by all possible means of objection if the arbitration panel exceeded its right of rectification as provided for in this section. The decision issued against a request for rectification may not be object of to independently.

Article (43):
The parties my request the arbitration panel which has issued the award to interpret any ambiguity in the text of the award. The interpretaion shall be deemed complementary in all respects to the original award and shall be subject as well as the rules relating to means of objection.

Article (44):
Whenever an order is issued for execution of the arbitration award, the latter becomes an executionary instrument and the clerk of the authority originally competent to try the case shall give the winning party the execution copy of the arbitration award, containing the order for execution and ending with the following phrase:

"All concerned government authorities and departments shall cause this award to be executed with all legally applicable means if such execution required application of force by the police."

FEES OF ARBITRATORS

Article (45):
If both opponents fail to agree on the fees, a decision may be issued for division of fees between them at the discretion of the authority originally competent to try the case; a decision also may be issued for payment of all such fees by one of the parties in dispute.

Article (46):

For additional analytical, business and investment opportunities information, please contact Global Investment & Business Center, USA at (202) 546-2103. Fax: (202) 546-3275. E-mail: ibpusa3@gmail.com Global Business and Legal Information Databank: www.ibpus.com

Any party may object to the estimate of the arbitrators' fees to the authority which issued the decision, the objection to be made within eight days from notification of the fees; the authority's decision on the said objection shall be final.

Article (47):
The concerned authorities shall execute these rules.

Article (48):
These rules shall be published in the Official Gazette and shall be effective from their date of publication.
The rules were published in the Official Gazette on 10-10-1405 corresponding to 28th June 1985.

SELECTED FORMS AND APPLICATIONS
APPENDIX VIII THE EXPORT INFORMATION SHEET
EIS FORM

The Royal Embassy of Saudi Arabia
Commercial Office, Washington DC
EXPORT INFORMATION SHEET (E.I.S.)

Please fill in the following information (type only, all information is required):

1. Exporter:	E.I.N.		Date	
Name				
Address			Phone	
City			State	Zip
Contact Person			Position	

2. Manufacturer/Producer (if different from above): ☐ Non-US

Name		
Address		
City	State	Zip

3. Saudi Importer: ☐ Agent ☐ Distributor ☐ Jt. Venture

Name	
Address	
City	Zip

4. Forwarding Agent: ☐ Bill of lading ☐ Airway Bill Number:

Name	
Phone	Shipment Date (mm-dd-yyyy)
Loading Port	Destination Port

5. Goods and Materials Exported:

HTS Code (10 digits)	Commodity Description	Qty	Unit Price	Total Price
	Subtotal From Additional Pages(s)			
	Total Invoice Value of Shipment (U.S. Dollars)			

Prepared by (Print Name): _____ Phone: _____

I certify that the information contained herein is complete, accurate

and true to the best of my knowledge. Signature: _____

For Official Use Only	EIS From 1048-595,
U.S. Saudi Arabian Business Council_____	Receipt Number _____
Saudi Arabian Consulate in _____	Serial Number _____

KINGDOM OF SAUDI ARABIA MINISTRY OF COMMERCE INTERNAL COMMERCE CONTROL CONTRACT OF AGENCY OR DISTRIBUTORSHIP

On this day _____/____/ 14 ____(H), corresponding to _____/_____/20___

this agreement has been made by and between:

(1) _____, whose business address is

in_____ C.R. No. _____dated _____, city of : _____

represented herein by _____, (hereinafter referred to as the *"First Party/Principal");*

(2)The Agent/Distributor _____, whose business address is

in_____, C.R. No. _____

dated _____ city of:_____

represented by _____

(hereinafter referred to as the *Second Party/Agent").*

RECITALS

WHEREAS, both parties desire to enter into an agency of distributorship arrangement to serve their mutual interests and to specify the rights and obligations of each party in such arrangement; and

WHEREAS, the Second Party (Saudi) desires that such relationshjp conform to the requirements of regulations with regard to foreign trade (import and export), specifically the Commercial Agencies Regulations and Amendments thereof in the Kingdom of Saudi Arabia, which regulations require a direct relationship between the business agent or distributor of products and the originator company abroad. Non-saudis are prohibited from engaging in import and export business and commercial agencies in the Kingdom of Saudi Arabia.

Both parties hereby agree as follows:

Article (1) The above recitals shall be considered an integral part of this contract.

Article (2) Both parties agree that the Second Party, as Agent or Distributor *("Agent")* for the First Party shall negotiate and conclude any agreements concerning the products or services subject to this distiburorship agreement on behalf of _____ and in the name of _____

Article (3) The scope of this agency contract covers the products and services provided by the First Party as hereunder specified.

_____

The Products included in this agency contract are:

_____

Article (4) The geographic area covered by this contract shall be _____(specify whether throughout the Kingdom or for a certain region.

Article (5) The term of this contract shall be _____ effective as from _____ renewable automatically for another period unless either party gives at least three months prior written notice of his intention to terminate the contract.

Reciprocal Obligations

Article (6) Because the Second Party is obligated to guarantee the quality of the products and materials which form the subject of this contract and to provide necessary maintenance and spare parts at reasonable prices when required by consumers, the First Party shall also be obligated to the Agent for the same obligations on such dates and shall provide such spare parts in such amount as may be specified by the Agent. In addition, the First Party shall provide to the Second Party at reasonable prices such spare parts and necessary maintenance through the date one year following the expiry date of this contract or from the time of appointing another agent.

Article (7) The Second Party is obligated under the law of importing country to provide under this Contract only products and materials that are compatible with the approved standard specifications in the importing country. The First Party shall guarantee the quality of these products and materials and ensure that they conform to approved standard specifications in the importing country; the Agent shall not be obligated to receive, or responsible for distribution of, any quantities received from the First Party that are contrary to such required standard specifications.

Article (8) Both parties shall execute this contract in accordance and acknowledged business practices and good faith. Such obligation shall extend to include all activities rendered as part of the contract requirements under generally accepted business practices.

Article (9) The Second Party shall undertake to:

(a) Provide the premises required for the Agent to run his business in the Kingdom with his own staff, exercise all reasonable care and diligence, and be entitled to make use of the services and technical expertise of the First Party as and when required.

(b) Perform all works necessary to execute contracts locally for promoting and marketing the products, make available the suitable storage areas, open new distribution centers as may be necessary and provide local services within the area covered by the Contract. The Second Party shall, in the performance of this Contract, be entitled to use the First Party's trademark but without any additions or modifications. He shall also exert his best efforts to make such trademark known throughout the area.

Article (10) The First Party shall undertake to :

(a) Pay the Second Party a commission in the amount of _____ of the value of the items sold within the Contract area even if the sales were made directly to a third party by the First Party. Schedule of Payments shall be as follows: _____

(b) Execute the Contract with diligence whether as to observation of good quality products and materials which form the subject of the Contract, or to insure safe and good delivery to the Second Party, or to fulfill obligations regarding quantities and dates specified in the Second Party's orders.

(c) Bear responsibility for the faults of himself and his employees, when such fault results in damage to the Second Party.

Expiry, Cancellation and Compensation

Article (11) This contract shall be terminated if performance by either party is rendered impossible, or, upon the death or the loss of competency, or bankruptcy of either party. This contract may also be terminated by revocation upon a substantial failure in execution by the other party.

Article (12) The Agent shall be entitled to compensation for damages which may arise out of the Principal's inability to meet his commitments, according to the Contract, or to business customs.

Article (13) If the Principal refuses to renew or continue work under this Contract, the terminated Agent shall be entitled to reasonable compensation for his activities that may have resulted in the apparent success in the business of the terminated Agent. Specifically, the terminated Agent shall be entitled to compensation for his promotional activities and efforts at client relations that result in goodwill that may accrue to the new Agent.

Article (14) The Principal may claim compensation from the Agent from damages caused as a result of the Agent's abandoning his Agency prior to the expiry of this contract or as a result of any breach of contract by the Agent.

For additional analytical, business and investment opportunities information,
please contact Global Investment & Business Center, USA
at (202) 546-2103. Fax: (202) 546-3275. E-mail: ibpusa3@gmail.com
Global Business and Legal Information Databank: www.ibpus.com

Article (15) Should this contract be improperly terminated or revoked, as a result of which either party sustains damages, the party improperly terminating the contract shall be obliged to compensate the other party for the damages such party sustained, taking into account the extent of efforts made and material and non-material capabilities provided to serve the Agency prior to such improper termination.

Concluding Articles

Article (16) Disputes arising between the parties hereto as a result of the performances under this Contract shall be settled amicably. Should this not be possible, the matter shall be referred to the Committee for Settlement of Commercial Disputes in the Kingdom of Saudi Arabia or to a local arbitration committee in accordance with the regulations for arbitration. In case of a dispute between the Principal and Agent, a new Agency Contract may be granted to a new Agent within the Agency area for the same products or services only after the authority considering the dispute shall have made a final award or decision.

Article (17) This Contract shall be governed by the provisions of regulations prevailing in the Kingdom of Saudi Arabia, specifically the Commercial Court Regulation, Commercial Agencies Regulations and amendments and implementing procedures thereof, and the Arbitration Regulations and the relevant implementing procedures.

Article (18) This Contract has been executed in three copies, with each party receiving one copy. The Second party shall present a certified copy to complete the Contract registration in the Commercial Agencies and Distributors Register with the Ministry of Commerce of the Kingdom of Saudi Arabia.

First Party (Principal)   Second Party (Agent)

Name: _____   Name: _____

Signature: _____   Signature: _____

For additional analytical, business and investment opportunities information, please contact Global Investment & Business Center, USA at (202) 546-2103. Fax: (202) 546-3275. E-mail: ibpusa3@gmail.com Global Business and Legal Information Databank: www.ibpus.com

BUSINESS TRAVEL

VISA REGULATIONS

All Americans seeking to visit the Kingdom must obtain entry visas from the nearest Saudi Arabian Royal Embassy or Consulate in the United States (see appendix II for addresses). **However, American citizens, upon the written recommendation of their embassy in the relevant country, can obtain entry visas to the Kingdom from any of the Saudi diplomatic missions all over the world (see appendix III for addresses).** An exit (or an exit and re-entry) visa is required for any person with a residence permit. Exit visas are issued by a Passport Department in the Kingdom on the request of the Saudi sponsor or employer.

Apart from the UMRAH or Hajj visa (a visit to Holy Makkah), the following three types of entry visa are issued by the Saudi Arabian Royal Embassy or Consulates in the U.S.:

A SHORT VISIT BUSINESS VISA

For a business visa, representatives of American corporations must contact Saudi Arabian companies to sponsor their visits to the Kingdom. An original letter of invitation, issued on the Saudi Arabian host company's letterhead, is required. The letter of invitation must include all passport details of the visiting representative. It must be signed and notarized by the general manager of the Saudi host company and be certified by the relevant local chamber of commerce and industry in the Kingdom. **The original letter of invitation can be sent to the visiting representative, or can be directly mailed or faxed to the relevant Saudi Arabian Royal Embassy or Consulate in the U.S.** Along with the letter of invitation, the following must be submitted:

(1) The white Visa Application Form (obtainable from any of the Royal Consulates General of Saudi Arabia in the U.S., see appendix II for address) filled out completely.

(2) A passport valid for at least six months from the date of submitting the Visa Application.

(3) One photograph.

(4) A letter from the U.S. company sponsoring the applicant.

(5) A money order for U.S. $54.00 made payable to the Royal Embassy or relevant Consulate General of Saudi Arabia in the U.S.

(6) A copy of the applicant's Resident Alien Card (i.e. Green Card), if applicable.

(7) A self-addressed stamped envelope with all mail applications.

An Employment Block Visa:

For additional analytical, business and investment opportunities information, please contact Global Investment & Business Center, USA at (202) 546-2103. Fax: (202) 546-3275. E-mail: ibpusa3@gmail.com Global Business and Legal Information Databank: www.ibpus.com

(1) The white Visa Application Form (obtainable from any of the Royal Consulates General of Saudi Arabia in the U.S., see appendix II for addresses) filled out completely.

(2) Two photographs.

(3) A passport valid for at least six months from the application's submittal date.

(4) A letter from the Saudi employer indicating the number and date of the applicant's employment block visa.

(5) A copy of the signed employment contract.

(6) a) A copy of the applicant's university degree and transcript, legalized by the Saudi Arabian Cultural Mission (see appendix II for address). or,

b) A copy of the applicant's technical, professional or academic diploma legalized by the Authentication Office of the U.S. Department of State (see appendix IX for address).

(7) A letter of release if applicant worked previously in the Kingdom.

(8) A money order for U.S. $267.00, made payable to the Royal Embassy or relevant Consulate General of Saudi Arabia in the U.S.

(9) A completed medical form (obtainable from the Royal embassy or any Consulates General of Saudi Arabia in the U.S.).

A FAMILY VISIT OR RESIDENT VISA:

Requirements for this type of visa and the UMRAH or HAJJ visas can be obtained from the Royal Embassy or Consulate general of Saudi Arabia near you.

CURRENCY

The **Saudi Riyal (SR)** is the unit of currency in the Kingdom of Saudi Arabia. It is divided into a hundred Halalah. The denominations of the Saudi currency are as follows:

Bills: 1, 5, 10, 50, 100, and 500 Riyals.
Coins: 5, 10, 25, 50, and 100 Halalahs.

Since July 1986, the Saudi Riyal has been pegged to the U.S. dollar with a fixed exchange rate of **SR3.75 to U.S. $1.00**.

SUPPLEMENTS

THE TOP 100 SAUDI COMPANIES

RANK 1995	Company	ASSETS	ACTIVITIES	LEGAL STATUS	TELEPHONE	FAX
1	Saudi Basic Industries Corp (SABIC)	41438	Industry	Joint stock	01-401-2033	401-2045
2	Dallah Al-baraka	36168	Diversified	Limited liability	02-671-0000	669-4680
3	Saudi Arabian Airlines (SAUDIA)	19837	Services	Government	02-686-0000	686-4552
4	Saudi Aramco Mobil Refinery Co.	5682	Industry	Limited liability	04-396-4000	396-0942
5	Arabian Oil Company	4723	Oil	Limited liability	03-76-0555	766-2385
6	Consolidated Contractors Int'l, Co., SAL	2859	Diversified	Limited liability	01-465-0311	464-5963
7	National Commercial Bank	69458	Banking	Partnership	02-644-6644	644-6644
8	Saudi American Bank	43605	Banking	Joint stock	01-477-4770 ext 200	
9	Riyadh Bank	53895	Banking	Joint stock	01-401-3030	404-2707
10	Saudi Consolidated Electric Co. (East)	27244	Services	Services	03-357-2300	858-6601
11	Alsuwaiket Trade & Contr Group	704	Diversified	Limited liability	03-357-9780	857-2904
12	Arab National Bank	30500	Banking	Joint stock	01-402-9000	402-7747
13	Saudi Consolidated Electric Co. (Central)	28438	Services	Joint stock	01-403-2222	405-3123
14	Saudi Consolidated Electric Co. (West)	16021	Services	Joint stock	02-651-1008	653-4139
15	Al-Rajhi Banking & Investment Corp.	28878	Banking	Joint stock	01-405-4244	403-2969
16	AlFaisalia Group	W	Diversified	Sole proprietor	02-643-6026	
17	Al Bank Al Saudi Al Fransi	24163	Banking	Joint stock	01-404-2222	404-2311
18	Saudi Cable Company	1568	Industry	Joint stock	02-669-4060	669-3935
19	A A Turki Group	W	Diversified	Sole	03-833-5588	833-9881

For additional analytical, business and investment opportunities information, please contact Global Investment & Business Center, USA at (202) 546-2103. Fax: (202) 546-3275. E-mail: ibpusa3@gmail.com
Global Business and Legal Information Databank: www.ibpus.com

	(ATCO)			proprietor		
20	Al Seif Group	W	Diversified	Limited liability	01-454-9191	454-2759
21	The Saudi British Bank	27109	Banking	Joint stock	01-405-0677	405-0660
22	Riyadh Cable	962	Industry	Limited partner	01-498-3947	498-1428
23	Jeraisy Group of Establishments	1512	Diversified	Sole proprietor	01-462-4000	462-5171
24	National Shipping Co. Saudi Arabia	3066	Services	Joint stock	01-478-5454	477-8036
25	Suleiman A. AlRajhi & Sons Co.	2017	Diversified	Joint liability	06-391-1555	391-1403
26	Saudi Hollandi Bank	14984	Banking	Joint stock	01-406-7888	403-1104
27	Savola	1819	Industry	Joint stock	02-647-7333	648-4119
28	Jamjoom Corp for Commerce & Industry	549	Diversified	Holding	02-647-7333	648-4119
29	Aggad Investment Group	698	Diversified	Limited partnership	01-476-7911	476-7895
30	Alhamrani & Alsuleiman United Co.	1131	Trading	Partnership	02-669-6690	660-0927
31	Almarai	W	Agribusiness	Limited liability	01-462-0088	462-4418
32	Saudi Cement Co.	2306	Industry	Joint stock	03-834-4500	834-5460
33	Saudi Cairo Bank	18096	Banking	Joint stock	02-660-8820	661-3044
34	Mahmood Saeed Collective Co.	1218	Diversified	Partnership	02-636-0020	637-9093
35	Al Bayan Group Holding Co., Ltd.	460	Diversified	Limited liability	01-477-2440	476-5777
36	National Co. for Cooperative Insurance	800	Services	Joint stock	01-482-6969	488-1719
37	Al-Subei for Money Exchange & Trade	1500	Trading and finance	Partnership	02-672-2288	672-5924
38	United Saudi Commercial Bank	10378	Banking	Joint stock	01-478-4200	478-3197
39	Arab Supply & Trading Corp (ASTRA)	1195	Diversified	Sole proprietor	04-422-0400	428-1584
40	Isam Khairi Kabbani Group	403	Diversified	Limited partners	02-667-2000	665-8079

For additional analytical, business and investment opportunities information, please contact Global Investment & Business Center, USA at (202) 546-2103. Fax: (202) 546-3275. E-mail: ibpusa3@gmail.com Global Business and Legal Information Databank: www.ibpus.com

41	Saudi Research & Marketing Group	90	Holding	Limited liability	01-441-0101	441-9569
42	Alhamrani Group of Companies	800	Diversified	Partnership	02-682-7777	683-6085
43	Saudi Catering & Contracting	893	Diversified	Sole proprietor	01-477-3713	478-0267
44	Yamama Saudi Cement Co.	1666	Industry	Joint stock	01-405-8288	403-3292
45	Saddik & Muhammad Attar Co.	89	Trading & services	Partnership	02-648-0033	647-0826
46	Eastern Province Cement Co.	1197	Industry	Joint stock	03-827-3330	827-1923
47	Haji Hussein Alireza & Co., Ltd.	W	Trading	Limited liability	02-642-3509	642-6435
48	Alpha Trading & Shipping Agencies, Ltd.	W	Trading	Limited liability	02-647-4242	647-9191
49	Ali Zaid al Quraishi & Bros.	242	Diversified	Partnership	02-697-1036	697-2938
50	Mohamad Al Mojil Group	1065	Sole proprietor-ship	Partnership	03-842-1111	842-5612
51	Petromin Lubricating Oil Company	650	Industry	Joint stock	02-661-3333	661-3322
52	Southern Province Cement Co.	668	Industry	Joint stock	07-227-1500	227-1407
53	Trading & Industrial Group Ltd.	600	Diversified	Holding	02-653-1680	651-9168
54	Belieli Saudi Heavy Industries	270	Industry	Limited liability	03-341-9304	341-0463
55	Rolaco	270	Diversified	Limited liability	02-651-8028	653-4280
56	Bin Zehefa Est.	352	Diversified	Sole proprietor	07-223-5523	222-0613
57	Taher Group	W	Holding	Limited liability	02-653-1975	653-1912
58	National Titanium Dioxide Co., Ltd. (CRISTAL)	856	Industry	Limited liability	02-651-9883	651-8757
59	National Pipe Co., Ltd.	495	Industry	Limited liability	03-857-7150	857-0963
60	SAPTICO	1469	Services	Joint stock	01-454-5000	454-1200
61	National Gas and Industrialization Co.	1081	Industry	Joint stock	01-401-4806	401-4088

62	Aluminum Products Co., Ltd. (ALUPCO)	373	Industry	Limited liability	03-857-0184	857-8311
63	Al Tayyar Travel Group	94	Services	Sole proprietor	01-463-3133	465-6049
64	Abdullah A.M. Al Khodari Sons	130	Diversified	Limited partnership	03-895-2840	898-6855
65	A.W. Aujan and Bros.	275	Trading & industry	Partnership	03-857-0777	857-7923
66	National Agricultural Development (NADEC)	1474	Agri-business	Joint stock		405-5522
67	The Saudi Investment Bank	6598	Banking	Joint stock	01-477-8433	477-1374
68	Abdullah Mohd. Bahlas Est.	W	Trading & industry	Sole proprietor	02-665-4996	667-4652
69	Abdulrahman Algosaibi G.T.B.	948	Trading	Sole proprietor	01-479-3000	477-1374
70	Abdul Ghani El-Ajou Group	880	Trading & industry	Group	01-404-1717	405-9052
71	Yanbu Cement Co.	1377	Industry	Joint stock	02-653-4584	653-1420
72	Alshamrany Industrial Group	185	Diversified	Partnership	03-843-1109	843-4430
73	Arabic Computer Systems, ltd.	70	Trading	Limited liability	01-476-3777	476-3196
74	Al Azizia Panda United Inc.	135	Trading	Joint stock	01-464-4992	463-3348
75	Arabian Cement Company, Ltd.	82	Industry	Joint stock	02-682-8270	682-9989
76	National Factory for Air Conditioners Co. WLL	W	Industry	Limited partnership	01-498-3730	498-5715
77	Tihama for Ad. Public Relations & Marketing	141	Services	Joint stock	02-644-4444	651-2228
78	Al Babtain Group	457	Diversified	Limited liability	01-241-1222	241-0228
79	Hoshanco	312	Diversified	Sole proprietor	01-476-6800	
80	Saudi Tourist & Travel Bureau, Ltd.	95	Services	Limited liability	02-644-3005	643-5811
81	SPIMACO	1606	Industry	Joint stock	01-477-4481	477-3961
82	Saudi Consolidated Electric Co. (South)	10844	Services	Joint stock	07-227-1111	227-1627

For additional analytical, business and investment opportunities information, please contact Global Investment & Business Center, USA at (202) 546-2103. Fax: (202) 546-3275. E-mail: ibpusa3@gmail.com Global Business and Legal Information Databank: www.ibpus.com

83	Al Huseini & Al Yahya Trading Co.	127	Trading	Limited liability	02-647-8888	648-6666
84	Sumama Co.	215	Diversified	Limited liability	01-463-4005	463-1651
85	Arabian Agricultural Services Co. (ARASCO)	117	Diversified	Limited liability	01-465-2551	464-5375
86	M.S. Suwaidi Est. for Contracting	W	Diversified	Sole proprietor	03-667-0304	667-1270
87	ABB Electrical Industries Co., Ltd.	310	Industry	Limited liability	01-498-0088	498-5487
88	Hussein Al Ali Est.	W	Diversified	Sole proprietor	03-586-6023	586-2044
89	Saudi Fisheries Company	286	Agri-business	Joint stock	03-857-3979	857-2493
90	Carrier Saudi Arabia	108	Diversified	Limited liability	01-491-1333	
91	Arabian Gulf Oil Co., Ltd.	131	Industry	Limited liability	02-691-6240	691-5731
92	Arabian Gulf Oil Co., Ltd. For Plastic Industries	396	Industry	Limited liability	02-680-1416	687-3275
93	Al Ruwaite Contracting Est.	269	Contracting	Sole proprietor	01-464-7847	465-5801
94	Muhammad Assad Aldrees & Sons Co.	400	Diversified	Partnership	01-476-3875	476-3875
95	Golden Grass Inc.	80	Diversified	Limited liability	01-478-3024	478-4630
96	Hail Agriculture Development Co.	702	Agri-usiness	Joint stock	06-533-1130	533-4937
97	Arabian Auto Agency	363	Trading	Limited liability	02-699-5595	669-2359
98	Saudi Gold Co.	W	Industry	Limited liability	01-498-0416	498-1272
99	Al Jazira Bank	3965	Banking	Joint stock	02-651-8070	653-2478
100	Arabian Drilling Co.	204	Services	Limited liability	03-857-6060	857-711

LARGEST LAW FIRMS

- **Abbas F. Ghazzawi Law Firm**, 94 Mohammed Al Taweel Street Mushrefah District, P.O. Box 2335, Jeddah, 21451, Saudi Arabia, Tel: (966)26654646, Fax: (966)26659155, Contact: H.E. Abbas Faiq Ghazzawi

- **Abdul Rahman Zahrani Law Office**, King Faysal Foundation Bldg., P.O. Box 55409, Riyadh, 11534, Saudi Arabia, Tel:(966)1-4627808, Fax:(966)1-4629519, Contact: Abdul Rahman Zahrani

- **Abdulaziz A. Al-Mohaimeed Law Firm**, Suite 601-607 Yamama Cement Co. Bldg. Al-Batha Street, P.O. Box 16545, Riyadh, 11474, Saudi Arabia, Tel:(966)1-4053274, Fax:(966)1-4029549, Contact: Abdulaziz Abdulrahman Al-Mohaimeed

- **Abdulnasir Al-Sohaibani Law Office**, P.O. Box 26525, Jeddah, 11496, Saudi Arabia, Tel: (966)24778552, Fax: (966)24771579, Contact: Abdulnasir Al-Sohaibani

- **Al Hasan & Al Akeel**, Suite 423, 4th Floor, AL Akaria Shopping Center, P.O. Box 8650, Riyadh, 11492, Saudi Arabia, Tel:(966)1-4634156, Fax:(966)1-4634160, Contact: Dr. Abdulatif Al Hasan

- **Al Tayar Consultants**, P.O. Box 51376, Jeddah, 21543, Saudi Arabia, Tel: (966)26516160, Fax: (966)26510226, Contact: Dr. Saleh Baker Al Tayar

- **Dr. Audhali Law Firm**, P.O. Box 1158, Al-Khobar, 31952, Saudi Arabia, Tel:(966)3-8643011, Fax:(966)3-8945837, Contact: Dr. Ahemed A. Audhali

- **Kadasah Law Firm**, P.O. Box 20883, Riyadh, 11465, Saudi Arabia, Tel:(966)1-4651371, Fax:(966)1-464-3789, Contact: Nassir A. Kadasah

- **Law Firm of Salah Al-Hejailan**, PO Box 1454, Al Dahna Centre, Al Ahsaa Street, Riyadh, 11431, Saudi Arabia, Tel:(966)1-4792200, Fax:(966)1-4791717, Contact: Salah AL-Hejailan

- **Law Office of Hassan Mahassni**, The Saudi Ceramic Company Building, 5th Fl, King Fahd Highway, Riyadh, 17411, Saudi Arabia, Tel: (966)14644006, Fax:(966)14651348, Contact: Hassan M.S. Mahassni

- **Law Offices of Abdulaziz H. Fahad**, P.O. Box 16206, Jeddah, 21464, Saudi Arabia, Tel:(966)2-6442663, Fax:(966)2-6435401, Contact: Abdulaziz H. Fahad

- **Law Offices of Ahmed Zaki Yamani**, PO Box 7159, Riyadh, 11462, Saudi Arabia, Tel:(966)1-4641115, Fax:(966)1-4648718, Contact: Joseph Parenteau

- **Law Offices of Dr Mujahid M Al-Sawwaf**, PO Box 5840, Jeddah, 21432, Saudi Arabia, Tel:(966)2-6690751, Fax:(966)2-6655052, Contact: Dr. Mujahid M. Al-Sawwa

- **Law Offices of Dr. Mohamed H. Hoshan**, Olaya Building, Olaya Road, P.O. Box 2626, Riyadh, 11461, Saudi Arabia, Tel:(966)1-4648353, Fax:(966)1-4632083, Contact: Dr. Mohamed H. Hoshan

- **Law Offices of Dr.A. Yehia Dennaoui**, P.O. Box 4386, Jeddah, 21491, Saudi Arabia, Tel:(966)2-6429344, Fax:(966)2-6446274, Contact: Dr. A. Yehia Dennaoui

- **Law Offices of Hassan Mahassni**, Al Hada Building, 5th Floor, 2013 Wali Al-Ahd Street. PO Box 2256, Jeddah, 21451, Saudi Arabia, Tel:(966)2-6513535, Fax:(966)2-6513636, Contact: Hassan Mahassni

- **Law Offices of His Royal Highness Prince Saad Al Faisal Bin Abdul Aziz**, Abalkhail Bldg, 8th Floor, Prince Fahad Street, P.O. Box 15836, Jeddah, 21454, Saudi Arabia, Tel:(966)2-6519373, Fax:(966)2-6519465, Contact: G. Cope Stewart III

- **Law Offices of Mohammed A.H. Touban**, Olaya Thamanin Street, P.O. Box 7606, Riyadh, 11472, Saudi Arabia, Tel:(966)1-4651460, Fax:(966)1-4632238, Contact: Mohamed A.H. Touban

- **Law Offices of Prince Saad Al Faisal BinAbdulAziz**, Abalkhail Building, 8th Floor, Prince Fahad Street, PO Box 15836, Jeddah, 21454, Saudi Arabia, Tel:(966)2-6519373, Fax:(966)2-6519465, Contact: G. Cope Stewart, III

- **Law Offices of Saud M.A. Shawwaf**, P.O. Box 2700, Riyadh, 11461, Saudi Arabia, Tel:(966)1-4656543, Fax:(966)1-4648480, Contact: Saud M.A. Shawwaf

- **Law Offices of Saudi Consulting Center**, Al-Ghamdi Building, King Abdul Aziz Road At Al-Sharkiya Street, Mursalact District, P.O. Box 57270, Riyadh, 11574, Saudi Arabia, Tel:(966)1-4560481, Fax:(966)1-4545209, Contact: Dr. Eid M. Al-Jhani

- **Legal Advisors**, King Faisal Foundation Building, King Fahad Road, PO Box 4288, Riyadh, 11491, Saudi Arabia, Tel:(966)1-4629886, Fax:(966)1-4632657, Contact: John E. Xefos

- **Legal Advisors Torki A. Al-Shubaiki**, King Faisal Foundation Building, King Fahad Road, Jeddah, 11491, Saudi Arabia, Tel: (966)24629886, Fax: (966)24632657, Contact: John E. Xefos

- **Nader Law & Translation Offices**, 19 Abo Zinadah Street, P.O. Box 3595, Jeddah, 21481, Saudi Arabia, Tel: (966)26652067, Fax: (966)26608709, Contact: Dr. Mohamed M. Jaber Nader

- **Saudi-American Legal Consultants**, Commercial Building #2, Diplomatic Quarter, P.O. Box 57270, Riyadh, 11574, Saudi Arabia, Tel: (966)14881563, Fax: (966)14880542, Contact: Stephen P. Matthews

- **The International Law Firm**, Sulaymaniyah Center, Tahlia Street, Riyadh, 11495, Saudi Arabia, Tel: (966)14628866, Fax: (966)14629001, Contact: Osama Mohammed

- **The Law Firm of Dr. Khalid Alnowaiser**, El-Khayyat Center, Tahlia Street, Entrance No.2 2nd Floor, Suite No. 211, Jeddah, 21523, Saudi Arabia, Tel: (966)26676375, Fax: (966)26611352, Contact: Khalid Abdulaziz Alnowaiser

- **Wohabe Law Offices**, Hweiriny Building Al-Ahsa Street, P.O. Box 15512, Riyadh, 11454, Saudi Arabia, Tel:(966)1-4776962, Fax:(966)1-4787506, Contact: Dr. Abdul Wahab Wohabe

GOVERNMENT AND BUSINESS CONTACTS

SAUDI CHAMBERS OF COMMERCE AND INDUSTRY IN SAUDI ARABIA

Council of Saudi Chambers of Commerce & Industry Riyadh Chamber of Commerce and Industry Building P.O.Box 16683, Riyadh 11474 Tel. (1)405-3200/405-7502 Fax: (1)402-4747	Abha Chamber of Commerce and Industry P.O.Box 72 ABHA Tel: (7)227-1818 Fax: (7)227-1919
AlAhsa Chamber of Commerce and Industry P.O.Box 1519 Al-Ahsa 31932 Tel: (3)582-0458 Fax: (3)587-5274	Albaha Chamber of Commerce and Industry P.O.Box 311 Albaha Tel: (7)725-4116 Fax: (7)725-0042

Arar Chamber of Commerce and Industry P.O.Box 440 ARAR Tel: (4)662-6544 Fax: (4)662-4581	Bishah Chamber of Commerce and Industry (Branch) P.O.Box 491, Bishah Tel: (7)622-5544/622-5524 Fax: (7)622-1511
Dammam Chamber of Commerce and Industry P.O.Box 719 Dammam 31421 Tel: (3)857-1111 Fax: (3)857-0607	Hafr Albaten Chamber of Commerce and Industry (Branch) P.O. Box 984 Hafr Albaten 31421 Tel: (3)722-0986 Fax: (3)722-0976
Hail Chamber of Commerce and Industry (Branch) P.O.Box 1292 Hail Tel: (6)532-1060/532-1064 Fax: (6)532-4644	Al-Jawf Chamber of Commerce and Industry P.O.Box 585 Sakaka, Al Jawf Tel: (4)624-9488/624-9060 Fax: (4)624-0108
Jeddah Chamber of Commerce and Industry King Khalid St., Ghurfa Bldg. P.O.Box 9549 Jeddah 21423 Tel: (2)642-3535/647-1100 Fax: (2)651-7373	Jizan Chamber of Commerce and Industry P.O.Box 201, Jizan Tel: (7)317-1519
Al-Majma`ah Chamber of Commerce and Industry P.O.Box 165 Al-Majma`ah 11952 Tel: (6)432-1571;432-0268 Fax: (6)432-2655	Makkah Chamber of Commerce and Industry Al Ghazzah St. P.O.Box 1086 Makkah Tel: (2)574-4020/574-5773 Fax: (2)574-1200
Medina Chamber of Commerce and Industry P.O.Box 443 Airport Rd., Medina Tel: (4)822-1590/822-5380	Najran Chamber of Commerce and Industry P.O.Box 1138, Najran Tel: (7)522-3738 Fax: (7)522-3926
Qaseem Chamber of Commerce and Industry On Intersection Al Wehdah St. and Alamarah St. P.O.Box 444, Buraidah, Qaseem Tel: (6)323-6104;323-5436 Fax: (6)324-7542	Riyadh Chamber of Commerce and Industry Dhabab St. P.O.Box 596 Riyadh 11421 Tel: (1)404-0044/404-0300/404-2700 Fax: (1)401-1103

Tabuk Chamber of Commerce and Industry P.O.Box 567 Tabuk Tel: (4)422-2736/422-0464 Fax: (4)422-7378	Taif Chamber of Commerce and Industry Al Saddad St. (Wadi Widj) P.O.Box 1005 Taif Tel: (2)736-4624;736-3025 Fax: (2)738-0040

SAUDI ARABIA MINISTRIES

MINISTRY	FUNCTIONS
Ministry of Agriculture Airport Road, Riyadh 11195 Tel: 401-6666 Fax: 403-1415	Implementation of economic plans and programs for agriculture. Water development. Desalination, irrigation, conservation of scarce water, fisheries, animal resources and locust control.
Ministry of Commerce P.O.Box 1774 Airport Rd., Riyadh 11162 Tel: 401-2220/401-4708 Fax: 403-8421	Foodstuff quality control, consumer protection, companies and commercial agents' registration, labeling regulation standards, international exhibits, hotels, bilateral trade agreements, and world trade organization.
Ministry of Communication & Transportation Airport Rd., Riyadh 11178 Tel: 404-2928/404-3000 Fax: 403-1401	Design, building and maintenance of road network. Coordination of surface transport including railroads and bus systems.
Ministry of Defense and Aviation Minister: H. R. H. Prince Sultan Bin Abdul Aziz Al-Saud Airport Rd., Riyadh 11165 Tel: 478-5900/477-7313 Fax: 401-1336 Economic Offset Secretariat Ministry of Defense and Aviation P.O.Box 27040, Riyadh 11417 Tel: 478-4145 Fax: 478-4123	Army, Navy, Air Force, construction of military bases, civilian airports and meteorology.
Ministry of Education Airport Rd., Riyadh 11148 Tel: 404-2888/404-2952 Fax: 401-2365	Provision of free general education in primary, intermediate and secondary schools. Royal Technical Institute programs for handicapped, antiquities and museums.

Ministry of Finance and National Economy Airport Rd., Riyadh 11177 Tel: 405-0000/405-0080 Fax: 405-9202	Government finance, including budgeting and expenditure of all ministries and agencies. Control of national economic growth. Zakat and income tax. Customs, Central Department of Statistics and National Computer Center.
Ministry of Foreign Affairs Minister: H. R. H. Prince Saud Al-Faisal Bin Abdul Aziz Al-Saud Nasseriya St., Riyadh 11124 Tel: 406-7777/441-6836 Fax: 403-0159	Political, cultural, and financial international relations. Monitors diplomatic relations between the Kingdom of Saudi Arabia and the outside world.
Ministry of Health Airport Rd., Riyadh 11176 Tel: 401-2220/401-2392 Fax: 402-9876	Health care and hospitals.
Ministry of Higher Education King Faisal Hospital St., Riyadh 11153 Tel: 464-4444 Fax: 441-9004	Universities and higher learning institutes.
Ministry of Industry and Electricity P.O.Box 5729 Omar bin al-Khatab Rd. North of Railway Station, Riyadh 11127 Tel: 477-2722/477-6666 Fax: 477-5451	Development of the Kingdom's industrial infrastructure and power projects. Foreign capital investment, industrial licensing, protection and encouragement of national industry, industrial statistics, industrial cities and SABIC.
Ministry of Information Nassiriya St., Riyadh 11161 Tel: 401-4440/401-3440 Fax: 402-3570	Television and radio broadcasts, publication of newspapers, magazines and relations with foreign press.
Ministry of Interior Minister: H.R.H. Prince Nayef Bin Abdul Aziz Al Saud P.O.Box 2993, Riyadh 11134 Tel: 401-1944 Fax: 403-1185 Directorate General of Passports	Public security, coastal guards, civil defense, fire stations, border police, special security and investigation forces, criminal investigation and traffic control.

Ministry of Islamic, Endowments Call(Dawa) and Guidance Affairs King Abdul Aziz St., Riyadh 11232 Tel: 473-0401 Fax: 477-2938	Administration of land controlled by religious trust.
Ministry of Justice University St., Riyadh 11137 Tel: 405-7777/405-5399	Administration of Sharia's Law and provision of legal services for all citizens of the Kingdom.
Ministry of Labor and Social Affairs Omar bin Al-Khattab St., Riyadh 11157 Tel: 477-1480/478-7166 Fax: 477-7336	Labor relations, manpower planning and general monitoring of employment situation. Labor permits and work visas, labor disputes, inspection, health and safety. Provisions of vocational and on-job training for handicapped. Social development and reform. Presidency for Youth and Welfare, Saudi Red Crescent Society and Social Security.
Ministry of Municipalities and Rural Affairs Nassiriya St., Riyadh 11136 Tel: 441-5434	Administration of municipalities throughout the Kingdom. Planning of cities and towns. Development of roads and basic infrastructure. Managing and maintaining services to keep cities and towns clean and healthy.
Ministry of Petroleum and Mineral Resources P.O.Box 757, Airport Rd., Riyadh 11189 Tel: 478-1661/478-1133 Fax: 479-3596	Administration and development of the Kingdom's oil, gas, oil refineries and mineral resources in conjunction with the General Petroleum and Mineral Organization (Petromin).
Ministry of Pilgrimage Omar bin Al-Khatib St., Riyadh 11183 Tel: 402-2200/402-2212 Fax: 402-2555	Provision of facilities for the annual visit of pilgrims to Makkah. Madinah and other Holy places in the Kingdom. Administration of land controlled by religious trust.
Ministry of Planning P.O.Box 1358 University St., Riyadh 11183 Tel: 402-3562/401-3333	National Planning.
Ministry of Post, Telegraph and Telephone Intercontinental Rd., Riyadh 11112 Tel: 463-7225 Fax: 405-2310	Development and maintenance of telecommunications and postal services.

Ministry of Public Works and Housing Washem St., Riyadh 11151 Tel: 402-2268/402-2036 Public Works Fax: 402-2723 Housing Fax: 406-7376	Supervision, construction and maintenance of Public Sector's projects. Public housing, evaluation of tenders, allocation of contracts and classification of contractors.

* Telephone codes for major cities in the Kingdom are: Riyadh(1) ;Jeddah, Makkah, Taif (2); Dammam, Dhahran, Jubail, Al-Ahsa (3) ; Yanbu, Tabul, Medina (4); Hail, Qaseem (6); and Abha and Najran (7). When calling Saudi Arabia from the U.S., dial 011 966 then city code, and finally the 7-digits phone number. Keep in mind time difference and official holidays (see page).

U.S. OFFICES AND GOVERNMENT AGENCIES RELATED TO DOING BUSINESS WITH THE KINGDOM OF SAUDI ARABIA

-U. S. Department of Commerce

Washington, DC 20230
Tel: (202)482-2000
Fax: (202)482-4576

Office of the Near East
14th and Constitution Ave., N.W.
Washington, DC 20230
Tel: (202)482-1860
Fax:(202)482-0878

-U. S. Trade Representative

600 17th St., NW, Room 201
Washington, DC 20508
Tel: (202)395-6890
Fax: (202)395-4549

-U.S. Department of Agriculture

5071 South Building, 14th and
Independence Ave., SW
Washington, DC 20205-1000
Tel: (202)720-3935
Fax: (202)690-2159

Office of the Near East, South Asia and Africa
5098 South Building, 14th and
Independence Ave., SW
Washington, DC 20205-1000
Tel: (202)720-7053
Fax: (202)720-6063

- Export Import Bank (EX-IM BANK)

811 Vermont Ave., NW
Washington, DC 20571
P:202-565-3946
F:202-565-3380

International Trade Commission

500 E St., SW
Washington, DC 20436
Tel: (202)205-2000
Fax: (202)205-2104

- U.S. DEPARTMENT OF STATE

Public Affairs Division
2201 C St., NW
Washington, DC 20520
Tel: (202)647-6575
Fax: (202)647-7120

Authentication Office U.S. Department of State

518 23rd St., N.W.
Washington, DC 20520
Tel: (202)647-5002
Fax: (202)663-3636

- U. S. DEPARTMENT OF TREASURY

1500 Pennsylvania Ave., NW
Washington, DC 20220
Tel: (202)622-1100
Fax: (202)622-0073

For additional analytical, business and investment opportunities information, please contact Global Investment & Business Center, USA at (202) 546-2103. Fax: (202) 546-3275. E-mail: ibpusa3@gmail.com Global Business and Legal Information Databank: www.ibpus.com

Biological Assessment Division U.S.D.A. APHIS
4700 River Rd., Unit 133
Riverdale, MD 20737
Tel: (301)734-8537
Fax: (301)734-5786

U.S.D.A. -APHIS,VS Veterinarian Services
2768 -A Riva Rd., Ste. 207
Annapolis, MD 21401
Tel: (301)962-7726
Fax: (301)261-8113

- Food and Drug Administration

Desk Officer, Africa and the Middle East
5600 Fishers Lane
Rockville, MD 20857
Tel: (301)827-4480
Fax: (301)443-0235

Fax: (202)622-0073

Deputy Assistant Secretary for Eurasia and the Middle East

1500 Pennsylvania Ave., NW, #3221
Washington, DC 20220
Tel: (202)622-0770
Fax: (202)622-0658

U. S. Department of Health and Human Services

200 Independence Ave., SW
Washington, DC 20201
Tel: (202)690-7000
Fax: (202)690-7203

ARAMCO

[P. O. Box 5000, Dhahran 31311; Tel: 966-3-875-6110; Fax: 873-8190]
SALES AND MARKETING OFFICES FOR CRUDE OIL AND PETROLEUM PRODUCTS

CRUDE OIL SALES AND MARKETING DEPARTMENT RM. 1-1072A

Name	Tilte	Work	Home
F.A.Al-Moosa, Fahad	Manager	Tel:873-8066 Fax:873-2173	Tel:891-0481 Fax:872-2000
	Secretary	874-1176	

SALES & MARKETING LOGISTICS DEPARTMENT, RM. T-1072B

Name	Title	Work	Home
M.S.Othman,Mohammad	Manager	Tel: 874-1985 Fax: 873-2173	Tel: 891-2556 Fax: 876-2556
	Secretary	874-1176	

PRODUCTS SALES & MARKETING DEPARTMENT, RM. T-1074A

Name	Title	Work	Home
R.D. Hansard, Bob	Manager(A)	Tel: 873-1867 Fax: 873-1926	Tel: 878-7338 Fax: 876-1431

| S.G.Clarke | Secretary | 873-1869 |

SALES & MARKETING : OVERSEAS OFFICES

Saudi Petroleum Overseas, Ltd.   Main Tel: 00 44 171 629 0800

Berkeley Square House   Main Fax: 00 44 171 409 0602

Berkeley Square, London W1X 5LE

Jon N. Deakin Managing Director   Direct Tel: 00 44 171 409 1162

Direct Fax: 00 44 171 409 0685

Saudi Petroleum International, Inc.   Main Tel: 001 212 832 4044

527 Madison Amenue, 22nd& 23rd Floor   Main Fax: 001 212 446 9200

New York, NY 10022

Thamer R. AL-Mushed President& CEO, SPII Tel: 001 212 735 0140

SAUDI COMMERCIAL BANKS OPERATING IN THE KINGDOM OF SAUDI ARABIA

The Arab National Bank
P.O.Box 56921, Riyadh 11564
Tel: 402-9000
Fax: 402-7747

Al-Bank Al-Saudi Al-Hollandi
P.O.Box 1467, Riyadh 11431
Tel: 406-7888/401-0288
Fax: 403-1104

Bank Al-jazira
P.O.Box 5859, Riyadh 11432
Tel: 403-6344/401-1636
Fax: 403-6344

Saudi British Bank
P.O.Box 9084, Riyadh 11413
Tel: 405-0677
Fax: 405-0660

Al-Bank Al-Saudi Al-Fransi
P.O.Box 56006, Riyadh 11554
Tel: 402-2222
Fax: 404-2311

United Saudi Commercial Bank
P.O.Box 25895, Riyadh 11476
Tel: 478-4200/478-8075
Fax: 478-3197

The National Commercial Bank
P.O.Box 3555, Jeddah
Tel: 644-6644
Fax 644-6644

Al-Rajhi Banking Investment Corporation
P.O.Box 28, Riyadh 11511
Tel: 405-4244
Fax: 405-2950

Saudi American Bank
P.O.Box 833, Riyadh 11421
Tel: 477-4770
Fax: 477-4770

Riyadh Bank
P.O.Box 229, Riyadh 11411
Tel: 401-4000/402-4011
Fax: 404-2705

For additional analytical, business and investment opportunities information,
please contact Global Investment & Business Center, USA
at (202) 546-2103. Fax: (202) 546-3275. E-mail: ibpusa3@gmail.com
Global Business and Legal Information Databank: www.ibpus.com

Saudi Cairo Bank
P.O.Box 42647, Riyadh 11551
Tel: 478-9345/476-0281
Fax: 479-1515

Saudi Investment Bank
P.O.Box 3533, Riyadh 11481
Tel: 477-8433
Fax: 477-6781

INTERNATIONAL ARAB/FOREIGN JOINT CHAMBERS OF COMMERCE

National U.S.-Arab Chamber of Commerce, Inc.

1100 New York Ave., N.W., Ste.550
Washington, D.C. 20005
Tel: (202)289-5920
Fax: (202)289-5938

National U.S.-Arab Chamber of Commerce

208 S. LaSalle St., Ste. 706
Chicago, IL 60604
Tel: (312)782-0320
Fax: (312)782-7379
*No certification of documents at this office.

National U.S.-Arab Chamber of Commerce

1330 Post Oak Blvd., Ste. 1600
Houston, TX 77056
Tel: (713)963-4620
Fax: (713)963-4609

National U.S.-Arab Chamber of Commerce

420 Lexington Ave., Ste. 2739
New York, NY 10170
Tel: (212)986-8024
Fax: (212)986-0216

U.S.-Arab Chamber of Commerce (Pacific), Inc.

One Hallidie Plaza, Ste. 504
(at Market and Fifth St., North)
San Francisco, CA 94102-2818
P.O.Box 422218
San Francisco, CA 94142-2218
Tel: (415)398-9200

Greece

Arab-hellenic Chamber of Commerce and Development
Leoforos Kifissias 180-2 Neo Psychico
Athens
Tel: 671-1210; 672-6882
Fax: 647-6577

Germany

Arabisch-Deutsche Vereinigung Fur Handel and Industrie
Ghorfa
Godesberger Allee 125/1
5300 Bonn-Bad Fodesberg 2
Tel: 373-637
Fax: 379-626

France

Chambre de Commerce Franco-Arabe
93, Rue Lauriston
75116, Paris
Tel: 45-532-012
Fax: 47-550-959

England

Arab-British Chamber of Commerce
6, Belgrave Square
London Swix SPH
Tel: 71-235-463
Fax: 24-566-88

Hungary

Arab-Hungarian Chamber of Comerce
P.O.Box 106, Budapest 62

Ireland

For additional analytical, business and investment opportunities information, please contact Global Investment & Business Center, USA at (202) 546-2103. Fax: (202) 546-3275. E-mail: ibpusa3@gmail.com Global Business and Legal Information Databank: www.ibpus.com

Fax: (415)398-7111

U.S.-Arab Chamber of Commerce (Pacific), Inc.

8939, South Sepulveda Blvd., Ste.430
Los Angeles, CA 90045
Tel: (310)646-1499

Argentina

Camara De Comercio Argentino-Arabe
Montevideo 513, 6 ME PISO
1019, Buenos Aires
Tel: 458-167

Austria

Austro: Arab Chamber of Commerce
Lobkowitzplatz 1. P.O.Box 181
1015 Vienna
Tel: 513-3965 - 0

Belgium

Arab-Belgium-Luxembourg Chamber of Commerce
60, Rue Mignot-Delstanche
1060 Bruxelles
Tel: 344-8204
Fax: 347-5764

Brazil

Camara de Commercio Arabe-Brasileira
Avenida Paulista 32617 Andar
01310 Sao Paulo
Tel: (11)283-4066

Arab-Irish Chamber of Commerce
63, Lower Mount Street (First Floor)
Dublin 2
Tel: 605-276
Fax: 602-425

Italy

Camera Di Commercio Italo-Araba
Piazzale Delle Arti 6
00196 Rome
Tel: 322-6753
Fax: 322-6901

Malta

Maltese-Arab Chamber of Commerce
Republic Street
Valetta-Malta
Tel: 272-33

Portugal

Camara de commercio ET Industria Arabe-Portuguesa
Avenida Fontes Pereira de Melo 19-8
1000 Lisboa
Tel: 547-371
Fax: 547-411

Switzerland

Arab Swiss Chamber of Commerce and Industry
70. Route de Florissant
CH, 12-11 Geneve 12
Switzerland
Tel: 022-473-202

Turkey

Turk-Arab Musterek Ticaret Odasei Ataturk Bulvari 149,
Bakanliklar Ankara Cable Birlik

SAUDI CHAMBERS OF COMMERCE AND INDUSTRY

Council of Saudi Chambers of Commerce & Industry
Riyadh Chamber of Commerce and Industry Building
P.O.Box 16683, Riyadh 11474
Tel. (1)405-3200/405-7502
Fax: (1)402-4747

Jizah Chamber of Commerce and Industry
P.O.Box 201, Jizan
Tel: (7)317-1519

Al-Majma'a Chamber of Commerce and

For additional analytical, business and investment opportunities information,
please contact Global Investment & Business Center, USA
at (202) 546-2103. Fax: (202) 546-3275. E-mail: ibpusa3@gmail.com
Global Business and Legal Information Databank: www.ibpus.com

Abha Chamber of Commerce and Industry
P.O.Box 72 ABHA
Tel: (7)227-1818
Fax: (7)227-1919

AlAhsa Chamber of Commerce and Industry
P.O.Box 1519 Al-Ahsa 31932
Tel: (3)582-0458
Fax: (3)587-5274

Albaha Chamber of Commerce and Industry
P.O.Box 311 Albaha
Tel: (7)725-4116
Fax: (7)725-0042

Arar Chamber of Commerce and Industry
P.O.Box 440 ARAR
Tel: (4)662-6544
Fax: (4)662-4581

Bishah Chamber of Commerce and Industry (Branch)
P.O.Box 491, Bishah
Tel: (7)622-5544/622-5524
Fax: (7)622-1511

Dammam Chamber of Commerce and Industry
P.O.Box 719 Dammam 31421
Tel: (3)857-1111
Fax: (3)857-0607

Hafar Albaten Chamber of Commerce and Industry(Branch)
P.O. Box 984 Hafar Albaten 31421
Tel: (3)722-0986
Fax: (3)722-0976

Hail Chamber of Commerce and Industry (Branch)
P.O.Box 1292 Hail
Tel: (6)532-1060/532-1064
Fax: (6)532-4644

Al-Jawf Chamber of Commerce and Industry
P.O.Box 585 Sakaka, Al Jawf
Tel: (4)624-9488/624-9060
Fax: (4)624-0108

Jeddah Chamber of Commerce and Industry
King Khalid St., Ghurfa Bldg.
P.O.Box 9549 Jeddah 21423
Tel: (2)642-3535/647-1100

Industry
P.O.Box 165 Almajma'a 11952
Tel: (6)432-1571;432-0268
Fax: (6)432-2655

Makkah Chamber of Commerce and Industry
Al Ghazzah St.
P.O.Box 1086 Makkah
Tel: (2)574-4020/574-5773
Fax: (2)574-1200

Medina Chamber of Commerce and Industry
P.O.Box 443 Airport Rd., Medina
Tel: (4)822-1590/822-5380

Najran Chamber of Commerce and Industry
P.O.Box 1138, Najran
Tel: (7)522-3738
Fax: (7)522-3926

Qaseem Chamber of Commerce and Industry
On Intersection Al Wehdah St. and Alamarah St.
P.O.Box 444, Buraidah, Qaseem
Tel: (6)323-6104;323-5436
Fax: (6)324-7542

Riyadh Chamber of Commerce and Industry
Dhabab St.
P.O.Box 596 Riyadh 11421
Tel: (1)404-0044/404-0300/404-2700
Fax: (1)401-1103

Tabuk Chamber of Commerce and Industry
P.O.Box 567 Tabuk
Tel: (4)422-2736/422-0464
Fax: (4)422-7378

Taif Chamber of Commerce and Industry
Al Saddad St. (Wadi Widj)
P.O.Box 1005 Taif
Tel: (2)736-4624;736-3025
Fax: (2)738-0040

Yanbu Chamber of Commerce and Industry
King Abdul Aziz St.

Fax: (2)651-7373

King Abdul Aziz St.
P.O.Box 58 Yanbu
Tel: (4)322-4257;322-4258
Fax: (4)322-6800

*Single digits in parenthesis before telephone and fax numbers are Saudi city codes.

SAUDI ARABIAN GOVERNMENT OFFICES, COMMERCIAL BANKS, AND COMPANIES IN THE U.S.

1. Royal Embassy of Saudi Arabia
601 New Hampshire Ave., N.W.
Washington, D.C. 20037
Tel:(202)342-3800

a) **Commercial Office**
Tel: (202)337-4088
Fax: (202)342-0271

b) **Consular Section**
Tel: (202)337-3767;3766;3765
Fax: (202)337-4084

c) **Information Office**
Tel: (202)337-4134
Fax: (202)944-5983

d) **Islamic Affairs Department**
Tel: (202)342-3700
Fax: (202)944-5982

e) **Medical Office**
Tel: (202)342-7393
Fax: (202)337-9251

2. Royal Consulate General of Saudi Arabia One Westheimer Plaza
5718 Westheimer St., Ste. 1500, Houston, TX 77057
Tel: (713)785-5577; Fax: (713)785-1163

3. Royal Consulate General of Saudi Arabia
2045 Sawtelle Blvd.
Los Angeles, CA 90025
Tel: (310)479-6000; Fax: (310)479-2752

15. Saudi Arabian Airlines (SAUDIA)

a) Trump Tower
725 Fifth Ave., 18th Flr.
New York, NY 10022
Tel: (212)751-7000
Fax: (212)751-7273

b) Building No. 54, Terminal 2
John F. Kennedy International Airport
Jamaica, NY 11430
Tel: (718)995-5112;5340;5341
Fax: (718)495-4282;4283

c) 2600 Virginia Ave., N.W., Ste. 903
Washington, D.C. 20037
Tel: (202)333-3800
Fax: (202)333-6086

d) 12555 Northborough Dr.
Houston, TX 77067
Tel: (713)873-1014
Fax: (713)872-5212;(800)252-3631

e) 2049 Century Park East, #2000
Los Angeles, CA 90067
Tel: (310)277-6900
Fax: (310)556-5637

16. The National Shipping Company of Saudi Arabia

a) Head Office: NSCSA America, Inc.
World Trade Center
401 East Pratt St., 26th Floor
Baltimore, MD 21202
Tel: (410)625-7000
Fax: (410)625-7050

b) 399 Hoes Ln., Ste. 100

4. Royal Consulate General of Saudi Arabia
866 UN Plaza, Ste. 480
New York, NY 10017
Tel: (212)752-2740; Fax: (212)688-2719

5. Saudi Arabian Cultural Mission
2600 Virginia Ave., N.W., Ste. 800
Washington, D.C. 20037
Tel: (202)337-9450; Fax: (202)337-2978

6. Saudi Arabian Armed Forces Office
1001 30th St., N.W..
Washington, D.C. 20007
Tel: (202)857-0122
Fax: (202)342-0588

7. Saudi Arabian National Guard Office
3000 K St., N.W., Ste. 320
Washington, D.C. 20007
Tel: (202)944-3344
Fax: (202)944-3340

8. Saudi Press Agency
1155 15th St., N.W., Ste. 1111
Washington, D.C. 20005
Tel: (202)861-0324
Fax: (202)872-1405

9. Saudi Arabian T.V.
1215 Jefferson Davies Hwy., Ste. 302
Crystal City, Arlington, Va. 22202
Tel: (703) 416-6800
Fax: (703) 416-6805

10. Saudi Arabian Mission to the UN
405 Lexington Ave., 56th Flr.
New York, NY 10017
Tel: (212)697-4830
Fax: (212)983-4895

11. Institute of Islamic and Arabic Studies in America
8500 Hilltop Rd.
Fairfax, Va. 22031
Tel: (703)641-4890
Fax: (703)641-4899

Piscataway, NJ 08854
Tel: (908)562-8989
Fax: (908)562-0909

17. ARAMCO Services Company

a) 1667 K St., N.W., Room 1200
Washington, D.C. 20006
Tel: (202)223-7750
Fax: (202)223-7756

b) P.O.Box 4534
Houston, TX 77210-4534
Tel. (713)432-4000
Fax: (713)432-8566

18. Saudi Research and Marketing
1310 G. St., N.W., Ste. 750
Washington, D.C. 20005
Tel: (202)638-7183
Fax: (202)638-1887

19. Al-Zamil Co., Inc.
2401 Fountain View, Ste. 420
Houston, TX 77057
Tel. (713)977-2689
Fax: (713)977-5731

20. ROYSPEC
(Purchasing Off. of King Faisal Hospital)
7470 Candlewood Rd.
Hanover , MD 21076
Tel:(410)850-0100
Fax:(410)850-5049

21. SABIC Americas, Inc.
Metro Center, One Station Place
Stamford, CT 06902
Tel: (203)353-5350
Fax: (203)353-5353

22. BURSON-MARSTELLER
(Agent for Saudi Basic Industries Corporation [SABIC])
230 Park Ave., South
New York, NY 10033
Tel: (212)614-4903
Fax: (212)614-4275;4263;4262

23. Saudi Petroleum International, Inc. (Subsidiary of ARAMCO)

For additional analytical, business and investment opportunities information, please contact Global Investment & Business Center, USA at (202) 546-2103. Fax: (202) 546-3275. E-mail: ibpusa3@gmail.com
Global Business and Legal Information Databank: www.ibpus.com

Fax: (703)641-4899

12. The Islamic Saudi Academy

a) 833 Richmond Hwy.
Alexandria, VA 22039
Tel: (703)780-0606
Fax: (703)780-8639

b) 11121 Pope's Head Rd.
Fairfax, VA 22030
Tel: (703)691-0000
Fax: (703)691-0454

13. Islamic Center
2551 Massachusetts Ave., NW
Washington, DC 20008
Tel: (202)332-8343
Fax: (202)234-5035

14. Saudi International Bank
520 Madison Ave.
New York, NY 10022
Tel: (212)355-6530
Fax: (212)758-5360

527 Madison Ave.,22nd floor
New York, NY 10022
Tel: (212)832-4044
Fax: (212)446-9200

24. Saudi Research and Marketing
Arab News
1310 G St., NW, Ste. 750
Washington, D.C. 20005
Tel: (202)638-7183
Fax: (202)638-1887

25. The World Bank, Office of the Executive Director for Saudi Arabia
1818 H St., N.W., Rm. D-12-025
Washington, D.C. 20433
Tel: (202)458-0190
Fax: (202)477-1759

26. International Monetary Fund, Office of the Executive Director for Saudi Arabia
700 19th St., N.W., Ste. 11306
Washington, D.C. 20431
Tel: (202)623-7283
Fax: (202)623-4760

27. U.S. - GCC Corporate Cooperation Committee, Inc.
1140 Connecticut Ave., N.W., Ste. 1210
Washington, D.C. 20036
Tel: (202)293-7499
Fax: (202)293-0903

28. U.S.-Saudi Arabian Business Council
1401 New York Ave., N.W., Ste. 710
Washington, D.C. 20005
Tel: (202)638-1212
Fax: (202)638-2894

29. U.S.-Saudi Joint Commission On Economic Cooperation
1401 New York Ave., Ste. 700
Washington, DC 20005
Tel: (202)879-4380
Fax: (202)638-1223/1224

HOTELS IN THE KINGDOM

Riyadh Hotels:	Jeddah Hotels:	Dammam, AlKhobar, Dhahran and Jubail Hotels:

For additional analytical, business and investment opportunities information,
please contact Global Investment & Business Center, USA
at (202) 546-2103. Fax: (202) 546-3275. E-mail: ibpusa3@gmail.com
Global Business and Legal Information Databank: www.ibpus.com

Riyadh Intercontinental Hotel
Al Maazar St.
P.O.Box 3636, Riyadh 11481
Tel: 465-5000

Riyadh Marriott Hotel
Al Maazar St.
P.O.Box 16294, Riiyadh 11464
Tel: 477-9300

Al-Khozama Hotel
Olaya St.
P.O.Box 4148, Riyadh 11491
Tel: 465-4650

Saudi Hotel
Al Nassiriya St.
P.O.Box 244, Riyadh 11411
Tel: 403-5051/402-4051/403-7141

Zahrat Al Sharq
Airport Rd.
P.O. Box 3616, Riyadh 11481
Tel: 403-8800

Riyadh Palace Hotel
Hay Alwazarat
P.O.Box 4561, Riyadh 11412
Tel: 401-5359/401-4444

Hyatt Riyadh Hotel
Airport Rd.
P.O.Box 18006, Riyadh 11415
Tel: 477-1111

Manhal Hotel
Airport Rd.
P.O.Box 17058, Riyadh 11484
Tel: 478-2500

Yanbu Hotels:

Yanbu Hayat Hotel
P.O. Box 300, Yanbu

Al Salam Meridian Hotel
Kylo 2, Makkah Rd.
P.O.Box 6582, Jeddah 21452
Tel: 631-4000

Al Attas and Oasis Hotel
Prince Fahd St.
P.O.Box 1299, Jeddah 21431
Tel: 642-0400/642-0418/642-0211

Al Kandara Palace Hotel
Airport St.
P.O.Box 473, Jeddah 21411
Tel: 631-2177/631-2944/631-2833

Hyatt Regency Hotel
P.O.Box 8483, Jeddah 21491
Tel: 669-0622

Makkah Hotels:

Makkah Intercontinental Hotel
Um Al-Jud
P.O.Box 1496, Makkah
Tel: 543-4455

Taif Hotels:

Masarah Intercontinental Hotel
Airport St.
P.O.Box 827 Taif
Tel: 732-8333

Al-Madinah Hotels:

Al Madinah Sheraton Hotel
Sultana Rd.
P.O.Box 1735, Al Madina
Tel: 823-0240/823-0004

Al-Gosaibi-Grand Metropolitan Hotel
Al-Khobar, North
P.O.Box 51, Dhahran Airport 31932
Tel: 864-2466/864-6466

Dhahran International Hotel
Dhahran Airport
P.O.Box 428, Dhahran 31932
Tel: 894-8555

Carlton al Muaibed Hotel
Dammam
P.O.Box 1235, Al Khobar 31952
Tel:864-5455

Dhahran Palace Hotel
P.O.Box 381, Dhahran 31932
Tel: 864-5444/864-5646

Al-Jubail International Hotel
P.O.Box 215, Al Jubail 31951
Tel: 361-0167

Al-Khaja Hotel
P.O.Box 45, Al-Khobar 31952
Tel: 864-7156/864-7162/864-3122

Al-Dossary Hotel
King St., Dammam
P.O.Box 5, Dammam, 31441
Tel: 832-2740/832-3782

Damm Obeiri Hotel
P.O.Box 1928, Dammam 31441
Tel: 832-2900/832-3782

Balhamar Hotel
P.O.Box 2259, Dammam 31451
Tel: 832-0117/822-0063/832-0181

Al Nemer Hotel
First St., Dammam
P.O.Box 509, Dammam 31421
Tel: 832-0641/832-0517

Tel: 322-4111/322-3888

MASS MEDIA AND ADVRTISING AGENCIES

A. Dailies

1. Al Jazeerah
Al-Nasirya St.
P.O.Box 354, Riyadh 11411
Tel: 402-1440-403-3361

2. Al-Riyadh
Arab Gulf Street
P.O.Boz 851, Riyadh 11421
Tel: 477-4710/ 4774610

3. Al-Nadwa
Al-Juffali
Al-Ghazza, Makkah
Tel: 542-3048/574-8150

4. Al-Madinah
Kilo 5, Makkah Rd.
P.O.Box 807, Jeddah 21421
Tel: 689-5168/688-0344

5. OKAZ
University Street
P.O.Box 1508, Jeddah 21441
Tel: 667-4020/667-4408

6. Al-Bilad
Ba-Kashab Bldg.
P.O.Box 7095, Jeddah 21462
Tel: 643-2465/643-7465

7. Al-Yaum
Near Coast Guard Offices
P.O.Box 565, Dammam 31421
Tel: 833-1091/833-1906

8. Riyadh Daily
Arab Gulf St.
P.O.Box 851, Riyadh 11421
Tel: 477-4710/477-4610
Fax: 479-4048

9. Arab News
Arab News Bldg., Off Sharafia
P.O.Box 4556, Jeddaj 21412

2. IQRAA
Al-Bilad Est.., Ba-Khashad Bldg.,
P.O.Box 6486, Jeddah 21442
Tel: 643-7465/6432465

3. Saudi Economic Survey
Apt. 17, 4th Flr., Attar Bldg.
P.O.Box 1989, Jeddah 21441
Tel: 642-8245

4. Saudi Business
Atab News Bldg., Off Sharafia
P.O.Box 4556, Jeddah 21412
Tel: 653-4743/653-4239

C. Advertising Agencies

1. Tihama
Foreign Ministry's Circle
P.O.Box 5455, Jeddah 21422
Tel: 644-4444 (20 Lines)

2. Marawah
Ba-Qadu Bldg., Prince Fahad St.
P.O.Box 3029,Jeddah 21471
Tel: 651-8204/ 651-8200

3. Saudi Advertising
Saudi Advert. International Co.
P.O.Box 6557, Jeddah 21452
Tel: 665-0380;660-2286

4. Transworld Publicity
North Murabba
P.O.Box 1482, Riyadh 11431
Tel: 403-8465/403-6898

5. Khoshaim
Al-Karwan Bldg., Batha Street
P.O.Box 3157, Riyadh 11471
Tel: 403-3053

6. Tac Tayyar
Room 504, 7th Floor, Al-Rajhy Bldg.
P.O.Box2999, Riyadh 11461
Tel:403-7545

For additional analytical, business and investment opportunities information,
please contact Global Investment & Business Center, USA
at (202) 546-2103. Fax: (202) 546-3275. E-mail: ibpusa3@gmail.com
Global Business and Legal Information Databank: www.ibpus.com

Tel: 653-4239/653-3723

Tel:403-7545

10. Saudi Gazette
Okaz Street, Mina Rd.
P.O.Box 5576, Jeddah 21432
Tel:667-4020/667-4408

7. Raed Advertising
Suite 1, Ali-Turki Bldg.
Prince Fahad Street
P.O.Box 1076, Jeddah 21431
Tel: 645-9782/644-8230

B. Weeklies

8. Marad Advertising
Saudi Research & Marketing Co.
P.O.Box 4556, Jeddah 21412
Tel: 453-4743;653-3723

1. Alyamamah
Al-Malaz Street
P.O.Box 6737, Riyadh 11452
Fax: 477-5162

BASIC LAWS AND REGULATIONS AFFECTING BUSINESS[4]

COUTRY	LAW TITLE
Saudi Arabia	Administrative / Public Law
Saudi Arabia	Amendment of 23 Clauses of Procedures before Sharee'ah Courts Implementing Rules
Saudi Arabia	Anti -Forgery Law
Saudi Arabia	Anti Money Laundering ("AML") Law
Saudi Arabia	Anti-Cyber Crime Law
Saudi Arabia	Anti-Human Trafficking Law
Saudi Arabia	Anti-Money Laundering and Counter-Terrorist Financing Rules
Saudi Arabia	Arms and Ammunitions Regulations
Saudi Arabia	Arms and Ammunitions Regulations
Saudi Arabia	Authorized Persons Regulations
Saudi Arabia	Banking Control Law
Saudi Arabia	Basic Law Of Government
Saudi Arabia	Civil Aviation Law - Approved 13 June 2009
Saudi Arabia	Code of law Practice
Saudi Arabia	Competition Law
Saudi Arabia	Contractor Classification Law
Saudi Arabia	Cooperative Health Insurance Law
Saudi Arabia	Cooperative Health Insurance Law
Saudi Arabia	Cooperative Insurance Companies Control Law
Saudi Arabia	Cooperative Insurance Companies Control Law
Saudi Arabia	Copyright Law
Saudi Arabia	Corporate Governance Regulations
Saudi Arabia	Corporate Income Tax
Saudi Arabia	Credit Information Law
Saudi Arabia	Currency Law
Saudi Arabia	Electricity Law
Saudi Arabia	Electricity Law implementing regulation
Saudi Arabia	Electronic Transactions Act

[4] For ordering tests of specific laws in English or French, Please contact Global Investment Center USA at ibpusa3@gmail.com

For additional analytical, business and investment opportunities information, please contact Global Investment & Business Center, USA at (202) 546-2103. Fax: (202) 546-3275. E-mail: ibpusa3@gmail.com
Global Business and Legal Information Databank: www.ibpus.com

Saudi Arabia	Electronic Transactions Law
Saudi Arabia	Foreign Investment Act
Saudi Arabia	Gass Supplies & Pricing Regulations
Saudi Arabia	GCC Common Law on Anti-dumping and Countervailing Measures and Safeguards
Saudi Arabia	General Environmental Law
Saudi Arabia	Government Lease and Evacuation of Real Estate Regulations
Saudi Arabia	Government Tendering & Procurement Regulations
Saudi Arabia	Government Tenders And Procurement Law
Saudi Arabia	Implementing Regulations of Commercial Data
Saudi Arabia	Implementing Regulations of Cooperative Insurance Companies Control Law
Saudi Arabia	Implementing Regulations of Copyright Law
Saudi Arabia	Implementing Regulations of Government Tender and Procurement Law
Saudi Arabia	Implementing Regulations of Income Tax Law
Saudi Arabia	Implementing Regulations of the Cooperative Health Insurance Law
Saudi Arabia	Implementing Regulations of the Law of Patents, Layout Designs of Integrated Circuits, Plant Varieties, and Industrial Designs Implementing Regulations
Saudi Arabia	Implementing Regulations of the Law of Trade Names
Saudi Arabia	Implementing Regulations of the Private Laboratories Law [2003]
Saudi Arabia	Implementing Regulations of Trademarks Law
Saudi Arabia	Implementing Rules for the Cooperative Insurance Companies Control Law
Saudi Arabia	Income Tax Law
Saudi Arabia	Investment Funds Regulations
Saudi Arabia	IT Criminal Act
Saudi Arabia	Kingdom of Saudi Arabia Capital Market Law
Saudi Arabia	Labor Law
Saudi Arabia	Law of Arbitration
Saudi Arabia	Law of Combating Money Laundering
Saudi Arabia	Law of Cooperative Associations
Saudi Arabia	Law of Criminal Procedure
Saudi Arabia	Law of Patents, Layout Designs of Integrated Circuits, Plant Varieties, and Industrial Models
Saudi Arabia	Law of Press Establishments
Saudi Arabia	Law of Printed Materials and Publication
Saudi Arabia	Law of Procedure before Shari'ah Courts
Saudi Arabia	Law of Provinces
Saudi Arabia	Law of Regions
Saudi Arabia	Law of Saudi Credit and Savings Bank
Saudi Arabia	Law of the Board of Grievances
Saudi Arabia	Law of the Council of Ministers
Saudi Arabia	Law of the Judiciary
Saudi Arabia	Law of the Judiciary
Saudi Arabia	Law of Time Share Properties
Saudi Arabia	Law of Travel Documents
Saudi Arabia	Market Conduct Regulations
Saudi Arabia	Merger and Acquisition Regulations
Saudi Arabia	Mining Investment Code
Saudi Arabia	Natural Gas Investment Taxation Law
Saudi Arabia	Offers of Securities Regulations
Saudi Arabia	Public Pension Agency Act

For additional analytical, business and investment opportunities information,
please contact Global Investment & Business Center, USA
at (202) 546-2103. Fax: (202) 546-3275. E-mail: ibpusa3@gmail.com
Global Business and Legal Information Databank: www.ibpus.com

Saudi Arabia	Real Estate Investment Regulations
Saudi Arabia	Regulations for Investment Funds
Saudi Arabia	Regulations for Money Changing Business
Saudi Arabia	Regulations for the Protection of Confidential Commercial Information
Saudi Arabia	Residence Regulations
Saudi Arabia	Rules for Enforcing Provisions of the Banking Control Law
Saudi Arabia	Saudi Arabia - Constitution
Saudi Arabia	Saudi Arabian Citizenship System
Saudi Arabia	Saudi Arabian Nationality Regulations
Saudi Arabia	Saudi Building Code Requirements
Saudi Arabia	Securities Business Regulations
Saudi Arabia	Shura Council Internal Regulations
Saudi Arabia	Shura Council Law
Saudi Arabia	Social Insurance Law
Saudi Arabia	Social Security Law
Saudi Arabia	Telecom Act
Saudi Arabia	Telecom Act Bylaws
Saudi Arabia	The Basic Law
Saudi Arabia	The Executive Rules of the Foreign Investment Act
Saudi Arabia	The Law Of Commercial Books
Saudi Arabia	The Law of Commercial Books
Saudi Arabia	The Law of Commercial Data
Saudi Arabia	The Law Of Commercial Register
Saudi Arabia	The Law of Commercial Register
Saudi Arabia	The Law of Private Laboratories
Saudi Arabia	The Law of the Board of Grievances
Saudi Arabia	The Law of the Council of Ministers
Saudi Arabia	The Law of Trade Marks
Saudi Arabia	Zakat Duty Regulations

BASIC TITLES FOR SAUDI ARABIA

IMPORTANT!
All publications are updated annually!
Please contact IBP, Inc. at ibpusa3@gmail.com for the latest ISBNs and additional information

TITLE
Saudi Arabia A "Spy" Guide - Strategic Information and Developments
Saudi Arabia Air Force Handbook
Saudi Arabia Banking & Financial Market Handbook
Saudi Arabia Business and Investment Opportunities Yearbook
Saudi Arabia Business and Investment Opportunities Yearbook Volume 2 Leading Export-Import, Business, Investment Opportunities and Projects
Saudi Arabia Business Intelligence Report - Practical Information, Opportunities, Contacts
Saudi Arabia Business Intelligence Report - Practical Information, Opportunities, Contacts
Saudi Arabia Business Law Handbook - Strategic Information and Basic Laws
Saudi Arabia Business Success Guide - Basic Practical Information and Contacts
Saudi Arabia Company Laws and Regulations Handbook
Saudi Arabia Constitution and Citizenship Laws Handbook - Strategic Information and Basic Laws

For additional analytical, business and investment opportunities information,
please contact Global Investment & Business Center, USA
at (202) 546-2103. Fax: (202) 546-3275. E-mail: ibpusa3@gmail.com
Global Business and Legal Information Databank: www.ibpus.com

TITLE
Saudi Arabia Country Study Guide - Strategic Information and Developments
Saudi Arabia Country Study Guide - Strategic Information and Developments Volume 1 Strategic Information and Developments
Saudi Arabia Criminal Laws, Regulations and Procedures Handbook - Strategic Information, Regulations, Procedures
Saudi Arabia Customs Tariffs and Regulations Handbook
Saudi Arabia Customs, Trade Regulations and Procedures Handbook
Saudi Arabia Customs, Trade Regulations and Procedures Handbook
Saudi Arabia Diplomatic Handbook - Strategic Information and Developments
Saudi Arabia Diplomatic Handbook - Strategic Information and Developments
Saudi Arabia Ecology & Nature Protection Handbook
Saudi Arabia Ecology & Nature Protection Laws and Regulation Handbook
Saudi Arabia Economic & Development Strategy Handbook
Saudi Arabia Economic & Development Strategy Handbook
Saudi Arabia Electoral, Political Parties Laws and Regulations Handbook - Strategic Information, Regulations, Procedures
Saudi Arabia Energy Policy, Laws and Regulation Handbook
Saudi Arabia Export-Import Trade and Business Directory
Saudi Arabia Fishing and Aquaculture Industry Handbook - Strategic Information, Regulations, Opportunities
Saudi Arabia Foreign Policy and Government Guide
Saudi Arabia Government and Business Contacts Handbook
Saudi Arabia Immigration Laws and Regulations Handbook - Strategic Information and Basic Laws
Saudi Arabia Industrial and Business Directory
Saudi Arabia Insolvency (Bankruptcy) Laws and Regulations Handbook - Strategic Information and Basic Laws
Saudi Arabia Internet and E-Commerce Investment and Business Guide - Strategic and Practical Information: Regulations and Opportunities
Saudi Arabia Investment and Business Guide - Strategic and Practical Information
Saudi Arabia Investment and Business Guide Volume 2 Business, Investment Opportunities and Incentives
Saudi Arabia Investment and Business Profile - Basic Information and Contacts for Succesful investment and Business Activity
Saudi Arabia Investment and Trade Laws and Regulations Handbook
Saudi Arabia Investment, Trade Strategy and Agreements Handbook - Strategic Information and Basic Agreements
Saudi Arabia Labor Laws and Regulations Handbook - Strategic Information and Basic Laws
Saudi Arabia Land Ownership and Agriculture Laws Handbook
Saudi Arabia Long-Term Economic Strategy and Reforms Handbook
Saudi Arabia Mineral & Mining Sector Investment and Business Guide - Strategic and Practical Information
Saudi Arabia Mining Laws and Regulations Handbook
Saudi Arabia Oil & Gas Sector Business & Investment Opportunities Yearbook
Saudi Arabia Oil and Gas Exploration Laws and Regulation Handbook
Saudi Arabia Oil, Gas & Minerals Laws and Regulations Handbook
Saudi Arabia Principal Industrial Sectors Handbook: Strategy and Business Opportunities
Saudi Arabia Principal Industrial Sectors Handbook: Strategy and Business Opportunities
Saudi Arabia Privatization Programs and Business Opportunities Handbook
Saudi Arabia Privatization Strategy Handbook
Saudi Arabia Recent Economic and Political Developments Yearbook
Saudi Arabia Starting Business (Incorporating) in....Guide
Saudi Arabia Tax Guide Volume 1 Strategic Information and Basic Regulations

TITLE
Saudi Arabia Taxation Laws and Regulations Handbook
Saudi Arabia Telecom Laws and Regulations Handbook
Saudi Arabia Telecommunication Industry Business Opportunities Handbook
Saudi Arabia Development Strategy Handbook
Saudi Arabia Transportation Policy and Regulations Handbook
Saudi Arabia: How to Invest, Start and Run Profitable Business in Saudi Arabia Guide - Practical Information, Opportunities, Contacts
Saudi Economic and Development Assistance Handbook

ISLAMIC BUSINESS, TRADE AND INVESTMENT LIBRARY

IMPORTANT!
All publications are updated annually!
Please contact IBP, Inc. at ibpusa3@gmail.com for the latest ISBNs and additional

1. Islamic Banking and Financial Law Handbook
2. Islamic Banking Law Handbook
3. Islamic Business Organization Law Handbook
4. Islamic Commerce and Trade Law Handbook
5. Islamic Criminal Law, Regulations and Procedures Handbook
6. Islamic Company Law Handbook
7. Islamic Constitutional and Administrative Law Handbook
8. Islamic Copyright Law Handbook
9. Islamic Customs Law and Regulations Handbook
10. Islamic Design Law Handbook
11. Islamic Development Bank Group Handbook
12. Islamic Economic & Business Laws and Regulations Handbook
13. Islamic Environmental Law Handbook
14. Islamic Financial and Banking System Handbook vol 1
15. Islamic Financial and Banking System Handbook Vol. 2
16. Islamic Financial Institutions (Banks and Financial Companies) Handbook
17. Islamic Foreign Investment and Privatization Law Handbook
18. Islamic Free Trade, Economic Zones Law and Regulations Handbook
19. Islamic International Law and Jihad (War) Law Handbook
20. Islamic Labor Law Handbook
21. Islamic Legal System (Sharia) Handbook Vol. 1 Basic Laws and Regulations
22. Islamic Legal System (Sharia) Handbook Vol. 2 Laws and Regulations in Selected Countries
23. Islamic Mining Law Handbook
24. Islamic Patent & Trademark Law Handbook
25. Islamic Taxation Law Handbook
26. Islamic Trade, Export-Import Laws and Regulations Handbook
27. Islamic Military and Defence Laws and regulations Handbook
28. Islamic Ownership Law, Regulations and Procedures Handbook

WORLD BUSINESS LAW HANDBOOKS LIBRARY

World Business Information Catalog, USA: http://www.ibpus.com
Email: ibpusa3@gmail.com

Price: $99.95 Each

TITLE
Abkhazia (Republic of Abkhazia) Business Law Handbook Volume 1 Strategic Information and Basic Laws
Afghanistan Business Law Handbook Volume 1 Strategic Information and Basic Laws
Aland Business Law Handbook Volume 1 Strategic Information and Basic Laws
Albania Business Law Handbook Volume 1 Strategic Information and Basic Laws
Algeria Business Law Handbook Volume 1 Strategic Information and Basic Laws
Andorra Business Law Handbook Volume 1 Strategic Information and Basic Laws
Angola Business Law Handbook Volume 1 Strategic Information and Basic Laws
Anguilla Business Law Handbook Volume 1 Strategic Information and Basic Laws
Antigua and Barbuda Business Law Handbook Volume 1 Strategic Information and Basic Laws
Antilles (Netherlands) Business Law Handbook Volume 1 Strategic Information and Basic Laws
Argentina Business Law Handbook Volume 1 Strategic Information and Basic Laws
Armenia Business Law Handbook Volume 1 Strategic Information and Basic Laws
Aruba Business Law Handbook Volume 1 Strategic Information and Basic Laws
Australia Business Law Handbook Volume 1 Strategic Information and Basic Laws
Austria Business Law Handbook Volume 1 Strategic Information and Basic Laws
Azerbaijan Business Law Handbook Volume 1 Strategic Information and Basic Laws
Bahamas Business Law Handbook Volume 1 Strategic Information and Basic Laws
Bahrain Business Law Handbook Volume 1 Strategic Information and Basic Laws
Bangladesh Business Law Handbook Volume 1 Strategic Information and Basic Laws
Barbados Business Law Handbook Volume 1 Strategic Information and Basic Laws
Belarus Business Law Handbook Volume 1 Strategic Information and Basic Laws
Belgium Business Law Handbook Volume 1 Strategic Information and Basic Laws
Belize Business Law Handbook Volume 1 Strategic Information and Basic Laws
Benin Business Law Handbook Volume 1 Strategic Information and Basic Laws
Bermuda Business Law Handbook Volume 1 Strategic Information and Basic Laws
Bhutan Business Law Handbook Volume 1 Strategic Information and Basic Laws
Bolivia Business Law Handbook Volume 1 Strategic Information and Basic Laws
Bosnia and Herzegovina Business Law Handbook Volume 1 Strategic Information and Basic Laws
Botswana Business Law Handbook Volume 1 Strategic Information and Basic Laws
Brazil Business Law Handbook Volume 1 Strategic Information and Basic Laws
Brunei Business Law Handbook Volume 1 Strategic Information and Basic Laws
Bulgaria Business Law Handbook Volume 1 Strategic Information and Basic Laws
Burkina Faso Business Law Handbook Volume 1 Strategic Information and Basic Laws
Burundi Business Law Handbook Volume 1 Strategic Information and Basic Laws
Cambodia Business Law Handbook Volume 1 Strategic Information and Basic Laws
Cameroon Business Law Handbook Volume 1 Strategic Information and Basic Laws
Canada Business Law Handbook Volume 1 Strategic Information and Basic Laws

For additional analytical, business and investment opportunities information,
Please contact Global Investment & Business Center, USA
at (202) 546-2103. Fax: (202) 546-3275. E-mail: ibpusa3@gmail.com

TITLE
Cape Verde Business Law Handbook Volume 1 Strategic Information and Basic Laws
Cayman Islands Business Law Handbook Volume 1 Strategic Information and Basic Laws
Central African Republic Business Law Handbook Volume 1 Strategic Information and Basic Laws
Chad Business Law Handbook Volume 1 Strategic Information and Basic Laws
Chile Business Law Handbook Volume 1 Strategic Information and Basic Laws
China Business Law Handbook Volume 1 Strategic Information and Basic Laws
Colombia Business Law Handbook Volume 1 Strategic Information and Basic Laws
Comoros Business Law Handbook Volume 1 Strategic Information and Basic Laws
Congo Business Law Handbook Volume 1 Strategic Information and Basic Laws
Congo, Democratic Republic Business Law Handbook Volume 1 Strategic Information and Basic Laws
Cook Islands Business Law Handbook Volume 1 Strategic Information and Basic Laws
Costa Rica Business Law Handbook Volume 1 Strategic Information and Basic Laws
Cote d'Ivoire Business Law Handbook Volume 1 Strategic Information and Basic Laws
Croatia Business Law Handbook Volume 1 Strategic Information and Basic Laws
Cuba Business Law Handbook Volume 1 Strategic Information and Basic Laws
Cyprus Business Law Handbook Volume 1 Strategic Information and Basic Laws
Czech Republic Business Law Handbook Volume 1 Strategic Information and Basic Laws
Denmark Business Law Handbook Volume 1 Strategic Information and Basic Laws
Djibouti Business Law Handbook Volume 1 Strategic Information and Basic Laws
Dominica Business Law Handbook Volume 1 Strategic Information and Basic Laws
Dominican Republic Business Law Handbook Volume 1 Strategic Information and Basic Laws
Ecuador Business Law Handbook Volume 1 Strategic Information and Basic Laws
Egypt Business Law Handbook Volume 1 Strategic Information and Basic Laws
El Salvador Business Law Handbook Volume 1 Strategic Information and Basic Laws
Equatorial Guinea Business Law Handbook Volume 1 Strategic Information and Basic Laws
Eritrea Business Law Handbook Volume 1 Strategic Information and Basic Laws
Estonia Business Law Handbook Volume 1 Strategic Information and Basic Laws
Ethiopia Business Law Handbook Volume 1 Strategic Information and Basic Laws
Falkland Islands Business Law Handbook Volume 1 Strategic Information and Basic Laws
Faroes Islands Business Law Handbook Volume 1 Strategic Information and Basic Laws
Fiji Business Law Handbook Volume 1 Strategic Information and Basic Laws
Finland Business Law Handbook Volume 1 Strategic Information and Basic Laws
France Business Law Handbook Volume 1 Strategic Information and Basic Laws
Gabon Business Law Handbook Volume 1 Strategic Information and Basic Laws
Gambia Business Law Handbook Volume 1 Strategic Information and Basic Laws
Georgia Business Law Handbook Volume 1 Strategic Information and Basic Laws
Germany Business Law Handbook Volume 1 Strategic Information and Basic Laws
Ghana Business Law Handbook Volume 1 Strategic Information and Basic Laws
Gibraltar Business Law Handbook Volume 1 Strategic Information and Basic Laws
Greece Business Law Handbook Volume 1 Strategic Information and Basic Laws
Greenland Business Law Handbook Volume 1 Strategic Information and Basic Laws
Grenada Business Law Handbook Volume 1 Strategic Information and Basic Laws
Guam Business Law Handbook Volume 1 Strategic Information and Basic Laws
Guatemala Business Law Handbook Volume 1 Strategic Information and Basic Laws
Guernsey Business Law Handbook Volume 1 Strategic Information and Basic Laws
Guinea Business Law Handbook Volume 1 Strategic Information and Basic Laws

For additional analytical, business and investment opportunities information,
Please contact Global Investment & Business Center, USA
at (202) 546-2103. Fax: (202) 546-3275. E-mail: ibpusa3@gmail.com

TITLE
Guinea-Bissau Business Law Handbook Volume 1 Strategic Information and Basic Laws
Guyana Business Law Handbook Volume 1 Strategic Information and Basic Laws
Haiti Business Law Handbook Volume 1 Strategic Information and Basic Laws
Honduras Business Law Handbook Volume 1 Strategic Information and Basic Laws
Hungary Business Law Handbook Volume 1 Strategic Information and Basic Laws
Iceland Business Law Handbook Volume 1 Strategic Information and Basic Laws
India Business Law Handbook Volume 1 Strategic Information and Basic Laws
Indonesia Business Law Handbook Volume 1 Strategic Information and Basic Laws
Iran Business Law Handbook Volume 1 Strategic Information and Basic Laws
Iraq Business Law Handbook Volume 1 Strategic Information and Basic Laws
Ireland Business Law Handbook Volume 1 Strategic Information and Basic Laws
Israel Business Law Handbook Volume 1 Strategic Information and Basic Laws
Italy Business Law Handbook Volume 1 Strategic Information and Basic Laws
Jamaica Business Law Handbook Volume 1 Strategic Information and Basic Laws
Japan Business Law Handbook Volume 1 Strategic Information and Basic Laws
Jersey Business Law Handbook Volume 1 Strategic Information and Basic Laws
Jordan Business Law Handbook Volume 1 Strategic Information and Basic Laws
Kazakhstan Business Law Handbook Volume 1 Strategic Information and Basic Laws
Kenya Business Law Handbook Volume 1 Strategic Information and Basic Laws
Kiribati Business Law Handbook Volume 1 Strategic Information and Basic Laws
Korea, North Business Law Handbook Volume 1 Strategic Information and Basic Laws
Korea, South Business Law Handbook Volume 1 Strategic Information and Basic Laws
Kosovo Business Law Handbook Volume 1 Strategic Information and Basic Laws
Kurdistan Business Law Handbook Volume 1 Strategic Information and Basic Laws
Kuwait Business Law Handbook Volume 1 Strategic Information and Basic Laws
Kyrgyzstan Business Law Handbook Volume 1 Strategic Information and Basic Laws
Laos Business Law Handbook Volume 1 Strategic Information and Basic Laws
Latvia Business Law Handbook Volume 1 Strategic Information and Basic Laws
Lebanon Business Law Handbook Volume 1 Strategic Information and Basic Laws
Lesotho Business Law Handbook Volume 1 Strategic Information and Basic Laws
Liberia Business Law Handbook Volume 1 Strategic Information and Basic Laws
Libya Business Law Handbook Volume 1 Strategic Information and Basic Laws
Liechtenstein Business Law Handbook Volume 1 Strategic Information and Basic Laws
Lithuania Business Law Handbook Volume 1 Strategic Information and Basic Laws
Luxembourg Business Law Handbook Volume 1 Strategic Information and Basic Laws
Macao Business Law Handbook Volume 1 Strategic Information and Basic Laws
Macedonia Business Law Handbook Volume 1 Strategic Information and Basic Laws
Madagascar Business Law Handbook Volume 1 Strategic Information and Basic Laws
Madeira Business Law Handbook Volume 1 Strategic Information and Basic Laws
Malawi Business Law Handbook Volume 1 Strategic Information and Basic Laws
Malaysia Business Law Handbook Volume 1 Strategic Information and Basic Laws
Maldives Business Law Handbook Volume 1 Strategic Information and Basic Laws
Mali Business Law Handbook Volume 1 Strategic Information and Basic Laws
Malta Business Law Handbook Volume 1 Strategic Information and Basic Laws
Man Business Law Handbook Volume 1 Strategic Information and Basic Laws
Marshall Islands Business Law Handbook Volume 1 Strategic Information and Basic Laws

For additional analytical, business and investment opportunities information,
Please contact Global Investment & Business Center, USA
at (202) 546-2103. Fax: (202) 546-3275. E-mail: ibpusa3@gmail.com

TITLE
Mauritania Business Law Handbook Volume 1 Strategic Information and Basic Laws
Mauritius Business Law Handbook Volume 1 Strategic Information and Basic Laws
Mayotte Business Law Handbook Volume 1 Strategic Information and Basic Laws
Mexico Business Law Handbook Volume 1 Strategic Information and Basic Laws
Micronesia Business Law Handbook Volume 1 Strategic Information and Basic Laws
Moldova Business Law Handbook Volume 1 Strategic Information and Basic Laws
Monaco Business Law Handbook Volume 1 Strategic Information and Basic Laws
Mongolia Business Law Handbook Volume 1 Strategic Information and Basic Laws
Montserrat Business Law Handbook Volume 1 Strategic Information and Basic Laws
Montenegro Business Law Handbook Volume 1 Strategic Information and Basic Laws
Morocco Business Law Handbook Volume 1 Strategic Information and Basic Laws
Mozambique Business Law Handbook Volume 1 Strategic Information and Basic Laws
Myanmar Business Law Handbook Volume 1 Strategic Information and Basic Laws
Nagorno-Karabakh Republic Business Law Handbook Volume 1 Strategic Information and Basic Laws
Namibia Business Law Handbook Volume 1 Strategic Information and Basic Laws
Nauru Business Law Handbook Volume 1 Strategic Information and Basic Laws
Nepal Business Law Handbook Volume 1 Strategic Information and Basic Laws
Netherlands Business Law Handbook Volume 1 Strategic Information and Basic Laws
New Caledonia Business Law Handbook Volume 1 Strategic Information and Basic Laws
New Zealand Business Law Handbook Volume 1 Strategic Information and Basic Laws
Nicaragua Business Law Handbook Volume 1 Strategic Information and Basic Laws
Niger Business Law Handbook Volume 1 Strategic Information and Basic Laws
Nigeria Business Law Handbook Volume 1 Strategic Information and Basic Laws
Niue Business Law Handbook Volume 1 Strategic Information and Basic Laws
Northern Cyprus (Turkish Republic of Northern Cyprus) Business Law Handbook Volume 1 Strategic Information and Basic Laws
Northern Mariana Islands Business Law Handbook Volume 1 Strategic Information and Basic Laws
Norway Business Law Handbook Volume 1 Strategic Information and Basic Laws
Oman Business Law Handbook Volume 1 Strategic Information and Basic Laws
Pakistan Business Law Handbook Volume 1 Strategic Information and Basic Laws
Palau Business Law Handbook Volume 1 Strategic Information and Basic Laws
Palestine (West Bank & Gaza) Business Law Handbook Volume 1 Strategic Information and Basic Laws
Panama Business Law Handbook Volume 1 Strategic Information and Basic Laws
Papua New Guinea Business Law Handbook Volume 1 Strategic Information and Basic Laws
Paraguay Business Law Handbook Volume 1 Strategic Information and Basic Laws
Peru Business Law Handbook Volume 1 Strategic Information and Basic Laws
Philippines Business Law Handbook Volume 1 Strategic Information and Basic Laws
Pitcairn Islands Business Law Handbook Volume 1 Strategic Information and Basic Laws
Poland Business Law Handbook Volume 1 Strategic Information and Basic Laws
Polynesia French Business Law Handbook Volume 1 Strategic Information and Basic Laws
Portugal Business Law Handbook Volume 1 Strategic Information and Basic Laws
Qatar Business Law Handbook Volume 1 Strategic Information and Basic Laws
Romania Business Law Handbook Volume 1 Strategic Information and Basic Laws
Russia Business Law Handbook Volume 1 Strategic Information and Basic Laws
Rwanda Business Law Handbook Volume 1 Strategic Information and Basic Laws
Sahrawi Arab Democratic Republic Volume 1 Strategic Information and Developments

For additional analytical, business and investment opportunities information,
Please contact Global Investment & Business Center, USA
at (202) 546-2103. Fax: (202) 546-3275. E-mail: ibpusa3@gmail.com

TITLE
Saint Kitts and Nevis Business Law Handbook Volume 1 Strategic Information and Basic Laws
Saint Lucia Business Law Handbook Volume 1 Strategic Information and Basic Laws
Saint Vincent and The Grenadines Business Law Handbook Volume 1 Strategic Information and Basic Laws
Samoa (American) A Business Law Handbook Volume 1 Strategic Information and Basic Laws
Samoa (Western) Business Law Handbook Volume 1 Strategic Information and Basic Laws
San Marino Business Law Handbook Volume 1 Strategic Information and Basic Laws
Sao Tome and Principe Business Law Handbook Volume 1 Strategic Information and Basic Laws
Saudi Arabia Business Law Handbook Volume 1 Strategic Information and Basic Laws
Scotland Business Law Handbook Volume 1 Strategic Information and Basic Laws
Senegal Business Law Handbook Volume 1 Strategic Information and Basic Laws
Serbia Business Law Handbook Volume 1 Strategic Information and Basic Laws
Seychelles Business Law Handbook Volume 1 Strategic Information and Basic Laws
Sierra Leone Business Law Handbook Volume 1 Strategic Information and Basic Laws
Singapore Business Law Handbook Volume 1 Strategic Information and Basic Laws
Slovakia Business Law Handbook Volume 1 Strategic Information and Basic Laws
Slovenia Business Law Handbook Volume 1 Strategic Information and Basic Laws
Solomon Islands Business Law Handbook Volume 1 Strategic Information and Basic Laws
Somalia Business Law Handbook Volume 1 Strategic Information and Basic Laws
South Africa Business Law Handbook Volume 1 Strategic Information and Basic Laws
Spain Business Law Handbook Volume 1 Strategic Information and Basic Laws
Sri Lanka Business Law Handbook Volume 1 Strategic Information and Basic Laws
St. Helena Business Law Handbook Volume 1 Strategic Information and Basic Laws
St. Pierre & Miquelon Business Law Handbook Volume 1 Strategic Information and Basic Laws
Sudan (Republic of the Sudan) Business Law Handbook Volume 1 Strategic Information and Basic Laws
Sudan South Business Law Handbook Volume 1 Strategic Information and Basic Laws
Suriname Business Law Handbook Volume 1 Strategic Information and Basic Laws
Swaziland Business Law Handbook Volume 1 Strategic Information and Basic Laws
Sweden Business Law Handbook Volume 1 Strategic Information and Basic Laws
Switzerland Business Law Handbook Volume 1 Strategic Information and Basic Laws
Syria Business Law Handbook Volume 1 Strategic Information and Basic Laws
Taiwan Business Law Handbook Volume 1 Strategic Information and Basic Laws
Tajikistan Business Law Handbook Volume 1 Strategic Information and Basic Laws
Tanzania Business Law Handbook Volume 1 Strategic Information and Basic Laws
Thailand Business Law Handbook Volume 1 Strategic Information and Basic Laws
Timor Leste (Democratic Republic of Timor-Leste) Business Law Handbook Volume 1 Strategic Information and Basic Laws
Togo Business Law Handbook Volume 1 Strategic Information and Basic Laws
Tonga Business Law Handbook Volume 1 Strategic Information and Basic Laws
Trinidad and Tobago Business Law Handbook Volume 1 Strategic Information and Basic Laws
Tunisia Business Law Handbook Volume 1 Strategic Information and Basic Laws
Turkey Business Law Handbook Volume 1 Strategic Information and Basic Laws
Turkmenistan Business Law Handbook Volume 1 Strategic Information and Basic Laws
Turks & Caicos Business Law Handbook Volume 1 Strategic Information and Basic Laws
Tuvalu Business Law Handbook Volume 1 Strategic Information and Basic Laws
Uganda Business Law Handbook Volume 1 Strategic Information and Basic Laws
Ukraine Business Law Handbook Volume 1 Strategic Information and Basic Laws

For additional analytical, business and investment opportunities information,
Please contact Global Investment & Business Center, USA
at (202) 546-2103. Fax: (202) 546-3275. E-mail: ibpusa3@gmail.com

TITLE
United Arab Emirates Business Law Handbook Volume 1 Strategic Information and Basic Laws
United Kingdom Business Law Handbook Volume 1 Strategic Information and Basic Laws
United States Business Law Handbook Volume 1 Strategic Information and Basic Laws
Uruguay Business Law Handbook Volume 1 Strategic Information and Basic Laws
Uzbekistan Business Law Handbook Volume 1 Strategic Information and Basic Laws
Vanuatu Business Law Handbook Volume 1 Strategic Information and Basic Laws
Vatican City (Holy See) Business Law Handbook Volume 1 Strategic Information and Basic Laws
Venezuela Business Law Handbook Volume 1 Strategic Information and Basic Laws
Vietnam Business Law Handbook Volume 1 Strategic Information and Basic Laws
Virgin Islands, British Business Law Handbook Volume 1 Strategic Information and Basic Laws
Wake Atoll Business Law Handbook Volume 1 Strategic Information and Basic Laws
Wallis & Futuna Business Law Handbook Volume 1 Strategic Information and Basic Laws
Western Sahara Business Law Handbook Volume 1 Strategic Information and Basic Laws
Yemen Business Law Handbook Volume 1 Strategic Information and Basic Laws
Zambia Business Law Handbook Volume 1 Strategic Information and Basic Laws
Zimbabwe Business Law Handbook Volume 1 Strategic Information and Basic Laws

For additional analytical, business and investment opportunities information,
Please contact Global Investment & Business Center, USA
at (202) 546-2103. Fax: (202) 546-3275. E-mail: ibpusa3@gmail.com